Praxis® II

Elementary Education: Multiple Subjects (5001)

Includes Subtests:

Reading and Language Arts (5002)
Mathematics (5003)
Social Studies (5004)
Science (5005)

By: Kathleen Jasper, Ed.D.

Kathleen Jasper

Kathleen Jasper LLC
Estero, FL 33928
www.kathleenjasper.com | info@KathleenJasper.com

Praxis® II Elementary Education: Multiple Subjects (5001)

Printed in the United States of America
ISBN: 9798613533251

kj Kathleen Jasper

Thank you for taking the time to purchase this book. I really appreciate it.

Would you mind leaving a review?

Did you purchase this book on Amazon? If so, I would be thrilled if you would leave an unbiased review at your convenience. Did you purchase this book from KathleenJasper.com? If so, you can leave a review on Facebook, Google, or directly on our website on the product page. Thank you for using my products.

Visit my Facebook Page.

I post videos, practice test questions, upcoming events, and other resources daily on my Facebook Page. Join us every Tuesday at 5 P.M. ET for our Facebook live math help session. https://www.facebook.com/KathleenJasperEdD.

Check out my other products.

I have built several comprehensive, self-paced online courses for many teacher certification exams. I also have other books, webinars and more. Go to https://kathleenjasper.com and use offer code **PRAXIS5001** for 20% off any of my products.

Join my private Facebook group.

Are you trying to become a teacher and are you looking for a community? Share insights, strategies and connect with other prospective teachers.

Go to: www.facebook.com/groups/certificationprep/ to request access.

Subscribe to my YouTube channel

Check out my enormous video library with tons of interesting and insightful content for teacher certification exams and more.

Subscribe here https://www.youtube.com/kathleenjasperedd.

If you have any questions, don't hesitate to reach out. It will be my pleasure to help.
Good luck on your exam.

–Kathleen Jasper, Ed.D.

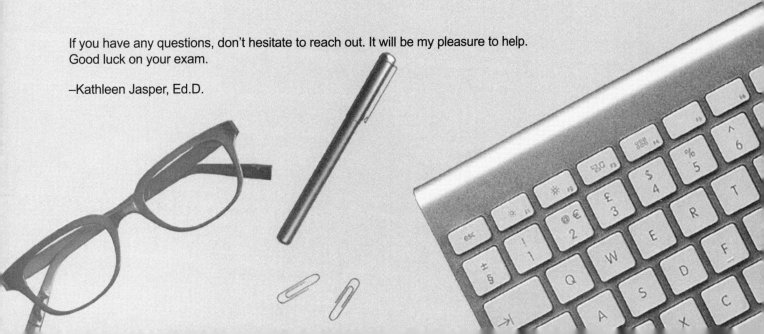

This page intentionally left blank.

Table of Contents

Algebraic Thinking

Geometry and Measurement, Data, Statistics, and Probability

United States History, Government, and Citizenship

Geography, Anthropology, and Sociology

World History and Economics

This page intentionally left blank.

Good Words List

When building test prep, one of our methodologies is to identify what we call *good words* in the answer choices to determine correct and incorrect answers. Good words are terms and phrases taken from the test specifications that highlight best practices. If you see these words or phrases in answer choices on the exam, slow down and have a closer look. There is a good possibility these words are in the correct answer choice. We have also included a list of bad words and phrases to avoid.

Good Words and Phrases

Accommodations. Modifying instruction or using supports to help special education students achieve. Accommodations do NOT involve lowering the standard or delaying learning.

Action research. The process of evaluating data in the classroom to identify issues and implementing effective and quick actions to solve problems.

Assessments. Using formative and summative data to monitor progress and measure outcomes.

Authentic instruction. Providing students with meaningful, relevant, and useful learning experiences and activities.

Balanced literacy. Reading and writing instruction that uses a variety of literary genres including literary and informational texts.

Bilingual instruction. Helping students use elements of their first language to support learning in English.

Celebrate culture. Finding materials and resources to celebrate the different cultures represented in your classroom.

Classroom management. A variety of skills and techniques that teachers use to keep students organized, orderly, focused, attentive, on task, and academically productive during class.

Close Reading. The process of reading and rereading a piece of text multipipe times for different purposes. This helps students with their comprehension.

Collaborative learning. These are strategies that are student-centered and self-directed rather than led by the teacher. Collaboration can also be working with colleagues or stakeholders to improve, create, or produce something.

Concept map. Visual representation of content. Especially useful for illustrating concepts like cause and effect, problem and solution, compare and contrast, etc.

Critical thinking. Higher-order thinking skills that involve evaluating, analyzing, creating, and applying knowledge.

Cultural responsiveness. Instruction as a pedagogy that empowers students intellectually, socially, and emotionally by celebrating and learning about other cultures. This includes recognizing the importance of including students' cultural references in all aspects of learning and designing a productive learning environment.

Data driven decisions. Using scores, writing samples, observations, and other types of qualitative and quantitative data to make instructional decisions.

Developmentally appropriate instruction (DAP). Choosing text, tools, and activities that are appropriate for the students' grade level.

Differentiated instruction. Providing all learners in a diverse classroom with different methods to understand instruction.

Diversity as an asset. Seeing diversity in the classroom as an opportunity to learn new things through the perspectives of others.

Evidenced-based. Providing instruction using materials with the best scientific evidence available.

Flexible grouping. The heart of differentiated instruction. It provides opportunities for students to be part of many different groups based on their readiness, interest, or learning style.

High expectations for ALL learners. Holding all students to high academic standards regardless of the students' achievement level, ethnicity, language, socioeconomic status.

Horizontal alignment. Organization and coordination of standards and learning goals across content areas in the same grade level.

Inclusive. Providing students with resources and experiences that represent their culture and ethnicity.

Interdisciplinary activities. Activities that connect two or more content areas; promotes relevance and critical thinking.

Interventions. Provides students with an opportunity to increase reading, writing, test taking, and study skills at their instructional level.

Intrinsic motivation. Answers that promote autonomy, relatedness, and competence are ways to apply intrinsic motivation. Be on the lookout for these answer choices.

Mentor texts. Pieces of literature that both teacher and student can return to and reread for many different purposes. They are texts to be studied and imitated.

Metacognition. Analysis of your own thinking.

Modeling. Demonstrating the application of a skill or knowledge.

Modifications. Changes to the curriculum and learning environment in accordance to a student's IEP. Modifications change the expectations for learning and the level of assessment.

Outcomes. The results of a program, strategy, or resources implemented in the classroom.

Performance assessment. An activity assigned to students to assess their mastery of multiple learning goals aligned to standards.

Primary resource. These are materials and information in their original form like diaries, journals, songs, paintings, and autobiographies.

Prior knowledge. What students know about a topic from their previous experiences and learning.

Progress monitor. Keeping track of student or whole class learning in real time. Quantifiable measures of progress, conferring, observing, exit tickets, and student self-assessments.

Recursive Teaching Methods. Using information or skills that is already known and acquired to learn new skills and knowledge.

Relevance, real-world, and relatable. Be sure to choose answers that promote real-world application and make learning relatable to students' lives.

Reliable. Consistent. Producing consistent results under similar conditions.

Remediation. Correcting or changing something to make it better.

Rigorous. A word used to describe curriculum that is challenging and requires students to use higher-order thinking skills.

Scaffolding. Using supports to help students achieve a standard that they would not achieve on their own.

Secondary resource. These are materials and information derived from the original like newspaper articles, history textbooks, and reviews.

Self-assessment. An assessment or evaluation of oneself or one's actions and attitudes, performance, and skills.

Specific and meaningful feedback. More than just a grade at the top of a paper, effective feedback includes positive aspects and how students can apply those positive aspects to improving. In addition, feedback should contain specific things the student should do to improve.

Standards-aligned. Ensuring that curriculum and instruction is aligned to the state-adopted standards.

Student centered/learner centered. A variety of educational programs, learning experiences, instructional approaches, and academic-support strategies that address students' distinct learning needs, interests, or cultural backgrounds.

Validity. Accuracy. How accurately knowledge or skills are measured.

Vertical alignment. Organization of standards and learning goals across grade levels. Structure for which learning and understanding is built from grade level to grade level.

Vocabulary in-context. Always teach vocabulary in context. It helps to relate the vocabulary to the real-world.

Wait time. Time between a question and when a student is called on or a response to a student's reply.

Word Consciousness. Students are aware and interested in words and word meanings. Students who are word conscious also notice when and how new words are used. Word conscious students are motivated to learn new words and to be able to use them skillfully.

Bad Words and Phrases

Bias. Inserting personal beliefs, stereotypes, and assumptions in the learning process. This can also include learning materials developed from the perspective of the dominant culture that exclude minority perspectives.

Extra homework. On this exam, students should be getting all of the instruction they need in class. In real life, we all assign homework. However, on this exam, extra homework is not the correct answer choice.

Extrinsic motivators. These are rewards of extrinsic value like pizza parties, recess time, etc. Students should be motivated by intrinsic motivators like self-confidence, sense of accomplishment, and feeling successful.

Homogenous grouping. Grouping by gender, English proficiency, or learning level is never a best practice on this exam or in your classroom. Homogenous groups should only be used in special circumstances and on a temporary basis.

Punitive solutions. Avoid answer choices that sound like punishments. For this exam, teachers are expected to be implementing positive behavior support methods so avoid any answer choices that sounds punitive.

Silent Independent Reading. When this practice is attached to a struggling reader scenario it is usually not the correct answer because if students are struggling, reading independently is not going to help the student get better.

Standardized Test Taking strategies. While students need to be strategic and learn how to approach their state exams, this concept is usually not the correct answer on the exam.

Worksheets. Do we use worksheets? Yes, absolutely. However, on this exam, using worksheets is probably not the correct answer, so avoid these answer choices.

This page intentionally left blank.

Reading and Language Arts Subtest

This page intentionally left blank.

The Reading and Language Arts Subtest of the Praxis Elementary Education exam is designed to test your knowledge and understanding of child development during elementary school years as it relates to reading, writing, and speaking. The assessment is not aligned to a particular grade or course, but it is aligned to the Common Core State Standards for English Language Arts.

The Reading and Language Arts Subtest is divided into the following four categories:

- Foundational Skills
- Literature and Informational Texts
- Language
- Writing

Each of these categories includes questions that test your knowledge of content as it relates to teaching and learning in the areas of reading, writing, and speaking. Solid foundational skills in reading are imperative for student success as students progress through their K-12 education. Therefore, exam questions are designed to ensure you are able to both apply content knowledge and identify teaching resources that are developmentally appropriate for students.

The four main categories are further broken down into subcategories: understanding of literature, text structures and organization, components of language in writing, literacy acquisition, reading instruction, and communication skills.

Test at a Glance	
Test Name	*Praxis*® Elementary Education Reading and Language Arts Subtest 5002
Format	Computer-based test (CBT)
Time	90 minutes; Approximately 1 minute 7 seconds per question
Number of Questions	Approximately 80 (field testing items may be added)
Passing Score	A scaled score of at least 157 for most states
Items Provided	Scratch paper and pencils
Format of Questions	Multiple choice (A, B, C, D), multiple response, order matching, grids; at least four item types other than multiple choice are included.

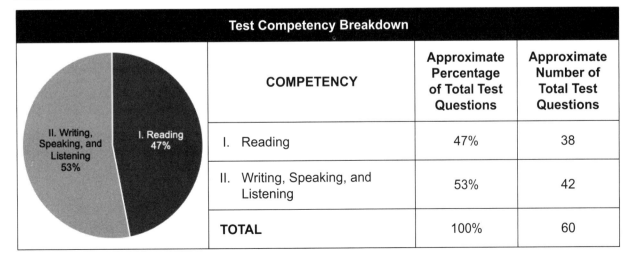

Test Competency Breakdown			
	COMPETENCY	**Approximate Percentage of Total Test Questions**	**Approximate Number of Total Test Questions**
	I. Reading	47%	38
	II. Writing, Speaking, and Listening	53%	42
	TOTAL	100%	60

I. Reading

Section I—reading—tests your knowledge of phonological awareness, phonics and word analysis, phonemic awareness, fluency, and text structure and complexity. Questions will include identifying developmentally appropriate teaching strategies and resources. Language acquisition and pedagogical approaches for English Language Learners are also addressed in this section.

The skills you need to know in this section include the following:

A. Foundational Skills

B. Literature and Informational Texts

A. Foundational Skills

Understands the role of phonological awareness in literacy development

Phonological awareness as a foundational skill for literacy

Phonological awareness is an overarching skill that includes identifying and manipulating units of oral language, including parts of words, syllables, onsets, and rimes.

Children who have phonological awareness are able to:

*   identify and make oral rhymes,

*   clap out the number of syllables in a word,

*   recognize words with the same initial sounds like *monkey* and *mother*,

*   recognize the sound of spoken language,

*   blend sounds together (*bl, tr, sk*), and

*   divide and manipulate words.

*Phonological awareness includes 2 very important subskills: phonemic awareness and phonics.

Phonemic awareness is understanding the individual sounds (or phonemes) in words. For example, students who have phonemic awareness can separate the sounds in the word cat into three distinct phonemes: /k/, /æ/, and /t/.

Phonics is understanding the relationship between sounds and the spelling patterns (graphemes) representing those sounds. For example, when a student sees that a c is followed by an e, i, or y, the student knows the c makes an /s/ sound.

Quick Tip

Think of phonological awareness as the umbrella encompassing many skills students need for literacy: syllabication, onsets, rimes, spelling, etc. Phonemic awareness and phonics are the subskills that support phonological awareness.

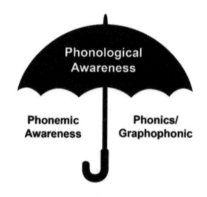

Phonemic Awareness	Phonics
Focus on phonemes/sounds	Focus on graphemes/letters and their corresponding sounds
Spoken language	Written language/print
Mostly auditory	Both visual and auditory
Manipulating sounds in words	Reading and writing letters according to sounds, spelling, patterns, and phonological structure

(Heggerty, 2003)

Phonemes, syllables, onsets, and rimes

Phonemes are the individual sounds in words. Usually, phonemes are expressed without a written letter because a letter can have different phonemes or sounds attached to it. For example, the letter *g* can make an /g/ sound, as in *game*, and a /j/ sound as in *gym*.

Syllables are units of pronunciation having one vowel sound, with or without surrounding consonants, forming the whole or a part of a word. For example, there are two syllables in *water* (*wa-ter*) and three in *elephant* (*el-e-phant*).

Onsets are the beginning consonant and consonant cluster. For example, the onset for the word **tack** is /t/. The onset for the word **track** is /tr/.

Rimes are the vowel and consonants that follow the onset. For example, in the word **tack** and **track**, the rime is *-ack*.

Common rimes include:

-ack	-ing	-ank	-or
-an	-op	-ay	-ock
-aw	-unk	-ide	-ight
-ick	-ain	-ink	-ame

Blending, segmenting, substituting, and deleting

Students must be able to break down words and understand different components of words. Teachers can help students do this in a number of ways.

Blending is the ability to string together the sounds that each letter stands for in a word. For example, when students see the word *black*, they blend the /bl/, the /a/ sound and the ending /k/ sound. Sometimes blending exercises focus just on the consonant blend, like the /br/ sound in the word *brick*.

Segmenting is breaking a word apart. This can be done by breaking compound words into two parts, segmenting by onset and rime, segmenting by syllables, or breaking the word into individual phonemes.

Examples of Segmenting		
Compound words	baseball	base ball
Onset and rime	dad	/d/ -/ad/
Syllables	behind	/be-hind/
Individual phonemes	cat	/c/ /a/ /t/
Segmenting phonemes into spoken words	dog	/d/ /o/ /g/

Substituting is replacing one phoneme with another in a word. For example, students say the word *play*, and the teacher asks them to change the first sound of play with */st/*. The students say the word *stay*. Another example is changing the ending sound of *play* to */ate/*, which forms the word *plate*.

Deleting is when students take words apart, remove one sound, and pronounce the word without the removed sound. For example, using the word *mice*, a teacher may ask students to delete the initial */m/* sound, resulting in the word *ice*. This skill is usually practiced orally.

Understands the role of phonics and word analysis in literacy development

Phonics and word analysis in literacy development

Phonics and morphology are foundational skills necessary for word analysis.

Phonics is the ability to map certain sounds in words based on written letters. For example, in the word *chain*, the *c + h* makes a */ch/* sound.

The essence of phonics is how letters represent different sounds in words. Students must have an understanding of spelling and phonemic awareness to master phonics.

Morphology is the study of words and their forms. Morphemes are smallest units of meaning in wordsx.

> **Quick Tip**
>
> Phonics involves letter-sound relationships. For example, when you see the letters ph in the word phone, you know the ph makes an /f/ sound. To understand that relationship, you must use phonics skills.

For example, in the word *firehouse*, there are two morphemes: *fire* and *house*. Both mean different things—*fire* means "hot, bright, lit", while *house* means "dwelling." When these meanings are combined in *firehouse*, they form a completely different meaning. However, it is important to understand the individual meanings to understand the combined meanings.

Word analysis is a process of using relationships between spelling and pronunciation to identify words. Word analysis requires students to identify meanings of words by using prefixes, root words, and suffixes. Teaching students to read using word analysis is an essential skill to building literacy (Kruidenier, 2002).

Words can be broken down by:

- inflected forms (-s, -es, -ed, -ing, -ly)
- contractions
- possessives
- compound words
- syllables
- base words

- root words
- prefixes
- suffixes
- beginning consonants
- end consonants
- medial consonants

- consonant blends (*bl, gr, sp*)
- consonant digraphs (*sh, th, ch*)
- short vowels
- long vowels
- vowel pairs (*oo, ew, oi, oy*)

Common letter-sound correspondences and spelling conventions

Letter-sound correspondence - Certain letters and combinations of letters make specific sounds. To read a word and pronounce the word correctly, the learner must be able to recognize letters and their corresponding sounds. Teaching this skill in isolation (one letter at a time) will help students become proficient.

Spelling conventions are the rules that English words follow. Common spelling conventions are found in the following tables.

The following tables includes examples of how teachers and students can use letter sound correspondence, spelling conventions, and graphemes to teach literacy. This table was adapted from the Common Core State Standards for English Language Arts and Literacy Appendix A.

Grapheme Type	Definition	Examples
Single letters	A single consonant letter can be represented by a phoneme.	b, d, f, g, h, j, k, l, m, n, p, r, s, t, v, w, y, z
Doublets	A doublet uses two of the same letter to spell a consonant phoneme.	ff, ll, ss, zz
Digraphs	Digraphs are a two-letter (di) combinations that create one phoneme.	th, sh, ch, wh, ph, ng (sing) gh (cough) ck
Trigraphs	Trigraphs are three-letter (tri) combinations that create one phoneme.	-tch -dge
Diphthong	Diphthongs are sounds formed by the combination of two vowels in a single syllable, in which the sound begins as one vowel and moves toward another. They can appear in the initial, middle or final position in a word.	aisle coin loud buy
Consonant blends	Consonant blends include two or three graphemes, and the consonant sounds are separate and identifiable.	s-c-r (scrape) c-l (clean) l-k (milk)
Silent letter combinations	Silent letter combinations use two letters: one represents the phoneme and the other is silent.	kn (knock) wr (wrestle) gn (gnarl)
Combination *qu*	These two letters always go together and make a */kw/* sound.	quickly
Single letters	A single vowel letter that stands for a vowel sound.	(short vowels) cat, hit, gem, pot, sub (long vowels) me, no, mute
Vowel teams	Vowel teams are combinations of two, three, or four letters that stand for a vowel sound.	(short vowels) head, hook (long vowels) boat, sigh, weigh (diphthongs) soil, bout

(Appendix A – Common Core State Standards)

The following table outlines rules students must know when beginning literacy.

Rule	Example
The letter *k* before *e, i,* or *y* makes a /k/ sound.	kite, key
The letter *c* before *a, o, u,* or any consonant makes a /k/ sound.	cat, cost, cut, clap
When *c* is followed by an *e, i,* or *y*, it makes an /s/ sound.	cycle, receive
The letter *q* is always followed by a *u*.	queen, quick
English words don't end in *i*; *y* is used instead.	my, fly
Use *ck* at the end of one-syllable words after a short vowel.	luck, tuck, stuck
Usually, *k* comes after a consonant or a long vowel sound.	look, skunk, book,
When *c* comes at the end of a two or more-syllable word, it makes a /k/ sound.	garlic, Atlantic
Always follow *k* with an e following a long vowel sound at the end of the word.	like, strike, hike, make
The letters *ss, ff, ll* are often doubled at the end of a one-syllable word that ends with that sound.	floss, fluff, chill
i before *e* except after *c*, except as in neighbor and weigh.	piece, receive, neighbor, weigh
The letter *g* before *e, i,* or *y* sounds like /j/.	gel, giant, gym
The letter *g* followed by any other letter sounds like a hard /g/.	glass, grow

(Osewalt, 2019)

High-frequency words vs. decodable words

High-frequency words are also referred to as sight words. These words occur most often in grade-level texts. Some sight words do not follow English language rules and cannot be sounded out. To read on grade level, students must have automaticity with high frequency words. These words should be memorized because they occur frequently. Examples include:

- want
- what
- said
- see
- by
- are
- why
- there

Decodable words can be sounded out and follow letter-sound correspondence and spelling conventions or rules. For example, a student can decode the word *expect* by segmenting the word: *ex-pe-ct*. It is not a word that occurs often like the word *said* or *there*. Therefore, a student may have to take a few seconds to decode the word.

Roots and affixes

Students can use roots and affixes to break apart difficult words into manageable pieces.

Roots are parts of words, without the prefix or suffix, that provide the basic meaning of the word.

Affixes are parts of a word added to the beginning and end of a word—prefixes and suffixes.

Structural analysis is the process of breaking words apart by prefixes, suffixes and roots, and interpreting meaning. This helps the reader determine the pronunciation and meaning of unknown words. This word identification technique is effective, especially when used along with phonic analysis and context clues.

Examples of Structural Analysis		
Roots	Parts of a word that provide the meaning of the word.	cred means believe (in**cred**ible) phon means sound (**phon**ological) auto means self (**auto**biography) bio means life (**bio**logy)
Prefixes	Additions at the beginning of root words that form a new word. The new word has a different meaning than the root word.	Prefixes that mean *not*: un- (unknown) dis- (disregard) im- (impossible) in- (inaccurate) mis- (misunderstand) ir- (irrational)
Suffixes	Additions at the end of root words that form a new word. The new word has a different meaning than the root word. Suffixes can change verb tense of a word. Suffixes can also indicate whether the word is plural or singular.	Suffixes that mean someone performing an action: -er (manager) Suffixes that mean an action or process: -ment (encouragement, engagement) Suffixes that mean a state or condition -ion (situation, location) Suffixes that change the verb tense: -ing present tense (jumping, walking) -ed past tense (jumped, walked)
Compound words	Two words put together	mailman sidewalk

Language acquisition

First language (L1) acquisition refers to the way children learn their native language. Second language (L2) acquisition refers to the learning of another language or languages besides the native language. Typically, language acquisition is associated with English language learners (ELLs).

Below are the stages an ELL goes through during second language acquisition.

Stage	Description
Stage 1: Pre-Production	This is commonly known as the silent period. At this stage, students are listening and deciphering vocabulary. Students may have receptive vocabulary (listening), but they are not speaking yet. In this stage, students benefit from repetition when trying to understand new words and phrases.
Stage 2: Early Production	This stage can last up to six months. Students at this stage understand about 1000 words in the new language. Students begin to form short phrases that may be grammatically incorrect. Students at this stage will use pictures to represent ideas in the new language.
Stage 3: Speech Emergence	At this stage, students will start to communicate with simple phrases and sentences. Students understand up to 3000 words during this stage. Students also begin to develop comprehension in the new language (L2).
Stage 4: Intermediate Fluency	During this stage, students have a robust vocabulary in the second language—6000 or more words. Students begin to communicate effectively in their writing and speech.
Stage 5: Advanced Fluency	At this stage, students are proficient and have comprehension and critical thinking in the second language. It can take 4–10 years for students to achieve academic proficiency in a second language.

(Chart adapted from Haynes, 2005)

World-class Instructional Design and Assessment (WIDA) – WIDA is an organization that supports multilingual students and creates standards and assessments to help with the instruction of ELLs. WIDA supports students, families, educators, and administrators with research-based tools and resources.

The WIDA framework includes five components that are interactive and interdependent. These components exemplify the WIDA vision for academic language development (WIDA, 2014).

1. Guiding Principles of Language Development
2. Developmentally Appropriate Academic Language in Sociocultural Contexts
3. Performance Definitions
4. Can Do Descriptors
5. Standards Matrices

Quick Tip

To be successful on the Reading and Language Arts portion of the Praxis exam, previewing the WIDA website is essential. There may be several questions on the exam related to the WIDA framework.

© 2022 Kathleen Jasper

The following are the WIDA descriptors for language acquisition. The beginning stage starts at 1, entering. The most proficient stage is 6, reaching.

Stage	Description
6 **Reaching**	• Specialized or technical language reflective of the content area at grade level • A variety of sentence lengths of varying linguistic complexity in extended oral or written discourse as required by the specified grade level • Oral or written communication in English comparable to proficient English peers
5 **Bridging**	• The technical language of the content areas • A variety of sentence lengths of varying linguistic complexity in extended oral or written discourse, including stories, essays, or reports • Oral or written language approaching comparability to that of English proficient peers when presented with grade-level material
4 **Expanding**	• Specific and some technical language of the content areas • A variety of sentence lengths of varying linguistic complexity in oral discourse or multiple, related paragraphs • Oral or written language with minimal phonological, syntactic, or semantic errors that do not impede the overall meaning of the communication when presented with oral or written connected discourse with occasional visual and graphic support
3 **Developing**	• General and some specific language of the content areas • Expanded sentences in oral interaction or written paragraphs • Oral or written language with phonological, syntactic, or semantic errors that may impede the communication but retain much of its meaning when presented with oral or written, narrative, or expository descriptions with occasional visual and graphic support
2 **Beginning**	• General language related to the content areas • Phrases or short sentences • Oral or written language with phonological, syntactic, or semantic errors that often impede the meaning of the communication when presented with one to multiple-step commands, directions, questions, or a series of statements with visual and graphic support
1 **Entering**	• Pictorial or graphic representation of the language of the content areas • Words, phrases, or chunks of language when presented with one-step commands, directions, or statements with visual and graphic support

(WIDA, 2012)

Linguistic complexity is the quantity and variety of language used by ELLs at the discourse level and refers to how ELLs express their ideas and understand interactions.

Language usage refers to the type and use of structures, phrases, and words. Some features include choices of intonation to convey meaning and types of grammatical structures (WIDA, 2004).

Effective Approaches for teaching ELLs

Most teachers will have the opportunity to teach students who are ELL. It is important that teachers understand effective instructional approaches to support these students. The following are a few examples of how teachers can support students who are ELL.

Approach	Description	Example
Visual	Using pictures, hands-on materials, and other visual tools	When teaching vocabulary, the teacher presents the word and a picture to resemble the concept that is being taught.
Cooperative Learning	Allowing students to work collaboratively in groups	When analyzing meaning in text, students engage in literature circles—small groups engaging in text analysis.
Honor the "Silent Period"	The "Silent Period" is part of the learning process. Allowing the student to stay quiet, observe, and learn will benefit the student's ability to continually learn in the classroom.	When teaching an English language arts class, the teacher allows students who are ELL to sit silently. The teacher does not call on these students or require them to speak during class.
Allow Use of Native Language	Allowing students to continue to use their native language until they build proficiency in their second language is a great way to scaffold learning of the second language.	During class, some students who are ELL explain some of their experiences to one another in their native language. The teacher understands this is an important part of language acquisition.

Literacy Theorists

When analyzing second language acquisition and ELL education, it is important to consider the main theorists in language acquisition. Below are two of the most eminent linguistic theorists.

- **B.F. Skinner** provided one of the earliest explanations of language acquisition. Well known for behaviorism, he claimed that language acquisition is based on environmental factors or influences. He said that language is based on reinforcement principles by associating words with meanings. Positive reinforcement will help children realize the value of words and phrases (Ambridge & Lieven, 2011).

- **Noam Chomsky** is known as the "Father of Modern Linguistics." He argued that all humans share the same underlying linguistic structure, irrespective of sociocultural difference. This was the basis for his theory of universal grammar.

Approaches for ELLs

When teaching students who are ELL, focusing on basic skills for recognizing words is effective. This is not only effective for students who are ELL, but it is also effective for those who are not ELL.

Syllable Type	Description	Example
Closed	A syllable with a single vowel followed by one or more consonants The vowel is closed in by a consonant. The vowel sound is usually short.	cat bat clock letter
Open	A syllable that ends with a single vowel The vowel is not closed in by a consonant. The vowel is usually long. The letter *y* acts like a vowel.	go no fly he
Vowel- Consonant-Silent e	A syllable with a single vowel followed by a consonant then the vowel *e* The first vowel sound is long, and the final *e* is silent. Can be referred to as the sneaky silent *e*	bike skate kite poke
Vowel Teams	A syllable that has two consecutive vowels. Vowel teams can be divided into two types: • Long vowel teams: Two vowels that make one long vowel sound. • Variant vowel teams: Two vowels that make neither a long nor a short vowel sounds but rather a variant. Letters *w* and *y* act as vowels.	Long vowel teams: eat, seat, say, see Variant vowel teams: stew, paw, book Exceptions: bread (makes a short vowel sound)
R-controlled **Also known as the "bossy r".**	A syllable with one or two vowels followed by the letter *r* The vowel is not long or short. The *r* influences or controls the vowel sound.	car far her fur sir
Consonant le (-al, -el) **Final stable**	A syllable that has a consonant followed by the letters *le, al,* or *el* This is often one syllable. This is the only syllable type without the vowel sound.	table stable local
Other Final Stable Syllables	A syllable that makes one sound at the end of a word Examples include: *sion, tion, ture, sure, age, cious, tious.*	tension, nation, culture, composure, rampage, gracious, infections

(Knight-McKenna, 2008)

Differentiates syllable patterns

Phonics helps students understand the structure of words in terms of consonant and vowel sounds. The table below lists the most common use of consonant and vowel sounds in words.

Syllable Pattern	Description	Example
CVC	consonant-vowel-consonant	bat, cat, tap
CVCe	consonant-vowel-consonant-silent *e*	make, take, bake
CCVC	consonant-consonant-vowel-consonant	trap, chop, grit
CVCC	consonant-vowel-consonant-consonant	tack, hunt, fast
VC-CV	Two or more consonants between two vowels	nap-kin pen-ny
V-CV and VC-V	One consonant between two vowels	e-ven de-cent
Consonant Blend	Consonant blends stick together	spec-trum

(National Governors Association, 2019)

Students can also use cuing systems to understand difficult words.

Cueing Systems

- **Syntactic** – The syntactic cueing system focuses on the structure of the sentence.

- **Semantic** – The semantic cueing system focuses on the meaning derived from the text.

Scenario: A student writes: I no go to park. This is a syntactic issue. You can understand the meaning, so this is not a semantic issue. The problem is in the structure of the sentence.

Understands the role of fluency in literacy development

Fluency

Fluency is reading without having to stop and decode (sound out) words. Fluency involves reading a paragraph from start to finish with very few errors.

Prosody is reading with expression while correctly using words and punctuation. Reading with prosody means the reader is conveying what is on the page, pausing at commas and periods, and using inflection based on punctuation.

Teachers perform **fluency checks** or fluency reads to measure students' reading progress. While the student reads, the teacher follows along. As the student reads, the teacher checks for **automaticity**, which is effortless, speedy word recognition. The teacher also checks the student's **accuracy** and **rate**.

FLUENCY CHECKS
- ☑ Prosody
- ☑ Automaticity
- ☑ Accuracy
- ☑ Rate

Teaching strategies to increase and monitor fluency:

- **Choral reading** – Reading aloud in unison with a whole class or group of students. Choral reading helps build students' fluency, self-confidence, and motivation.

- **Repeated reading** – Reading passages again and again, aiming to read more words correctly per minute each time.

- **Running records** – Following along as a student reads, marking when he or she makes a mistake or miscues.

- **Miscue analysis** – Looking over the running record, analyzing why the student miscued, and employing strategies to help the student with miscues.

Scenario: A teacher is following along as a student is reading. The teacher makes a mark when the student struggles or says a word incorrectly. When the student is finished reading, both the teacher and the student look over the miscues and discuss how to fix the issues. The teacher and student are engaging in a fluency read, a **running record**, and a **miscue analysis**.

The impact fluency has on comprehension

Fluency is necessary for comprehension. For students to understand text, they must first read through the text with fluency. This way they can focus on meaning rather than sounding out words.

Comprehension is the essence of reading. This is when students begin to form images in their minds as they read. They are able to predict what might happen next in a story because they understand what is happening in the story. Students who are in the comprehension stage of reading do not need to decode (sound out) words. They read **fluently** with **prosody, automaticity, and accuracy**.

Critical thinking is when students can apply certain concepts to their reading and extract meaning from the text. Students in the critical thinking stage are using high level skills to relate meaning in the text to themselves and to real life.

Metacognition is thinking about thinking. When students have metacognition, they understand the processes in their minds and can employ a variety of techniques to understand text. Strategies for boosting **comprehension, critical thinking**, and **metacognition** are:

- **Predicting** – Asking students what they think will happen next

- **Questioning** – Having students ask questions based on what they are reading

- **Read aloud/think aloud** – Teacher or student reads and stops to think aloud about what the text means

- **Summarizing** – Asking students to summarize what they just read in their own words

Scenario: A teacher is modeling the reading process by reading aloud and stopping to think aloud through difficult words and areas in the text. The teacher is using a *read aloud/think aloud* technique to model the cognitive process and increase students' *metacognition, critical thinking*, and **comprehension**.

*All of the above strategies are considered higher-order/critical thinking and can be employed before, during, and after reading.

Cognitive Endurance

When students read through large sections of text and build meaning from that text, students have cognitive endurance. Students are not wasting cognitive energy on decoding words. Instead, students are reading fluently, using their cognitive energy towards comprehension and critical thinking, not word recognition and meaning.

According to Lyon and Moats (1997), a young reader has only so much attentional capacity and cognitive energy to devote to a particular task. If the reading of the words on the page is slow and labored, readers simply cannot remember what they have read, much less relate the ideas they have read about to their own background knowledge. Fluent readers use less cognitive energy and are able to spend more time developing comprehension on the reading, rather than decoding words. Meaning and understanding of words can be lost in the decoding phase. That is why building automaticity and cognitive endurance is essential in developing comprehension.

Cognitive Endurance

The use of mental activities and skills to perform tasks such as learning, reasoning, understanding, remembering, and paying attention helps to build cognitive endurance. Building cognitive endurance allows readers to use stored cognitive energy for tasks like comprehension. If students are struggling to decode words, they are using more cognitive energy to decode and less to comprehend.

Remember: Independent reading means a student is reading at >95% accuracy.

B. Literature and Informational Text

Understands how to use key ideas and details to comprehend literature and informational text

Key details of literary text

Key details are specific pieces of information in a text. These can include characters, setting, and plot. The key details help the reader summarize important information in the story. These specific key details will help build comprehension of the text.

The moral of a story is the lesson that story teaches about how to behave in the world. Fables use morals to convey meaning.

Theme is the overall feeling or underlying topic of the text. Students will often have to identify the theme of a story in reading comprehension assessments.

Citing textual evidence refers to using the text to support answers. Asking students to defend positions using the text is part of the Common Core State Standards for literacy. Citing textual evidence can be used when asking for key details in the story, theme, moral, or central idea.

Key details and/or central idea of information text

Key details are the facts and information that support the central idea of the text.

Central idea is what the text is mostly about or what the author is trying to inform you about. Central idea often has to be inferred using text evidence.

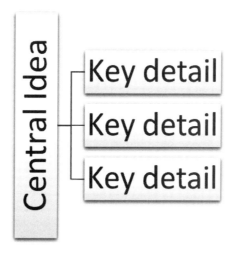

Inferences from a text

An inference is when a student reaches a conclusion based on evidence that is NOT explicitly stated in the text. Using clues and information helps students answer inference questions. Because inferences require students to make educated assumptions based on clues in the text, inference is considered a higher-order thinking skill.

Most often, students will be required to look at a passage and make inferences about meaning and author's purpose. The following is an example of that.

There are many reasons to use alternative energy sources. One reason is to reduce the amount of pollutants and greenhouse gasses in the atmosphere. Reducing these pollutants and greenhouse gasses can help reduce climate change, which is causing the Earth to get warmer.

People can use different types of renewable resources in their daily lives. For example, wind power and solar power can provide electricity to homes and businesses without the use of fossil fuels. Reducing fossil fuel dependence helps keep the Earth's atmosphere clean.

If people value life on Earth, they will start to use alternative energy sources as a primary provider of energy. The more people who commit to using alternative energy sources, the less pollution will impact Earth. It cannot happen soon enough.

1. What can be inferred about the last line in paragraph 1?

   A. Alternative resources are expensive.

   B. Pollutants and greenhouse gasses are only in certain parts of the atmosphere.

   C. People should be worried about the Earth getting warmer.

   D. Another reason to use alternative energy sources is they are less expensive.

2. What is the author's purpose for writing this piece?

   A. To inspire people to become climate change activists.

   B. To educate people about how renewable resources can benefit people and the environment.

   C. To scare people into recycling and using renewable resources.

   D. To promote a renewable resource company and increase its sales.

Question 1 is an inference question. The answer is not explicitly stated. However, because the author wants to reduce greenhouse gasses that cause the Earth to get warmer, the reader can infer that the Earth warming is a bad thing and that people should be concerned about it. Therefore, **C** is the best answer.

Question 2 is an author's purpose question. While the reader has no real idea why the author wrote this, based on the text, the reader can infer that the author wrote this to educate people about renewable energy sources and how they can help the environment. Therefore, **B** is the best answer.

Quick Tip

When teaching students to navigate reading passages and questions, showing them the process of elimination is very helpful, especially with inference questions. In question 1 above, answers A, B and D can be eliminated because they all contain elements that disqualify them as answers. In question 2 above, answers A, C and D can be eliminated, leaving B as the best answer.

Summarizes information from a text

Students will often have to summarize the most important information in the text. This is a high-level skill because students must have the comprehension and understanding of the text before they can summarize the important parts of the text. Using graphic organizers can help students summarize information from a text.

A **story map** is a graphic organizer that helps students learn the elements of a book or story by identifying characters, plot, setting, problem, and solution.

A **Venn diagram** can help students compare and contrast ideas and characters in the text.

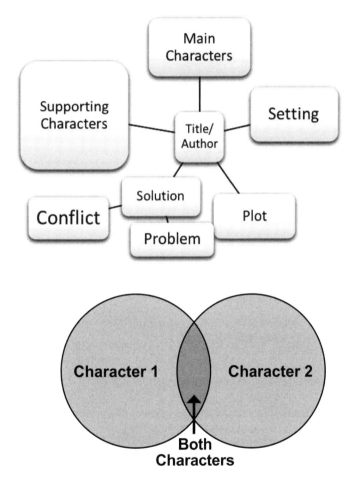

A **main idea and details** graphic organizer helps students organize and categorize specific information in the text. This helps students to pick out the most important parts of the text so they can summarize effectively.

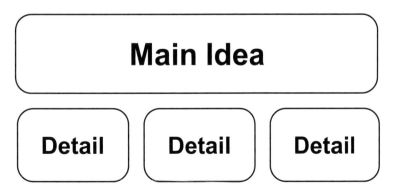

Characters, setting, and plot of a literary text

Characters are who the story is about. The characters in the story can be humans, animals, or even fictional creatures depending on the type of text. Understanding the characters will help students determine important components of the story.

Setting refers to the place and time in which the story is occurring.

Sequencing is understanding how a series of events occur in a specific and logical order. This is an important concept for students to develop because it allows students to recognize patterns that make the text and the world understandable and predictable.

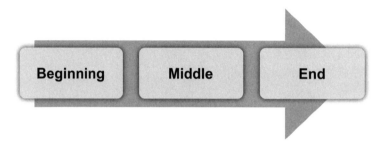

Plot Structure

Mapping plot structure allows readers and writers to visualize the key features of stories that help the student unfold important parts of the story or plot. Most stories follow a standard plot structure.

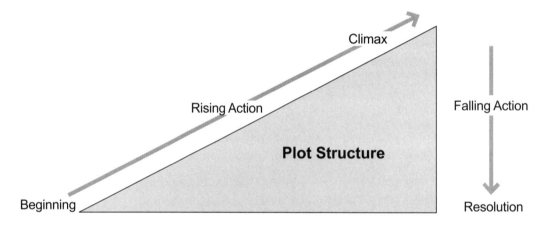

Relationships among individuals, events, ideas, and concepts in informational text

When analyzing relationships among individuals, events, ideas, and concepts, students must organize key details quickly and employ critical thinking to find meaning in informational text. Some skills students will use in the process are:

- Locate key words and vocabulary to build meaning.

- Identify persuasive/informational/narrative elements in the text.

- Determine text structures (chronological, cause and effective, problems solution).

Understands how features and structures of text across genres affect comprehension

Elements of literature across genres

Poems

Meter is a stressed and unstressed syllabic pattern in verse or within the lines of a **poem** (Literary Devices, 2019).

Narrative Poetry

Narrative poetry tells a story, often making use of the voices of a narrator and characters. The entire story is usually written in metered verse. The **poems** that make up this genre may be short or long, and the story may be complex.

Fixed verse poetry has a set formula; **free verse poetry** has little or no pre-established guidelines.

> **Quick Tip**
>
> The purpose of poetry is to convey images. Not all poems rhyme. Not all poems are short or long, but all poems use imagery.

Epic Poetry

Originating in Greece, this long narrative focuses on the trials and tribulations of a hero or god-like character who represents the cultural values of a race, nation, or religious group. The fate of the people is in the hands of the hero. Epic poetry typically takes place in a vast setting and covers a wide geographic area. The protagonist in an epic poem possesses superhuman abilities and must prove himself or herself via feats of strength. Gods or supernatural beings frequently take part in the action to affect the outcome.

Haiku

A haiku is a Japanese poem consisting of 3 lines and 17 syllables.

Each line has a set number of syllables:

- Line 1 – 5 syllables

- Line 2 – 7 syllables

- Line 3 – 5 syllables

Example:

The sky is so blue. (5 syllables)
The sun is so warm up high. (7 syllables)
I love the summer. (5 syllables)

> **Quick Tip**
>
> A teacher might use a haiku poem to teach students syllabification.

Limerick

A limerick is a humorous verse of three long lines and two short lines rhyming (aabba). These poems are effective for teaching rhythm and rhyme. They are particularly fun to recite and can help with memorization.

A limerick consists of five lines:

- The first line of a limerick poem usually begins with "There was a..." and ends with a name, person, or place.

- The last line of a limerick is normally a little farfetched or unusual.

- A limerick should have a rhyme scheme of aabba.

Example:

"There Was an Old Man with a Beard" by Edward Lear

There was an Old Man with a beard,
Who said, "It is just as I feared!—
Two Owls and a Hen
Four Larks and a Wren
Have all built their nests in my beard!"

Sonnet

A sonnet is a poem of 14 lines using any of a number of formal rhyme schemes, typically with 10 syllables per line.

Example:

"Sonnet 18" by William Shakespeare

Shall I compare thee to a summer's day?
Thou art more lovely and more temperate:
Rough winds do shake the darling buds of May,
And summer's lease hath all too short a date;

Sometime too hot the eye of heaven shines,
And often is his gold complexion dimm'd;
And every fair from fair sometime declines,
By chance or nature's changing course untrimm'd;

But thy eternal summer shall not fade,
Nor lose possession of that fair thou ow'st;
Nor shall death brag thou wander'st in his shade,
When in eternal lines to time thou grow'st:
So long as men can breathe or eyes can see,
So long lives this, and this gives life to thee.

Dramas are stories that can be acted out in front of people or an audience. Dramas include plays, screenplays, and performances.

For students to have a depth and breadth of understanding of structural elements of literature in dramas, they must understand elements of dramas and plays.

Element	Definition	Example
Playwright	The person who writes the play, or the "author" of the play	William Shakespeare
Dialogue	These are the lines the characters speak in the play. Most of a play script is made up of this. Quotation marks show what characters are saying.	Bob: "Let's go to the park." Mike: "What would we do there?" Bob: "Play football!"
Stage Direction	These notes tell the actor what to do or how to say a line. They can also give information about the setting of the play. Stage directions are usually written in brackets.	[Bob enters with rage and throws his book down on the ground as he begins conversation.]
Cast of Characters	This list at the beginning of a play gives readers an idea of how many characters will be in the play.	Bob: A middle-aged man Mike: Friend of Bob
Plot	The main events of a play or drama.	Turning Point / Beginning Problem / Solution

(Enterainism, 2019)

Text features

Text features are parts of the text used for understanding. The table below shows examples of text features found in print or digital informational text.

Text Feature	Description	Example
Information in Print		
Heading	Bold words or phrases that separate the text by main ideas.	**Reptiles in the Wild** Reptiles are cold-blooded; they rely on heat from their surroundings to stay warm or to stay cool. Reptiles have lungs. Most species of reptiles eat other animals and lay eggs on land to breed.
Glossary	Used to find the meanings of important words in the text.	**Glossary** **Cold-blooded** - Having a body temperature varying with that of the environment; poikilothermic **Reptile** - A vertebrate animal of a class that includes snakes, lizards, crocodiles, turtles, and tortoises. They are distinguished by having dry, scaly skin and typically laying soft-shelled eggs on land.
Index	Used to reference certain aspects of the text using page numbers where those ideas are found. An index is in alphabetical order.	**R** Rattlesnakes 23 Reptiles in the Wild 34 Respiratory Systems 15 Reproduction 44
Graphs/Charts	Representation of data in visual form.	 Diet of a Reptile
Sidebar	More information found on the side or bottom of a website.	
Hyperlink	Used to point the reader to additional information. Brings the reader to another website or file and is usually indicated with a different color text that is underlined.	www.Reptiles.com/american-aligator

Structures of informational text

Test structure is how information in text is organized. For example, text will often have a chronological order, cause and effect, problem and solution, or narrative structure.

Chronological

The text goes in order by time or events. Sometimes this includes dates, but that is not always the case.

Cause/Effect

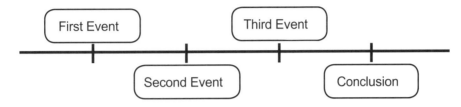

This is when the organization of the text results in is a relationship between events or things, where one is the result of the other or others.

Cause:
Why something happened

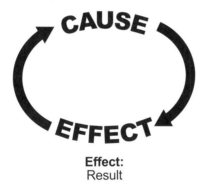

Effect:
Result

Key Words for Cause and Effect

- Consequently
- Therefore
- As a result of
- Reason -- why
- Because of
- May be due to
- If/then

Example:

- **Cause** – David makes faces in front of the class.
- **Effect** – The other students laugh.

Problem/Solution

A **problem** is something that arises in the story that the character wants to change or fix. The solution is how the character was able to fix the problem.

Example:

- **Problem** – Mean Jean won't let anyone play at recess.
- **Solution** – A new friend asks Jean to play.

Quick Tip

Problem and solution can easily be mapped out. If the author is giving the main character a conflict, he/she is guiding you to predict possible solutions as you read.

Structural elements

Understanding structural elements of text can positively impact students' literacy skills. When students understand the structure of text, they can construct, examine, and extend the meaning in text, which leads to a depth of understand of the text.

Text structure refers to how the information is organized in the text and can help students identify the following elements of the text.

- **Main idea and details** – The story or passage has an overarching viewpoint or idea and then supports that idea with details throughout the text.
- **Chronological order** – The story or passage goes in order by time.
- **Cause and effect** – The story or passage presents something that happens and then the result or effect of that action.
- **Inferences** – A conclusion based on evidence and reasoning that is not explicitly stated. A logical "guess" based on something that is happening in the story.
- **Key details** – Words or phrases that help the reader answer questions about the text. Key details give information by asking questions like who, what, where, when, and why.

Understands the concept of point of view using evidence from the text

Author's point of view

Understanding the **author's point of view** will help with comprehension of the text. The following table outlines different points of view used in text.

First Person	Second Person	Third Person Objective	Third Person Limited Omniscient	Third Person Omniscient
A narrator in the story recounts his or her own perspective, experience or impressions. The pronouns *I, we, me, us*, are used in the text.	The story is written in the perspective of *you*.	The narrator remains a detached observer, telling only the stories action and dialogue.	The narrator tells the story from the viewpoint of one character in the story.	The narrator has unlimited knowledge and can describe every character's thoughts and interpret his/her behaviors.

*Third person narrative is often used in informational text because it is the most objective point of view.

Multiple account of the same event or topic

Point of view impacts the reader's understanding of the story. Stories are often told from different points of view or told from different characters' perspectives. This affects the structure, outcome, and tone of the story. An example of this is the *The True Story of the 3 Little Pigs!* by Jon Scieszka. In this rendition, the story is told from the wolf's point of view. The wolf narrates how he saw the day unfold. Because the wolf is telling the story, his point of view is different from the pigs' points of view. This is an effective way to compare multiple accounts of the same topic or event.

Allowing students to analyze the shifting points of view or perspectives in a story fosters critical thinking and comprehension. Because analyzing different perspectives is a high-level skill, students have to move beyond what is obvious or explicitly stated and evaluate the story in a complex manner.

Point of view impacts the overall structure of a literary or information text

Point of view impacts the relationship the reader has with the story. The world the author is attempting to create depends on the point of view.

According to the Common Core State Standards, students must compare and contrast the points of view from which different stories are narrated, including the difference between first- and third-person narrations. Students who have mastered this skill will be able to:

• Compare and contrast the points of view from which different stories are narrated, including the difference between first- and third-person narrations

• Identify basic points of view as first person and third person

• Determine a narrator's or speaker's point of view in the story

• Compare the point of view in different stories

• Contrast the point of view in different stories

Understands how to integrate and compare written, visual, and oral information from texts and multimedia sources

Visual and oral elements

When students are beginning to read, visually and orally enhanced books can help them move through the text and derive meaning. In addition, using multimedia to explain text or allowing students to use multimedia to represent their understanding of the text can increase comprehension of text.

• **Picture books** – These books contain illustrations that are just as important, and sometimes more important, than the words in the book. These books present material in the form of illustrations and short pieces of text. An example of a picture book is *The Very Hungry Caterpillar* by Eric Carle. Using bold, graphic art, this book walks students through several concepts: counting, days of the week, and the life cycle of a butterfly.

• **Graphic novels** – These books are like comic books but longer. They can be fictional or informational. They contain graphic depictions of what is happening in the story, and the dialogue is set apart like it is in a comic book.

• **Pattern books** – These books have a predictable sequence because they use a strong repetitive pattern that allows children to predict what is coming next as they read. Types of pattern books include rhyme, repeated words or phrases, and familiar expressions. Pattern books can be used to increase young readers' confidence and fluency.

• **Multimedia presentations** – These include information presented with slides, video, or digital representations.

Compare different versions of text with different themes

Compares the written version of a literary text with oral, staged, or filmed version

Because students have different learning preferences—audio, visual, kinesthetic—using different mediums when analyzing text is effective in helping students comprehend text. The following are a few examples of how this can be accomplished in the classroom.

Oral/audio version of text – In centers, students use headphones and listen to the story as they follow along in the text. This exercise can increase fluency and comprehension.

Staged version of text – In groups, students act out certain parts of the text. This is often referred to as reader's theater because students read their parts of the text like they would in a play. This activity helps with fluency and comprehension.

Film version of text – Using YouTube or media resources, students can watch the film version of the text and identify similarities and differences between the book and the film version. This helps to cultivate critical thinking.

Compare different versions of text that address the same topic

Most language arts academic standards require students to compare different versions of text. Written versions of a text will often vary from oral, staged, or filmed versions. Classroom activities in this area should focus on the unique characteristics of a medium—books, film, audio. To accomplish this, teachers can ask students to explain how the ideas in the alternative media clarify a topic or text.

A **theme** refers to what the author wants the reader to learn or know. The theme is usually not stated. Instead, the theme is implied or understood through the language, circumstances, tone and other elements of the story.

The Common Core State Standards for English language arts requires students to compare and contrast themes across texts, often informational and literary.

Common Themes Within Stories	
Acceptance	Characters who respect and accept others' differences
Courage	Brave characters who have the strength to overcome a fear or accept risk
Perseverance	Characters who never give up even during difficult times
Cooperation	Characters who work together to solve a problem or reach a goal
Compassion	Characters who want to help others feel better
Kindness	Friendly characters who are kind and generous to others
Loyalty	Characters who trust each other and never turn their backs on their friends
Honesty	Characters who find that it is best to tell the truth

Compare informational texts that address the same topic

Informational texts present facts and information to inform the reader about a topic. Informational texts are usually object.

Analyzing elements of two or more informational texts is an example of critical thinking. Teachers can help students develop their critical thinking by asking guided questions.

- What domain-specific vocabulary can you find in both texts, and how does it impact the story/article?

- How is the structure of the text alike and different, and what effect does it have on the overall meaning?

- What inferences can be made from each of the texts?

In all of the questions above, students are required to use their critical thinking skills. When answering critical thinking questions on the Praxis exam, be sure to identify the Bloom's verb that corresponds to critical thinking: analyze, evaluate, create, apply.

Critical thinking comes from the top tiers of the pyramid. Analyzing two or more texts requires students to use higher-order thinking skills.

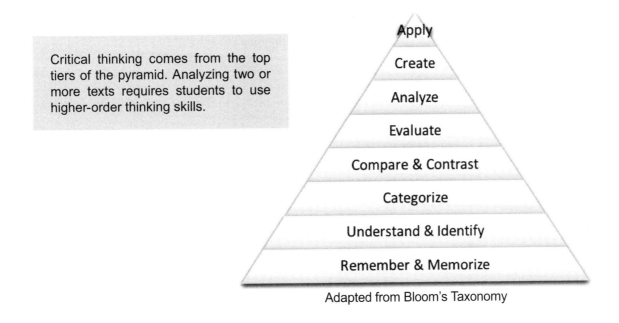

Adapted from Bloom's Taxonomy

Interpret visual and multimedia elements in literary and informational texts

Visual and multimedia elements in literary and informational texts allow students to observe key information in different mediums. Examples are illustrations, photographs, movies, maps, audio/music, and animation. These can contribute to the meaning and tone of a text.

Illustrations help the reader develop a clear idea of the tone of the passage by pulling information from the pictures and drawing conclusions about the text. Visual elements are just as important as text and allow the reader to gain an understanding and comprehension. Questions to ask when looking at multimedia in a text could be:

- What does the picture tell you that the text does not?

- How can the picture support your answer?

- Can you figure out the meaning of the vocabulary using evidence from the picture?

- Does the map give you more information and help you draw conclusions?

- What clues does the photograph give you?

Evaluate key claims in a text and support claims with evidence

The Common Core State Standards emphasize using evidence from texts to present careful analyses, well-defended claims, and clear information. Rather than asking students questions they can answer solely from their prior knowledge and experience, the standards call for students to answer questions that depend on them having read the texts with care (Common Core State Standards, 2019).

Using text to support ideas and thoughts is a critical thinking skill. Arguments are claims backed by reasons that are supported by evidence. Having students use the text to support their claims and their answers will allow the teacher to see if they are comprehending the text. Sample questions to use when asking students to cite evidence from the text include:

- Why do you think that?

- What reason can you give to convince me to believe that?

- Where in the text can you find evidence to support your answer?

Quick Tip

When trying to decipher among answer choices on the exam, if there is an answer choice that requires students to cite, use, or identify evidence from text to support their claims, it is the correct answer choice.

Knows the role of text complexity in reading development

<u>**Factors that measure text complexity**</u>

When developing a balanced literacy approach in the classroom, teachers must use several data points to measure text complexity. It is important for teachers to select appropriate text levels because classrooms consist of students with varying abilities.

Measures of Text Complexity	
Qualitative	This type of data cannot be quantified. Instead, this data often comes in the form of anecdotal responses or scenarios.
	Example: While a teacher is observing students as they read, she notices some students are struggling. She decides to intervene with a different text or targeted interventions.
Quantitative	This is data that can be quantified. When analyzing this type of data, teachers often look over reading levels, words per min and other measures that can be represented as numbers.
	Example: A teacher uses students' correct words per min to determine the Lexile levels of subsequent books they will use.
Reader and Task	These are the reader variables (motivation, knowledge, and experience) and task variables (purpose and complexity generated by the task assigned and the question posed). These variables can be measured both qualitatively and quantitatively.
	Example: A teacher chooses books that students have expressed interest in. The teacher understands the students are more likely to engage in text they are motivated to read.

(Lapp, Moss, Grant, & Johnson, 2015)

<u>**Features of text-leveling systems**</u>

Text-leveling systems allow teachers to implement reading strategies to meet the needs of students. Identifying the different levels in the classroom will allow the teacher to drive instruction, focus on areas of improvement, and enrich students' individual needs. This data should be used to make instructional decisions.

There are several types of leveling systems. The following table outlines text-leveling systems teachers can use in the classroom.

	Grade Level	Guided Reading	Lexile Level (CCSS)	DRA Level	Reading Level
Emergent	Kindergarten	A	BR	A-1	1
		B		2-3	2
		C		4	3-4
		D		6	5-6
Early	Grade 1	E	190L-530L	8	7-8
		F		10	9-10
		G		12	11-12
		H		14	13-14
		I		16	15-17
		J		18	18-20
Transitional	Grade 2	K	420L-650L	20	18-20
		L		24	
		M		28	
	Grade 3	N	520L-820L	30	
		O		34	
		P		38	
Fluent	Grade 4	Q	740L-940L	40	
		R			
		S			
	Grade 5	T	830L-1010L	50	
		U			
		V			
	Grade 6	W	925L-1070L	60	
		X			
		Y			
Proficient	Grade 7	Z	970L-1120L	70	
	Grade 8	Z	1010L-1185L	80	
	Grade 9-12	Z(+)	1050L-1385L		

Balanced Literacy Program

Using a balanced literary approach is key when teaching students how to read. Teachers can use various types of literature to implement a balanced literacy program in the classroom.

Type of Literature	Definition	Examples
Fable	A short story that conveys a moral, typically with animals as characters	*The Three Little Pigs*
Legend	A narrative that features human actions that take place within human history and demonstrate human values. There is no proof that these stories happened, yet they are told over and over again. These stories are often passed down by word of mouth	*The Legend of Sleepy Hallow*
Biography	An account of a person's life story written by an outside author	*A Biography of Martin Luther King Jr.*
Realistic Fiction	A genre consisting of stories that could have actually occurred to people or animals in a believable setting	*Ramona the Pest*
Fantasy	Stories set in an imaginary universe, where the locations, events, or people are not from the real world	*A Wrinkle in Time*

Another way teachers can implement a balanced literacy program is to use a combination of informational and literary texts.

Text Type	Examples
Informational Text	• Written primarily to inform • Literary nonfiction • History/social science texts • Science/technical texts • Digital texts
Literary Text	• Adventure • Folktales • Legends • Fables • Fantasy • Realistic fiction • Myths

Multicultural literature – Using multicultural literature helps students to see themselves in the literature they read (text to self). The challenge for teachers is identifying authentic, reliable books by and about people of color and First/Native Nations (CCBC, 2018).

II. Writing, Speaking, and Listening

Section II—writing, language, and speaking and listening—tests your knowledge of English language conventions, semantics and etymology, writing (i.e., writing process, types of writing) and research process, appropriate vocabulary choice as it relates to student development, and communication, collaboration, and presentation skills. Questions will include identifying developmentally appropriate teaching strategies and resources.

The skills you need to know in this section include the following:

A.   Writing

B.   Language

C.   Speaking and Listening

A. Writing

Understands the characteristics of common types of writing

Common types of writing

There are four main modes of writing:

Opinion/argumentative – Writing that persuades or convinces using support, details, and examples from the text in logical order. In early grades, this is called opinion writing.

Informative/explanatory – Writing that informs, explains, or tells "how to" without using opinions (just the facts).

Descriptive – Writing that describes or helps form a visual picture using sensory details and spatial order.

Narrative – A first-person account that tells a story as it happens using sensory details and chronological order.

> **Quick Tip**
>
> Selecting the correct mode for the appropriate occasion and audience is key. Students should understand which mode to use based on what they are trying to say and to whom they are trying to say it.

Genres and subgenres

Genres are categories of artistic composition characterized by similarities in form, style, or subject matter. The main genres recognized in English language arts instruction are fiction, nonfiction, poetry, folklore and drama. Subgenres are particular categories within a genre. For example, historical fiction is a subgenre of fiction. See the following table for examples.

Genre of Writing	Subgenre
Fiction	**Realistic fiction** – Fictional stories that could be true.
	Historical fiction – Fictional stories set during a real event or time in history. These stories will have historically accurate events and locations.
	Science fiction – Fictional stories that focus on space, the future, aliens, and other galaxies.
	Fantasy – Fictional stories that include monsters, fairies, magic, and/or other fantastical elements.
Nonfiction	**Informational text** – Text that informs the reader, such as a social science textbook or informational brochure.
	Biographies – Text that tells the life of another person. The author is not the person in the biography.
	Autobiographies – Text that describes one's own life. The author is the person in the autobiography.
	Persuasive writing – Writing that takes a position; the main goal is to persuade the audience to think or believe something.
Poetry	**Limerick** – A humorous verse of three long and two short lines rhyming (aabba).
	Sonnet – A poem of 14 lines using any of a number of formal rhyme schemes.
	Epic – A long narrative that focuses on the trials and tribulations of a hero or god-like character who represents the cultural values of a race, nation, or religious group.
	Haiku – A Japanese poem consisting of 3 lines and 17 syllables. Each line has a set number of syllables: line 1 has 5 syllables; line 2 has 7 syllables; line 3 has 5 syllables.
Folklore	**Fable** – A short story that includes animals who speak and act like humans. There is usually a moral at the end of a fable.
	Myth – A story that showcases gods or goddesses and typically outlines the creation of something.
	Legend – A story that may have once been true but is exaggerated, usually about extraordinary human beings.
	Fairy tale – A story that has both human and magical creatures in it.
Dramas	**Comedy** - Entertainment consisting of jokes and satirical sketches intended to make an audience laugh.
	Tragedy – A play dealing with tragic events and having an unhappy ending, especially concerning the downfall of the main character.

Evaluates effectiveness of writing

Teachers must often evaluate the effectiveness of writing. However, students must also evaluate the effectiveness of their own wiring. Rubrics are used by both the teacher and student to evaluate writing.

Rubrics are used to convey expectations and criteria of an assessment and are often used to grade students' writing. Rubrics also provide teachers with a framework to implement specific and meaningful feedback.

Rubrics should be given to students:

- **Before** writing to convey explicit expectations

- **During** writing so students can check their progress

- **After** writing to communicate grades/progress

Example Rubric

	1 - Minimal	2 - Meets	3 - Exceeds
Mechanics (Syntactic)	Many spelling, grammar, and punctuation errors; sentence fragments; incorrect use of capitalization	Some spelling and grammar errors; most sentences have punctuation and are complete; uses uppercase and lowercase letters	Correct spelling, grammar, and punctuation; complete sentences; correct use of capitalization
Ideas and Content (Semantic)	Key words are not near the beginning; no clear topic; no beginning, middle, and end; ideas are not ordered.	Main idea or topic is in first sentence; semi-defined topic; attempts beginning, middle, and end sections; some order of main idea and details in sequence.	Interesting, well-stated main idea or topic sentence; uses logical plan with an effective beginning, middle, and end; good flow of ideas from topic sentence to details in sequence.
Organization	Very unorganized and confusing	Organized enough to read and understand the ideas	Very organized and easy to understand

Understands the characteristics of effective writing

Appropriateness of a particular piece of writing

According to the Common Core State Standards (2019), students must demonstrate the following:

- Adapt their communication in relation to audience, task, purpose, and discipline.
- Set and adjust purpose from reading, writing, speaking, listening, and language use as warranted by the task.
- Appreciate nuances, such as how the composition of an audience should affect tone when speaking and how the connotations of words affect meaning.
- Know that different disciplines call for different types of evidence.

There are three elements that shape the content in a piece of writing: tone, purpose, and audience.

1. **Tone** refers to the overall feeling of the piece of writing. When writing a narrative vs. an opinion, the tone or position may be different depending on the content. The tone will convey a specific attitude toward the audience and the subject. For example, *Pete the Cat* by Eric Litwin and James Dean expresses an optimistic tone. Pete the Cat runs into various obstacles but is able to prevail by having a positive attitude.

2. **Purpose** refers to the reason for the piece of writing. Is the student writing to persuade, to entertain, or to explain? For example, if a student is writing her state representative to pass a new law, the student should write a persuasive essay. However, if a student is writing to her grandmother to describe how summer camp is going, the student should write a narrative. Establishing a purpose for the piece of writing is an important step in the writing process.

3. **Audience** refers to the individuals the writer expects to read the piece of writing. As explained above, a student will write differently in a letter to her grandmother than she will in a letter to her congressional representative. Understanding the audience is a key component of the writing process.

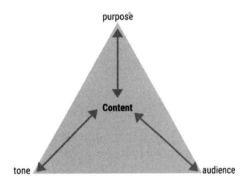

Development, organization, or style of writing

Teachers must guide students in using structure to enhance their writing. This helps students to develop and organize their writing.

Structures of Writing

- **Description** – Gives the reader descriptive information so images of what is being written can be visualized. Gives the reader a good mental picture.
- **Definition** – Defining specific topics and giving information to the reader.
- **Examples** – Used to give more information or a specific example to help with the content that is being given.

Students can use the different types of text structures to organize their writing. The following table outlines the types of text structures used in writing.

Text Structure	Definition	Example
Compare and Contrast	Analyzes two or more items to establish similarities/ differences.	*The hungry bunny eats grass, while the hungry hawk eats rabbits.*
Chronological Sequence	Gives information in order of occurrence.	*First, settlers arrived in the colonies and built their homes. Next, settlers began to farm. Finally, settlers set up a government.*
Spatial Sequence	Describes things as they appear.	*The store was located just south of the old bridge and to the east of Dr. Miller's office.*
Cause and Effect	Gives reason/explanation for happening.	*One of the reasons grasses are producers is because grasses make their own food. This allows grasses to produce energy in the form of carbohydrates for animals to eat.*
Problem and Solution	Sets up a problem and outlines a solution.	*The third pig knew the wolf would be coming to the neighborhood, so he built his house out of strong brick.*
Description	Descriptive details about characteristics, actions, etc.	*The traveler came upon a beautiful meadow with vibrant green grass and a cloudless sky.*

Revisions to strengthen a piece of writing

The secret to good writing is good editing and revisions. Effective writing teachers help students focus their efforts on the revision process. Well-written essays need to be proofed, revised, and even reorganized.

Emphasis on revision – Revising pieces thoughtfully over time, not developing a new piece of writing each day (much writing will not leave draft form).

Conference/assessment notes – Keeping a log or portfolio on each student's writing progress.

Spelling and vocabulary – Connecting to both writing, reading, and language use.

Meaningful feedback – Providing students with specific details as you review their work.

Quick Tip

Communicating expectations is key. Be sure to use rubrics and allow students to use those rubrics before they begin the writing process and as they are writing.

Clear and coherent writing

Writing clearly and coherently is challenging for elementary-age students. Therefore, teachers must provide students with tools to help with the writing process. There are several ways teachers can help students write clearly and coherently.

- **Organization** – It is important that students organize their writing by first mapping what they are going to write. Mind maps and other graphic organizers can help students do this.

- **Transitional words** – These words connect parts of a paragraph to one another. Helping students identify the right transitional words is useful in coherent writing.

- **Cooperative learning** – Peer reviews, brainstorming sessions, and editing roundtables can help students revise their writing in an effective manner. It is important to remember that for cooperative learning to be effective, it must be organized, and everyone in the group must have a role.

- **Frameworks** – These formulas allow students to follow a step by step structure as they write. This allows students to plug their information into the pre-established formula. As the students get more proficient in writing, they can modify or abandon the formula.

- **Rubrics** – These assessment tools outline expectations for student writing. Students should not have to guess what the teacher wants to see in the writing assignment. Rubrics outline a set of parameters that help students focus their writing.

Planning, revising, and editing in the writing process

As stated above, students must use a variety of approaches to write clearly and coherently. Students must also understand the writing process and how to apply the process as they construct their writing.

Stages of the Writing Process

- **Pre-writing** – Brainstorming, considering purpose and goals for writing, using graphic organizers to connect ideas, and designing a coherent structure for a writing piece.

- **Drafting** – Working independently to draft the sentence, essay, or paper.

- **Peer review** – Students evaluate each other's writing in the peer review process.

- **Revising** – Reworking a piece of writing based on structure, tone, and clear connections.

> **Quick Tip**
>
> The peer reviewer reads for content and understanding. The peer reviewer reads through the writing in its entirety and then conferences with his or her partner about suggestions for revision. Then the student revises his or her draft based on that feedback.

- **Editing** – Editing based on conventions and mechanics.

- **Rewriting** – Incorporating changes as they carefully write or type their final drafts.

- **Publishing** – Producing and disseminating the work in a variety of ways, such as a class book, bulletin board, letters to the editor, school newsletter, or website.

Knows the developmental stages of writing (e.g., picture, scribble)

Grade appropriate student writing

Early on, children begin to understand that writing is a form of communication and their marks on paper convey a message (Mayer, 2007).

- **Preliterate drawing** – The student uses drawing to stand for writing and believes that the drawings/writing are communicating a purposeful message.

- **Preliterate scribbling** – The student scribbles but intends the scribbles to be writing. During this stage, the student holds the pencil correctly.

- **Emergent** – The student uses random letters or drawings. Students at this stage also use letter sequences and may write long strings of numbers in random order.

- **Transitional** – The student continues to use a variety of different strategies to spell more difficult words. Students at this stage often use inventive or phonetic spelling.

Preliterate to Emergent	
Scribbling	Random marks or scribbles often occur on a page with drawings. Children may say, "This says Tommy!" (child's name). Toddlers use the terms drawing and writing to describe their marks; however, 3- and 4-year-olds generally understand the difference between the two.
Emergent	
Mock Handwriting or Wavy Scribble	Children produce lines of wavy scribbles as they imitate adult cursive writing. Children will often pretend they are writing something they have seen their parents write such as a grocery list or a letter.
Mock Letters	Children attempt to form alphabetic representations, which also often appear in their drawings. Writing in this stage is often vertical versus horizontal. Children make shapes that resemble conventional letters.
Transitional	
Conventional Letters	Children begin to write letters, usually from their name or a family member's name. As children's mock letters become more and more conventional, real letters of the alphabet begin to appear. Children will often create strings of letters across a page and "read" them as real sentences or a series of sentences.
Invented Spelling (also known as approximated or phonetic spelling)	Children write words using phonemic awareness. The words are not spelled correctly but do resemble the sounds of the words. For example, invented spelling of the word *was* may be *wuz*, or the invented spelling of the word *other* may be *uther*.
Fluent	
Conventional Spellings	Children's approximated spellings gradually become more and more conventional. The child's own name is usually written first, followed by words such as mom, dad, and love. Initially, children may incorrectly copy words. Eventually, words will be written correctly. Adults can support the child's move to conventional spelling by being patient and by continuing to serve as a good writing model.

Knows the importance of digital tools for producing and publishing writing and for interacting with others

Digital tools for producing, publishing, and interacting with others

Using digital tools can enhance writing in the classroom. Digital tools can be used for prewriting, freewriting, revisions, collaboration, and proofing/editing. The following are just a few of the digital tools available to teachers and students.

Internet – The Internet can be used for research and general information on a topic. It is also an effective tool for prewriting. For example, students may research a topic on the Internet before writing, or a teacher may use a video from the Internet to introduce a topic before writing.

Word processing software – This is also referred to as Microsoft® WORD. However, the test questions will not refer to it as Microsoft® WORD. This tool is helpful during the free writing process. Students can open up a blank page and type whatever comes to mind. They can move sentences and paragraphs around using the editing tools.

Document sharing software – This is also referred to as Google® Docs. However, the test questions will not refer to it as Google® Docs. With this tool, students can write collaboratively in one document. The document is saved in real time, and students can suggest changes and revisions in the document.

Editing software – This software identifies errors in grammar and spelling and suggests revisions.

Online plagiarism checker – Teachers can copy and paste excerpts of student work or upload student writing into these websites, and the software will search the Internet to determine if the work is that of the student's or if it was copied from another source. These sites will often give the teacher a percentage of what was copied without proper citations.

Citation software – These tools help students properly cite and organize sources in their writing.

References to Use with Writing

- **Online Dictionary** – Electronic resource that lists the words of a language (typically in alphabetical order) and provides their meaning. Dictionaries often provide information about pronunciation, origin, and usage.

- **Online Encyclopedia** – Electronic resources that provide information on many subjects. Encyclopedias are typically arranged alphabetically.

- **Online Thesaurus** – An electronic word list in groups of synonyms and related concepts.

Using Resources

A dictionary is an effective tool for looking up words and determining parts of speech. However, when teaching vocabulary, it is best to teach in context and not just using a dictionary to find word meaning.

Internet sources

- **Keyword search** – Using specific words to search for information using the Internet.

- **Databases** – A structured set of data held in a computer, especially one that is accessible in various ways.

- **Bulletin boards** – Computer application used to share information.

Knows the research process

Research process

The **research process** is broken down into seven steps.

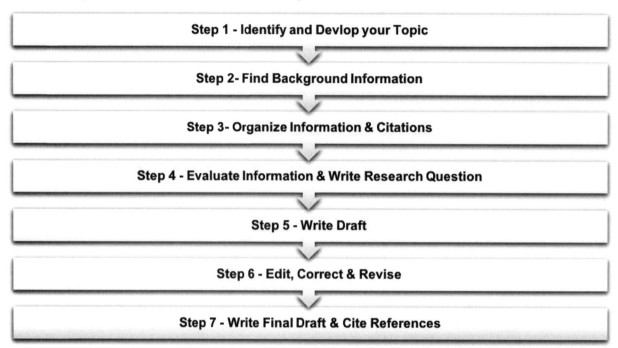

Step 1 - Identify and Devlop your Topic

Step 2- Find Background Information

Step 3- Organize Information & Citations

Step 4 - Evaluate Information & Write Research Question

Step 5 - Write Draft

Step 6 - Edit, Correct & Revise

Step 7 - Write Final Draft & Cite References

(Cornell University Library, 2016)

Primary and secondary sources

Students will use a variety of primary and secondary sources when they write research papers. It is important that teachers help students identify relevant primary and secondary resources and cite them appropriately.

	Humanities	Sciences
Primary Sources (original source)	• Diaries, journals, letters • Interviews with people who lived during a particular time (e.g., survivors of genocide in Rwanda or the Holocaust) • Songs, plays, novels, stories • Paintings, drawings, sculptures • Autobiographies	• Published results of research studies • Published results of scientific experiments • Published results of clinical trials • Proceedings of conferences and meetings
Secondary Sources (interpretation of the original source)	• Biographies • Histories • Literary criticism • Book, art, theater reviews • Newspaper articles that interpret	• Publications about the significance of research or experiments • Analysis of a clinical trial • Review of the results of several experiments or trials

Reliable and unreliable sources

Evaluating Sources

It is important to evaluate source information for relevancy. This is especially important when using Internet sources. Understanding credibility in resources is essential for scoring well on the exam.

Sources	Definition	Examples
Reliable Sources	A trustworthy source of information	• Published results of research studies • Published results of scientific experiments • Published results of clinical trials • Proceedings of conferences and meetings
Unreliable Sources	An unqualified and unreliable source to support ideas	• Online blogs about a particular topic • Chats or discussion forums on the Internet • Websites from private companies

Paraphrasing and plagiarizing

It is imperative that students learn from a young age how to paraphrase information into their own words. Teachers can help students do this by showing students how to take notes that summarize a topic or idea. Teachers can also encourage students to cite information when the student has taken an idea or excerpt from a text.

Paraphrasing – Restating a text, passage, or work to express the meaning in another form (Merriam-Webster Dictionary, 2019).

Plagiarizing – Passing off the ideas or words of another as one's own; using another's work without crediting the source (Merriam-Webster Dictionary, 2019).

IMPORTANT: Even when a student paraphrases content, if the idea or information was obtained from someone else's work, it MUST be cited in the text.

Credible print and digital sources

Evaluating Sources

It is important to help students discern between reliable and unreliable sources of information. It is the responsibility of the teacher to provide multiple reliable resources to students for research purposes. There are several types of resources teachers can use in the classroom to help students find reliable information.

- **Peer-reviewed journals/articles** – These academic sources are found in databases and are considered credible. The sources have been vetted and verified. Academic journals are one of the most reliable and credible resources to use in the classroom. When possible, teachers should use peer-reviewed academic journals for research purposes.

- **Websites** – Websites are helpful for a general audience, for background information, to evaluate different perspectives on a topic, and for current news events. Things like ads and heavy political or controversial opinion statements are red flags that the site is biased and unreliable.

- **Print sources (books, newspapers, magazines)** – Books are a good place to start the search for historical information or context. Magazines and newspapers will be useful for current events in an easy-to-understand format.

B. Language

Knows the conventions of standard English grammar, usage, mechanics, and spelling when writing, speaking, reading, and listening

Parts of speech

Most elementary classrooms will focus on 8 different parts of speech when teaching the writing process: nouns, verbs, adjective, adverbs, pronouns, prepositions, interjections, and conjunctions.

Noun	Verb
A person, place, or thing	Shows action
EX: John, the school, a rock	EX: run, walk, read

Adjective	Adverb
Describes a noun	Describes a verb, adjective or another adverb and usually ends in *ly*
EX: pretty, large, young	EX: quickly, bravely, somberly

Pronoun	Preposition
Used in place of a noun	Shows the relationship between nouns and between pronouns.
EX: he, she, they, we	EX: at, on, of, over

Interjection	Conjunctions
A word or phrase that expresses a strong emotion.	Joins two words or phrases and shows a connection.
EX: Wow, Whoa, Jeez	EX: but, and, yet, so

Errors in usage, mechanics, and spelling

When correcting student writing, there are an infinite number of things to look for in usage mechanics and spelling. The following are a few areas where students make the most mistakes in their writing.

Fragments and run-ons are perhaps the most common errors in student writing.

Fragments are any group of words that do NOT create a complete sentence. Fragments come in several forms. Other forms of fragments include predicates without a subject, subjects without a predicate, and phrases that are neither a subject nor predicate.

Incorrect	*I suspect he can't read a map. Because he always gets lost.*	"Because he always gets lost" is not an independent clause; it is a dependent clause because it relies on the other clause to make its meaning clear. **Correction:** *I suspect he can't read a map because he always gets lost.* *Because he always gets lost, I suspect he can't read a map.*
Incorrect	*Walking down the street.*	Here, we only have the verb phrase, walking down the street. There is no subject. **Correction:** *John was walking down the street.*

Run-ons are multiple sentences in a row lacking clear grammatical structure and punctuation.

Incorrect	*He went to the store he maxed out his credit card again and when his dad found out he got in a lot of trouble.*	This example is missing conjunctions and punctuation. There are many ways to correct this sentence, but the best two ways are listed below. **Correction:** *He went to the store and maxed out his credit card again, and when his dad found out, he got in a lot of trouble.* *He went to the store and maxed out his credit card again. When his dad found out, he got in a lot of trouble.*

Pronoun/Antecedent Agreement

Pronouns must agree with the noun they replace or the antecedent.

Antecedent Agreement	
My <u>mother</u> went to the store, and <u>she</u> bought some cookies from the bakery.	The pronoun is <u>she</u> and the antecedent is <u>mother</u>.
Good <u>bosses</u> make sure <u>their</u> employees get a raise every year.	The word <u>bosses</u> is plural; therefore, the plural pronoun—<u>their</u>—is correct.
The <u>dog</u> barked constantly, so <u>its</u> owner put a shock collar on <u>it</u>.	The pronoun <u>it</u> agrees with the antecedent <u>dog</u>. Also, <u>its</u> is the correct possessive pronoun to use here.
The <u>team</u> lost so many of <u>its</u> games, the coach decided to quit.	Even though there may be 10 people on a <u>team</u>, the <u>team</u> is singular. Therefore, <u>it</u> is the correct pronoun here. Beware of collective nouns; they can be tricky on the exam.
The <u>board members</u> were tired, so <u>they</u> delayed the vote until the next meeting.	There are multiple <u>board members</u>—plural. Therefore, the pronoun <u>they</u> is correct.
Antecedent Disagreement	
The <u>university</u> had <u>their</u> annual gala to raise funds.	While there may be thousands of people who are part of the university, <u>university</u> is a singular noun. In this case, the plural pronoun <u>their</u> does not agree with the singular antecedent <u>university</u>.
	Whenever you see the pronouns **they, their**, or **them**, slow down to determine whether the subject is singular or plural.
	Correction: Replace their with <u>its</u>.
	The <u>university</u> had <u>its</u> annual gala to raise funds.
<u>Some</u> of the <u>marbles</u> rolled out of its bag.	<u>Some</u> and <u>marbles</u> indicate this is a plural antecedent.
	Correction: Replace its with their.
	<u>Some</u> of the <u>marbles</u> rolled out of <u>their</u> bag.
<u>A student</u> should go to <u>their</u> locker during lunch.	<u>A student</u> is singular, so a singular pronoun is needed here.
	Correction: Replace their with <u>his or her</u>.
	<u>A student</u> should go to <u>his or her</u> locker during lunch.
	Better yet, change the subject to match the pronoun their.
	<u>Students</u> should go to <u>their</u> lockers before lunch.
	*Notice the noun-noun agreement here: multiple students have multiple lockers.

Pronoun Case

Pronouns have distinctive cases based on sentence function.

Subjective Pronouns Occur in the subject of the sentence.	Objective Pronouns Occur in the predicate of the sentence (after the action verb or prepositional phrase).	Possessive Pronouns Show possession in the sentence.
I – *I went to the store.* The pronoun <u>I</u> is the subject of the sentence.	**me** – *Sally went to the store with <u>me</u>.* The pronoun <u>me</u> is the object of the preposition <u>with</u>.	**my/mine** – *I need to increase <u>my</u> GPA.* *That pencil is <u>mine</u>.* <u>My/mine</u> is the possessive form of the pronoun <u>me/I</u>.
he/she – *<u>She</u> went to the store.* The pronoun <u>she</u> is the subject of the sentence.	**him/her** – *Sally went to the store for <u>him</u>.* The pronoun <u>him</u> is an object of the preposition <u>for</u>. *Mom gave <u>her</u> all the money.* The pronoun <u>her</u> is the indirect object of the verb <u>gave</u>.	**his/her/hers** – *Mark needs to increase <u>his</u> GPA.* The pronoun <u>his</u> is the possessive form of the pronoun <u>he</u>. *Her car was parked outside.* The pronoun <u>her</u> is the possessive form of the pronoun <u>she</u>.
we – *<u>We</u> went to the store.* The pronoun <u>we</u> is the subject of the sentence.	**us** – *Sally went to the store with <u>us</u>.* The pronoun <u>us</u> is the object of the preposition <u>with</u>.	**our/ours** – *Sally and I need to increase <u>our</u> grade-point averages.* The pronoun <u>our</u> is possessive. *That big dog is <u>ours</u>.*
they – *<u>They</u> went to the store.* The pronoun <u>they</u> is the subject of the sentence.	**them** – *My brother went to the party with <u>them</u>.* The pronoun <u>them</u> is the object of the preposition <u>with</u>.	**their/theirs** – *The cars in the parking lot are theirs.* The pronoun <u>theirs</u> is the plural possessive because there are multiple cars belonging to multiple people.

Here are some common ways in which pronoun case is assessed on the exam. We almost always see examples like these on the test. They can be tricky because people often use pronoun case incorrectly in their everyday speech.

Sample Question:

Choose the portion of the sentence that needs to be corrected. If there is no error, choose E.

I was happy when the <u>president</u> of the <u>university</u> came to see my <u>brother</u> and <u>I</u> on Saturday. <u>No error</u>.
                A   B   C   D   E

The answer is **D**. In this case, the pronoun <u>I</u> is used incorrectly. <u>I</u> is a subject pronoun, and should not be used in the predicate. Instead, the pronoun <u>me</u> should be used. When you see questions like this, take out the other person in the sentence to see if the sentence reads correctly.

Correct: *The president came to see <u>me</u>.*

Incorrect: *The president came to see <u>I</u>.*

Be careful—sometimes we use I in the predicate even though it is a subjective pronoun. Look at the examples below and determine which one uses the underlined portion correctly.

A. *I was disappointed to see that my sister received a higher score on her math exam <u>than me</u>.*

B. *I was disappointed to see that my sister received a higher score on her math exam <u>than I</u>.*

In this case, B is correct because if you take this sentence out all the way, it should read:

✓ *I was disappointed to see that my sister received a higher score on her math exam <u>than I did</u>.*

✓ *I was disappointed to see that my sister received a higher score on her math exam <u>than I received</u>.*

Quick Tip

When trying to determine what pronouns to use, look at the surrounding words.

Ask yourself:

- Is this a comparison? Do I see the word <u>than</u>? If so, use <u>I</u>.
  She is taller than I. She is taller than I am.

- Is this a prepositional phrase? Do I see the word <u>to</u> or <u>with</u>? If so use <u>me</u>.

  The president came <u>to</u> see my son and <u>me</u>.

  Sally came <u>with</u> Kim and <u>me</u>.

Pronoun Number and Person

The pronoun must match the number of items in the antecedent.

Antecedent Agreement	
Every time a person comes into the restaurant right before closing time, the cook and bartender roll their eyes.	In this case, the antecedent includes two people: the cook and the bartender. *Their* is a plural pronoun. The plural antecedent matches the plural pronoun.
Antecedent Disagreement	
The teacher told the student to bring their permission slip tomorrow.	In this case, the antecedent includes one student, but *their* is a plural pronoun. The singular antecedent does not match the plural pronoun. Correction: Change the pronoun to <u>his</u> or <u>her</u>. *The teacher told the student to bring her permission slip tomorrow.* Correction: Change the antecedent, the pronoun, and the object to be plural. *The teacher told the students to bring their permission slips tomorrow.*

Pronoun Shift

When writing, it is important to stay with the same voice. However, students often use more than one point of view when they write.

First Person Pronouns	Second Person Pronouns	Third Person Pronouns
I, me, mine, myself, we, us, ours, ourselves	you, yours, yourself, yourselves	he, she, it, him, her, his, hers, its himself, herself, itself, they, them, their, theirs, themselves

Incorrect	*When I buy new clothes, you have to remember to cut the labels off.* *We were starving after 1st period, but you can't get food at our school until lunch.* *She was not sure which road to take, so you ended up getting lost.*
Correct	*When I buy new clothes, I have to remember to cut the labels off.* *We were starving after 1st period, but we can't get food at our school until lunch.* *She was not sure which road to take, so she ended up getting lost.*

Subject/Verb Agreement

When writing, students must have subject verb agreement. This seems like an easy concept. However, sometimes prepositional phrases can make it difficult to align subject and verbs in a sentence.

Singular Nouns/Verbs	
John is late for work. He buys roses for his wife on her birthday.	In simple cases, singular subjects are paired with singular verbs.
Peanut butter and jelly is my favorite kind of sandwich. Room and board is a monthly expense she must include in her budget.	When the two words are joined with and but are treated as a single unit, use the singular noun.
Fifty dollars is a lot for me to spend this week. Seventy-five cents is too much to pay for the can of beans.	When the subject refers to an amount of money, use a singular verb.
Neither Ann nor John is available for a meeting at noon. Either Ann or John is available for a meeting at noon.	When two singular nouns are joined with **either/or** or **neither/nor** in the subject, use a singular verb. Remember—only one of the nouns is completing the action
Plural Nouns/Verbs	
They are late for work. The children buy roses for their mother on her birthday.	In simple cases, plural subjects are paired with plural verbs.
John and Ann are available for a meeting at noon. The bikes and the car fit into the garage.	If the subject includes multiple nouns that are joined by and, use the plural verb.* *In most cases. See above.
Neither the bikes nor the car fits into the garage. Either the car or the bikes fit into the garage.	When a singular noun and a plural noun are joined with **either/or** or **neither/nor** in the subject, make the verb agree with the noun closest to it.

How will the question look on the exam?

The board of directors are having their meeting today.

A.   The board of directors are having their meeting today.

B.   The board of directors is having their meeting today.

C.   The board of directors are having a meeting today.

D.   The board of directors are having its meeting today.

E.   The board of directors is having its meeting today.

The correct answer is **E**. There are two errors in the sentence given, and they have to do with the fact that the board is a collective noun. In addition, the board is the subject. The prepositional phrase is *of directors*. Therefore, you should use the board when determining the verb and pronoun in the sentence.

The board of directors **is** having **its** meeting today.

Quick Tip

Be aware of prepositional phrases when analyzing subject/verb agreement. Test makers will often squeeze in a prepositional phrase to confuse you.

✗   The use of cell phones and computers are prohibited.

In this case, <u>the use</u> is the subject, not cell phones and computers.

Therefore, the verb should be in singular form.

✓   The use of cell phones and computers <u>is</u> prohibited.

Inappropriate Shift in Verb Tense

A shift in verb tense occurs when two or more activities in a sentence are happening within the same time period. Typically, the verb tense in a sentence should remain consistent. However, there are always exceptions to the rule.

Incorrect	*She is <u>driving</u> in the car and <u>turned</u> down the wrong street.*	In this case, <u>is driving</u> is present tense and <u>turned</u> is past tense. **Correction**: Make the verb tenses match. *She <u>is driving</u> in the car and turns down the wrong street.* *She <u>was driving</u> in the car and turned down the wrong street.*
Correct	*As I <u>drove</u> along the highway, I <u>saw</u> two eagles and <u>thought</u> of the amazing trip I <u>had</u>.*	In this case, <u>drove</u>, <u>saw</u>, <u>thought</u>, and <u>had</u> are all past-tense verbs. The tense remains consistent throughout the sentence.

Misplaced and Dangling Modifiers

A misplaced modifier is a word, phrase, or clause that is improperly separated from the word it modifies or describes. The separation makes the sentence confusing.

Incorrect	*Yolanda realized too late that it was a mistake to walk the neighbor's dog in high heels.*	*I saw the magnificent owls skiing down the mountain.*	*Sitting in the kennel, I saw the dog.*
Correct	The phrase <u>in high heels</u> <u>is</u> modifying <u>the neighbor's</u> <u>dog</u>. The dog is not in high heels; Yolanda is in high heels. **Correction:** Rearrange the sentence so that "in high heels" no longer modifies "the neighbor's dog". *Yolanda realized too late that that it was a mistake to wear high heels while walking the neighbor's dog.*	The phrase <u>skiing down the</u> <u>mountain</u> is modifying <u>owls</u> instead of I. **Correction:** *While I was skiing down the mountain, I saw the magnificent owls.*	The phrase <u>sitting in the</u> <u>kennel</u> is modifying <u>I</u> instead of <u>the dog</u>. **Correction:** *I saw the dog that was sitting in the kennel.*

Quick Tip

Misplaced phrases are often subject or predicate location issues.

By moving the phrase to the other part of the sentence, you can usually correct the problem.

Example:

The professor returned the exam with a smile. (The exam isn't smiling.)

With a smile, the professor returned the exam to the student.

Example:

She notified the man in an email that he would be fined. (The man is not in an email.)

In an email, she notified the man that he would be fined.

Frequently Confused Words

Standardized English tests often include questions about frequently confused words.

accept - to agree to receive or do

except - not including .

coarse – rough

course - a direction; a school subject; part of a mealw

---

adverse - unfavorable, harmful

averse - strongly disliking; opposed

complement - an addition that improves

compliment - to praise or express approval; an admiring remark

---

advice - recommendations about what to do
advise - to recommend something

council - a group of people who manage or advise

counsel - advice; to advise

---

affect - to change or make a difference to
effect - a result; to bring about a result

elicit - to draw out a reply or reaction

illicit - not allowed by law or rules

---

aisle - a passage between rows of seats

isle - an island

ensure - to make certain that something will happen

insure - to provide compensation

---

all together - all in one place, all at once
altogether - completely; on the whole

foreword - an introduction to a book

forward - onwards, ahead

---

along - moving or extending horizontally on
a long - referring to something of great length

principal - most important; the head of a school

principle - a fundamental rule or belief

---

aloud - out loud
allowed - permitted

sight - the ability to see

site - a location

---

altar - a sacred table in a church
alter - to change

stationary - not moving
stationery - writing materials

---

amoral - not concerned with right or wrong
immoral - not following accepted moral standards

allusion - indirect reference
illusion - false idea

---

assent - agreement, approval
ascent - the action of rising or climbing up

allude - to make indirect reference to
elude - to avoid

---

bare - naked; to uncover
bear - to carry; to put up with

capital - major city, wealth, assets
capitol - government building

---

bated - in phrase with bated breath; in great suspense
baited - with bait attached or inserted

conscience - sense of morality
conscious - awake, aware

---

censure - to criticize strongly
censor - to ban parts of a book or film

eminent - prominent, important
imminent - about to happen

---

cereal - a breakfast food
serial - happening in a series

everyday - routine, common
every day - each day, all the day

Wrong Word Use

Common words are often misused in speech and text. In this case, one usually is misused for the other. Here are some that typically appear on the *Praxis®* exam.

Commonly Confused Words	Examples in Context
then/than • Then is used to mark time. • Than is used for comparisons.	**Incorrect**: *This is farther **then** I thought.* **Correct**: *This is farther **than** I thought.*
between/among • Between involves two things. • Among involves three or more things.	**Incorrect**: *That matter must be discussed **between** Jeff and his brothers.* **Correct**: *That matter must be discussed **among** Jeff and his brothers.*
number/amount • Number is used for quantifiable nouns (things you can count). • Amount is used for non-quantifiable nouns (things you don't count).	**Incorrect**: *There were a large **amount** of people there.* **Correct**: *There were a large **number** of people there.* **Incorrect**: *The **amount** of dollars she made was staggering.* **Correct**: *The **amount** of money she made was staggering.* **Correct**: *The **number** of dollars she made was staggering.*
many/much • Many is used for count nouns. • Much is used for non-count nouns.	**Incorrect**: ***Much** of the people had left.* **Correct**: ***Many** of the people had left.* **Correct**: ***Much** of the cake was left over after the party.*
less/fewer • Fewer is used for count nouns. • Less is used for non-counts.	**Incorrect**: *There are even **less** people here now.* **Correct**: *There are even **fewer** people here now.* **Correct**: *The population is **less** this year than last year.*
imply/infer • The speaker implies. • The listener infers.	**Incorrect**: *The author **inferred** that Ned was the killer.* **Correct**: *The author **implied** that Ned was the killer.*

Sentence types

Sentences vary in structure. They range from simple, to compound, complex and compound-complex.

Sentence Type	Description	Example
Simple sentence	one independent clause	"I like her."
Compound sentence	two independent clauses and a coordinating conjunction	"I like her, and I like him."
Complex sentence	independent clause and a dependent clause	"Although I like her, I do not like him." "I went to the gym for the first time in months; I felt great afterward."
Compound-Complex sentence	two independent clauses and one dependent clause	I've never liked horror movies, but because my husband likes them, I now watch horror movies all the time.

Sentences also vary in content. In this case, there are four types of sentences: declarative, interrogative, imperative, and exclamatory.

Sentence Type	Examples
Declarative Tells about something and ends with a period.	I have a yellow dress. My sister is in third grade. I like to read novels.
Interrogative Asks something and ends with a question mark.	When are we eating dinner? How do you know what to do after school? What is your favorite color?
Imperative Tells someone to do something and ends with a period.	Clean your classroom. Do your homework, please. Pick up those pencils.
Exclamatory A sentence that shows strong feelings and ends with an exclamation mark.	The cat has fleas! The building is on fire! Watch out for the car!

Parallel Structure

Parallel structure is when the sentence follows the same grammatical pattern.

Ex: He was skiing, snowboarding, and running (all verbs have -ing ending)

Incorrect: He was <u>skiing</u>, <u>snowboarded</u>, and <u>ran</u>.

> **Sample Question**
>
> After reaching level three, you have three chances to defeat the dragon, finding the treasure chest, and collect the magic sword.
>
> A.   After reaching level three, you have three chances to defeat the dragon, to find the treasure chest, and collect the magic sword.
>
> B.   After reaching level three, you have three chances to defeat the dragon, find the treasure chest, and collect the magic sword.
>
> C.   After reaching level three, you have three chances to defeating the dragon, finding the treasure chest, and collecting the magic sword.
>
> D.   No error.
>
> The correct answer is **B**. Here, the phrase <u>you have three chances to</u> connects each of the parallel form items: <u>defeat</u>, <u>find</u>, and <u>collect</u>.

Varieties of English

When students engage with text, they will often encounter dialect and register.

Dialect refers to a variation of a language that is characteristic of the users of that language,

Register refers to a variation of a language that is determined by use—a situation or context. For example, when a character switches to a different dialect to reflect what is happening in the text.

Varieties of English (e.g., dialects, registers) used in stories, dramas, or poems support the overall meaning of text.

Variety of English	Example
Dialect	*Huckleberry Finn* by Mark Twain Jim: "We's safe, Huck, we's safe! Jump up and crack yo' heels. Dat's de good ole Cairo at las', I jis knows it." Huck: "I'll take the canoe and go see, Jim. It mightn't be, you know."
Register	People speak differently in church than they do on the street. Also, people speak differently at work than they do with friends.

(Definitions from Merriam-Webster and literary examples from literacydevices.net)

Understands how to determine the meaning of words and phrases

Meaning of words

Young readers will often use context clues when trying to figure out the meaning of words. For students to be successful at this skill, teachers must show how authors use context in writing. Students must infer a word meaning by using the paragraph or surrounding text. There are several types of context clues that can guide the reader to the meaning of the unknown word. Teachers can use different strategies to help students use context clues as they read.

Context Clue	Definition	Examples
Root word and affix	Breaking apart the word can give more information about the meaning. Looking for the root word and the prefix or suffix can help determine the meaning.	*People who study birds are experts in* **ornithology**. *ornitho* – birds
Contrast	Using another example to give the opposite of what the word means.	*Unlike mammals, snakes lay eggs.* The word <u>unlike</u> prompts the student to think of the opposite of laying eggs.
Logic	Using information from the sentence to logically allow the reader to find the meaning of the word.	*Smaller animals are always on the lookout for* **predators** *that may harm their young.* Smaller animals tend to get eaten by bigger animals. Also, the word <u>harm</u> is helpful here.
Definition	Using the definition of the word in the sentence to give meaning.	*Frugivorous birds eat fruit and prefer it over other foods.* <u>Frugivorous</u> is defined in the sentence.
Example or illustration	Using a specific example to bring meaning to the word or emphasizing the meaning of the word through pictures.	*Some animals like to hide their food in* **inconspicuous** *spots that are hidden from all other animals.* <u>Inconspicuous</u> means discrete or hidden.
Grammar	Understanding verb tense of the words will allow you to use the context clues to find meaning.	*Many animals* **hibernate** *during the winter months and wake during the spring.* <u>Hibernate</u> and <u>wake</u> are both present tense and are oppositely related.

Identifies and interprets figurative language

Figurative language is writing or speech that is not meant to be taken literally. Writers use figurative language to express ideas in vivid or imaginative ways.

Device	Definition	Examples
Simile	Using *like* or *as*.	*She was as thin as a rail.*
Imagery	A description that conveys a clear picture to the reader.	*The big, juicy burger with its melted cheese and ripe tomatoes made my mouth water.*
Metaphor	Applying word or phrase to an individual or thing.	*He was a lion filled with rage.*
Personification	Attributing human characteristics to something not human.	*The cat judged me from across the room.*
Onomatopoeia	The formation of a word from a sound associated with it.	*Sizzle, kurplunk, POW!, BAM!*
Hyperbole	Exaggerated statements or claims not meant to be taken literally.	*The cake must have weighed 500 pounds!*
Idioms	A word or phrase that means something different from its literal meaning.	*It's raining cats and dogs.*
Alliteration	When words that start with the same sound are used repeatedly in a phrase or sentence.	*Paul picked purple pickles in pink pants.*
Irony	Expression of one's meaning by using language that normally signifies the opposite, typically for humorous or emphatic effect.	*It was raining on National Picnic Day.*
Foreshadow	When the author uses clues or imagery to express what might happen next.	*The dark spot on the ceiling grew bigger and bigger.* This is written before a pipe bursts and floods the house.

Analyzes word choice and tone

Just as the words people speak can affect the overall tone of what is being said, the words people write can affect the overall tone of a piece of writing. Teachers must help students understand how word choice and tone affect writing. Word choice can impact the overall tone of the piece. Below are a few examples of the different types of word choices that can affect tone.

Denotation – The formal definition of a word.

Connotation – An idea or feeling that a word invokes in addition to its literal or primary meaning.

Allusion - An expression designed to call something to mind without mentioning it explicitly; an indirect or passing reference. There are three types of allusion: biblical, literary and historical.

When teaching students to select words to achieve the maximum desired effect, have them consider the following.

- **Meaning** – Students can choose words for either their denotative meaning, which is the definition found in a dictionary, or the connotative meaning, which are the emotions, circumstances, or descriptive variations the word evokes.

- **Specificity** – This helps students choose language that is concrete and directly related to the topic. Abstract words can be powerful tools when creating poetry, fiction, or persuasive rhetoric.

- **Audience** – Determining what audience students are writing to can help determine if the writing is meant to engage, amuse, entertain, inform, or incite.

- **Level of Diction** – The level of diction an author chooses directly relates to the intended audience. Diction is classified into four levels of language:

  1. **Formal** which denotes serious discourse.

  2. **Informal** which denotes relaxed but polite conversation.

  3. **Colloquial** which denotes language in everyday usage.

  4. **Slang** which denotes new, often highly informal words and phrases that evolve as a result sociolinguistic constructs such as age, class, wealth status, ethnicity, nationality, and regional dialects.

- **Tone** – Tone is an author's attitude toward a topic.

- **Style** - Word choice is an element in the style.

(Nordquist, 2019)

Understands characteristics of conversational academic, and domain-specific language

Vocabulary

Three tiers of vocabulary

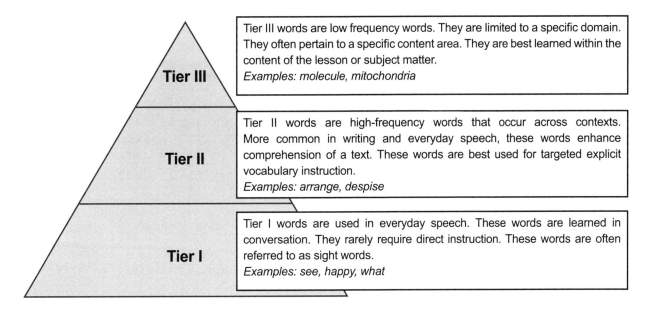

Tier III words are low frequency words. They are limited to a specific domain. They often pertain to a specific content area. They are best learned within the content of the lesson or subject matter.
Examples: molecule, mitochondria

Tier II words are high-frequency words that occur across contexts. More common in writing and everyday speech, these words enhance comprehension of a text. These words are best used for targeted explicit vocabulary instruction.
Examples: arrange, despise

Tier I words are used in everyday speech. These words are learned in conversation. They rarely require direct instruction. These words are often referred to as sight words.
Examples: see, happy, what

Word choice, order, and punctuation

It is important for students to understand that language is used in different ways to convey meaning and communicate ideas.

- **Word choice** – The words students choose to use in their writing can affect the overall tone and impact of the writing.

- **Order** – The way an essay or piece of writing is organized can impact the meaning and tone of the work.

- **Punctuation** – The punctuation used in writing can affect the momentum, flow, and meaning in the writing.

C. Speaking and Listening

Knows the characteristics of effective collaboration to promote comprehension

Communicate for a variety of purposes with diverse partners

Communicating and collaborating with diverse partners is essential for learning. Classrooms can use a wide variety of strategies to engage and encourage students working together.

Activity	Definition	Example
Jigsaw	A cooperative learning activity in which each student becomes an expert on a small piece of information that is part of a much larger piece.	Teachers arrange students in groups. Each group member is assigned a different piece of information. Group members then join with members of other groups assigned the same piece of information and research and/or share ideas about the information. Eventually, students return to their original groups to try to "piece together" a clear picture of the topic at hand.
Think-Pair-Share	A cooperative learning activity in which students work together to solve a problem or answer a question about an assigned reading.	**Think:** Teachers begin by asking a specific question about the text. Students "think" about what they know or have learned about the topic. **Pair**: Each student should be "paired" with another student or a small group. **Share**: Students share their thinking with their partner. Teachers expand the "share" into a whole-class discussion.
Reading Response Journals	A writing activity where students use journals to react to what they read by expressing how they feel and asking questions about the text.	After reading a storybook in class, the teacher asks students to use their reading response journals to respond to the story emotionally, make associations between ideas in the text and their own ideas, and record questions they may have about the story.
Evidence-Based Discussion	The teacher sets the expectation that students use evidence in the text to support claims they make during the discussion.	The class is discussing World War II. Students are split into groups and answer questions on the board. Students must identify where in the text their answer or claim is supported.
Literature Circles	A small-group, cooperative learning activity where students engage and discuss a piece of literature/text	A teacher divides students into groups. Every student in each group has a role. A teacher distributes an article from the newspaper. Students read the article and then discuss the article. Students engage using their role to understand the text.

Identifies the characteristics of active listening

Active listening is engaging in the conversation by asking questions and restating parts of the conversation. This shows comprehension or understanding of what the speaker is saying. There are questions a teacher can ask to show the speaker she is listening to what the speaker is saying. A teacher can use this technique to improve relationships, make students feel cared for, make students feel understood, and make learning easier. Feedback is a big part of active listening.

Steps in the active listening process are as follows:

- Look at the person. Put everything else away and pay attention to the speaker.

- Listen to the words and understand how the speaker is feeling.

- Be interested in what the person is talking about.

- Restate what is being said.

- Ask questions for clarification.

- Be aware of your own opinions and feelings on the subject.

- Restate what the speaker has said. For example, "I hear you when you say, 'I am feeling frustrated with this assignment.'"

Appropriate feedback for active listening can be done verbally and nonverbally.

ACTIVE LISTENING

 Active listening statements

- Good idea because...
- I agree because...
- I like that opinion because...
- I like your point because...
- I want to add to that...
- I also want to share...

 Clarifying Questions

- Why do you think that?
- What do you mean when you say...?
- What else do you think?
- Can you say the whole thing over?
- How can you prove that...?
- Do you have an idea?

 Sharing your thinking

- I think... because...
- I knew that... because it says in the text...
- If you look at the text it says...
- I'd like to share my perspective on that...
- My thinking was that... because...

 Disagreeing respectfully

- I disagree with... because...
- I don't agree with that because the text says...
- I have another idea...
- I have a different perspective because...
- When I thought about it, I thought that...

Verbal Signals	Non-Verbal Signals
• "I'm listening"	• Appropriate eye contact (when culturally appropriate)
• Disclosures	• Facial expressions
• Statements of validation	• Body language
• Support statements	• Silence
• Reflecting/mirroring statements	• Touching (when culturally appropriate)

Knows the characteristics of engaging oral presentations

Oral presentations

When teaching students to engage in oral presentations, teachers should focus on certain principles. Teaching these skills can help students understand how to successfully give presentations that are clear and coherent. Using the Common Core State Standards to review grade-level expectations will help with using the characteristics appropriately in different grade levels.

Characteristic	Explanation
Volume	Using appropriate volume to deliver a clear presentation.
Articulation	Articulation is defined as the movement of the tongue, lips, and jaw in order to make the specific speech sounds.
Awareness of Audience	Understanding what the audience needs and delivering that information as effectively as possible.

It is important that students understand that effective and engaging presentations:

- have clear objectives

- are useful to the audience

- are practiced or rehearsed

- contain visuals and other helpful tools

- include audience participation in some form

This page intentionally left blank.

1. When a student has awareness of phonemes in words, syllables, onset-rime segments, and spelling, he or she is demonstrating:

    A. Phonological awareness

    B. Phonics mastery

    C. Phonemic awareness

    D. Structural analysis

2. Phonemic awareness includes the ability to:

    A. Form compound words and combine word parts

    B. Spell accurately and decode unfamiliar words

    C. Pronounce individual sounds in words

    D. Differentiate between homonyms and spell accurately

3. Which is NOT a best practice for vocabulary instruction?

    A. Model using context clues

    B. Teaching prefixes, suffixes, and roots

    C. Explicit instruction using a dictionary

    D. Using word walls for target vocabulary

4. Students are using the tiles below. They use the first tile (tr) and match it with the others to make words. The students are working on:

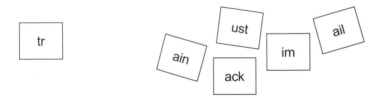

    A. Syllables and rime

    B. Onset and rime

    C. Onset and segmentation

    D. Deletion and rime

5. A student is struggling during reading. The student often stops when encountering high-frequency words and tries to decode them. This interrupts the reading and makes it difficult for the student to understand meaning in the text. Which of the following interventions should the teacher employ?

   A. The teacher should have the student focus on spelling because spelling is phonics, and phonics is a necessary part of the comprehension process.

   B. The teacher should have the student take a diagnostic test and then have the reading coach work with the student where the student's skills are weak.

   C. The teacher should use a running record to record the miscues a student demonstrates during one minute of reading.

   D. The teacher should focus on fluency and automaticity strategies for this student because proper fluency and automaticity will reduce the cognitive demand needed for decoding, leaving more cognitive space for comprehension.

6. When a teacher asks students to make predictions about a text, he or she is fostering the students':

   A. Fluency

   B. Comprehension

   C. Decoding skills

   D. Automaticity

7. Which of the following is an example of prosody?

   A. Reading text quickly and without errors

   B. Decoding confusing words for meaning

   C. Determining meaning in words by analyzing prefixes and suffixes

   D. Reading text, pausing at commas, and using inflection for meaning

Use the passage below to answer questions 8-10.

THE ANT AND THE DOVE

By Aesop

An Ant came down to the brook; he wanted to drink. A wave washed him down and almost drowned him. A Dove was carrying a branch; she saw the Ant was drowning, so she cast the branch down to him in the brook. The Ant got up on the branch and was saved. Then a hunter placed a snare for the Dove, and was on the point of drawing it in. The Ant crawled up to the hunter and bit him on the leg; the hunter groaned and dropped the snare. The Dove fluttered upwards and flew away.

8. In the fable, the words Ant and Dove are capitalized. Why might the author do this?

   A. The author is attempting to give the animals human-like characteristics, using Ant and Dove as their proper names.

   B. The author is following proper grammar by capitalizing Ant and Dove because they are proper nouns in the English language.

   C. The author is trying to distract the reader from the fact that these characters are animals.

   D. The author is attempting to draw attention to the moral of the fable.

9. In the fable, the word snare (highlighted in the text) most likely means a:

    A. Target

    B. Trap

    C. Gun

    D. Blanket

10. Which of the following sentences summarizes the meaning of the fable?

    A. It is important to pay attention because you never know when there will be friend or foe nearby.

    B. A dove should stay in the sky, and an ant should not go near the water if it wants to survive in nature.

    C. It is important to work as a team because every living organism needs others to survive.

    D. It is important to help those in need because you never know when you will be in need yourself.

Students in a 5th grade language arts and reading class are creating stories using different literary elements. Use the student writing sample below to answer questions 11–13.

(1) Bridgett could not wait to tell her parents about the A+ she earned on her math exam. (2) She had worked for days, studying meticulously for the exam. (3) She looked over her notes, practiced her questions, and didn't let anyone distract her from her goal. (4) That was how Bridgett was, she was determined and resilient. (5) It paid off, and Bridgett was able to achieve the score she wanted: an A+.

11. What literary element is the student focusing on in the paragraph above?

    A. Foreshadowing

    B. Sequence

    C. Imagery

    D. Characterization

12. The teacher suggests that the student change sentence 3 to:

    She looked over her notes, practiced her questions, and focused on the goal.

    This change reflects which of the following English grammar concepts?

    A. Subject-verb agreement

    B. Pronoun-antecedent agreement

    C. Parallel structure

    D. Sentence variety

13. Which sentences in the piece show that the student has an understanding of vocabulary and complex sentence structure. Choose all that apply.

   A. Sentence 1

   B. Sentence 2

   C. Sentence 3

   D. Sentence 4

   E. Sentence 5

14. Which of the following edits would be most effective for sentence 4?

   A. Change the comma to a semicolon.

   B. Change the comma to a colon.

   C. Change the comma to a conjunction.

   D. Leave the sentence as is.

Use the poem below to answer questions 15–17.

The Road Not Taken (an excerpt)

By Robert Frost

Two roads diverged in a yellow wood,
And sorry I could not travel both
And be one traveler, long I stood
And looked down one as far as I could
To where it bent in the undergrowth;

Then took the other, as just as fair,
And having perhaps the better claim,
Because it was grassy and wanted wear;
Though as for that the passing there
Had worn them really about the same,

And both that morning equally lay
In leaves no step had trodden black.
Oh, I kept the first for another day!
Yet knowing how way leads on to way,
I doubted if I should ever come back.

I shall be telling this with a sigh
Somewhere ages and ages hence:
Two roads diverged in a wood, and I—
I took the one less traveled by,
And that has made all the difference.

15. What is the pattern of the poem above?

   A. ABABA

   B. ABAAB

   C. AABBA

   D. ABBAB

16. The author uses stanza 1 and stanza 2 in the poem above primarily to show:

   A. An image

   B. A comparison

   C. Repetition

   D. Alliteration

17. The third-person objective point of view allows the reader to understand:

   A.   only the feelings of the narrator.

   B.   only the feelings of one character.

   C.   the feelings of all the characters.

   D.   the feelings of the main characters.

18. A teacher is working with students on phonemes. She says the word **place** and asks the students to say the word without the **p** sound. This is called:

   A.   Deletion

   B.   Substitution

   C.   Blending

   D.   Segmenting

19. A student is scribbling from left to write. What stage of the writing process is the student in?

   A.   Preliterate

   B.   Emergent

   C.   Transitional

   D.   Fluent

20. Students are working in collaborative groups. They are reading text together and discussing meaning. What can the teacher do to ensure that all students in the group have an opportunity to listen and be heard?

   A.   Make the groups as large as possible.

   B.   Assign an administrator to each group.

   C.   Limit the groups to 3–5 students.

   D.   Assign times when each student can speak.

21. Match the stage of writing to the activity.

1.	writing strings of words		A.	preliterate
2.	writing his or her name		B.	emergent
3.	scribbling in a pattern		C.	transitional
4.	scribbling randomly		D.	fluent

22. Which of the following is the benefit of using document-sharing software instead of using word processing software?

   A.   Document-sharing software allows the students to see their grammar and spelling mistakes in real-time.

   B.   Document-sharing software allows the teacher to determine easily if a student has plagiarized material from the internet.

   C.   Document-sharing software allows the student to incorporate a rubric into the writing assignment.

   D.   Document-sharing software allows several students to collaborate on a piece of writing in real-time.

23. A teacher is helping her ELLs understand living situations (shopping, going to school, eating dinner, etc.) in English. The students are matching icons and pictures to living scenarios written in English. What stage of English language proficiency are the students in?

    A. Entering

    B. Emerging

    C. Developing

    D. Bridging

24. A teacher is using a piece of informational text with students. What tier are the words shaded below?

    The DNA molecule contains all the genetic information for living organisms. The DNA molecule contains nucleotides. Those nucleotides make up the nitrogen bases of the DNA molecule.

    A. I

    B. II

    C. III

    D. I & III

25. Why is it important for a teacher to integrate oral, written, and visual elements from texts when teaching comprehension?

    A. Integrating oral, written, and visual elements from texts helps to make the material interesting to students, which helps students comprehend the text.

    B. Integrating oral, written, and visual elements from texts enhances the meaning of complex text, which helps students comprehend the text.

    C. Integrating oral, written, and visual elements from texts helps to make classical text modern so students can understand the text.

    D. Integrating oral, written, and visual elements from texts makes reading the text easier for students to understand than if those elements were not integrated.

26. Which three of the following are qualitative measures of text complexity?

    A. Predictability of text

    B. Familiarity of topics in the text

    C. Total word count

    D. Single vs. multi-themed

27. If a teacher wants to encourage students' critical thinking when engaging with text, what would be the best activity?

    A. Work in collaborative groups to identify complex vocabulary.

    B. Engage in paired reading of poems and identify images in the poems.

    C. Participate in a reading competition where those who read the most pages win.

    D. Work in literature circles and evaluate how different texts are related.

28. Which of the following is considered a best practice when planning lessons for ELLs?

    A. Using the WIDA standards to guide pedagogy and practice with ELLs.

    B. Using the Internet to research exciting activates for students who are learning English.

    C. Consult with a peer teacher who has experience with ELL instruction.

    D. Group all ELL students together to apply interventions effectively.

29. A teacher is engaging in a running record with students individually. As the student reads, the teacher indicates, with a tally mark, any time a student makes a mistake in the reading. After one minute, the teacher stops the student, tallies the mistakes, and determines the student's words per minute. The teacher is measuring the student's:

    A. Accuracy and comprehension

    B. Fluency and comprehension

    C. Accuracy and rate

    D. Rate and prosody

30. Why is it important for students to work on fluency?

    A. Fluency helps a student read quickly, which helps the student get through the reading with enough time to answer comprehension questions.

    B. Fluency reduces the amount of time a student spends decoding words, which helps the student apply cognitive energy to understanding the text.

    C. Fluency helps a student increase correct words per minute measures, which helps the teacher group students into comprehension centers.

    D. Fluency allows the students to decode words more efficiently, which helps the student focus on complex vocabulary rather than sight words.

31. Which of the following are considered text structures? Choose all that apply.

    A. Cause and effect

    B. Problem and solution

    C. Chronological patterns

    D. Character development

32. Which of the following words would be most effective to use when teaching root word analysis?

    A. Pizza

    B. Tree

    C. Computer

    D. Social

Use the passage below to answer questions 33–36.

An Excerpt from *Emma* by Jane Austen

Emma Woodhouse, handsome, clever, and rich, with a comfortable home and happy disposition, seemed to unite some of the best blessings of existence; and had lived nearly twenty-one years in the world with very little to distress or vex her.

She was the youngest of the two daughters of a most affectionate, indulgent father; and had, in consequence of her sister's marriage, been mistress of his house from a very early period. Her mother had died too long ago for her to have more than an indistinct remembrance of her caresses; and her place had been supplied by an excellent woman as governess, who had fallen little short of a mother in affection.

Sixteen years had Miss Taylor been in Mr. Woodhouse's family, less as a governess than a friend, very fond of both daughters, but particularly of Emma. Between *them* it was more the intimacy of sisters. Even before Miss Taylor had ceased to hold the nominal office of governess, the mildness of her temper had hardly allowed her to impose any restraint; and the shadow of authority being now long passed away, they had been living together as friend and friend very mutually attached, and Emma doing just what she liked; highly esteeming Miss Taylor's judgment, but directed chiefly by her own.

The real evils, indeed, of Emma's situation were the power of having rather too much her own way, and a disposition to think a little too well of herself; these were the disadvantages which threatened alloy to her many enjoyments. The danger, however, was at present so unperceived, that they did not by any means rank as misfortunes with her.

Sorrow came—a gentle sorrow—but not at all in the shape of any disagreeable consciousness—Miss Taylor married. It was Miss Taylor's loss which first brought grief. It was on the wedding-day of this beloved friend that Emma first sat in mournful thought of any continuance. The wedding over, and the bride-people gone, her father and herself were left to dine together, with no prospect of a third to cheer a long evening. Her father composed himself to sleep after dinner, as usual, and she had then only to sit and think of what she had lost.

33. It can be inferred from the passage that Miss Taylor is:

   A.   A demanding woman, especially where Emma is concerned

   B.   A meek woman, afraid to impose any rules or regulations

   C.   A self-centered woman who only cares about her own well-being

   D.   A dignified woman, who is easy to get along with

34. The main idea of the passage above is:

   A.   Emma and her father are left alone after Miss Taylor gets married, and they have to fend for themselves.

   B.   Emma Woodhouse develops a bond with her governess and is lost when her governess marries and moves out of the house.

   C.   Emma Woodhouse is used to getting her own way and thought too much of herself, which causes her problems in life.

   D.   Emma Woodhouse's mother dies when Emma is young, leaving Emma and her father to care for one another.

35. The word disposition, highlighted in paragraph 1, most likely means:

   A. Personality

   B. Social status

   C. Occupation

   D. Situation

36. Which of the following lines supports the idea that Miss Taylor was not strict with Emma?

   A. Emma Woodhouse, handsome, clever, and rich, with a comfortable home and happy disposition, seemed to unite some of the best blessings of existence; and had lived nearly twenty-one years in the world with very little to distress or vex her.

   B. Sixteen years had Miss Taylor been in Mr. Woodhouse's family, less as a governess than a friend, very fond of both daughters, but particularly of Emma.

   C. Even before Miss Taylor had ceased to hold the nominal office of governess, the mildness of her temper had hardly allowed her to impose any restraint.

   D. The real evils, indeed, of Emma's situation were the power of having rather too much her own way, and a disposition to think a little too well of herself

37. Which of the following lines is an example of personification?

   A. She was as tall as a pine tree.

   B. The turtle moved along the grass slowly.

   C. Her hair was spun gold blowing in the breeze.

   D. The road had risen happily to meet her feet.

38. Which of the following are considered text features? Choose all that apply.

   A. Headings

   B. Readability

   C. Graphs

   D. Bolded words

39. Which of the following words would be considered a tier II vocabulary word?

   A. She

   B. Examined

   C. Lithosphere

   D. Place

40. What would be the most appropriate and effective approach to determining students' comprehension while reading a story in class. Check all that apply.

   A. Ask students to summarize the main points of the text.

   B. Ask students to identify important vocabulary within the text.

   C. Ask students to sound out difficult words in the text.

   D. Ask students to predict what might happen next in the text.

41. Which of the following words is a CVCe word? Check all that apply.

    A. Back

    B. Bake

    C. Tack

    D. Take

42. If a teacher wants to focus on morphology, what would be the most appropriate activity in which to have students engage?

    A. Fluency reads for time

    B. Comprehension checks after reading

    C. Comparing two texts to relate their similarities

    D. Breaking words down into prefixes, suffixes, and roots

43. Which of the following is considered an open syllable?

    A. Late

    B. Track

    C. Play

    D. Cat

44. If a teacher is helping students understand syntax, which of the following would be most effective?

    A. Students work collaboratively to understand meaning in text.

    B. Students identify improper spelling and grammar in a piece of text.

    C. Students use a word wall to identify important words in the text.

    D. Students identify point of view while reading a story.

45. Which of the following is a component of fluency?

    A. Reading comprehension

    B. Identifying text structure

    C. Summarizing events in a text

    D. Reading with prosody

46. Which of the following is a component of phonemic awareness?

    A. Identifying individual sounds in words

    B. Understanding correct spelling of words

    C. Identifying proper endings in words like *-ing* and *-ed*

    D. Memorizing high-frequency words

Use the following excerpt from George Gershwin's opera Porgy and Bess to answer questions 47–48.

"Say, who is you? Whar is you? Dog my cats ef I didn' hear sumf'n. Well, I know what I's gwyne to do: I's gwyne to set down here and listen tell I hears it ag'in."

47. The piece above would be best used as a lesson in:

   A. Characterization

   B. Personification

   C. Dialect

   D. Syntax

48. The work above would be best classified as a:

   A. Narrative

   B. Autobiography

   C. Speech

   D. Persuasive essay

49. Students are engaging in cooperative learning as they analyze informational text. Each student in the group has a role. What is the most effective way to use the role of the administrator of the group?

   A. To ensure all students get a chance to read aloud

   B. To keep the group on task

   C. To make sure every student in the group is heard

   D. To make sure all norms are followed in the group

50. Students are engaging in a group discussion regarding literature they have read in class. Which of the following statements would most align with someone who is being an active listener?

   A. "What did you think about the text? I thought it was interesting."

   B. "I wonder why it ended that way. What do you think?"

   C. "When you say, 'the text was difficult to read,' do you mean because of the vocabulary or because of the subject?"

   D. "You are just like the main character. She has the same personality as you have."

51. Which of the following would be the most appropriate example of persuasive writing?

   A. *As she walked through the room, she remembered her childhood and was transported back in time.*

   B. *Picturesque mountains and pristine grass are the backdrop to the beautiful 19th century campus.*

   C. *In 1969, the United States made it to the moon, making the U.S. the most powerful nation in the world.*

   D. *This is the most pressing issue of our time, and young people should get out and vote.*

52. Students are in the brainstorming stage of writing a research paper. Which of the following is the most appropriate activity for this stage?

    A. Students are engaged in a peer review to evaluate each other's work for clarity and consistency.

    B. Students are searching terms on the Internet and looking at different publications for ideas.

    C. Students are using academic journals to compile a bibliography for their papers.

    D. Students are working together using document-sharing software to edit their papers.

53. Which of the following activities would be most appropriate to help students avoid plagiarism?

    A. Use the abstract of a research study.

    B. Use note cards to summarize ideas in the text.

    C. Use academic journals for scholarly research.

    D. Conduct peer reviews during class.

54. A teacher wants to show students the difference between reliable resources and unreliable resources. Which of the following activities would be most effective to teach this?

    A. Students compare and contrast social media for quotes found in online magazines and blogs.

    B. Students compare and contrast an academic journal with an online magazine.

    C. Students look at the differences between information found on a .gov website and a .org website.

    D. Students compare and contrast primary and secondary resources.

55. Which of the following is used in an online magazine or blog to give the reader immediate access to material related to the content being communicated in a publication?

    A. Bibliography

    B. Citation

    C. Hyperlink

    D. Index

56. Which of the following is an example of a student using evidence from the text to support an argument about the central theme in the text?

    A. "In the beginning of the story, the boy says, 'Go away, I don't need any friends.'"

    B. "The main character is lonely."

    C. "The tone of the story is sad but then happy at the end."

    D. "I like the main character because he reminds me of my friend."

57. Which of the following perspectives does third-person omniscient narrative give the reader?

    A. Only the narrator's perspective

    B. Only the main character's perspective

    C. No one's perspective

    D. Everyone's perspective

58. Which of the following is true regarding meter in poetry?

    A. It contributes to the rhyme in the poem.

    B. It contributes to the rhythm of the poem.

    C. It contributes to the vocabulary in the poem.

    D. It contributes to the structure of the poem.

59. The teacher is using a text where each chapter is written in first-person from a different character's perspective. What would be the benefit of using this novel?

    A. Students can check to see if the narrator switches point of view anywhere in the text.

    B. Students can analyze each character's perspective of events occurring in the text.

    C. Students can each read for the different characters in the text.

    D. Students can identify similarities among all the characters in the text.

60. Which of the following is an example of a teacher using quantitative measures for evaluating text complexity?

    A. Counting how many times a student miscues while reading the text

    B. Asking students how the text relates to their lives

    C. Using lexile to determine reading level

    D. Evaluating survey data to see what book students like most

61. Which of the following is the most important thing for students to consider when they are writing a persuasive essay?

    A. Audience

    B. Readability

    C. Point of view

    D. Tone

62. Which of the following words depends on context for its meaning?

    A. Swim

    B. Read

    C. Relax

    D. Restate

63. Which of the following is most aligned with tone in text?

    A. The overall feeling of the text

    B. The central theme of the text

    C. The setting in the text

    D. The interaction among characters in the text

64. Which of the following are important elements of oral presentations?

    A. Tone, point of view, volume

    B. Articulation, awareness of audience, volume

    C. Articulation, vocabulary, point of view

    D. Awareness of audience, tone, volume

65. Which TWO would be considered expository writing?

    A. A brochure on the Grand Canyon

    B. A letter from a husband to a wife during the Civil War

    C. An op ed in the local newspaper discussing new bridge construction

    D. An excerpt from a social studies textbook on WWII

Use the following sentences to answer questions 66-67.

She knew it was a mistake to walk the dog in high heels.

66. Which of the following is the error in the above sentence?

    A. Subject-verb agreement

    B. Pronoun-antecedent

    C. Misplaced modifier

    D. Parallel structure

67. Which of the following would be the most effective revision for the sentence above?

    A. Rearrange the sentence so *high heels* modifies the subject in the sentence.

    B. Change the pronoun "she" to a name of a person.

    C. Put a comma after the word *mistake*.

    D. Change the verb phrase to *walk* to *walking*.

68. What would be the most effective tool for students to use for free writing?

    A. Wiki

    B. Word processing software

    C. Presentation software

    D. Search engine

69. If a student is in the revising stage of writing, what is the student doing?

    A. Reading another student's writing and marking spelling errors

    B. Fixing grammar and spelling mistakes

    C. Brainstorming ideas

    D. Modifying the writing in terms of organization and content

1) The American alligator is a reptile. 2) The American alligator is an apex predator. 3) An apex predator is a predator at the top of the food chain. 4) Other apex predators are lions and tigers. 5) The American alligator lays eggs in sticks, leaves and mud.

70. Which of the following would strengthen the paragraph in terms of complex sentences?

    A.   Change sentences 1 and 2 by combining them with punctuation.

    B.   Delete sentence 4.

    C.   Use varied vocabulary for the term predator.

    D.   Add a comma after leaves in sentence 5.

71. What would be appropriate feedback to share with the student who wrote the paragraph above?

    A.   *"You use the term American alligator a lot. Try combining sentences to give the paragraph varied language."*

    B.   *"Your writing does a great job describing your knowledge about the American alligator. Consider deleting sentence 4 so it doesn't take away from your overall theme."*

    C.   *"Good job! Keep up the great work!"*

    D.   *"Consider using a closing statement at the end."*

72. Which of the following activities would benefit the student who wrote the essay above?

    A.   Showing a video tutorial on how to format a research paper

    B.   Allowing the student to use spell check

    C.   Using small group instruction on combining sentences with different punctuation

    D.   Facilitating a whole-group presentation on vocabulary

73. Which of the following words in the writing is considered a tier III word?

    A.   Apex predator

    B.   Reptile

    C.   Alligator

    D.   Food chain

74. Which TWO of the following words would be considered tier II words?

    A.   Better

    B.   Opinion

    C.   The

    D.   Amphibian

75. Which of the following would be considered the publishing stage of the writing process?

    A. Editing grammar mistakes in a research paper

    B. Reading another student's paper for content and understanding

    C. Brainstorming new ideas to write about

    D. Mailing a letter to the editor of a newspaper

76. Which of the following should students do to avoid plagiarism?

    A. Use as many direct quotes as possible and cite them with the author and page number

    B. Paraphrase as much as possible and cite those ideas within the paper and in the bibliography

    C. Put a Works Cited page at the end of the paper with all the authors used in it

    D. Use quotation marks around any writing that was taken from another piece of writing

77. A student is writing words, reproduced below. What stage of writing is the student in?

    We went to the uther gas stashun.

    A. Pre-literate

    B. Emergent

    C. Transitional

    D. Fluent

78. Which of the following would be an effective activity to help students think and listen critically?

    A. Collaborative discussions where students evaluate what each other is saying and repeat pieces of those discussions back before presenting a new idea

    B. A debate where students use proper parliamentary procedures to state their opinions and cite evidence to support their opinions

    C. Literature circles where every student plays a role in the outcome of the discussion

    D. An activity where students work together to build a website

79. Which TWO of the following would be considered a primary source?

    A. Martin Luther King's I Have a Dream speech

    B. President Reagan's letters to his wife

    C. A biography on the life of Andrew Jackson

    D. A social studies textbook

80. What figurative language is being used in the excerpt below?

    The steak sizzled and popped on the hot grill.

    A. Personification

    B. Simile

    C. Onomatopoeia

    D. Metaphor

#	Answer	Category	Explanation
1.	A	I	All these individual skills fit under the umbrella of phonological awareness. Phonological awareness is a broad set of skills that includes identifying and manipulating units of oral language—parts such as phonemes in words, syllables, and onsets and rimes. Students with phonological awareness also understand conventional spelling. Remember, phonemic awareness is a sub-skill of phonological awareness and only deals with the smallest unit of sound—the phoneme. Signs of strong phonemic awareness include being able to hear rhyme and alliteration. Although they are often used interchangeably, when talking about reading skills, phonological awareness is usually the correct term.
2.	C	I	Phonemic awareness is understanding the individual sounds—or phonemes—in words. When you see the word *phonemic*, think of the root word *phone*, which is related to sound. Answers A, B, and D all reference words and spelling, which is connected to phonics.
3.	C	I	When teaching vocabulary, students must have the opportunity to interact with words in an authentic manner. Answer A is a best practice because using context clues allows the students to figure out new vocabulary by evaluating words and ideas around the vocabulary words. Answer B is also a best practice because analyzing prefixes, suffixes, and roots is a way to deconstruct a word by understanding its word parts. Answer D is also a best practice because word walls are interactive. Out of all the answers, answer C is *not* the best practice. Dictionaries are amazing tools to use as a supplement to instruction. However, explicitly using a dictionary is not an authentic practice in vocabulary instruction.
4.	B	I	In this activity, the students are using onset and rime. Onsets are the beginning consonant and consonant cluster; in this case, tr is the onset. Rime is the vowel and consonants that follow. Some common rimes are: *-ack, -an, -aw, -ick, -ing, -op, -unk, -ain, -ank, -ay, -ide, -ink, -or, -ock, -ight, -ame, -eat, -ine.*
5.	D	I	If the student is stopping when encountering high-frequency words (sight words) to decode them, the student is struggling with fluency. Having automaticity when reading is essential in the comprehension process. Automaticity does reduce the cognitive demand needed for decoding. That reduced cognitive demand can then be applied to the comprehension process. Focusing on spelling (answer A) is not the best approach. A diagnostic test (answer B) is unnecessary because the teacher can already see the problem is fluency. Answer C is not the best choice because it is essentially repeating what the teacher can already see: the student is having trouble with fluency.
6.	B	I	Predicting is a high-level skill and coincides with comprehension. Students cannot predict what is going to happen unless they have an understanding of the text's meaning. Fluency and decoding are skills used in the emergent stage of reading. Prediction is used in the later stages of reading. Automaticity has to do with fluency. Comprehension involves making predictions and asking questions.

#	Answer	Category	Explanation
7.	D	I	Prosody is reading with expression while using the words and punctuation correctly. Reading with prosody means the reader is conveying what is on the page, pausing at commas and periods, and using inflection based on punctuation.
8.	A	I	In a fable, animal characters take on human roles. By capitalizing the words *Ant* and *Dove*, the author is using them as proper names when they would normally be common nouns.
9.	B	I	In context, the word snare is associated with hunter. We can assume it is not a blanket. If it were a gun, the hunter would not "place it for the Dove." The hunter would aim it at the Dove. Therefore, we can assume it is not a gun. A target does not make sense. Therefore, a trap is the best answer here. This is a *vocabulary in context* question.
10.	D	I	In a fable, animals carry out humanistic situations, and there is always a moral conveyed at the end of the story. In this case, answer D fits that description. The moral in answer D accurately describes what happened in the story.
11.	D	I	This excerpt is detailing the type of person Bridgett is. Therefore, characterization is the best answer here.
12.	C	II	Proper parallel structure means the list within a sentence is cohesive. As is, sentence 3 is not parallel. The first two items in the list are: *looked over her notes* and *practiced her questions*. Those items contain past tense verbs. However, the third item in the list is not parallel to the first two items. Changing that last part of the list to *focused on the goal* makes the list parallel.
13.	B, C, D, E	II	These answers showcase the author's ability to use complex vocabulary and sentence structure. In sentence 2, she uses a comma to separate a descriptive dependent clause. She also uses the term *meticulously*. In sentence 4, the author uses two independent clauses with proper punctuation—the comma. The author also uses the term *resilient* in sentence 4. In sentence 5, the author uses punctuation properly in a complex sentence. Sentence 1 is not a complex sentence and does not contain high-level vocabulary.
14.	A	II	There are two independent clauses in this sentence: *That was how Bridgett was* and *she was determined and resilient*. When separating two independent clauses, a semicolon is needed. A comma separates a dependent clause from an independent clause.
15.	B	I	Look at the last words in the stanza to determine the pattern: wood (A), both (B), stood (A), could (A), undergrowth (B).
16.	B	I	The poem makes a comparison between the two paths in the woods. While there is imagery in the poem, the two stanzas are there to compare. Alliteration and repetition are not used in this poem.
17.	C	I	In third-person objective, the narrator remains a detached observer, telling only the story's action and dialogue.
18.	A	I	Go with the obvious when you have a chance. The teacher is asking students to remove a sound or to delete a sound.
19.	B	II	Scribbling is part of the emergent stage. The student is mimicking the process of writing by using directionality. This is the beginning stage—the emergent stage—of writing.

#	Answer	Category	Explanation
20.	C	II	A good rule of thumb when administering cooperative learning is to keep the groups under six students when possible. Too many students in a group can limit students' abilities to interact effectively. Having an administrator is a good practice, but limiting groups to fewer students is the best answer here.
21.	1-D 2-C 3-B 4-A	II	See chart on page 46.
22.	D	I	Document-sharing software is beneficial because students can collaborate on a piece of writing in real-time. This is why teachers use Google Docs. You will not see the words Google Docs on the test because that is a brand name.
23.	A	I	According to the WIDA standards for English Language Acquisition, using pictorial representations is a characteristic of the entering stage.
24.	C	II	Tier III words are low frequency words. They are limited to a specific domain. They often pertain to a specific content area; in this case, the content area is biology. They are best learned within the content of the lesson or subject matter.
25.	B	I	When answering questions about reading, look for those "good" words. Answer B has words like *complex text* and *comprehend*.
26.	A, B, D	I	Qualitative measures are those that convey information but cannot be quantified with numbers. Predictability, familiarity, and themes are all qualitative measures because they cannot be quantified with numbers. Word count can be quantified. Therefore, answer C is eliminated.
27.	D	I	When you see the words "critical thinking" in the question stem, think Bloom's Taxonomy. Critical thinking is a high-level skill. Therefore, the correct answer will have the high-level verb in the answer choice. Answer D has the word *evaluate*, which goes with critical thinking. Answer choices A, B, and C contain the words *identify* and *participate*. Those are not high-level skills.
28.	A	I	WIDA is the authority on ELL education and Second Language Acquisition. When you can, go with WIDA.
29.	C	I	This is a timed fluency read. Timing has to do with rate. Tallying miscues has to do with accuracy.
30.	B	I	Fluency is important because it reduces cognitive energy needed to decode words. Students can then apply that cognitive energy to understanding the text. Fluency frees up the brain to work on more complex tasks, like predicting, questioning, and evaluating—all essential skills in comprehension.
31.	A, B, C	I	The key words here are *text structure*. Cause and effect, problem and solution, and chronological patterns are all text structures. Character development is a technique in writing but is not a text structure.
32.	C	I	To use a root word analysis, the word must have a root word. The only word in the answer choices that has a root word is computer. Its root word is *compute*. Pizza, tree, and social do not have root words.

#	Answer	Category	Explanation
33.	D	I	Look at the main adjectives in the answer choices: *demanding, meek, self-centered,* and *dignified.* In the passage, the author refers to Miss Taylor favorably. Therefore, *demanding* (answer A) and *self-centered* (answer B) are out. *Meek* means *timid,* and she was never characterized that way. Answer D is the best choice here.
34.	B	I	When thinking about main idea, go with the most general and correct answer possible. B is the only answer that is both general and correct. The words "fend for themselves" in answer A disqualifies the answer choice. Answer C is not the main idea, and the passage doesn't mention "problems later in life." Answer D is somewhat related but is not the main idea.
35.	A	I	Use context clues around the word *disposition.* The words around *disposition* are *clever* and *comfortable.* These words describe a personality more than they describe social status, occupation, or situation.
36.	B	I	The term "less as a governess than a friend" is the reason answer B is correct. It directly answers the question.
37.	D	I	Personification is when non-human or inanimate objects take on human qualities. In this example, a road cannot rise. A road is inanimate. Answer A is a simile. Answer C is a metaphor. Answer B is just a sentence. Therefore, D is the best answer here.
38.	A, C, D	I	Readability is the quality of being legible or decipherable. It is not a text feature. All the other choices are text features.
39.	B	I	In this case, she and place are sight words. They are high-frequency, tier I words. *Lithosphere* is a tier III word because it is specific to a content area like science. *Examined* is tier II word. It is not a sight word and is not an academic-specific word.
40.	A, D	I	Summarizing and predicating are high-level comprehension skills. Identifying words and sounding out words (decoding) are not comprehension skills.
41.	B, D	I	CVCe stands for consonant, vowel, consonant, silent *e* pattern. Therefore, *bake* and *take* fit the CVCe pattern.
42.	D	I	Morphology is the study of the form of words. Breaking down words using prefixes suffixes and roots is a component of morphology. Answers A, B, and C all have to do with text. Answer D focuses on words.
43.	C	I	The word *play* has a long a sound at the end of the word. It is an open vowel sound. Be careful, don't pick A—*late.* While late has a vowel at the end of the word, the sound at the end of the syllable is a *t* sound. *Track* and *cat* also have closed syllables with a *k* sound and *t* sound, respectively.
44.	B	I	Syntax is all about the structure of a word or sentence. It includes the proper spelling and grammar of a word or sentence. Semantics has to do with meaning. Since we are talking about syntax here, the best answer choice is B. All the other answers have to do with meaning, which is semantics.

#	Answer	Category	Explanation
45.	D	I	Prosody is reading with expression while using the words and punctuation correctly. Reading with prosody means the reader is conveying what is on the page, pausing at commas and periods, and using inflection based on punctuation. Prosody and fluency are related skills. All the other answer choices have to do with comprehension.
46.	A	I	When you see the phonemic awareness, think individual sounds in words. Spelling and word endings (answers B and C) are related to phonics. High-frequency words are related to fluency.
47.	C	II	In the excerpt, the author is using dialect.
48.	A	II	This is a narrative piece. The author is speaking in his own words and dialect.
49.	C	II	The administrator does all of the tasks listed in the answer choices. However, in cooperative learning, the most important thing is that everyone in the group has a chance to speak and be heard.
50.	C	II	In answer C, the student is repeating back what was said. This is a characteristic of active listening.
51.	D	II	Answer A is a narrative. Answer B is a descriptive. Answer C is informational. Answer D is persuasive. The words "Most pressing issue of our time" are claim-based and persuasive.
52.	B	II	Brainstorming is the prewriting stage. Answer B is the best choice here because students haven't started writing yet and are looking for ideas. All the other answer choices are when the student has already started writing.
53.	B	II	Summarizing reduces plagiarism because students put the ideas in their own words. They still have to cite what they are summarizing.
54.	B	II	The teacher wants to compare reliable sources with unreliable sources. Academic journals are more reliable than online magazines. Therefore, Answer B is the best answer here.
55.	C	I	When reading online, a hyperlink will take you to additional content. Hyperlinks are typically activated by clicking on a highlighted word or image on the screen.
56.	A	II	Answer A uses evidence from the text because the statement says, "In the beginning of the story..." That is text evidence. All the other answer choices relate to what the student thinks or feels, but they are not supported with evidence from the text.
57.	D	II	Third-person narrative omniscient gives the reader everyone's perspective.
58.	B	II	Meter in poetry is the rhythmical pattern of stressed and unstressed syllables in verse.
59.	B	II	First-person narrative in this case helps the reader understand the different perspectives of each character.
60.	C	I	Quantitative measures can be quantified by numbers. Therefore, answers A and C are the best answer choices. The question also includes text complexity. That eliminates answer A and leaves C. Lexile levels are numerical and indicate text complexity and readability.
61.	A	II	Audience is number one when deciding on a persuasive essay.

#	Answer	Category	Explanation
62.	B	II	Because *read* can be past tense or present tense and can mean multiple things, context is important. *He read his book yesterday.* In this sentence, *read* is a verb in the past tense; *yesterday* is a context clue. *He needed to get a read on his opponent.* In this sentence, *read* is a noun.
63.	A	II	Tone has to do with feeling in text. The tone of a text can be informational, serious, angry, ominous, etc.
64.	B	II	The only three directly related to oral presentations are articulation (how you articulate words), awareness of audience (an essential component of giving a presentation), and volume (speaking loudly enough so people can hear). Vocabulary, point of view, and tone are not related to an oral presentation.
65.	A, D	II	Expository writing is informational writing. Therefore, answers A and D are most appropriate here.
66.	C	II	In this case, the words *high heels* are modifying *the dog*. It reads as if the dog is wearing the high heels. This is a misplaced modifier.
67.	A	II	The only logical revision would be to fix the misplaced modifier.
68.	B	II	Word processing software is Microsoft Word. This is the best tool because students can free-write by typing in their documents. Answers A, C, and D are not related to free writing.
69.	D	II	Revising a document is a general edit for structure, content, and information. Answer A is peer review. Answer B is line editing, which is different from revising; it is focused on grammar and spelling. Answer C is prewriting.
70.	A	II	Because the question is focused on complex sentence structure, combining sentences 1 and 2 is the best answer because it is concerned with complex sentenecs. Combining 1 and 2 would make it a complex sentence.
71.	B	II	When giving feedback on student writing, always start with a positive comment first, and then suggest ways to strengthen the piece. Answer B does that.
72.	C	II	A workshop on complex sentences and combining sentences with punctuation would be most beneficial to this student based on the writing.
73.	A	II	While many of these words are complex, *apex predator* is a content area-specific term, making them tier III words.
74.	B, D	II	These words are not high-frequency (sight words), and they are not domain or content-specific. *Amphibian* can probably be a tier II or III word. However, because the question says to pick two answers, the only correct choices are answers B and D.
75.	D	II	Once that letter is out in the world, it is published. Hitting send on an email is publishing. Submitting a paper or letter is also publishing.
76.	B	II	To avoid plagiarism, paraphrase and summarize. Then students should cite where that information came from. Students must also use a bibliography to give credit to authors whose ideas the students used in the paper.
77.	C	I	This is the transitional stage of writing because the student is using strings of letters, and they are mostly correct. The student is spelling phonetically (using sounds in the words).

#	Answer	Category	Explanation
78.	A	II	The key words in this question are *think and listen critically*. The word *critically* indicates a high-level function. Therefore, we should look for the answer that has the high-level Bloom's Taxonomy words; in this case, Answer A contains the verb *evaluate*.
79.	A, B	II	Primary sources are sources that come directly from the person writing them. Speeches and letters are primary sources. Biographies and textbooks are secondary sources.
80.	C	II	An onomatopoeia is the formation of a word from a sound associated with it (sizzle, kurplunk, BAM!)

This page intentionally left blank.

1. Which word has the prefix that means half?

   A. Semicolon

   B. Bilateral

   C. Tricycle

   D. Dichotomy

2. Which word is correctly broken up by onset and rime?

   A. /mon/ -/key/

   B. /t/- /ap/

   C. /hand/- /y/

   D. /pro/-/tect/

3. A student is reading with proper tone, stopping at punctuation, and reading fluently. The student is displaying:

   A. Fluency

   B. Prosody

   C. Tone

   D. Application

4. Students are using the tiles below. They match first tile (tree) with the others to make words. The students are working on which TWO concepts (check two):

   tree   house   top

   A. Syllables

   B. Rime

   C. Segmentation

   D. Compound words

5. Which word has a vowel team?

   A. Pineapple

   B. Relief

   C. Jumpstart

   D. Underhand

6. How many phonemes are in the word "glass"?

    A. 1

    B. 3

    C. 4

    D. 5

7. The sun kissed the flowers as it rose in the east.

   What is this an example of?

    A. Personification

    B. Alliteration

    C. Metaphor

    D. Simile

8. A teacher is working with a student on initial sounds. The teacher says pet and asks the student to replace the initial consonant to make other words, such as *get, vet*, and *set*. What is this an example of?

    A. Segmenting

    B. Blending

    C. Structural analysis

    D. Substituting

9. Pick the two complex sentences:

    A. When he was younger, Mike had many dogs.

    B. I like to go to the movies when it rains; it is a fun place to go and hang out.

    C. Frank likes to walk around the block.

    D. I like to watch the rain fall outside my window.

Use the following student work to answer questions 10–12.

1) I don't like bats, they are scary little creatures. 2) When thinking about standing in a dark cave surrounded by animals that hang upside down, it gives me the chills. 3)They eat insects and are great at keeping the population under control. 4) There are many different types of bats, but I don't think I would like to run into any of them.

10. What is the author's tone in the passage? Select three options.

    A. Excited

    B. Disgust

    C. Objection

    D. Dislike

11. What is the author's purpose for writing this passage?

    A. Inform readers about a type of bat

    B. Persuade the reader not to like bats

    C. Give her opinion on why she thinks bats are horrible

    D. Explain why bats are great at flying at night and not active during the day

12. What mistake did the student make in the paragraph above?

    A. The student should use a semicolon or a period in place of the comma in sentence 1.

    B. No comma is needed in sentence 2.

    C. A comma is needed before the conjunction in sentence 3.

    D. No comma is needed before the conjunction in sentence 4.

13. When walking around the classroom, the teacher is taking anecdotal notes on student learning and student behavior. What kind of data is she collecting?

    A. Qualitative

    B. Quantitative

    C. Summative

    D. Criterion-referenced

14. Sara is the shortest of the four girls.

Which of the following statements about the sentence is true?

    A. The sentence is written correctly.

    B. The subject and verb do not agree

    C. The word "girls" should be possessive

    D. "shortest" modifies Sara incorrectly

Use the passage below to answer questions 15–16.

A Dog was crossing the river over a plank, carrying a piece of meat in her teeth. She saw herself in the water and thought that another dog was carrying a piece of meat. She dropped her piece and dashed forward to take away what the other dog had: the other meat was gone, and her own was carried away by the stream.

And thus, the Dog was left without anything.

15. What is the author trying to convey as the moral to this fable?

    A. If you look down at others, you are looking down at yourself.

    B. You are what you eat.

    C. When you become greedy, you can lose it all.

    D. You can never have the meat and the fight.

16. In the phrase, *She dropped her piece and dashed forward*, what word could be used to replace *dashed*?

    A.   Walked

    B.   Bolted

    C.   Dawdled

    D.   Crawled

17. A teacher is working with students to be active listeners when a student is presenting. What is a way for the teacher to encourage listening?

    A.   Ask and answer questions on what a speaker says in order to gather additional information or clarify something that is not understood.

    B.   Take notes to gather information about what the speaker is presenting about.

    C.   Listen to the oral presentation and discuss in small groups after the presentation is finished.

    D.   Allow questions to be answered during the presentation.

Using the fable: The Oak and the Reeds, answer questions 18–21

A Giant Oak stood near a brook in which grew some slender Reeds. When the wind blew, the great Oak stood proudly upright with its hundred arms lifted to the sky. (1) But the Reeds bowed low in the wind and sang a sad and mournful song.

"You have reason to complain," said the Oak. "The slightest breeze that ruffles the surface of the water makes you bow your heads, while I, the mighty Oak, stand upright and firm before the howling tempest."

"Do not worry about us," replied the Reeds. (2) "The winds do not harm us. We bow before them and so we do not break. (3) You, in all your pride and strength, have so far resisted their blows. But the end is coming."

As the Reeds spoke a great hurricane rushed out of the north. The Oak stood proudly and fought against the storm, while the yielding Reeds bowed low. (4) The wind redoubled in fury, and all at once the great tree fell, torn up by the roots, and lay among the pitying Reeds.

18. What type of literary element is the author using in the highlighted sentence, "When the wind blew, the great Oak stood proudly upright with its hundred arms lifted to the sky?"

    A.   Alliteration

    B.   Personification

    C.   Articulation

    D.   Hyperbole

19. Which sentences from the fable use figurative language? Select all that apply.

    A.   1

    B.   2

    C.   3

    D.   4

20. Which of the following sentences summarizes the meaning of the fable?

    A.   Put up a fight even when it is foolish; you could win at the end.

    B.   Better to go adapt with change than resist with pride.

    C.   You never know who is going to help you in the end. Be nice to your enemies.

    D.   Be stubborn until the end and don't listen to your inner voice.

21. The word *redoubled* has both a:

    A.   Prefix and suffix

    B.   Beginning and prefix

    C.   Word phrase and suffix

    D.   Verb tense and suffix

22. Which of the following are essential skills in reading comprehension?

    A.   Decoding, spelling, word knowledge

    B.   Decoding, word recognition, fluency

    C.   Spelling, fluency, understanding the text

    D.   Decoding, monitoring, speed

23. A teacher is evaluating the cognitive function of an ELL student using the WIDA standards in the area of reading. The student is using a series of extended sentences. What level is her student demonstrating?

    A.   Bridging

    B.   Developing

    C.   Emerging

    D.   Entering

24. Mrs. Smith is teaching a science lesson on cell growth. *Nucleus, membrane,* and *lysosome* are words being used to label the cell. These words are examples of what kind of vocabulary?

    A.   Tier I

    B.   Tier II

    C.   Tier III

    D.   Context vocabulary

25. What stage of writing is a student in if she is using symbols and other drawings to represent letters and words?

    A.   Transitional

    B.   Fluent

    C.   Emergent

    D.   Developmental

26. Which of the following would be the most effective resource to use to access additional information in a digital text?

    A.   A glossary

    B.   An index

    C.   A hyperlink

    D.   A website

27. Which two syllables are present in the word *apart*? Choose TWO answers.

    A.   Open

    B.   Closed

    C.   Vowel team

    D.   R-controlled

28. Which of the following would be an appropriate description of how graphic novels are used for inferencing?

    A.   Readers use dialogue to tell the story.

    B.   Readers summarize the story, explaining beginning, middle, and end.

    C.   Readers use pictures to understand text.

    D.   Readers decode words in the text.

29. When using qualitative measures of text complexity, which of the following is true?

    A.   Qualitative measures use a computer algorithm to describe the text.

    B.   Qualitative measures help to evaluate attributes of a text that canot be quantified.

    C.   There is no way to predict the text and know the measure of complexity.

    D.   Qualitative measures can only measure the level of meaning and not give clarity of language.

30. Which THREE of the following can be classified as expository writing?

    A.   Diary

    B.   Educational speech

    C.   Scientific report

    D.   Opinion column

    E.   Research report

31. Which context clue can be used to determine the meanings of a word within the sentence by using opposites?

    A.   Root words and affix

    B.   Definition

    C.   Contrast

    D.   Example or illustration

32. The sentence, "I like to go outside and play after school," is an example of what type of sentence?

    A.   Interrogative

    B.   Imperative

    C.   Declarative

    D.   Exclamatory

33. Evaluate the sentences below:

    1.   A teacher from Alabama displayed artwork to her class.

    2.   The teacher displayed artwork from Alabama to her class.

    How does the meaning of sentence 1 differ from the meaning of sentence 2?

    A.   Sentence 1 ends in a prepositional phrase.

    B.   The adjective phrase *from Alabama* modifies different nouns.

    C.   The subject of sentence 1 is *the teacher*, while the subject of sentence 2 is *artwork*.

    D.   They do not have the same predicates.

34. Which of the following would be the most reliable source for a research paper?

    A.   .org

    B.   .net

    C.   .edu

    D.   .com

35. When using technology, which of the following tools would be used to facilitate personal writing?

    A.   Interactive whiteboards

    B.   Blogging programs

    C.   Slide-share programs

    D.   Interactive discussions

36. Which of the following is an aspect of social linguistics?

    A.   Process

    B.   Automaticity

    C.   Prosody

    D.   Dialect

37. According to WIDA, at what level would a student's linguistic complexity be if the student is using short sentences while speaking and writing?

    A.   Entering

    B.   Developing

    C.   Expanding

    D.   Reaching

38. The word *happily* is what part of speech in the sentence below?

   The teacher walked <u>happily</u> with her students to the bus after a long day at school.

   A. Verb

   B. Adverb

   C. Pronoun

   D. Subject

39. What syllabication pattern is represented in the word *sister*?

   A. cvc

   B. cvvc

   C. vc-cv

   D. v-cv

40. A teacher is discussing Native Americans and their influences on a territory. What type of vocabulary is needed to understand context and word meaning?

   A. Tier I

   B. Tier II

   C. Tier III

   D. Concept vocabulary

41. Pick all the examples of secondary sources:

   A. Newspaper articles

   B. Photographs

   C. Diary

   D. Biographies

42. The revised sentence below reflects an improvement in which of the following aspects of writing?

   Original Sentence

   The pilot viewed the sky to determine how the trip would go.

   Revision

   The aviator surveyed the clouds to predict the trip's success.

   A. Conventions

   B. Organization

   C. Sentence fluency

   D. Word choice

43. Two gerbils sat in the cage side by side; a furtive, timid one and a glossy, bold one watched each other warily.

The sentence is an example of:

   A.   Simple sentence

   B.   Compound sentence

   C.   Complex sentence

   D.   Compound-complex sentence

44. Which of the following is typically included in the conclusion of an oral presentation?

   A.   Expand on the thesis statement.

   B.   Identify details to support the thesis statement.

   C.   Attempt to build rapport with the audience.

   D.   Move to gain the audience's attention.

45. In a discussion about whether vendors at the mall should stop selling junk food, which of the following statements best demonstrates active listening?

   A.   "In my opinion, it would be a mistake for the mall to remove junk food from the food court because no one would want to eat there anymore."

   B.   "Peter thinks that our health should come before eating foods we like, but Leo says that people should not take away our right to choose what we want to eat."

   C.   "How many of you would actually go to the mall if they stopped selling junk food?"

   D.   "What if we wrote a letter to the mall to voice our opinion on why we would like them to continue to sell the food we like?"

46. Which is the proper sequence of stages of phonetic spelling?

   A.   Beginning sounds, middle sounds, ending sounds, vowel sounds

   B.   Beginning sounds, ending sounds, middle sounds, vowel sounds

   C.   Middle sounds, vowel sounds, beginning sounds, and ending sounds

   D.   Vowel sounds are used first, followed by beginning sounds, middle sounds, and ending sounds.

47. Which literary device is being used in the sentence below?

He was as proud as a lion.

   A.   Simile

   B.   Metaphor

   C.   Personification

   D.   Imagery

© 2022 Kathleen Jasper

48. Which of the following is considered a primary source?

    A. Biography

    B. Newspaper article

    C. Textbook

    D. Autobiography

49. Students are breaking down words using prefixes and suffixes. They are conducting a:

    A. Structural analysis

    B. Semantic analysis

    C. Phonics analysis

    D. Rubric analysis

50. If a teacher wants students to understand prefixes, which group of words would be most appropriate to analyze?

    A. Cat, bat, sat, trap

    B. Uneven, unruly, undone

    C. Station, transition, lamination

    D. Prescription, transcript, manuscript

51. In which of the following sentences is the underlined word used correctly?

    A. The <u>drivers</u> slowed down as they approached the intersection.

    B. Florida is <u>further</u> away than New York than Alabama.

    C. The <u>principle</u> of the school had a hard tone in her voice when speaking.

    D. It is nice to give someone a <u>complement</u> when they do something nice.

52. Students are writing papers for their social science class. The papers outline where landmarks are on a map of the United States. The papers would be classified as what genre of writing?

    A. Interpretive

    B. Analytical

    C. Expository

    D. Persuasive

53. When a student is using clues to find a word's meaning, the student is using

    A. context

    B. a dictionary

    C. the headings

    D. the denotative meaning

54. Students are in the prewriting phase. Which of the following would NOT be an activity they are doing?

    A. Brainstorming

    B. Editing

    C. Webbing

    D. Outlining

55. What stage of the research process are students in if they are rearranging the essay based on content and organization.

    A. Prewriting

    B. Peer review

    C. Revising

    D. Editing

56. An example of a quantitative measure of a piece of text would be:

    A. Student interest survey

    B. Lexile level

    C. Text purpose

    D. Readability

Read the passage below to answer questions 57–58.

(1) When the two sisters returned from the ball, Cinderella asked them whether they had been well entertained and whether the beautiful lady was there. (2) They replied she was, but she had run away as soon as midnight had struck. She ran away so quickly, that she dropped one of her dainty glass slippers, which the king's son had picked up, and was looking at most fondly during the remainder of the ball; indeed, it seemed beyond a doubt that he was deeply enamored of the beautiful creature to whom it belonged. (3)They spoke truly enough; for, a few days afterwards, the king's son caused a proclamation to be made, by sound of trumpet all over the kingdom, to the effect that he would marry her whose foot should be found to fit the slipper exactly. (4) So, the slipper was first tried on by all the princesses, then by all the duchesses, and next by all the persons belonging to the court; but in vain. (5) It was then carried to the two sisters, who tried with all their might to force their feet into its delicate proportions, but with no better success.

- Henry W. Hewet, Cinderella, Project Guttenberg 2004

57. It can be inferred by the text that the king's son is

    A. Determined

    B. Oblivious

    C. Energetic

    D. Potent

58. In sentence 4, what is the meaning of *but in vain*?

    A. The slipper fit.

    B. It was a failure.

    C. It was done with anger.

    D. It was working for everyone.

© 2022 Kathleen Jasper

59. Metacognition is an important skill necessary for students to comprehend text. What would be the best activity to foster metacognition in students?

   A. Round robin reading

   B. Read-aloud/think-aloud

   C. Silent sustained reading

   D. Popcorn reading

60. A student is using a webpage to research information for a project. Which of the following is NOT a text feature of an online source?

   A. Sidebar

   B. Hyperlink

   C. Glossary

   D. Heading

61. Which is NOT a characteristic of a fable?

   A. Anthropomorphized inanimate objects

   B. Mythical creatures

   C. Exaggerated version of historical events

   D. Contains a moral message

62. During independent reading, a student notices the characters in his chapter book exhibit distinct behaviors.

   Which story element is the student picking up on?

   A. Plot

   B. Setting

   C. Point of view

   D. Characterization

63. Read the poem below and answer the question that follows.

   The blue ocean gleams.
   Shimmering like precious gems.
   An endless treasure.

   This is an example of:

   A. Limerick

   B. Sonnet

   C. Haiku

   D. Free verse

64. A teacher is asking students to compare two texts with similar themes and evaluate their meanings and how they relate to each other. This is an example of:

    A. Critical thinking

    B. Qualitative thinking

    C. Complexity of text

    D. Text to self

65. Students should be given rubrics because:

    A. rubrics show comprehension.

    B. rubrics show miscues.

    C. rubrics convey standards and tested items.

    D. rubrics communicate expectations and guidelines.

66. When students are asked to support claims or opinions through information found in the text, students are engaging in:

    A. Reading response journals

    B. Double entry journals

    C. Reading text to self

    D. Evidence-based discussion

67. A student is copying text from the Internet and including it in a research paper. The student also fails to summarize and cite the phrases used. What is this an example of?

    A. Paraphrasing

    B. Plagiarizing

    C. Citing

    D. Sources

68. A speech outlining a political view about the importance of the First Amendment would be considered what type of writing?

    A. Persuasive

    B. Informative

    C. Expository

    D. Narrative

69. Which of the following is the overall feeling in text?

    A. Purpose

    B. Tone

    C. Content

    D. Audience

70. When reviewing a student's paper, the teacher notices that the grammar and phrases are not coherent. What part of the writing is incorrect?

    A. Semantic

    B. Organization

    C. Syntactic

    D. Ideas and content

71. Which sentence is written correctly?

    A. Jim went to the store with Kim and I.

    B. Jim went to the store with Kim and me.

    C. Jim went to the store with I.

    D. Jim go to the store with Kim and me.

72. Which sentence uses the semicolon correctly?

    A. I went to the store; and I bought ice cream.

    B. We were excited to see the president of the university; he gave a wonderful speech.

    C. She is very happy with her purchase; but she wants to evaluate the cost.

    D. Before we agree on a title; we should consult the team.

73. Which type of figurative language is being used when the teacher reads, "The oranges were so ripe and juicy, they practically beckoned the girl to eat them?"

    A. Simile

    B. Metaphor

    C. Personification

    D. Irony

74. What can students do to be sure they are using the correct mode of writing?

    A. Understand how to use imagery in writing.

    B. Evaluate what type of audience they are writing to.

    C. Identify language patterns in writing.

    D. Use a dictionary to select appropriate words.

75. A teacher is working with students to help them maximize sentence variety in their writing. What would be most effective in achieving this goal?

    A. Individual conferences with specific and meaningful feedback

    B. Detailed feedback on the back of student writing samples

    C. Parent/teacher conferences

    D. Extra homework in the area of writing

76. A teacher shows a video of hurricanes before students begin to free-write on the topic of hurricanes. What stage of writing are the students in?

    A. Prewriting

    B. Drafting

    C. Editing

    D. Revising

77. Volume, articulation, and awareness of audience are all elements of a(n):

    A. Digital presentation

    B. Oral presentation

    C. Group presentation

    D. Collaborative presentation

78. A teacher understands the importance the role of speaking, listening, and viewing play in language acquisition is for second language learners. Which way of presenting a lesson would be the most beneficial?

    A. Silent reading

    B. Lecture of materials

    C. Choral speaking and reading

    D. Popcorn reading

79. Which mode of writing conveys factual information with data and is free from bias?

    A. Expository

    B. Narrative

    C. Argumentative

    D. Persuasive

80. Group discussions and debates are an effective way to teach:

    A. Handwriting skills

    B. Reading skills

    C. Comprehension skills

    D. Speaking and listening skills

This page intentionally left blank.

#	Answer	Category	Explanation
1.	A	I	The prefixes in the answer choices are *semi, bi, tri,* and *di. Semi* means half. *Bi* and *di* mean two. *Tri* means three.
2.	B	I	Onset is the beginning consonant and consonant cluster. Rime is the vowel and consonants that follow. In this case, the only answer choice with a definitive onset and rime is B. The /t/ is the onset. The /ap/ is the rime. The other answer choices are broken up by syllables, not onset and rime.
3.	B	I	Prosody is reading with expression while using the words and punctuation correctly. Reading with prosody means the reader is conveying what is on the page, pausing at commas and periods, and using inflection based on punctuation.
4.	A, D	I	*Treehouse* and *treetop* are compound words. They also have two syllables and are broken up by those syllables in the tiles. Rime and segmentation are not used in this activity.
5.	B	I	Remember a vowel teams are a combination of two, three, or four letters stands for a vowel. While it may be tempting to choose A, *pineapple* is a compound word, and the e and a do not make one vowel sound. In *relief*, the *i* and *e* team up to make a long *e* sound.
6.	C	I	Phonemes are individual sounds in words. The word glass has four individual sounds *g	l	a	ss*.
7.	A	II	The sun is carrying out a human task in this excerpt. The sun cannot actually kiss anything. Therefore, personification is the best answer choice here.
8.	D	I	The key word in the question is *replace*. *Replace* also means *substitute*. The students are changing out, replacing, or substituting one sound for another in this activity.
9.	A, B	II	Complex sentences contain two clauses. Answer A includes a dependent clause: *when he was younger*; it also includes an independent clause: *Mike had many dogs*. Answer B includes two independent clauses separated by a semicolon. The other two choices only include one clause.
10.	B, C, D	II	This is when looking at the answer choices first is beneficial. Choices B, C, and D all express a negative connotation.
11.	C	II	This is an opinion piece with a tone of strong dislike for bats.
12.	A	II	In sentence 1, the author combines two independent clauses with a comma. When connecting two independent clauses, a semicolon or a comma plus a conjunction are needed. A comma alone is not enough. All other punctuation in the writing is correct.
13.	A	II	Anecdotal notes are qualitative because they cannot be quantified by numbers. They are representations of observations. Therefore, A is the best answer. Summative and criterion-referenced are types of assessments that typically produce quantitative data in the form of scores.
14.	A	II	This sentence is written correctly. The word *shortest* is correct because the sentence is describing two or more girls. The subject, *Sara*, agrees with the verb *is*. The word *girls* is not possessive.

#	Answer	Category	Explanation
15.	C	I	In this fable, the dog sees her reflection and wants what is in the reflection. That represents greed. She ends up dropping her meat while trying to take what she sees in the reflection.
16.	B	I	The word *dash* means to *hurry*. Therefore, *bolted* is the best answer here.
17.	B	II	The key phrase in the question stem is *to encourage listening*. Listening is the main skill. Answers A, C, and D all involve speaking. Answer B is the best choice because it only focuses on listening.
18.	B	I	The Oak is acting humanlike in this fable—it stood proudly, arms lifted to the sky. Therefore, personification is the best choice here.
19.	A, B, C, D	II	All of the sentences use some form of personification. In sentence 1, the reeds bow low. In sentences 2 ad 3, the reeds are talking and describing the tree as prideful. In sentence 4, the wind has fury. All of these sentences give inanimate objects or non-humans human characteristics.
20.	B	I	In this case, the reeds bend and bow and survive the storm. The stubborn trees that do not bend are destroyed by the storm.
21.	A	I	In *redoubled*, *re-* is the prefix, and *-ed* is the suffix.
22.	B	I	In reading comprehension, decoding is necessary for complex words; word recognition and fluency are necessary for automaticity. Spelling is not a comprehension skill. Spelling is a part of phonics, which contributes to fluency. Speed is not a skill needed for comprehension.
23.	B	I	This is an intermediate skill, so *bridging* and *entering* can be eliminated because *bridging* is the highest level and *entering* is the lowest level. Because the student is using sentences, *emerging* can also be eliminated.
24.	C	II	This is academic vocabulary that is specific to a content area (biology). Therefore, these are Tier III words.
25.	C	II	The use of pictures and symbols is indicative of the emergent stages of writing. Developmental is not a stage of writing. Transitional and fluent are stages of writing where the student is using letters and strings of words to make sentences.
26.	C	I	A hyperlink will take the reader from the original digital text to other websites or blogs with additional information.
27.	A, D	I	The beginning syllable is an open syllable, and the second syllable is an r-controlled syllable.
28.	C	I	The word *graphic* in graphic novels means *picture*. The main components of graphic novels are pictures. Students can use those pictures to make inferences in text. Dialogue and summary are not the best answers because they do not address pictures in the text. Graphic novels are not used for decoding words.
29.	B	I	Qualitative measures of text evaluate non-numerical attributes.
30.	B, C, E	II	Expository writing is informational writing. A diary is narrative writing, and an opinion piece is persuasive writing.
31.	C	I	The key word in the question stem is *opposites*. Therefore, *contrast* is the best answer. When students are reading and using contrast to determine words, they are figuring out a word based on the opposite of the meaning in the text. Example: *She was joyful about moving to another town, but she was also melancholy.* If students are determining what melancholy means, the word *but* indicates that *melancholy* is the opposite of *joyful*. They can ascertain that *melancholy* means *sad*.

#	Answer	Category	Explanation
32.	C	I	A declarative sentence declares something and ends with a period. An interrogative sentence asks a question and ends in a question mark. An imperative sentence tells someone to do something and ends in a period. Finally, an exclamatory sentence shows strong feelings and ends in an exclamation point.
33.	B	I	In this sentence, the phrase *from Alabama* modifies *the **teacher*** in sentence 1 and modifies *artwork* in sentence 2.
34.	C	I	Out of all the websites, .edu would be the most reliable because it comes from a university. Websites ending in .org, .net, and .com can all come from companies that may or may not be sharing reliable information.
35.	B	II	Blogs are used to communicate personal information and opinions.
36.	D	I	Dialect is a particular form of a language which is sometimes particular to a specific region or social group. This is an aspect of social linguistics.
37.	A	I	Using short sentences is an entering stage of language acquisition. Therefore, A is the best answer.
38.	B	II	Adverbs describe verbs and typically end in *-ly*. The adverb *happily* describes the verb walked in this sentence.
39.	C	I	When dividing a word into VC-CV pattern, the first thing to be identified would be the vowels, then the consonants. In this case, the consonants are next to each other, which would allow you to break the word apart correctly to show syllables and how to pronounce.
40.	C	I	The teacher is working in specific content area; therefore, Tier III words should be taught in context.
41.	A, D	I	Secondary sources are interpretations and analyses based on primary sources. In this case, newspaper articles and biographies interpret information. Photographs and diaries are firsthand accounts of something.
42.	D	II	In this sentence, the writer replaces *pilot* with *aviator* and *viewed* with *surveyed*. This is an example of using word choice to enhance writing.
43.	B	II	A simple sentence has a subject and a predicate. A compound sentence has at least two independent clauses joined by a comma, semicolon, or conjunction. A complex sentence is made from one independent clause and one or more subordinate clauses. A compound-complex sentence is made from two independent clauses and one or more dependent clauses. In this case, there are two independent clauses separated with a semicolon. Therefore, this is a compound sentence.
44.	A	I	Moving to gain the audience's attention, identifying details to support the thesis, and building rapport with the audience all happen during the presentation. Expanding on the thesis happens at the conclusion of an oral presentation. The presenter revisits the thesis at the end of the presentation and expands on what was presented.
45.	B	II	In this example, the person speaking is summarizing what two people have said. That is active listening. In the other examples, the speaker is simply stating his or her opinion.

#	Answer	Category	Explanation
46.	B	I	When students begin to spell words, the beginning and ending sounds are typically written first because they are the hard consonants. Vowel sounds come later. For example, when a student writes the word Sun the progression is S, Sn, Sun.
47.	A	II	A simile is a figure of speech that compares two different things and uses the words *like* or *as*.
48.	D	II	An autobiography is written from the point of view of the person it is describing. It is straight from the person who experienced the story. Therefore, an autobiography is a primary source. All the other sources listed are secondary sources.
49.	A	I	Using prefixes and suffixes to determine meaning is breaking down the structure of the word. This is considered a structural analysis.
50.	B	I	In this case, the only group of words that has the same prefixes throughout is B. They all have the prefix *un-*. It is tempting to pick D. However, answer D includes words that share same root word: *script*.
51.	A	I	All are incorrect except for A. When talking about distance, *farther* is correct. *Further* indicates a placement. The head of school is the princi**pal**. Comp**le**ment is to complete; comp**li**ment is a favorable comment about someone.
52.	C	II	The papers are informational; therefore, expository is the best answer here.
53.	A	I	Using clues to find the meaning of a word is using context.
54.	B	II	Editing happens after students have finished writing and are proofing for grammatical and mechanical mistakes.
55.	C	II	Revising occurs when the writer rearranges the essay based on content, understanding, organization, and flow. Editing is line editing for grammar, spelling, punctuation, etc. In this case, the writer is revising. Prewriting happens before writing. A peer review is when students suggest modifications to other students' essays.
56.	B	I	A Lexile level is a number given to reading levels. All the other choices are qualitative measures.
57.	A	I	The king's son is determined to find Cinderella in this passage.
58.	B	II	Sometimes it is helpful to read above and below the vocabulary words or phrases in the question. In this case, the slipper was tried by the duchesses and other princesses. Based on context, we can determine the slipper does not fit, and its a failure.
59.	B	I	Metacognition means *thinking about thinking*. Answer B is the only choice that includes the word think. In a read-aloud/think-aloud, a teacher models her process of reading and thinking for students.
60.	C	I	Glossaries are typically located in the back of a textbook. Answers A, B, and D are all components of an online source.
61.	B	I	Mythical creatures are characteristics of epic poetry, not fables. In a fable, inanimate objects are animated, animals take on human-like characteristics, and historical events are exaggerated.
62.	D	I	Plot is the overall meaning of the text or why the story is happening. Setting is where the story takes place. Point of view is the perspective from which the story is being told. Characterization is the development of the characters and their behaviors and personalities in the text.

#	Answer	Category	Explanation
63.	C	I	The poem exhibits the syllable pattern 5, 7, 5—five syllables in the first line, seven syllables in the second line, and five syllables in the third line. This is a haiku poem.
64.	A	I	The key word here is *evaluating*. *Evaluate* and *critical thinking* always go together.
65.	D	II	Rubrics should explicitly state what students are expected to do for a task. Rubrics reduce ambiguity and bias.
66.	D	II	A big part of English language arts instruction is encouraging students to support claims. Evidence-based discussions require students to find information in the text to support their claims.
67.	B	II	Copying directly from the Internet and not citing is plagiarism. An English language arts teacher's job is to show students how to use information ethically. That includes teaching students—from the very beginning—how to paraphrase and cite information from the Internet or text.
68.	A	II	Typically, political writing is persuasive. The writer is trying to get the reader to agree to a particular side.
69.	B	II	Tone is the overall feeling in a text. The text can be informational with a neutral tone. The text can also be argumentative with a more intense tone.
70.	C	II	Syntax has to do with the structure in writing—typically the grammar, spelling, and mechanics in an essay. Semantics relates to meaning. Organization is the flow of the essay—introduction, details, conclusion. Ideas and content can be connected to meaning or semantics.
71.	B	II	When evaluating which pronoun (I or me) to use in a sentence that involves yourself and another person, try removing the second person to see which pronoun makes the most sense. • Jim went to the store with ~~Kim and~~ *I*. • Jim went to the store with ~~Kim and~~ *me*. Now it's easy to see that me is the correct choice.
72.	B	II	A semicolon is used to separate two independent clauses. Answer B is the only choice where the semicolon is separating two independent clauses. Answers A and C have a conjunction after the semicolon. Never use a semicolon before a coordinating conjunction. Answer D uses a semicolon to separate a dependent clause from an independent clause, which is incorrect.
73.	C	II	The author says the oranges are *beckoning me to eat them*. Oranges are not human, but the author applies human-like traits to the oranges. Therefore, the answer is personification.
74.	B	II	Modes of writing are persuasive, expository, narrative, and descriptive. To determine what mode to use, the writer should consider the audience.
75.	A	II	Individual conferences with detailed and specific feedback are the very best thing a teacher can do during writing instruction. Answer B is good, but answer A is even better.
76.	A	II	This is the prewriting stage. In the question, the phrase before *they begin to free-write* is used to describe the activity. Students are activating their background knowledge during this prewriting activity.

#	Answer	Category	Explanation
77.	B	II	Volume, articulation, and audience awareness are all elements of oral skills.
78.	C	II	Answer C is the only answer choice that includes activities indicative of speaking, listening, and viewing. Quick tip: Just say no to popcorn reading and silent sustained reading.
79.	A	II	Expository writing is the type of writing used in textbooks and informational material. The author of the expository writing should remain free from bias and convey factual information.
80.	D	II	Students participating in a debate are required to listen to other points of view and communicate their own point of view in an effective manner.

This page intentionally left blank.

Mathematics Subtest

This page intentionally left blank.

The mathematics subtest of the *Praxis®* Elementary Education exam is designed to test your knowledge of what math students need in elementary school and what they will need to know to be successful in middle and high school math courses. The assessment is not aligned to a particular grade or course, but is aligned to the Common Core Mathematics Standards for both elementary and middle grades.

Test at a Glance	
Test Name	*Praxis®* Elementary Education Mathematics Subtest 5003
Format	Computer-based test (CBT)
Time	65 minutes; 1 minute 18 seconds per question
Number of Questions	Approximately 50 (field testing items may be added)
Passing Score	A scaled score of at least 157 for most states
Items Provided	On-screen scientific calculator (TI-30XS Multiview), work pad, and pencil
Format of Questions	Multiple choice, multiple response, drag and drop, numeric entry

Test Competency Breakdown			
	COMPETENCY	**Approximate Percentage of Total Test Questions**	**Approximate Number of Total Test Questions**
	I. Numbers and Operations	40%	20
	II. Algebraic Thinking	30%	15
	III. Geometry, Measurement, Data, Statistics, and Probability	30%	15
	TOTAL	100%	50

You are not provided a hand-held calculator, but the online calculator is the same as a handheld TI-30XS Multiview. ETS® (Educational Testing Service, writers of *Praxis®* exams) does provide training through Texas Instruments for the calculator (visit https://ibt2calc.ets.org/practicetest for calculator training access). We strongly suggest you access and complete their training. Several questions will require the use of a calculator, and this calculator can perform certain functions that will save you time.

Section I, numbers and operations, tests your knowledge of the foundations of the base-10 number system. Skills include knowing basic terminology associated with the number system, knowing how to represent and move in the place value system, how to use the place value system to compose and decompose numbers, how to represent numbers in different forms, including fractions, decimals, percents, and scientific notation, and how to solve problems using all four operations.

The skills you need to know in this section include the following:

A. Understands the place value system

B. Understands operations and properties of rational numbers

C. Understands proportional relationships and percents

D. Knows how to use basic concepts of number theory

E. Knows a variety of strategies to determine the reasonableness of results

A. Understands the place value system

Cardinal and ordinal numbers

A **cardinal number** is a number that says how many of something there are. Cardinal numbers are used specifically for counting. An **ordinal number** is a number that tells the position of something in a list. Ordinal numbers are used specifically when referring to the order of an object.

Cardinal Numbers	Ordinal Numbers
1	1st
2	2nd
3	3rd
4	4th
5	5th

Example:

1. Classify the bold number in each statement as cardinal or ordinal.
    - *Statement 1: There are **4** puppies in the line.*
    - *Statement 2: The dachshund is the **2nd** puppy in line.*

Solution:

Statement 1, the number 4 is a cardinal number because 4 is the count of the number of puppies. Statement 2, 2nd is an ordinal number because it is referring to the order of the dachshund in the line of puppies.

Base-10 number system

Our number system is called the **base-10 number system**, which is a system based on the digits 0, 1, 2, 3, 4, 5, 6, 7, 8, and 9.

Snap cubes and a place value mat are useful for making meaning of the base-10 system. The example below shows 7 cubes, representing 7 digits, in the 1s place.

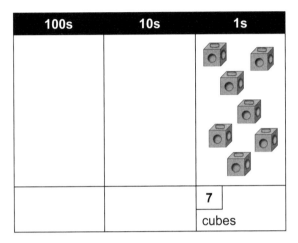

When using snap cubes, remember that the base-10 system contains the digits 0 through 9, so if 10 cubes are in the 1s column, they connect to form 1 group in the 10s column. Once a group of 10 is formed, single digits can then be added again to the 1s column. The number represented on the left is 10, and the number represented on the right is 14. We could continue this pattern into the 100s column if we reached 10 groups in the 10s column, making 1 group of 100.

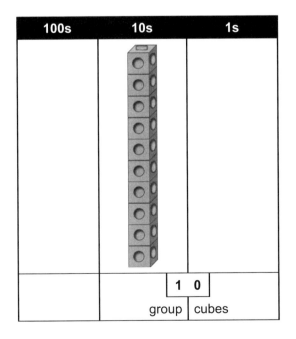

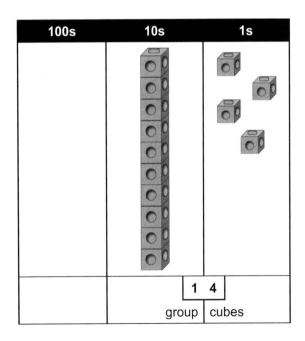

Place value

The value of a certain digit is determined by the place where it resides within a number. In our number system, each "place" has a value of ten times the place to its right or $\frac{1}{10}$ of the number to its left. The place value of each digit in a number is included in the word form of a number.

Take the number, 2,487,905.631, as an example. This number is read as two *million*, four hundred eighty-seven *thousand*, nine *hundred* five, and six hundred thirty-one *thousandths*.

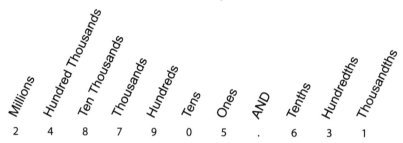

It is important to know how to manipulate a number using the base 10 system. Moving the decimal point to the left (to create a smaller number), is the same as dividing by increments of 10 or multiplying by increments of $\frac{1}{10}$. Conversely, moving the decimal point to the right (to create a larger number) is the same as multiplying by increments of 10. Increments of 10 include 10, 100, 1000, 10,000...etc.

Knowledge of place value helps students to compose and decompose larger numbers, thus creating a better understanding of the relative size of a number.

Test Tip

Exam items may ask you to describe or manipulate a number or the place value of a number in terms of multiplication or division by 10 or a power of 10.

Examples:

2. For the number 42,103.68, the place value 4 is how many times larger than the place value of the 0?

    A. 4
    B. 100
    C. 1,000
    D. 40,000

    Solution: C

    The correct answer choice is C because the 0 is three places to the right of 4, which would be $10 \times 10 \times 10 = 1,000$ times larger.

3. Select all of the statements that are true about the number below.

    23,401.07

    ☐ The 2 is in the thousands place.
    ☐ The 4 is in the hundreds place.
    ☐ There are no 10s in this number.
    ☐ 7 is in the tenths place.
    ☐ There is a 0 in the oneths place.
    ☐ The 2 is in the ten-thousands place.

    Solution:

    The statements that are true are the second, third, and last statements. There is a 4 in the hundreds place, there are no 10s in the number, and the 2 is in the ten-thousands place. The first statement is not true because 3 is in the thousands place. The fourth statement is not true because 7 is in the hundredths place. The fifth statement is not true because there is no place value called the oneths.

Rounding

In addition to being able to compose and decompose numbers, you will be expected to round to a given place value. Questions involving rounding will require you to know place values. To round, look at the number to the right of the place value to which you are rounding. If the number to the right is between 0 and 4, the number does not change. If the number to the right is between 5 and 9, the place value to which you are rounding is rounded up 1.

Example:

4. A teacher asked the class to round the number 507,291 to the nearest ten-thousands. Of the responses she received below, which one is correct?

    A. 507,000
    B. 508,000
    C. 510,000
    D. 600,000

    Solution: C

    The correct response is C. The digit in the ten-thousands place is 0. The number to its right, 7, is greater than 4, which means 0 should be rounded up one to 1. Thus, the new rounded number would be 510,000.

    Remember: after rounding to the correct place value, all the numbers to the right of the place value round to become zeros.

Expanded form

Another way to teach place value is by writing numbers in expanded form. A number written in **expanded form** is written so that the place value of each number is represented as part of a sum. The number 872 written in expanded form would be $800 + 70 + 2$. When writing a number in expanded form, each digit that is not zero should have its own **addend**.

An extension of expanded form is **expanded notation** where each digit is written as a product of its place value. 872 written in expanded notation would be $(8 \times 100) + (7 \times 10) + (2 \times 1)$.

Vocabulary Lookout

Test questions may use terms that are part of a basic operation problem. Know what each of these terms mean. Vocabulary terms used most often include:

- addend
- sum
- difference
- product
- quotient

Scientific notation

When numbers are very large or very small, they are often written in scientific notation. **Scientific notation** is a number greater than or equal to 1 and less than 10 multiplied by a power of 10. When a number is written in scientific notation, the number multiplied by the power of ten must have only 1 number in front of the decimal point.

Students in elementary learn patterns of how multiplying by a power of ten changes the placement of the decimal point in a number. They also learn how the number of zeros in a large number and the exponent when this number is written as a product of a number and a power of 10 are related.

Consider the number 4,000,000. Instead of writing this number out, we could multiply the 4 by a power of 10. Because there are six zeros after the 4, the power of 10 we are multiplying by will be 10^6. Thus 4,000,000 in scientific notation is 4×10^6. In elementary school, students are not expected to be familiar with the terminology and exact definition of scientific notation, but the test may use the terminology in questions.

Examples:

5. Write the number 4,030,122 in expanded form.

    Solution:

    To write in expanded form, think about the verbal form of the number. 4,030,122 is read, "Four million, thirty thousand, one hundred twenty-two."

    In expanded form 4,030,122 is written as $4,000,000 + 30,000 + 100 + 20 + 2$.

6. Select all of the numbers that are equivalent to 68,500.
    - ☐ 68.5×10^3
    - ☐ 6.85×10^2
    - ☐ 6.85×10^4
    - ☐ 685×10^2
    - ☐ $6,850 \times 10^1$

    Solution:

    The question did not ask for the number to be written in scientific notation, so it is important to look at each option carefully. If we had been asked to write the number in scientific notation, the correct answer would have been 6.85×10^4 because there can only be one digit in front of the decimal point. Other correct representations of 68,500 include 68.5×10^3, 685×10^2, and $6,850 \times 10^1$.

7. Which of the following is equivalent to 0.9?

    A. $900 \times \frac{1}{1,000}$
    B. 9×10^1
    C. $90 \times \frac{1}{10}$
    D. 0.9×10

    Solution: A

    The first answer choice is the same as dividing by a power of 10^3. 900 divided by 10^3 moves the decimal point 3 places left, resulting in 0.9, which is the correct answer choice. Option B equals 90, and options C and D both equal 9.

    Testing Tip

    Test questions may have numeric expressions with numbers written in a form which typically would not be used to test your knowledge of equivalent forms.

B. Understands operations and properties of rational numbers

When learning to add and subtract in kindergarten through second grade, students learn to approach a problem from different points of view. Various points of view help students understand operations and number facts and prepare them for solving for an unknown value in later grades.

The tables that follow outline how students learn addition and subtraction. Be familiar with the terms in these charts and what they represent. You may be expected to identify the problem situation (e.g., add to, take apart) given a scenario.

	RESULT UNKNOWN	CHANGE UNKNOWN	START UNKNOWN
ADD TO *A number is given, and more is being added to the number to find a sum.*	*Word Problem* Jon had 2 apples. Kevin gave him 3 more apples. How many apples does Jon have now? $2 + 3 = ?$	*Word Problem* Manda has one cat. She found a couple more cats on the playground. Now she has three cats. How many cats did she find on the playground? $1 + ? = 3$	*Word Problem* The teacher has some paperclips on her desk. A student comes up and places two more paperclips on the teacher's desk. Now there are five paperclips total. How many paperclips were on the teacher's desk to start? $? + 2 = 5$
	Picture Problem 	*Picture Problem* 	*Picture Problem*
TAKE FROM *A number is given, and some is being taken from this number to find a difference.*	*Word Problem* Tory had five flowers. She gave away three flowers. How many flowers does she have now? $5 - 3 = ?$	*Word Problem* Seven bees are flying around a flower. A bunch of them fly away leaving two near the flower. How many bees flew away? $7 - ? = 2$	*Word Problem* Sally started out with a bunch of star stickers. She gives four away, leaving her with one for herself. How many star stickers did she start with? $? - 4 = 1$
	Picture Problem 	*Picture Problem* 	*Picture Problem*

	TOTAL UNKNOWN	ADDEND UNKNOWN	BOTH ADDENDS UNKNOWN
PUT TOGETHER/ TAKE APART *Often referred to as part, part, whole. Part of the number is given, then another part is given to make a total amount.*	*Word Problem* Sally knitted three gloves on Monday and knitted three more on Tuesday. How many total gloves did Sally knit? $3 + 3 = ?$	*Word Problem* Darrell has collected five rare bird feathers. Two feathers are blue and the rest are white. How many feathers are white? $2 + ? =$ $5 - 2 =$	*Word Problem* Brock has six forks to place in two buckets, bucket A and bucket B. How many forks can go in bucket A and how many forks can go in bucket B? The addends will vary. $2 + 4 = 6$ $5 + 1 = 6$ $3 + 3 = 6$
	Picture Problem	*Picture Problem*	*Picture Problem*

	DIFFERENCE UNKNOWN	BIGGER UNKNOWN	SMALLER UNKNOWN
COMPARE *Two values are given for a total, with the size of one being compared to the size of the other.*	*Word Problem* **How many more?** There are five butterflies on a purple flowering bush. There are three butterflies on a yellow flowering bush. *How many more* butterflies are on the purple flowering bush? $3 + ? = 5$	*Word Problem* **"More" Version** Tory has four *more* tickets than Paula. Paula has 3 tickets. How many tickets does Tory have? $3 + 4 = ?$	*Word Problem* **"More" Version** Joseph has two *more* dollars than Stephen. Joseph has five dollars. How many dollars does Stephen have? $5 - 2 = ?$
	Word Problem **How many fewer?**	*Word Problem* **"Fewer" Version**	*Word Problem* **"Fewer" Version**
	Kevon has three oranges. Natasha has six oranges. *How many fewer* oranges does Kevon have than Natasha? $6 - 3 = ?$	Elvin has one *fewer* notebook than Josiah. Elvin has four notebooks. How many notebooks does Josiah have? $? - 4 = 1$	Petra has three *fewer* fish than Deana. Deana has eight fish. How many fish does Petra have? $? + 3 = 8$

Beginning in third grade, students work with multiplication and division as an extension of addition and subtraction. The table that follows outlines how students learn multiplication and division. Be familiar with the terms in the chart and the type and composition of problems that each scenario represents.

	UNKNOWN PRODUCT	GROUP SIZE UNKNOWN	NUMBER OF GROUPS UNKNOWN
EQUAL GROUPS	Word Problem *Multiplication*	Word Problem *How many in each group? Division*	Word Problem *How many groups? Division*
	There are 3 bags with 6 plums in each bag. How many plums are there in all? $3 \times 6 = ?$	If 18 plums are shared equally into 3 bags, then how many plums will be in each bag? $3 \times ? = 18$ and $18 \div 3 = ?$	If 18 plums are to be packed 6 to a bag, then how many bags are needed? $? \times 6 = 18$ and $18 \div 6 = ?$
	Measurement Example	*Measurement Example*	*Measurement Example*
	You need 4 lengths of string, each 5 inches long. How much string will you need altogether? $4 \times 5 = ?$	You have 12 inches of string, which you will cut into 6 equal pieces. How long will each piece of string be? $6 \times ? = 12$ and $12 \div 6 = ?$	You have 14 inches of string, which you will cut into pieces that are 7 inches long. How many pieces of string will you have? $? \times 7 = 14$ and $14 \div 7 = ?$
ARRAYS	*Array Example*	*Array Example*	*Array Example*
	There are 3 rows of apples with 6 apples in each row. How many apples are there? $3 \times 6 = ?$	If 18 apples are arranged into 3 equal rows, how many apples will be in each row? $3 \times ? = 18$ and $18 \div 3 = ?$	If 18 apples are arranged into equal rows of 6 apples, how many rows will there be? $? \times 6 = 18$ and $18 \div 6 = ?$
AREA	*Area Example*	*Area Example*	*Area Example*
	What is the area of a 4 cm by 5 cm rectangle? $4 \times 5 = ?$	A rectangle has area 12 square centimeters. If one side is 6 cm long, how long is a side next to it? $6 \times ? = 12$ and $12 \div 6 = ?$	A rectangle has area 14 square centimeters. If one side is 7 cm long, how long is a side next to it? $? \times 7 = 14$ and $14 \div 7 = ?$

Compare problems occur first with whole numbers (e.g., two times as much) and then phase in unit fractions (e.g., one-half as much) in the fifth grade. Either grade level scenario is a possibility on the test.

	UNKNOWN PRODUCT	GROUP SIZE UNKNOWN	NUMBER OF GROUPS UNKNOWN
	Word Problem	*Word Problem*	*Word Problem*
COMPARE	A blue hat costs \$6. A red hat costs 3 times as much as the blue hat. How much does the red hat cost? $6 \times 3 = ?$	A red hat costs \$18, and that is 3 times as much as the cost of a blue hat. How much does a blue hat cost? $3 \times ? = 18$ and $18 \div 3 = ?$	A red hat costs \$18, and a blue hat costs \$6. How many times as much of the blue hat does the red hat cost? $? \times 6 = 18$ and $18 \div 6 = ?$
	Measurement Example	*Measurement Example*	*Measurement Example*
	A rubber band is 6 cm long. How long will the rubber band be when it is stretched to be 3 times as long? $6 \times 3 = ?$	A rubber band is stretched to be 18 cm long, and that is 3 times as long as it was at first. How long was the rubber band at first? $3 \times ? = 18$ and $18 \div 3 = ?$	A rubber band was 6 cm long at first. Now it is stretched to be 18 cm long. How many times longer is the rubber band now than it was at first? $? \times 6 = 18$ and $18 \div 6 = ?$
	Unit Fraction Example	*Unit Fraction Example*	*Unit Fraction Example*
	The oak tree is 15 feet tall. The palm tree is 1/5 as tall as the oak. How tall is the palm tree? $15 \times \frac{1}{5} = ?$	The palm tree is 3 feet tall. This is 1/5 as tall as the oak tree. How tall is the oak tree? $? \times \frac{1}{5} = 3$ and $3 \div \frac{1}{5} = ?$	The oak tree is 15 feet tall. The palm tree is 3 feet tall. What fraction of the height of the oak tree is the height of the palm tree? $3 \times ? = 15$ and $3 \div 15 = ?$

(National Governors Association Center for Best Practices, Council of Chief State School Officers, 2016)

Manipulatives (Physical models)

It is important to understand how manipulatives are used to represent counting, patterns, operations, physical attributes of geometric figures, and formulas. It's not enough to know that snap cubes exist; you also need to be aware of how they are used. Below is a list of commonly used manipulatives.

Quick facts:

1. ***Attribute blocks*** come in five different geometric shapes and with different colors. Attribute blocks can be used for sorting, patterns, and teaching attributes of geometric figures.

2. ***Base-10 blocks*** are visual models in powers of 10 that represent ones, tens, hundreds, and thousands. These blocks can be used to teach place value, regrouping with addition or subtraction, fractions, decimals, percents, and area and volume.

3. ***Bar diagrams*** are used to represent parts and whole and are often used with finding a missing value in a number sentence (e.g., $5 + ? = 12$).

4. ***Counters*** come in different shapes and colors (e.g., bears, bugs, chips) and are used for sorting and counting.

5. ***Geoboards*** are pegboard grids on which students stretch rubber bands to make geometric shapes. They are used to teach basic shapes, symmetry, congruency, perimeter, and area.

6. ***Fraction strips*** help to show the relationship between the **numerator** (top number of a fraction) and **denominator** (bottom number of a fraction) of a fraction and how parts relate to a whole.

7. ***Snap cubes*** are cubes that come in various colors that can be snapped together from any face. Snap cubes can be used to teach number sense, basic operations, counting, patterns, and place value.

8. ***Tiles*** are 1-inch squares that come in different colors. Some more common topics tiles can be used to teach include counting, estimating, place value, multiplication, fractions, and probability.

	Manipulative Representations	
Attribute Blocks	• Sorting • Patterns • Attributes of figures	
Base-10 Blocks	• Place value • Whole number operations • Comparing numbers • Regrouping with addition and subtraction • Area and volume	
Bar Diagram	• Solve for an unknown value using one of the four operations • Solve word problems	Kelly added 6 more stamps to her collection. Now she has 18 stamps. How many did she have before? 18 | ? | 6 |
Counters	• Sorting • Counting	
Geoboard	• Perimeter • Area • Properties of basic shapes • Congruency and Similarity	
Fraction Strips	• Perform operations with fractions • Represent fractional parts	1 / $\frac{1}{2}$ $\frac{1}{2}$ / $\frac{1}{4}$ $\frac{1}{4}$ $\frac{1}{4}$ $\frac{1}{4}$ / $\frac{1}{8}$ $\frac{1}{8}$ $\frac{1}{8}$ $\frac{1}{8}$ $\frac{1}{8}$ $\frac{1}{8}$ $\frac{1}{8}$ $\frac{1}{8}$ $\frac{1}{2} = \frac{1}{4} + \frac{1}{4} = \frac{1}{8} + \frac{1}{8} + \frac{1}{8} + \frac{1}{8}$
Snap Cubes	• Combine like terms • Represent ratios • Distributive property • Multiply polynomials • Factoring polynomials	
Tiles	• Perform operations with fractions • Represent fractional parts	

Adding and multiplying using visual models

On the *Praxis*® exam, you may have to identify appropriate manipulatives for an operation, or you may be asked to identify a problem that a manipulative is modeling. You may also be asked to identify an array that appropriately represents a multiplication problem.

Examples:

8. Model the problem below using both a manipulative and a number line.

    Dory has 5 books. Kelvin gives her 4 more books. How many books does Dory have now?

    Solution:

    This problem is an add-to problem where the total is unknown. Using snap cubes, we can start with 5 and then add 4 more to the 5 to find the total. Students should conclude that there are 9 total cubes.

    Using a number line, start at the first addend, 5, then move 4 spaces right, the value of the second addend to find the total number of books.

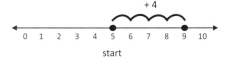

9. Use groups and arrays to model the problem below.

    Tina ordered 4 boxes of tennis balls. Each box contains 3 tennis balls. How many tennis balls did Tina order?

    Solution:

    To model using groups, show that there are 3 tennis balls in each of the 4 boxes, or 4 groups of 3.

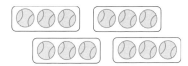

    An array puts groups into organized lines, preparing students for additional math topics, such as area. To model with an array, create 4 rows of 3 tennis balls each, showing this model is also equivalent to 12 tennis balls.

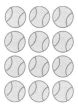

Order of operations

Please Excuse My Dear Aunt Sally (PEDMAS) is an acronym used to remember the order of operations.

Please, or parentheses, includes all grouping symbols, which may include brackets [ ]. If there is math that can be computed inside grouping symbols, do that FIRST, then the grouping symbols may be removed.

Excuse, or exponents, means anything raised to a power should be simplified after all operations inside of grouping symbols have been simplified.

My **D**ear, or multiplication and division, are essentially the same "type" of operation. Therefore, these operations are performed in order from left to right, just as you would read a book. All multiplication and division should be completed BEFORE any addition or subtraction that is not inside parentheses.

Aunt **S**ally, or addition and subtraction, are also essentially the same "type" of operation and are also done in order from left to right. These operations should always come last unless they are inside parentheses.

On the *Praxis®* exam, you will be expected to recognize order of operations in various problems. When solving all problems, pay close attention to the order in which you are solving.

Example:

10. Simplify the expression and write the solution in the box.

$$1 + 2(28 - 12) + 2 \times 10$$

Solution: 53

$1 + 2(28 - 12) + 2 \times 10$
$1 + 2(16) + 2 \times 10$
$1 + 32 + 2 \times 10$
$1 + 32 + 20$
$33 + 20$
53

Strategies for problem solving

You should be familiar with a variety of strategies that students may use to solve problems; also know the best strategy to use based on the problem type. Typically, test questions will expect you to *apply* a strategy rather than *identify* the strategy by name.

Examples of common problem-solving strategies:

- Draw a picture

- Find a pattern

- Guess and check

- Make a chart or table

- Work the problem backward

- Act it out

- Estimating or rounding

Example:

11. Robert was at a friend's house for three and a half hours. He left his friend's home at 6:15 p.m. What time did he arrive?

    Solution: 2:45 p.m.

    This is a good problem for using the problem-solving strategy of working backwards. Starting with 6:15 and going back 30 minutes to account for the half hour puts the time at 5:45. Working backwards another 3 hours to address his remaining time Robert was at his friend's house, puts him arriving at 2:45 p.m.

Properties of operations

Know the properties of operations for the exam, including how and when they are used. As students become more proficient with addition and multiplication, these properties allow them to fluently rewrite and simplify problems.

Property of Operations	Rule	Description
Commutative Property of Addition	$a + b = b + a$	Changing the order of two numbers being added does not change their sum.
Commutative Property of Multiplication	$a \cdot b = b \cdot a$	Changing the order of two numbers being multiplied does not change their product.
Associative Property of Addition	$(a + b) + c = a + (b + c)$	Changing the grouping of the addends does not change their sum.
Associative Property of Multiplication	$a \cdot (b \cdot c) = (a \cdot b) \cdot c$	Changing the grouping of the factors does not change their product.
Additive Identity Property of 0	$a + 0 = 0 + a = a$	Adding 0 to a number does not change the value of that number.
Multiplicative Identity Property of 1	$a \cdot 1 = 1 \cdot a = a$	Multiplying a number by 1 does not change the value of that number.
Inverse Property of Addition	For every a, there exists a number $-a$ such that $a + (-a) = (-a) + a = 0$	Adding a number and its opposite results in a sum equal to 0.
Inverse Property of Multiplication	For every a, there exists a number $^1/_a$ such that $a \cdot \dfrac{1}{a} = \dfrac{1}{a} \cdot a = \dfrac{a}{a} = 1$	Multiplying a number and its multiplicative inverse results in a product equal to 1.
Distributive Property of Multiplication over Addition	$a \cdot (b + c) = a \cdot b + a \cdot c$	Multiplying a sum is the same as multiplying each addend by that number, then adding their products.
Distributive Property of Multiplication over Subtraction	$a \cdot (b - c) = a \cdot b - a \cdot c$	Multiplying a difference is the same as multiplying the minuend and subtrahend by that number, then subtracting their products.

We often think of a property as only reading one way, but we can read the definition of properties from left to right or from right to left. Let's consider this idea with the distributive property:

Usually, we think of applying the distributive property by multiplying all the terms on the inside of a set of parentheses by a factor multiplied on the outside of the parentheses. For example, $2(x + 3) = 2x + 6$.

We can also apply the distributive property by looking at the right side of the equation and rewriting it as a product of two factors. Our example then becomes, $2x + 6 = 2 \cdot x + 2 \cdot 3 = 2(x + 3)$. The step in the middle is not necessary, but it is helpful in visualizing the factor that each term has in common.

Opposites and reciprocals

Make sure that you understand that the **opposite** of a number is the same number with a different sign, so the opposite of 5 is -5 and the opposite of -2 is 2. Important facts about opposites include,

- The sum of a number and its opposite equals 0. For example, $5 + (-5) = 0$.

- Zero does NOT have an opposite.

In addition to opposites, know that the multiplicative inverse, or **reciprocal**, of a number is what the number is multiplied by to get 1. To find a reciprocal, write the number as a fraction, if it is not already a fraction, then flip the fraction. For example, to find the multiplicative inverse of 3, write it as a fraction, $\frac{3}{1}$, then flip the fraction to $\frac{1}{3}$. Thus, the multiplicative inverse of 3 is $\frac{1}{3}$ because $3 \times \frac{1}{3} = 1$. Important facts about multiplicative inverses include,

- The product of a number and its reciprocal is 1.

- Zero does NOT have a reciprocal.

Examples:

12. Which of the following is an example of applying the distributive property to the expression $4 + 14a$?
    A. $2(2 + 7a)$
    B. $2 \times 2 + 14a$
    C. $4 + (2 \times 7a)$
    D. $18a \times 1$

    Solution: A

    If we apply the distributive property to $4 + 14a$, we get $4 + 14a = 2 \cdot 2 + 2 \cdot 7a = 2(2 + 7a)$, which is option A.

13. Which of the following is an example of the commutative property of addition?
    A. $(2 + x) + 3 = 2 + (x + 3)$
    B. $4 + (y + w) = 4 + (w + y)$
    C. $5a + b + 1 = 5a + b$
    D. $2(3x + 8) - 1 = 6x + 16 - 1$

    Solution: B

    The commutative property of addition changes the order of two addends in an addition statement. In choice B, although there are parentheses, they don't serve a purpose. Notice the w and y change order from the left side of the equation to the right side of the equation. This is an example of the commutative property of addition.

Ordering and comparing various forms of numbers

In upper elementary grades and into middle school, students are presented with and expected to know different ways to write the same number. This includes writing numbers as fractions, decimals, percents, in scientific notation, and as a product using exponents. On the *Praxis®* exam, you should be familiar with writing numbers in different forms, comparing the size of the numbers, and knowing where various forms of numbers are located on a number line.

Unit fractions

A unit fraction is a fraction with a numerator of 1. Students learn unit fractions using fractional pieces of circles or bars and also by breaking up a number line into fractional pieces. From the number line, students learn the placement of fractions and their size relative to one another and to 0 and 1. The table that follows gives examples of some, not all, unit fractions.

Unit Fraction	Manipulative Representation	Number Line Representation
$\frac{1}{2}$		The fraction $\frac{1}{2}$ is the same distance from both 0 and 1.
$\frac{1}{4}$		The fraction $\frac{1}{4}$ is closer to 0 than 1, and $\frac{1}{4}$ is less than $\frac{1}{2}$.
$\frac{1}{5}$		The fraction $\frac{2}{5}$ is closer to 0 than 1, and $\frac{3}{5}$ is greater than $\frac{1}{2}$.

Working with unit fractions leads to decomposing fractions and writing an equation, representing the decomposition by showing the sum of the unit fractions is equal to the original fraction. To **decompose** a fraction means to break it into parts.

Example:

14. Which of the following is a decomposition of $\frac{3}{4}$?

   A. $\frac{1}{4} + \frac{1}{4} + \frac{1}{4} = \frac{3}{4}$

   B. $\frac{3}{4} = 0.75 = 75\%$

   C. $\frac{1}{4} + \frac{3}{4} = \frac{4}{4} = 1$

   D. $\frac{1}{2} < \frac{3}{4}$

   Solution: A

   The correct answer choice is A because decomposing a fraction means to break a fraction up into the sum of smaller parts with the same denominator. Options B, C, and D do not break the fraction into smaller parts.

Number Representation

The same number can be written several ways. Be prepared to know how to write a number in different forms and to recognize equivalent forms of the same number. Also, be prepared to compare numbers written in different forms.

Fractions, Decimals, and Percents	
Fractions, decimals, and percents are all interchangeable and are acceptable in any of the three forms. Base-10 blocks create an effective visual when first learning percents and decimals as values out of 100.	
Base-10 Blocks	To represent a number out of 100 pictorially, we can use a base-10 block with 100 squares. The image to the right has 30 squares shaded or 30 out of 100, which is $\frac{30}{100}$, 0.30, or 30%.
Fraction	To write a number out of 100 as a fraction, place the number over 100 and reduce. The fraction $\frac{30}{100}$ may also be written as $\frac{3}{10}$.
Decimal	To convert a fraction to a decimal, always divide the numerator (top number) by the denominator (bottom number); numerator ÷ denominator. $30 \div 100 = 0.30$ or 0.3
Percent	To convert a decimal to a percent, move the decimal point two place values to the right. Moving the decimal point two places to the right is the same as multiplying by 100. Example: To convert 0.43 to a percent, move the decimal 2 places to the right: $0.43 = 43\%$ This is the same as $0.43 \times 100 = 43$. Moving the decimal is the shortcut; make sure you always know the math behind the shortcuts.

Application problems for fraction, decimal, and percent conversions often include having to find the percent of a number. To find **the percent of a number**, change the percent to a decimal and multiply the decimal by the number. For example, 12% of 40 is $0.12 \times 40 = 4.8$.

Examples:

15. Choose a number from the list that is greater than 70% but less than 80%. Write your answer in the box.

0.85 1 0.75 2^2

☐

Solution:

To solve, rewrite each of the numbers in the question and answer choices as a decimal so that they are easy to compare.

- $70\% = 0.7$

- $80\% = 0.8$

The correct choice should be between 0.7 and 0.8.

- 0.85 is not between 0.7 and 0.8, NO

- $\frac{65}{100} = 0.65$, is not between 0.7 and 0.8, NO

- 1 is not between 0.7 and 0.8, NO

- 0.75 is between 0.7 and 0.8, YES *Remember 0.7 and 0.70 are the same number.*

- $2^2 = 4$, is not between 0.7 and 0.8, NO

16. Select all the expressions that are equivalent to 0.75.

   ☐ $\frac{75}{100}$

   ☐ $\frac{3}{5}$

   ☐ 75%

   ☐ $5^2 + 50$

   ☐ 0.750

   ☐ $1 - \frac{1}{4}$

Solution:

To solve, rewrite each of the numbers as a decimal so that they are easy to compare.

- $\frac{75}{100} = 0.75$, YES

- $\frac{3}{5} = 0.6$, NO

- $75\% = 0.75$, YES

- $5^2 + 50 = 25 + 50 = 75$, NO $(75 \neq 0.75)$

- $0.750 = 0.75$, YES

- $1 - \frac{1}{4} = \frac{3}{4} = 0.75$, YES

17. In a recent survey of 60 people, 15% of the people responded that they eat dinner out more than twice a week. What fraction of people do not eat dinner out more than twice a week?

Solution:

To find the *fraction* of people who do not eat dinner out more than twice a week, we need to know the *actual number of people* this represents. To find this number, we need to first find the percent of people who do not eat out more than twice a week. If 15% eat out more than twice a week, then $100\% - 15\% = 85\%$ represents those who do not eat out more than twice a week.

Next, find 85% of 60 people.

$0.85 \times 60 = 51$

Thus, 51 people don't eat out more than twice a week, which is $\frac{51}{60}$ of those surveyed.

Testing Tip

Know what the "set-up" of problems looks like. You may be required to identify expressions or problems that could be used to find the percent of a number, the unit rate, the total cost, etc. Remember, there is more than one way to write expressions, so your answer may not match exactly to answer choices listed in a question.

Example:

To find the percent of a number, we typically convert the percent to a decimal, but on the *Praxis*® exam, a possible answer choice may represent the decimal as a fraction. Both produce the same results. Instead of listing 0.85×60, an answer choice may be $\frac{85}{100} \times 60$.

Proportional relationships

A **ratio** is a comparison of two numbers using a fraction, a colon, or the word "to". Ratios have the same units. When ratios have different units, they are referred to as a **rate**.

RATES AND RATIOS		
Verbal Statement **Manipulatives/ Picture**	Four dogs for every three cats	
Fraction **Colon**	$\dfrac{4 \text{ dogs}}{3 \text{ cats}}$	4 dogs : 3 cats OR 4:3

Rates are often expressed as **unit rates** and are read using the word "per" instead of "to". It is common to reference a unit rate in everyday language.

A **unit rate** is a rate with a denominator of 1. Examples of unit rates include 60 miles per hour $\left(\frac{60 \text{ miles}}{1 \text{ hour}}\right)$, $3 per box $\left(\frac{\$3}{1 \text{ box}}\right)$, or 22 students per teacher $\left(\frac{22 \text{ students}}{1 \text{ teacher}}\right)$. Any rate can be converted to a unit rate by dividing the numerator of the fraction by the denominator.

When two ratios are equivalent, they can be set equal to one another to form a **proportion**.

Test items that contain proportional relationships may involve any of the following:

- a scale

- equivalency statements

- descriptions of similar figures

> **Remember**
>
> **Ratio:** $\frac{2 \text{ feet}}{3 \text{ feet}}$ same units
>
> **Rate:** $\frac{25 \text{ miles}}{3 \text{ hours}}$ different units
>
> **Proportion:** $\frac{3 \text{ inches}}{14 \text{ miles}} = \frac{x \text{ inches}}{84.5 \text{ miles}}$

Proportions: Given a scale

A scale is typically given using a colon, and questions involving a scale include a map, a blueprint, or a model. The units may or may not be part of the scale, but they will be given in the problem or in an accompanying picture.

Example:

18. A model of a new parking garage being built downtown has a height of 12.5 inches. If the scale of the model to the actual building is 2:15 and represents inches to feet, how tall is the actual parking garage?

Solution: 93.75 feet

Set up the first part of the proportion using the scale.

$$\frac{2 \text{ inches}}{15 \text{ feet}}$$

> **How do I know to use a proportion?**
>
> ✓ Contains a scale (2:15).
>
> ✓ Each of the numbers contains units.
>
> ✓ There are 3 numbers with units, and the problem asks for a 4th number with units.

Next, finish setting up the proportion by using what we call **matchy-matchy**. Match the units in the first fraction with the units in the second fraction; if inches are in the numerator in the first fraction, inches must also be in the numerator for the second fraction.

$$\frac{2 \text{ inches}}{15 \text{ feet}} = \frac{12.5 \text{ inches}}{x \text{ feet}}$$

Last, cross multiply and solve the equation to find the value of the variable.

$2x = 12.5(15)$ *Note: Once you cross-multiply, the fraction has been eliminated.*

$$\frac{2x}{2} = \frac{187.5}{2}$$

$x = 93.75$ feet

Proportions: Given an equivalency statement

An equivalency statement is a statement that describes a rate using words, such as a number of envelopes stuffed every 20 minutes or a number of chaperones for every 15 students. Equivalency statements will have a constant rate and will also have three numbers with units and will ask for a fourth number.

Example:

19. A pie crust machine can press 15 pie crusts into pie tins in 20 minutes. How many pie crusts can be pressed into pie tins in 4 hours?

Solution: 180 minutes

Set up the first part of the proportion using the equivalency statement.

$$\frac{15 \text{ crusts}}{20 \text{ minutes}}$$

> **How do I know to use a proportion?**
>
> ✓ Contains an equivalency statement that represents a rate.
>
> ✓ Each of the numbers contains units.
>
> ✓ There are 3 numbers with units, and the problem asks for a 4th number with units.

Next, finish setting up the proportion, remembering **matchy-matchy**. Be careful because the time for the second fraction is in hours. Convert hours to minutes so that the units are the same.

4 hours = 4 · 60 minutes = 240 minutes

$$\frac{15 \text{ crusts}}{20 \text{ minutes}} = \frac{x \text{ crusts}}{240 \text{ minutes}}$$

Last, cross-multiply and solve the equation to find the value of the variable.

$20x = 240(15)$

$20x = 3600$

$x = 180$ pie crusts

Proportions: Given a description of similar figures

Some word problems describe a situation that is proportional without explicitly using the term proportional. This is often the case with similar figures. The side lengths of similar figures are proportional, which is why the problem does not have to state anything about proportionality.

Example*:*

20. The height of a tree can be found using similar triangles. A 12-foot tall tree casts a 7-foot shadow. If a nearby tree casts a 5-foot shadow, how tall is the tree?

    Solution:

    Draw a picture and label the lengths.

    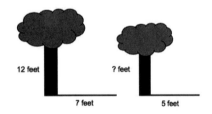

    12 feet   ? feet

    7 feet   5 feet

How do I know to use a proportion?
✓ Contains similar figures that can be drawn.
✓ Each of the numbers contains units.
✓ There are 3 numbers with units, and the problem asks for a 4th number with units.

Next, use the picture to set up the proportion. Notice that the labels on the picture are already in the right place for a proportion.

$\frac{12}{7} = \frac{x}{5}$ *Note: The units are not included here because they are all the same.*

Cross-multiply and solve the proportion for the variable.

$7x = 12(5)$

$7x = 60$

$x = 8\frac{4}{7}$ feet

Proportions: Given similar figures

Questions that contain a proportional relationship may only include a figure. In this instance, the shapes should be the same shape but a different size.

Examples:

21. The rectangles below are similar. What is the length of the missing side, x?

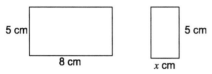

Solution: 3.125 cm

Be careful when setting up the proportion for this question because the second rectangle is rotated so that the shorter side is the length. If the first fraction in the proportion is set up as the shorter side over the longer side, make sure it is the same in the second fraction.

$$\frac{5}{8} = \frac{x}{5}$$

$$8x = 25$$

$$x = 3.125 \text{ cm}$$

> **How do I know to use a proportion?**
>
> The problem stated the figures are similar.
>
> There are 3 numbers with units, and the problem asks for a 4th number with units.

22. An artist made a scale drawing of a mural he is painting on the side of a building. The building is 10 feet tall and 80 feet wide. The scale of inches to feet used to make the drawing is 3:40. How wide is the scale drawing?

   A. 6 inches
   B. 0.75 inches
   C. 24 inches
   D. 5 inches

Solution: A

The scale, 3:40, is one fraction of the proportion. Although we have both the length and width of the building, the question is asking for the width of the scale drawing, so only the width of the actual building should be used in the second fraction of the proportion along with the unknown, x. The length of the building is extra information.

$$\frac{3}{40} = \frac{x}{80}$$

$$40x = 240$$

$$x = 6 \text{ inches}$$

The correct answer is A.

23. The height of building AB can be measured using similar triangles. A small puddle at point C reflects the top of building AB so that a person standing on the top of ED can see the reflection of AB in the puddle. Using the information in the sketch below, find the height of building AB.

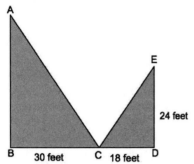

A. 36 feet
B. 39 feet
C. 40 feet
D. 45 feet

Solution: C

To solve, set up a proportion using the dimensions of the two triangles.

$$\frac{x}{30} = \frac{24}{18}$$

$$18x = 720$$

$$x = 40 \text{ feet}$$

The correct answer is C.

24. A factory produces 10 pillows every 45 minutes. If the factory runs 8 hours each day, how many pillows will it produce in a 5-day work week?

A. 36
B. 106
C. 533
D. 888

Solution: C

This problem contains the equivalency statement, 10 pillows every 45 minutes. The question asks for the final answer in hours, so first convert 45 minutes to hours, which is $45 \div 60 = 0.75$ hour. The final answer also asks for the number of pillows over 5 days. This problem can be solved by either using 40 hours in the proportion or using 8 and multiplying the answer by 5. To speed up the problem solving and not forget the last step, we suggest using 40 in the original problem.

$$\frac{10}{0.75} = \frac{x}{40}$$

$$0.75x = 400$$

$$x = 533.\overline{3}$$

The company cannot make $0.\overline{3}$ of a pillow, so C is the correct solution.

Percent of change (Increase/Decrease)

Questions that require finding the percent of increase or decrease will either ask for the percent of increase/decrease or the percent of change. To find the percent of change, begin by finding the following fraction:

$$\frac{\text{new number} - \text{original number}}{\text{original number}}.$$

Next, convert the fraction to a decimal, and then convert the decimal to a percent. If the percent is positive, the percent of change was an increase. If the percent is negative, the percent of change was a decrease. **The negative sign is not included** in the answer of a percent decrease. It is instead denoted with the word *decrease*.

Example:

25. Last month Michael ran an average of 5 miles per day. This month, he ran an average of 6 miles per day. Find the percent of increase for Michael's mileage from last month to this month.

    A. 16%
    B. 17%
    C. 20%
    D. 183%

    Solution: C

    Find the fraction using the original and new numbers, then convert the fraction to a decimal and then percent.

    $$\frac{\text{new-original}}{\text{original}} = \frac{6-5}{5} = \frac{1}{5} = 0.2 = 20\% \text{ increase.}$$

    The correct answer is answer choice C.

Percent of total

When a question asks what percent a situation represents, this requires writing numbers as a fraction, converting the numbers to decimals, and then converting the decimal to a percent.

Example:

26. At a local baseball tournament of 1,500 players, 500 of the players did not record a strikeout at the plate. What percent of the players, to the nearest whole percent, did record a strikeout during the tournament?

    A. 67%
    B. 69%
    C. 33%
    D. 46%

    Solution: A

    First find the number of those striking out: $1500 - 500 = 1,000$

    Next, write this number as a fraction out of the total number of players: $\frac{1000}{1500}$

    Convert to a decimal and then a percent: $\frac{1000}{1500} = 0.6667 = 67\%$. The correct answer choice is A.

D. Knows how to use basic concepts of number theory

Numbers are classified into various groups based on their properties. Notice that for each of the types of numbers defined in the table that follows, the numbers continue forever, hence the, "…" at the end. The arrows at the end of a number line represent the concept of the numbers continuing forever. Numbers in the Real Number System that are addressed at various stages in grades K–6 are classified further into the groups shown in the table.

Classification of Numbers	
Real Number System	
Counting Numbers	1, 2, 3, 4, 5, 6, …
Whole Numbers	0, 1, 2, 3, 4, 5, 6, …
Integers	…, −5, −4, −3, −2, −1, 0, 1, 2, 3, 4, 5, …
Rational Numbers	Any number that can be written as a fraction $^a/b$, where a and b are any integer. Rational numbers include all terminating and repeating decimals. Example: 0.2, $4\frac{1}{2}$, 7, $\frac{1}{3}$
Additional Classifications	
Prime	A positive integer that only has 1 and itself as factors. Example: 2, 3, 13, 29 **Note: 1 is neither prime nor composite, and 2 is the only even prime number.**
Composite	A positive integer that has factors other than 1 and itself. Example: 4, 12, 27, 44
Even	A number that is divisible by 2
Odd	A number that is not divisible by 2

Terms used to classify real numbers may be sprinkled throughout the test. Know what type of number each of these terms represent in the event the term is used in a problem.

It is possible that you get a question that tests your knowledge of number sense. For example, why is $\frac{0}{1}$ a number but $\frac{1}{0}$ not defined? (For the first fraction, we can say that 1 goes into 0 zero times, so the result is 0. For the second fraction, a number cannot be divided into 0 parts, so a denominator of zero makes no sense and is not possible).

Important Number Facts

- 1 is neither prime nor composite.
- 2 is the only even prime number.
- 0 is an even number.
- The sum of two even numbers is always even.
- The sum of two odd numbers is always even.
- The sum of an even number and an odd number is always odd.

Factors and multiples

Prime factorization refers to finding all the prime numbers, when multiplied together, result in a composite number. For example, the prime factorization of 24 is 2 · 2 · 2 · 3 or 2^3 · 3. A common method for finding the prime factorization of a number is using factor trees. Using a factor tree to find the prime factorization of 24 is shown below.

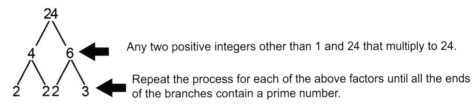

Any two positive integers other than 1 and 24 that multiply to 24.

Repeat the process for each of the above factors until all the ends of the branches contain a prime number.

Prime factorization is one method for finding the greatest common factor and the least common multiple.

The **greatest common factor,** or GCF, is the largest number that divides into all numbers in a given set. The GCF can only be as large as the smallest number in the set.

The **least common multiple**, or LCM, is the smallest multiple (for students in elementary grades, multiples are found by skip counting) that all the numbers in a set have in common.

Besides using a factor tree, a list may also be used to find the GCF or LCM. The larger the numbers in a set, the less practical the method of using a list becomes.

Factors and Multiples		
Factor Tree	Greatest Common Factor (GCF) of 8 and 12: *Find the factors each number has in common; for 8 and 12, they have a pair of 2s in comon. Next, multiply all the factors each has in common; if no common factors exist, the GCF=1.* (2)(2) = 4 Least Common Multiple (LCM) of 8 and 12: *Find each factor in both numbers. For 8 and 12, the prime factors are 2 and 3. Next, multiply each factor the greatest number of times it occurs between the numbers. The 2 occurs three times in 8 and the 3 occurs only once in 12.* (2)(2)(2)(3) = 24	8 = (2)(2)(2) 12 = (2)(2)(3)
List	Greatest Common Factor (GCF) of 8 and 12: 8: 1, 2, 4, 8 12: 1, 2, 3, 4, 6, 12 Least Common Multiple (LCM) of 8 and 12: 8: 8, 16, 24, 32 12: 12, 24, 36	

Examples:

27. Find the least common multiple (LCM) of 12 and 15.

    A. 3
    B. 30
    C. 60
    D. 180

    Solution: C

    To find the LCM of 12 and 15, make a list of the multiples of each number. The smallest multiple they share is 60.

    12: 12, 24, 36, 48, 60, 72, 84, 96   **15**: 15, 30, 45, 60, 75

28. Which number has the same prime factors as 24?

    A. 15
    B. 12
    C. 34
    D. 19

    Solution: B

    We saw previously that the prime factors of 24 are $24 = 2^3 \cdot 3$. Thus, we are looking for which of the answer choices has a combination of 2s and 3s for its prime factors as well. We can eliminate A because 5 is a factor. We can eliminate C because 17 is a prime factor of 34. We can also eliminate D because 19 is a prime number. Answer choice B, 12, contains the prime factors 2^2 and 3, which is what we want; thus, B is the correct answer.

Estimation is a strategy used to quickly find an answer that is close to the actual answer. Estimation is also used to check the reasonableness of a solution. The following table lists three ways to estimate a solution.

Testing Tip

Know the names of the estimation strategies. They are one of the few terms that may be on the exam.

Strategy	Definition/What It Looks Like
Estimation	Finding a rough calculation or approximation; different estimation strategies are helpful in different situations.
3 Types of Estimation	
Compatible Numbers	Estimating by rounding pairs of numbers to numbers that are easy to add, subtract, multiply, or divide. Example: $31.8 \div 5.2$ becomes $30 \div 5$, so the estimated value is 6.
Clustering	Estimating sums or products when all the numbers are close to a single value. Example: $42 + 38 + 40 + 41$ becomes $40 + 40 + 40 + 40$, so the estimated value is 160.
Front-End Estimation	Estimating by rounding to the greatest place value or the number in front. Example: $412 + 58 + 1{,}780$ would become $400 + 60 + 2{,}000$, so the estimated value is 2,460.

II. Algebraic Thinking

Algebraic thinking tests your knowledge of identifying, manipulating, and performing operations on expressions and equations that are found in algebra. This includes being able to solve equations and inequalities with one variable using properties of operations, identifying and creating linear equations and functions from a table, and applying properties of arithmetic and geometric sequences to find missing numbers or figures in a pattern.

The skills you need to know in this section include the following:

A. Knows how to evaluate and manipulate algebraic expressions, equations, and formulas

B. Understands the meanings of the solutions to linear equations and inequalities

C. Knows how to recognize and represent patterns (e.g., number, shape)

A. Knows how to evaluate and manipulate algebraic expressions, equations, and formulas

Expressions and Equations

An **algebraic expression** is a mathematical phrase that contains terms that include numbers (constants), variables, or a combination of numbers and variables. A **term** in an expression is separated by a $+$ or a $-$ sign. The following list contains examples of algebraic expressions and the number of terms in each expression.

Expression	Number of Terms
$2a + 7$	2
$x^2 + 3xy - y$	3
8	1
$a^2 b^5 c^3$	1
$y - 2$	2

An **equation** is two algebraic expressions separated by an equal sign. The equal sign is what differentiates an equation from an expression.

Examples:

29. How many terms do each of the math phrases have?
    $2xy - y$ $3a$ $a + b - c + 4$

    Solution:

    Remember that terms are separated by addition or subtraction signs. The first expression has two terms: $2xy$ and y. The second expression has one term, and the third expression has four terms, $a, b, c,$ and 4.

30. Select all the choices that represent an expression.
    ☐ $2x + 7 = 5$ ☐ $A = bh$
    ☐ $ab - 8$ ☐ $3(4h + 3g)$
    ☐ $\frac{2}{5}x + x^2$ ☐ $y = 2x - 1$

    Solution:

    The expressions are all the answer choices without an equal sign. Therefore, $ab - 8$, $\frac{2}{5}x + x^2$, and $3(4h + 3g)$ are all expressions.

Polynomials

Polynomials are algebraic expressions that do not have a variable in the denominator of a fraction. *Praxis®* exam questions may require you to identify characteristics about a polynomial, including the name and degree.

Polynomials may be named by the number of terms they have or their degree. For the *Praxis®* exam, be familiar with the names of polynomials by terms. The **degree of a polynomial** is the largest sum of exponents in one term.

Polynomial	Number of Terms	Name by Term Number	Degree
$3a^2b^3$	1	monomial	5
$x^2 + 7$	2	binomial	2
$a^2b^2 + ab^5 + 3a$	3	trinomial	6*

*Note: $ab^5 = a^1b^5$, which is a degree of 6.

Equations

The equations you will have to solve on the *Praxis®* exam are linear or a factored form of a quadratic, which is similar to solving a linear equation. A linear equation is an equation with all the variables having a power of 1. An example of a linear equation is $y = 2x + 4$. You do not need to identify whether or not an equation is linear.

A factored quadratic equation looks like $(x + 3)(x - 5) = 0$. If we performed the multiplication between the parentheses, the power of x would be 2, which is what makes it a quadratic equation. You do not need to know how to identify quadratic equations. These terms are discussed here to be able to note the differences when solving.

The **independent variable** in an equation represents where numbers are input in order to find the value of the **dependent variable**, which is the output value. In testing scenarios, x is typically the independent variable, and y is the dependent variable. The value of y depends on what is substituted in for x.

Example:

31. Jenny has completed 10 sketches for her art portfolio. She adds 3 sketches each month. This can be represented by the equation $y = 3m + 10$, where y is the total number of sketches in her portfolio and m is the number of months that she has added 3 sketches to the total. Which variable is the independent variable?

    A. m
    B. y
    C. 3
    D. 10

    Solution: A

    There are two variables in the equation: y and m. The value of the total number of art projects, y, is going to depend on the number of months that have passed, so y is the dependent variable, making m the independent variable.

Translating verbal statements into expressions and equations

The following lists and examples include common math vocabulary used in verbal statements. Be familiar with these phrases. You may be expected to translate verbal expressions presented in different scenarios, so be prepared.

Verbal statements

Verbal Statements			
Addition Words	• *Sum* • Plus • Add • Altogether • Total • Increased by	**Subtraction Words**	• *Difference* • Minus • Take Away • Less, *Less than* • *Subtracted from* • Decreased by
Multiplication Words	• *Product* • Times • Multiply • *Of* • Double, twice	**Division Words**	• *Quotient* • Divide • Ratio • Split into Parts
Equal	• *Is* • Equal • Equivalent to	**Grouping Symbols**	• *Quantity* • 2 Operations in a row • (Example: *times the sum of*…)

IMPORTANT – The *italicized and underlined* terms in the table above are prevalent in assessment questions. Be sure to memorize these terms.

Examples:

Write a mathematical statement for each verbal expression in questions 32–35.

32. Four times the quantity of a number, x, plus three.

> **Solution:** $4(x + 3)$

> Verbal Expression Breakdown:

four	4
times	$\times$
the quantity	( )
a number	x
plus	+
three	3

> **Testing Tip**
>
> When the phrases *less than* or *fewer than* are in a math sentence, the numbers in the sentence will be "flipped."
>
> Example: 5 less than 10 is written 10-5.

The tricky part here is the phrase *the quantity*. When you have two operations in a row, or the phrase *the quantity*, the numbers and operations following go into the parentheses because they are *the quantity*. The math statement that represents the verbal statement is $4(x+3)$. (We don't need the multiplication symbol between the 4 and the parentheses).

33. The quotient of double a number, y, and 15.

    Solution: $\dfrac{2y}{15}$ OR $2y \div 15$

34. Eight subtracted from the product of 3 and m.

    Solution: $3m - 8$

    Subtracted from can be tricky because it switches the order of the terms given in the problem. Since 8 is subtracted from the product, the product of 3 and m needs to come first.

35. Four times the difference of a number and twelve is eighty-seven. Which of the following choices represents the math sentence?

    A. $4 \times x - 12 = 87$
    B. $4(x - 12) = 87$
    C. $4(12 - x) = 87$
    D. $12 - 4x = 87$

    Solution: B

    When two operations are in a verbal statement with no numbers in between, this represents a quantity. Four times the difference of two numbers should be interpreted as having to subtract two numbers in the order they appear before multiplying by 4, which would mean the subtraction problem has to be in parentheses so that it comes first in the order of operations.

36. Jessica and Emily both collect coins. Emily has four less than twice as many coins as Jessica. If c represents the number of coins Jessica has, which expression represents the number of coins Emily has?

    A. $4 < 2c$
    B. $4 - 2c$
    C. $2(4 - c)$
    D. $2c - 4$

    Solution: D

    Four less than twice as many coins as Jessica is calculated by finding two times the number of coins Jessica has, then subtracting four. Remember, less than switches the order of the numbers being subtracted in the problem. The less than symbol is not an option because the word "is" would need to be present. For example, 4 **is** less than 5 is represented $4 < 5$ whereas 4 less than 5 is equivalent to $5 - 4$.

37. Jarrod is using a verbal statement to represent the addition of two terms in an expression. Which word could he use to represent addition?

    A. sum
    B. product
    C. difference
    D. quotient

    Solution: A

    The answer to an addition problem is called the sum.

Write equations and inequalities given a word problem

In addition to translating verbal expressions, you will be expected to write an equation, inequality, or system of equations given a real-world scenario. The process is the same as translating a verbal expression, but you will have to make some inferences. For example, John earns $15 per hour will translate to $15h$.

Examples:

38. Heather buys some tomatoes for $2 each and three onions for $1.25 each. She spent less than $9 on tomatoes and onions. Which option represents this scenario?

    A. $2t + 1.25 < 9$
    B. $2t + 1.25 > 9$
    C. $2t + 3.75 < 9$
    D. $2t + 3.75 \leq 9$

    Solution: C

    We don't know how many tomatoes Heather bought, so let t represent the number of tomatoes purchased. We do know the tomatoes were $2 each, so $2t$ represents the cost of the tomatoes. She purchased 3 onions for $1.25 each, making the cost of the onions $3 \times 1.25 = \$3.75$. If she spent less than $9, the total cost of the tomatoes and onions, $2t + 3.75$, is less than 9, or $2t + 3.75 < 9$. Therefore, C is the correct answer choice.

39. Brenden is three years older than Darrel. The sum of their ages is 32. Which system of equations represents this scenario?

    A. $\begin{cases} B + D = 3 \\ B - D = 32 \end{cases}$

    B. $\begin{cases} B = D + 3 \\ B + D = 32 \end{cases}$

    C. $\begin{cases} D = 3 - B \\ B - D = 32 \end{cases}$

    D. $\begin{cases} D = 3 + B \\ B + D = 32 \end{cases}$

    Solution: B

    Use the answer choices to find the solution. We know that the sum of their ages equals 32 from the problem. Looking at the second equations that equal 32 in each choice, we can eliminate option A and option C because they are subtracting not adding to get 32.
    This leaves the first equations to evaluate. The options are either $B = D + 3$, which reads Brenden is Darrel's age plus 3, or $D = 3 + B$, which reads Darrel is Brenden's age plus 3. We know Brenden is three years older than Darrel, so the first equation from answer choice B is correct.

40. A gym membership costs $18 per month plus a $10 application fee. Which equation represents the total cost of the membership after m number of months?

    A. $y = 18m + 10$
    B. $18m + y = 10$
    C. $10 - y = 18m$
    D. $18(y + m) = 10$

    Solution: A

The application fee is a flat rate, so in an equation, it is represented by adding 10. The cost per month can be represented by $18m$ because members pay $18 each month. The total paid after any given number of months can be found using the equation $y = 18m + 10$.

Performing operations on expressions

When generating equivalent expressions, the commutative, associative, and distributive properties are often used for operations. On the test, be prepared to recognize equivalent expressions through the application of these properties. Remember, each of these properties can be applied from either side of the equal sign.

Property	Rule	Example
Properties of Operations		
COMMUTATIVE PROPERTY of Addition/Multiplication	$a + b = b + a$ $a \cdot b = b \cdot a$	$2x + 3 + 6x = 2x + 6x + 3$
ASSOCIATIVE PROPERTY of Addition/Multiplication	$(a + b) + c = a + (b + c)$ $(a \cdot b) \cdot c = a \cdot (b \cdot c)$	$(4x + 3) + 5 = 4x + (3 + 5)$
DISTRIBUTIVE PROPERTY of Multiplication over Add. /Sub.	$a \cdot (b + c) = a \cdot b + a \cdot c$ $a \cdot (b \cdot c) = a \cdot b - a \cdot c$	$4(2x + 1) = 8x + 4$

Examples:

41. Which of the following is an equivalent expression to $(2x - 8 - 4x) - (3x + 2 - 5x)$?
    A. -10
    B. $-10x - 10$
    C. $14x - 10$
    D. $-10x - 6$

    Solution: A

To simplify this expression, first "distribute" the minus sign to each of the terms in the second set of parentheses.

$$(2x - 8 - 4x) - (3x + 2 - 5x)$$
$$= 2x - 8 - 4x - 3x - 2 + 5x$$

Next, rearrange the expression using the commutative property to make it easy to combine like terms.

$$= 2x - 8 - 4x - 3x - 2 + 5x$$
$$= 2x + 5x - 4x - 3x - 8 - 2$$

Last, combine like terms to get -10. Therefore, the correct answer choice is A.

42. Which of the following is an equivalent expression for $3 - \left(5y + 9 - 8y\right) - 2\left(-2 - 3y\right) - 7$?

    A. $3y + 10$
    B. $-16y + 7$
    C. $9y - 9$
    D. $-16y$

Solution: C

Distribute while paying attention to negative signs, rearrange to combine like terms, and simplify:

$$3 - \left(5y + 9 - 8y\right) - 2\left(-2 - 3y\right) - 7$$
$$= 3 - 5y - 9 + 8y + 4 + 6y - 7$$
$$= -5y + 8y + 6y + 3 + 4 - 9 - 7$$
$$= 9y - 9$$

The correct answer choice is C.

Solving for a variable

On the *Praxis®* exam, you will have to solve for a variable in a formula after substituting in given values. This means you will have to use inverse operations to solve.

In addition, you may have to rearrange an equation so that it is in a different form. This often occurs when writing an equation for a table. We write the equation in slope-intercept form, $y = mx + b$, but the answers may be listed in standard form, $Ax + By = C$. You do not need to know the technical terms. You will just need to know how to get from one form to the other.

The table that follows lists a formula, scenario, and solution for many of the common formulas and scenarios. Understanding these will prepare you for most formulas you may encounter on the *Praxis®* exam.

Formula/Equation	Given Information	Solution	Solution Explanation
$F = \dfrac{9}{5}C + 32$	The temperature is $8°C$. Find the temperature in $°F$.	$F = \dfrac{9}{5}(8) + 32$ $= \dfrac{72}{5} + 32$ $= 14.4 + 32$ $= 46.4$	Subtittute 8 for C. Multiply $\dfrac{9}{5}$ and 8. Divide 72 and 5 to simplify the fraction. Solution.
$C = \dfrac{5}{9}(F - 32)$	The temperature is $70°F$. Find the temperature in $°C$.	$C = \dfrac{5}{9}(70 - 32)$ $= \dfrac{5}{9}(38)$ $= \dfrac{190}{9}$ ≈ 21.1	Substitute 70 for F. Subtract. Multiply $\dfrac{5}{9}$ and 38. Solution.
$K = \dfrac{5}{9}(F - 32) + 273$	The temperature is $90°F$. Find the temperature in $°K$.	$K = \dfrac{5}{9}(90 - 32) + 273$ $= \dfrac{5}{9}(58) + 273$ $= \dfrac{290}{9} + 273$ $\approx 32.2 + 273$ ≈ 305.2	Substitute 90 for F. Subtract. Multiply $\dfrac{5}{9}$ and 58. Divide 290 and 9. Solution.
$V = lwh$	Find the width, w, if the length is 4 meters, the height is 6.5 meters, and the volume is 260 cubic inches.	$260 = (4)(w)(6.5)$ $260 = 26w$ $\dfrac{260}{26} = \dfrac{26w}{26}$ $10 = w$ or $w = 10$	Substitute given values. Simplify. Divide both sides by 26. Solution.
$A = \dfrac{1}{2}bh$	Find the height of a triangle with a base of $12\dfrac{1}{2}$ inches and an area of 50 square inches.	$50 = (0.5)(12.5)h$ $50 = 6.25h$ $\dfrac{50}{6.25} = \dfrac{6.25h}{6.25h}$ $8 = h$ or $h = 8$	Substitute given values. Simplify. Divide both sides by 6.25. Solution.
$Ax + By = C$	Given $y = 3x + 5$, rewrite in the form $Ax + By = C$.	$y - 3x = 3x - 3x + 5$ $-3x + y = 5$ $-1(-3x + y) = -1(5)$ $3x - y = -5$	Subtract $3x$ from both sides. Simplify and rewrite with x before y. Multiply by -1 to make x positive. Simplify for solution.

Evaluating expressions and equations

Evaluating an expression or equation means to substitute given values into the variables and simplify the math expression. When evaluating, it is important to remember to follow order of operations and be very careful about negative signs.

Example:

43. Evaluate the expression for $x = -2$. Write your answer in the box.
$$-x^2 - 4x - 1$$

Solution: 3

Substitute -2 into the expression. Pay close attention to all the negative and minus signs.

$$-(-2)^2 - 4(-2) - 1$$
$$= -(4) - 4(-2) - 1$$
$$= -4 - (-8) - 1$$
$$= -4 + 8 - 1$$
$$= 4 - 1 = 3$$

C. Understands the meanings of the solutions to linear equations and inequalities

Solve equations or inequalities with one variable

The table below outlines the types of linear equations and inequalities to understand for the *Praxis*® exam. Steps to solving and useful tips are in the sections that follow.

Equation/Inequality Type	Example
Multistep Linear Equations	$-2(2x+3) - 5 = -(5-x)$
Multistep Linear Inequalities	$5 - 4(x-2) < 2x - (x+7)$
Compound Linear Inequalities	$-3 < 2x - 8 < 10$ $x + 3 > -4$ or $x + 3 \leq 7$

Multistep linear equations

To solve multistep linear equations, isolate the variable using inverse operations, remembering what is done to one side has to be done to the other to keep the expressions equal. The steps that follow outline one way to approach multistep equations.

1. Distribute any numbers outside of parentheses on both sides of equation, if necessary.

2. Combine like terms **on the same side** of the equal sign.

3. Move variables to one side of the equation using inverse operations (add or subtract).

4. Isolate the variable term using inverse operations (add or subtract).

5. Divide both sides by the coefficient with the variable.

6. Look out for no solution or infinitely many solutions.

When an equation has **no solutions** or **infinitely many solutions**, the variable terms are eliminated when moved to one side. This leaves only numbers on both sides of the equation.

- No Solutions: Equation in the form $a = b$.

   Example: 2 = 3; because 2 does not equal 3, there are no solutions.

- Infinitely Many Solutions: Equation in the form $a = a$.

   Example: 2 = 2; because 2 equals 2, any solution will work for the equation, so there are infinitely many solutions.

Examples:

44. Solve: $2(x + 3) = 2x - 8$

   Solution:

$$2x + 6 = 2x - 8$$
$$\underline{-2x \qquad\quad - 2x}$$
$$6 = -8$$

   Because 6 does not equal -8, there are **no solutions**.

45. Solve: $-2(2x + 3) - 5 = -(5 - x)$

   Solution:

$-2(2x + 3) - 5 = -(5 - x)$ 1. Distribute on both sides of the equation.

$-4x + (-6) - 5 = -5 + x$ 2. Combine like terms on the same side. Inverse operations not needed when combining on the same side.

$-4x + (-11) = -5 + x$

$-4x - 11 = -5 + x$ 3. Move variables to one side of the equation by adding or subtracting. *It is always best to move smaller variables to avoid negative values.*

$\underline{+4x \qquad\qquad + 4x}$

$-11 = -5 + 5x$ 4. Isolate the variable term by adding or subtracting.

$\underline{+5 \quad\; +5}$

$\dfrac{-6}{5} = \dfrac{5x}{5}$ 5. Divide both sides by the coefficient with the variable.

$x = -\dfrac{6}{5}$

46. Solve: $-2x + 3 - 6x = -8x + 3$

Solution:

$$-8x + 3 = -8x + 3$$
$$\underline{+8x \qquad + 8x}$$
$$3 = 3$$

Because 3 equals 3, any solution will work for $-2x + 3 - 6x = -8x + 3$, so there are **infinitely many solutions.**

Multistep linear inequalities

Multistep linear inequalities are solved just like multistep equations. An additional step of flipping the inequality symbol is necessary only if dividing by a negative. Solutions to inequalities may include a number line (number line solutions are covered in the next topic).

Examples:

47. Solve: $-2x + 3 < 5$

Solution:

$$-2x + 3 < 5$$
$$-2x < 2$$
$$x > -1$$

To solve, subtract 3 from both sides of the inequality. Next, divide by a -2, and **flip < to > because you are dividing by a negative number**.

48. Choose the answer choice that represents the solution set of the inequality.

$$2x - 9 < 5x - 12$$

A. $x < 1$

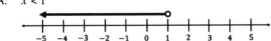

B. $x > 1$

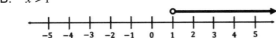

C. $x < 1$

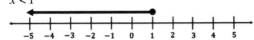

D. $x > 1$

Solution: B

The inequality can be solved a few different ways. There is no rule that says move all the variables to the left. They may be moved to the right side of the inequality as well. When solving inequalities, moving the variable with the smaller coefficient will help eliminate having to divide by a negative and then remembering to flip the inequality symbol. Either way works. Solving moving variables to the left and solving moving the smaller variable are both displayed below. Choose what is more comfortable for you.

DIVIDING BY A NEGATIVE	VARIABLE ON THE RIGHT
$2x - 9 < 5x - 12$ $\underline{-5x \quad\quad - 5x}$ $-3x - 9 < -12$ $\underline{+9 \quad +9}$ $\dfrac{-3x < -3}{-3 \quad -3}$ $x > 1$	$2x - 9 < 5x - 12$ $\underline{-2x \quad\quad - 2x}$ $-9 < 3x - 12$ $\underline{+12 \quad\quad +12}$ $\dfrac{3 < 3x}{3 \quad 3}$ $1 < x \rightarrow x > 1$

If the coefficient on the variable is negative, remember to flip the inequality when dividing.

If the variable is on the right, you may need to flip the sentence to match the answer choices.

After the inequality is solved, answer choices A and C can be eliminated. Because the inequality symbol is a greater than symbol, 1 is not part of the solution set, so the graph should be an open circle on 1 that points to the right. The correct answer choice is B.

Compound Linear Inequalities

A compound inequality is two simple inequalities joined together by the word "and" or "or".

The solution set of inequalities joined by the word "and" is the intersection of the two inequalities, making solutions **between** the two solution values. Typically, "and" inequalities are written as a single math sentence with less than/less than or equal to symbols as shown in the table that follows.

Solutions to inequalities joined by "or" are a union of two different problems. These two problems are always solved independently of one another.

COMPOUND INEQUALITIES	
AND	$x + 2 > -4$ and $x + 2 < 6$
AND	$-4 < x + 2 < 6$
OR	$x + 4 > 1$ or $2x + 1 < 10$

Typically, "and" inequalities like the second example in the table are more prevalent on exams because they look different than simple inequalities.

Example:

49. Solve. $-6 \le 4x + 6 < 10$

A. $-3 \le x < 1$

B. $-3 \le x < 1$

C. $-3 < x \le 1$

D. $-3 < x \le 1$

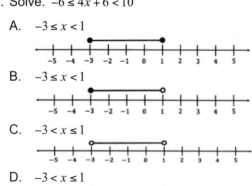

Compound Inequality Help

When solving a compound inequality such as $-6 \le 4x + 6 < 10$ think about it as two separate inequalities.

It is helpful to place your finger over the < 10 and start to isolate the variable for $-6 \le 4x + 6$ by subtracting 6 from -6 and $4x + 6$.

Then, place your finger over the $-6 \le$, and repeat the same process for $4x + 6 < 10$.

Repeat these steps for division by 4 to get the solution.

Solution: B

$$-6 \le 4x + 6 < 10$$
$$\underline{-6 \qquad -6 \ -6}$$
$$-12 \le 4x < 4$$
$$-3 \le x < 1$$

A compound inequality is a way of writing two inequalities together. Written separately, we would have $-6 \le 4x + 6$ and $4x + 6 < 10$. Writing them as one inequality saves time and also helps to make the solution clearer. When solving, think about solving each side separately and follow steps to isolate the variable in the middle.

The solution to the inequality shows that x is between -3 and 1, which means the values of x that are solutions all fall between -3 and 1. Because the first inequality symbol is a less than or equal to symbol, -3 is also included in the solution set. Conversely, 1 is not in the solution set because the second inequality shows that x is less than 1 but does not include 1.

To graph this on a number line, draw a point, or circle, on or just above -3. The circle should be filled in and is often referred to as a **closed circle** because the value where the point is drawn is part of the solution set. Next, draw an open point, or circle, on or just above 1. An open point or **open circle** means that value is not included in the solution. Last, draw a line connecting the two points to show that all the values between the points are part of the solution set.

The correct answer choice is B because the graph has a closed circle on -3 and an open circle on 1.

Graphing Linear Inequalities

The following table displays the various possibilities of graphs of inequalities based on the algebraic solution.

Algebraic Representation	Verbal Representation	Graph Representation
$x < 2$	x is less than 2.	
$x > 2$	x is greater than 2.	
$x \le 2$	x is less than or equal to 2.	
$x \ge 2$	x is greater than or equal to 2.	
$-2 < x \le 2$	x is greater than -2 and less than or equal to 2.	
$x < -2$ or $x \ge 2$	x is less than or equal to -2 or greater than 2.	

Examples:

50. Which of the following is the graph of the solution to $-5 \le -4x + 1 \le 13?$

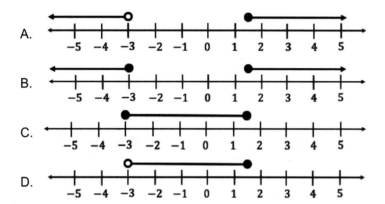

Solution: C

The solution of the inequality is $-3 \le x \le 1.5,$ so the solution set is between -3 and 1.5 and includes both -3 and 1.5. Therefore, the graph that represents the solution is answer choice C.
Remember to flip the inequality symbols because you are dividing by a negative. Because both symbols in the inequalilty are $\le$, both circles must be filled in, which eliminates answer choices A and D immediately.

51. Which of the following inequalities does the graph represent?

A. $-2 < x \le 6.5$
B. $-2 < x < 7$
C. $x < -2$ or $x > 6.5$
D. $-2 < x \le 7$

Solution: B

The graph displays solutions that are between -2 and 7 but do not include either -2 or 7. Therefore, the algebraic representation should have x between two values but not equal to either of them. The correct answer choice is B.

D. Knows how to recognize and represent patterns (e.g., number, shape)

Predicting missing terms in algebra refers to arithmetic sequences and geometric sequences. For these types of questions, you will be asked to find a number in a pattern or the sum of numbers where the same number is either added or multiplied each time. Patterns may be presented as a list, a table, or in pictorial form.

Arithmetic Sequences

An arithmetic sequence is a list of values where the difference between one term and the next term is always the same value. This value is called the **common difference**.

For example, given the sequence 2, 5, 8, 11, ... the common difference is 3 because 3 is the difference between each value. To continue the pattern, 3 is added to each of the previous terms to get the next term.

Geometric Sequences

A geometric sequence is a list of values where the difference between one term and the next term is always a multiple of the same value. This value is called the **common ratio**.

For example, given the sequence 1, 2, 4, 8, ... the common ratio is 2 because we are multiplying each previous term by 2 to get the next number in the list.

You do NOT need to know the technical terms or vocabulary associated with sequences. You only need to identify the common difference or ratio and apply it to find additional numbers in the sequence.

Examples:

52. Given the sequence 4, 2, 1, $\frac{1}{2}$, ... find the 6th term.

    A. $-\frac{1}{8}$

    B. $\frac{1}{16}$

    C. $16\frac{1}{2}$

    D. $\frac{1}{8}$

Solution: D

To solve this problem, first determine if the sequence is arithmetic or geometric and determine what the common difference or ratio is.

From the first term, 4 to the second term, 2:
The difference is 2.
The ratio is $\frac{1}{2}$. Note: it appears we are dividing by 2, which is the same as multiplying by $\frac{1}{2}$.

Looking at the next set of numbers in the sequence, we have the following:

From the second term, 2 to the third term, 1:
The difference is 1.

The ratio is $\frac{1}{2}$.

The sequence is geometric with a common ratio of $\frac{1}{2}$ because from one term to the next, each previous term is being multiplied by $\frac{1}{2}$ to get the next term. Now we can find the 6th term.

Because the 6th term is easy to find, we can do the math or use the general rule.

Math: 5th term: $\frac{1}{2} \times \frac{1}{2} = \frac{1}{4}$; 6th term: $\frac{1}{2} \times \frac{1}{4} = \frac{1}{8}$

53. How many triangles are in the 4th figure based on the pattern below?

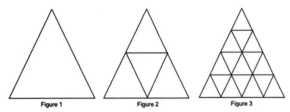

Figure 1   Figure 2   Figure 3

A. 4
B. 16
C. 32
D. 64

Solution: D

There is 1 triangle in the first figure, 4 triangles in the second figure, and 16 triangles in the third figure. From one figure to the next, the number of triangles is multiplied by 4. The next number in the sequence would be $16 \times 4 = 64$ The correct answer choice is D.

54. Find the sum of the first 4 terms of a geometric sequence when the first number is 160 and the common ratio is $\dfrac{1}{2}$.

A. 160
B. 240
C. 300
D. 150

Solution: C

A geometric sequence means we are multiplying by the same number each time. To find the sum of the first four numbers, we need to find the 2nd, 3rd, and 4th terms.

1st term: 160

2nd term: $160 \times \dfrac{1}{2} = 80$

3rd term: $80 \times \dfrac{1}{2} = 40$

4th term: $40 \times \dfrac{1}{2} = 20$

Sum: $160 + 80 + 40 + 20 = 300$

55. How many sticks will be needed to form the 5th figure in the sequence below?

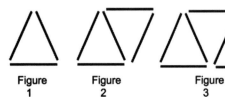

Figure 1   Figure 2   Figure 3

Solution:

In Figure 1, there are 3 sticks. In Figure 2, there are 5 sticks. In Figure 3, there are 7 sticks. Each figure has 2 more sticks than the one before it.

Following the pattern, in the fourth figure, there will be 9 sticks, and in the fifth figure, there will be 11 sticks. The pattern for determining the number of sticks is illustrated in the table that follows.

Figure #	Number of Sticks
1	3
2	5
3	7
4	9
5	11
6	13
7	15

+ 2
+ 2
+ 2
+ 2
+ 2
+ 2

Testing Tip

When looking for a pattern, it is helpful to create a table to organize your information, especially if the problem asks for an answer that requires finding three or more items in the sequence.

Writing an equation (function rule) from a table

To write an equation of a line, or a function rule, from a table, it is easiest to use slope-intercept form, $y=mx+b$, where m represents the slope and b represents the y-intercept. When writing an equation given a table, two different scenarios may occur, one where the y-intercept is part of the table, and one where it is not. In both cases, find the slope of the line, then determine the y-intercept based on the information given.

To find the equation of a line when y-intercept is included:

Write the equation of a line for the table below.

x	y
-1	3
0	1
3	-5
8	-15

Slope:

To find the slope, m, from a table, use any two points, stack them vertically, and subtract.

$$\begin{array}{r} (-1, 3) \\ -(0, \ 1) \\ \hline -1 \quad 2 \end{array}$$

Then, use the two differences to write the slope, $\dfrac{\text{change in } y}{\text{change in } x} = \dfrac{2}{-1} = -2$.

Before beginning the process of finding the y-intercept, look to see if one of the x values in the table is 0. If so, its y value is the y-intercept, b, and no further solving is required. For the table above, the y-intercept is included in the table and is 1.

The equation of the line for this table is $y = -\frac{2}{1}x + 1$ or $y = -2x + 1$.

Note: Answer choices may be in standard form. You still need to find the equation of the line in slope-intercept form, then convert the equation to standard form. The equation above would be $2x + y = 1$ in standard form.

To find the equation of a line when y-intercept is NOT included:

Write an equation of the line for the table.

x	y
-3	-6
3	-2
6	0
18	8

First, find the slope:

$$\begin{array}{r}(-3,-6)\\ -(6,\ \ 0)\\ \hline -9\ -6\end{array}$$

Slope: $\dfrac{-6}{-9} = \dfrac{2}{3}$

Because the y-intercept is not included in the table, choose a point, and substitute this point and the slope you just found into the slope-intercept form of an equation, $y=mx+b$. The point will replace x and y, and the slope will replace m.

x	y
-3	-6
3	-2
6	0
18	8

Point: $(3, -2)$

Slope: $\dfrac{2}{3}$ (from above)

$y = mx + b$

$-2 = \dfrac{2}{3}(3) + b$

Solve the equation for b.

$-2 = \dfrac{2}{3}(3) + b$

$-2 = 2 + b$

$-4 = b$

© 2022 Kathleen Jasper

Once b is found, substitute b and m, the slope, back into $y=mx+b$.

$$y = \frac{2}{3}x - 4$$

Note: When b is negative, the sign between x and b becomes a minus.

Example:

56. Which of the following is the equation of the line represented by the table?

x	y
-1	-3
0	-1
1	1
2	3
3	5

A. $y = x - 1$

B. $y = -2x - 3$

C. $y = 2x - 1$

D. $y = \frac{1}{2}x - 1$

Solution: C

Knowing that the y-intercept, b, is in the form $(0, y)$ we can see that the table includes the y-intercept, $(0, -1)$. Therefore, $b = -1$.

To find the slope, m, choose two points in the table, and find the difference of the y-coordinates and the difference of the x-coordinates.

$$\begin{array}{r} (3, 5) \\ -(2, 3) \\ \hline 1 \quad 2 \end{array}$$

Avoiding Errors
The method we use to find slope is different than the formula, but it produces the same result. We use this method to avoid subtraction errors.

Because slope is $\dfrac{\text{change in } y}{\text{change in } x}$ the slope for the equation of the line represented by the table is $\dfrac{2}{1}$.

Therefore, we have: $m = \dfrac{2}{1}$ and $b = -1$. Substituting into $y=mx+b$ we get $y = \dfrac{2}{1}x - 1$ or $y = 2x - 1$, which is answer choice C.

III. Geometry and Measurement, Data, Statistics, and Probability

Section III of the test encompasses both geometry and statistics. Geometry includes identifying and manipulating geometric figures, the coordinate plane, and formulas. In addition, geometry also includes understanding both the U.S. and metric measurement systems and conversions within each system. Statistics includes representations of data, measures of central tendency and spread (mean, median, mode, range), and probability.

The skills you need to know in this section include the following:

A. Understands how to classify one-, two-, and three-dimensional figures

B. Knows how to solve problems involving perimeter, area, surface area, and volume

C. Knows the components of the coordinate plane and how to graph ordered pairs on the plane

D. Knows how to solve problems involving measurement

E. Is familiar with basic statistical concepts

F. Knows how to represent and interpret data presented in various forms

G. Is familiar with how to interpret the probability of events

A. Understands how to classify one-, two-, and three-dimensional figures

Objects in geometry each have their own nomenclature based on letters or symbols or a combination of both. For the test, you need to know the foundational figures in geometry and have a good understanding of their definitions and properties.

*   Angle: $\angle$

*   Line: $\leftrightarrow$

*   Ray: $\rightarrow$

*   Segment: $-$

*   Parallel: $\parallel$

*   Perpendicular: $\perp$

*   Triangle: $\triangle$

When naming rays, the endpoint of the ray must be the first letter, but any other point on the ray can be used as the second letter. When naming a line, any two points on the line can be used. When naming a line segment, the beginning point and ending point must be used.

OBJECT	DEFINITION	NAMING
LINE	A collection of points that extends forever in both directions. Use any two points on a line to name it.	Line AB $\overleftrightarrow{AB}$
RAY	Has one endpoint and extends in one direction forever. Use the endpoint first and then any other point on the ray to name it.	Ray AB $\overrightarrow{AB}$
LINE SEGMENT	Part of a line that has two endpoints. Use each endpoint to name the line segment.	Segment AB $\overline{AB}$
PARALLEL LINES	Two lines in the same plane that are exactly the same distance apart. Lines may also be named using a lowercase letter.	Parallel lines a and b $a \parallel b$
PERPENDICULAR LINES	Two lines in the same plane that intersect at a $90°$ angle.	Perpendicular lines a and b $a \perp b$

Examples:

57. Which of the following are used to name a line?

    I.   The word, line, followed by any two points on the line
    II. A lowercase letter
    III. A small line drawn over any two points on the line ($\leftrightarrow$)
    IV. A small line symbol over a lowercase letter ($\leftrightarrow$)

A. I and II
B. I and IV
C. I, II, and III
D. I, II, III, and IV

Solution: C

A line can be named using the verbal description, line AB, with a line symbol over the AB, $\overleftrightarrow{AB}$ or with a single lowercase letter, such as a.

58. Which of the following is an object with one endpoint and extends infinitely in one direction?

    A. point
    B. line
    C. line segment
    D. ray

Solution: D

A point does not extend infinitely, a line extends infinitely in both directions, and a segment has two endpoints. A ray has one endpoint and extends infinitely in the other direction.

Angles

Angle pairs that may appear on the test include complementary angles and supplementary angles. These pairs of angles may share a side, or they can be two separate angles. What is important to remember is their name and the sum of their angles.

Angle Name	Example	Definition
Complementary Angles	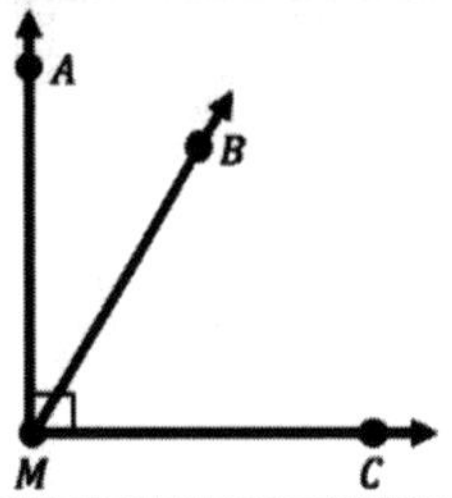	**Two angles that add to $90°$** Note: The angles may share a side, as pictured, or may be two separate angles.
Supplementary Angles	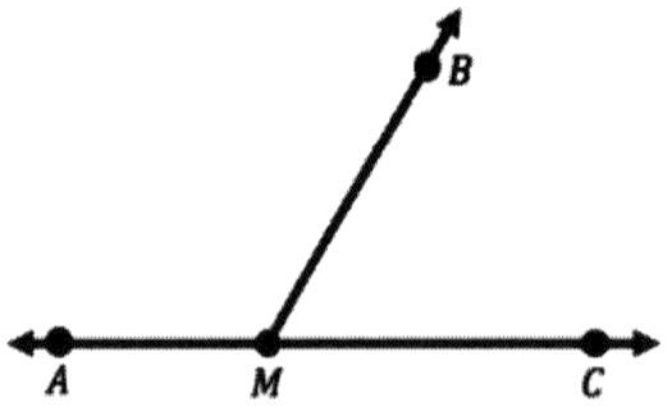	**Two angles that add to $180°$** Note: The angles may share a side, as pictured, or may be two separate angles.

The terms complementary angles and supplementary angles may appear in problems without an accompanying sketch, so knowing their names is important.

Example:

59. The complement to angle A is $42°$. What is the measure of angle A?

    A. $42°$
    B. $48°$
    C. $58°$
    D. $138°$

Solution: B

Complementary angles add to $90°$. Therefore, subtract $90 - 42$ to find the measure of angle A. The measure of angle A, $m\angle A = 48$.

Triangles

One of the most important facts to remember about a triangle is that the sum of the measures of the angles inside a triangle is $180°$. Often *Praxis®* exam items give only one or two angles, and the third is needed in order to solve the problem.

Additional triangle facts that you should know include classifying triangles by sides and angles. The tables that follow provide definitions, characteristics, and examples of possible vocabulary and images that may be used in a *Praxis®* exam question.

Triangle	Definition and Characteristics	Examples
Classification by Sides		
Scalene	A triangle with no congruent sides	
Isosceles	A triangle with two congruent sides Angles opposite the congruent sides are also congruent.	
Equilateral	A triangle with all sides congruent Angles in an equilateral triangle are all congruent, equal to $60°$.	

Triangle	Definition and Characteristicss	Examples
Classification by Angles		
Acute	A triangle with all angle measures less than $90°$.	
Right	A triangle with one angle equal to $90°$.	
Obtuse	A triangle with one angle greater than $90°$.	

Example:

60. What is the BEST way to classify the triangle?

    A. Right, scalene
    B. Right, isosceles
    C. Acute, scalene
    D. Acute, equilateral

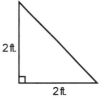

Solution: B

Because the triangle has two congruent sides, it is isosceles, and because it contains a right angle, it is also a right triangle.

Pythagorean Theorem

If two sides of a right triangle are given, the Pythagorean Theorem is a way to find the third side.

Pythagorean Theorem: $a^2 + b^2 = c^2$ where a and b represent the lengths of the **legs** (two sides that make the right angle) of the triangle and c represents the length of the **hypotenuse**.

It is likely that a question involving the Pythagorean theorem will most likely appear on the *Praxis®* exam. There are several real-world situations where the Pythagorean theorem may be applied to find a missing length, which makes it a good exam topic.

Pythagorean triples are whole numbers that satisfy the Pythagorean Theorem. Memorizing Pythagorean triples is a good test-taking strategy because **they are often embedded in exam items** or are the answer to an exam question. Although other Pythagorean triples exist, the following list appears most often on exam items:

- $3 - 4 - 5$

- $6 - 8 - 10$

- $5 - 12 - 13$

    The longest side will always be the hypotenuse.

Examples:

61. Find the missing side of the right triangle.

A. $\sqrt{313}$

B. 6

C. 5

D. $2\sqrt{3}$

Solution: C

Side lengths 12 and 13 are part of a Pythagorean triple, so the missing leg is 5. The Pythagorean Theorem could also be used to solve:

$$a^2 + b^2 = c^2$$
$$12^2 + b^2 = 13^2$$
$$144 + b^2 = 169$$
$$b^2 = 25$$
$$\sqrt{b^2} = \sqrt{25}$$
$$b = 5$$

62. Michael leaves his house and rides his bike 3 miles east. He then rides another 5 miles north before stopping at a convenience store. If he took the shortest distance home, how many miles would he ride from the store back to his house? Round to the nearest tenth of a mile.

    A. 5.8
    B. 4.5
    C. 4.0
    D. 8.0

Solution: A

The shortest distance between two points is a line. The path Michael takes from his house to the store and back home again is a right triangle. Draw a picture to help determine the length of the shortest distance.

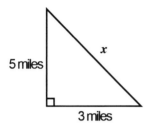

Using the Pythagorean Theorem, we get the following:

$$a^2 + b^2 = c^2$$
$$3^2 + 5^2 = x^2$$
$$9 + 25 = x^2$$
$$34 = x^2$$
$$\sqrt{34} = \sqrt{x^2}$$
$$x = \sqrt{34} \approx 5.8$$

Be Careful

You may be tempted to use the Pythagorean triple technique here. However, this is not a 3-4-5 triangle because the hypotenuse is not 5. Instead, 5 is the measure of one of the legs.

Attributes of two-dimensional and three-dimensional figures

To help solve problems involving geometric figures on the *Praxis*® exam, know attributes of basic geometric figures. When geometric figures are named, their unique properties are understood to be true by the reader. The most commonly used figures and their attributes are given in the table that follows.

Figure Name	Image	Attributes
Rectangle		• All angles equal • Opposite sides have the same length • A special type of parallelogram • Opposite sides parallel
Square		• All angles equal • All sides have the same length • A special type of parallelogram • A special type of rectangle • Opposite sides parallel
Circle		• Diameter goes through the center of the circle to the edge of the circle • Radius starts at the center of the circle and ends on the edge of the circle • The radius is half the length of the diameter.
Cube		• All sides of a cube are squares • All sides have the same length • All angles equal
Sphere		• Perfectly symmetrical • Radius starts at the center and ends at any point on the sphere • The distance around a sphere is the circumference of a circle

Nets

A net is the resulting two-dimensional shape when a three-dimensional figure is opened and laid flat; think of the net as the pattern for the three-dimensional figure. Nets are useful when teaching surface area and characteristics of three-dimensional figures. On the *Praxis*® exam, questions with a net will ask you to pair a net with the name of its corresponding three-dimensional figure. To determine the name of a three-dimensional figure, use the following tips:

- A **prism** will have *two bases*. All other shapes are the sides of the prism.

- A **pyramid** will have *one base*. All other shapes are the sides of the pyramid.

- The **shape of the base** is used to name the prism or pyramid.

Know the names of the two-dimensional figures in the table that follows to correctly identify the base name of a three-dimensional figure. The key to getting a question with a net correct is identifying and naming the base(s).

Number of Sides	Name	Image
3	Triangle	
4	Rectangle	
4	Square	
5	Pentagon	
6	Hexagon	
7	Heptagon	
8	Octagon	

The table that follows lists the names of prisms and pyramids and gives an example of a possible net. When naming a three-dimensional figure, consider the following:

1. There is more than one way to draw the net of a figure.

2. Sometimes the figure is turned on its side, and the bases are located on the sides of the figure.

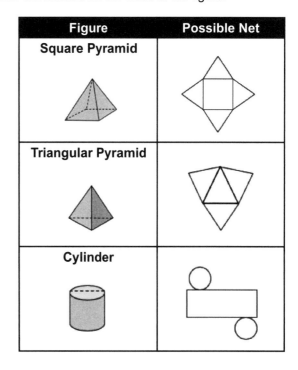

Figure	Possible Net
Rectangular Prism	
Cube	
Triangular Prism	

Figure	Possible Net
Square Pyramid	
Triangular Pyramid	
Cylinder	

Examples:

63. Which of the following is a possible net for a cube?

A.

C.

B.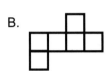

D.

Solution: B

The net of a cube should have four squares attached in one row and two squares on either side of the row that are able to be folded to create the top and bottom. The correct solution is answer choice B. Choice A does not have enough squares to create a cube, and answer choice D does not have four squares in one row. Answer choice C does not have two squares on opposite sides of the row of four.

64. Which of the following could be used to construct a triangular prism?

A. 4 triangles
B. 3 triangles, 4 squares
C. 2 triangles, 3 rectangles
D. 2 triangles, 4 rectangles

Solution: C

A prism has an identical top and bottom, and the base shape is part of the name of the prism. In this case, a triangle is the shape of the top and bottom, or two bases. Thus, three rectangles would connect the triangles to form a triangular prism. The correct answer choice is C.

65. Name the net.

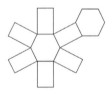

A. Pentagonal prism
B. Hexagonal prism
C. Octagonal prism
D. Hexagonal pyramid

Solution: B

The shape of the base is a hexagon, which is a 6-sided figure. Because the net has two bases, the figure is a prism. Therefore, the net makes a hexagonal prism, which is answer choice B.

Transformations

Transformations change the location or size of a figure. Types of transformations you will see on the *Praxis®* exam include translations, rotations, and reflections. Translations, rotations, and reflections create a new image that is *congruent* to, or the same size as, the original image.

Transformations are typically performed on a coordinate plane so that the exact changes are reflected in the coordinates of the vertices of the image. When a figure is transformed, the vertices contain a prime mark (similar to an apostrophe) to delineate between the original figure and the transformed figure. For example, if rectangle ABCD is rotated, the new rectangle will be named A'B'C'D'. If a question is only looking for the type of transformation, the axes and figures may not contain any labels.

Translation

Another term for translation is slide. A translation changes the position of an image by moving it left, right, up, or down. The figure will look exactly the same but in a different place.

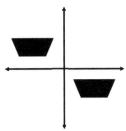

Rotation

A rotation spins or rotates a figure about a point or line. A rotated figure will be in a different place and will have a different orientation.

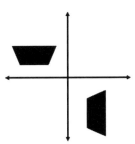

Reflection

Another term for a reflection is flip or a mirror image. Reflections "flip" an image over a line or axis. Each vertex point of the new figure will be the exact same distance from the line as the original image, in the direction of the reflection. You may have to be able to identify the axis over which the reflection occurred. The axis that the figures are on either side of will be the axis over which the figure was reflected.

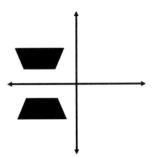

Examples:

66. The coordinate plane below shows what type of transformation?

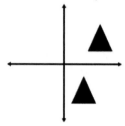

    A. Translation
    B. Rotation
    C. Reflection over the-axis
    D. Reflection over the -axis

Solution: A

Sliding one of the images up/down and left/right will produce the second image. Therefore, answer choice A is the correct answer.

67. What transformation occurred from one image to the other?

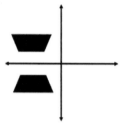

    A. Reflection over the x-axis
    B. Rotation about the origin
    C. Reflection over the y-axis
    D. translation

Solution: A

The two images are mirror images of one another, or one is flipped over the x-axis to get the second image.

B. Knows how to solve problems involving perimeter, area, surface area, and volume

The possible scenarios of real-world geometry problems are endless. *Praxis®* exam questions typically, but not always, include a combination of formulas so that multiple skills are assessed at one time. You will not have to recall every formula listed in the table that follows. If you remember the basic formulas for area, it is much easier to find surface area and volume because surface area is just several area formulas added together, and volume is the area of the base times the height of the object.

The most common formulas used on standardized math assessments include:

- Perimeter of a rectangle or square
- Area of a circle
- Area of a rectangle or square
- Area of a triangle
- Volume of a sphere
- Volume of a rectangular prism (box)
- Pythagorean Theorem

Measurement	Formula	Picture and Description
Perimeter Rectangle or Square	Rectangle: $P = b + h + b + h = 2b + 2h$ Square: $P = 4s$	Add all the sides of the figure for both the rectangle and square.
Area Rectangle	$A = bh$	The base (b) and height (h) are always perpendicular to one another for all figures.
Area Parallelogram	$A = bh$	The base (b) and height (h) are always perpendicular to one another, so a dotted line is added to show the height.
Area Trapezoid	$A = \frac{1}{2}h\left(b_1 + b_2\right)$	Because a trapezoid can have either base at the bottom, the base lengths are averaged, then multiplied by the height (h).
Area Triangle	$A = \frac{1}{2}bh$	The base and height are always perpendicular to one another, so a dotted line is added to show the height for different types of triangles.
Area Circle	$A = \pi r^2$	The area of a circle uses the radius, which is the length from the center of the circle to a point on the circle.
Circumference Circle	$C = \pi d = 2\pi r$	The circumference measures the distance around the outside of a circle.

Measurement	Formula	Picture and Description
Surface Area Prism	$SA = 2lw + 2wh + 2lh$ or $SA = Ph + 2B$ P is perimeter of base; h is height of prism for 2nd formula	The surface area (SA) of a prism is found by finding the area of all six sides and adding these areas together.
Surface Area Cylinder	$SA = 2\pi r^2 + \pi dh$ or $SA = 2\pi r^2 + 2\pi rh$	Surface area of a cylinder formula uses both radius and diameter. The radius is always half of the diameter.
Surface Area Sphere	$SA = 4\pi r^2$	Remember $r^2 = r \cdot r$
Volume Prism	$V = lwh$ or $V = Bh$	Multiply all three sides together to find the volume of a prism.
Volume Cylinder	$V = \pi r^2 h$ or $V = Bh$	Find the area of the circle, then multiply by the height.
Volume Sphere	$V = \frac{4}{3}\pi r^3$	Multiply r^3 times 4 and pi, if not in terms of pi, then divide this answer by 3.
Pythagorean Theorem	$a^2 + b^2 = c^2$	Used to find a missing side of a right triangle only.
Approximations of pi (π)	$\pi \approx 3.14$ or $\frac{22}{7}$	Know both the decimal approximation and the fraction approximation for pi.

The examples below represent some of the common types of problems representative of those that may appear most often on the *Praxis*® exam.

Perimeter

Examples:

68. Stacey wants to plant one row of bushes along the length of her front yard. The length of Stacey's front yard is 6 less than three times the width. If the perimeter of her yard is 284 feet, what is the length of the yard?

   A.   37 feet
   B.   74 feet
   C.   105 feet
   D.   210 feet

   Solution: C

To solve, draw a picture and label the sides. The length is given in terms of the width. Therefore, the width is w, and the length is $3w$ - 6 (less than switches the order).

The question gave the perimeter of the yard, which is a BIG hint that the perimeter of a rectangle formula is needed to solve. Substitute the expressions for the length and width into the perimeter formula to find the width.

$$w + \left(3w - 6\right) + w + \left(3w - 6\right) = 284$$
$$8w - 12 = 284$$
$$8w = 296$$
$$w = 37$$

Be Careful

Solving the equation finds the width, but the question asks for the length. Substitute w into the expression for length, $3w - 6$.

$3\left(37\right) - 6 = 111 - 6 = 105$ feet. The correct answer choice is C.

69. Find the perimeter of a square with an area of 100 square feet.

A. 1,000 feet
B. 40 feet
C. 20 feet
D. 10 feet

Solution: B

Because the sides are the same length, find what number was multiplied by itself to get the length of each side. In this case, $100 = 10 \cdot 10$, so the side lengths are 10 feet. Therefore, the perimeter is

$$P = 4s$$
$$P = 4\left(10\right) = 40 \text{ feet.}$$

Circumference

Example:

70. At a local horse training facility, a fenced-in training ring is in the shape of a circle and has a diameter that measures 57 feet. Six flags are attached to the fence that surrounds the ring. The flags are evenly spaced out around the circle. What is the length of the fence between any two flags? Round to the nearest tenth.

A. 104.1π feet
B. 4.2π feet
C. 8.3π feet
D. 9.5π feet

Solution: D

The flags are posted along the outside of the ring, which is a circle. The length around the outside of a circle is its circumference, and the formula for the circumference of a circle is $C = \pi d$. Substituting in the diameter, d, of 57, the length around the entire fence is 57π. The question asks for the length between any two flags. If there are 6 flags evenly spaced, divide the circumference by 6, $57\pi \div 6 = 9.5\pi$. The correct answer is D.

Area

Example:

71. A rectangular playground is being refurbished and covered in rubber mulch. Each bag of rubber mulch covers 1,500 square inches. If the playground measures 30 feet by 10 feet, how many bags of rubber mulch are needed?

    A. 29 bags
    B. 30 bags
    C. 31 bags
    D. 28 bags

Solution: A

To solve, find the area of the playground, but because the area the mulch covers is given in inches, the sides of the playground need to be converted to inches first. Multiply each side by 12 to convert to inches, then find the area of the playground.

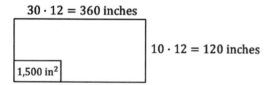

Playground area: $360 \cdot 120 = 43,200 \text{ in}^2$

Each bag of mulch covers 1,500 square inches, therefore divide the total area by 1,500 to get the number of bags needed.

$43,200 \div 1,500 = 28.8$

Because bags of mulch cannot be split, 29 bags are needed to cover the playground, which is answer choice A.

Quick Tip

When converting feet to inches in geometry word problems, always convert **before** finding the area.

Surface Area

Examples:

72. Which of the following formulas could be used to find the area of a label on a soup can if h represents the height of the can and r represents the radius of the top?

   A. πr^2
   B. $2\pi rh$
   C. $2\pi rh + 2\pi r^2$
   D. $4\pi r^2$

   Solution: B

   A soup can is in the shape of a cylinder, and the label covers the surface area of the cylinder, excluding the top and bottom. The formula for finding the surface area of a cylinder is $2\pi rh + 2\pi r^2$, where the $2\pi r^2$ represents the area of the circles on the top and bottom. Since a label does not cover the top and bottom of a soup can, the area of the label would be $2\pi rh$. The correct answer is B.

73. A wastepaper basket is in the shape of a rectangular prism, as shown below. If the wastepaper basket is covered with decorative paper on the outside, what is the surface area of the faces with paper?

   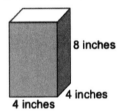

   8 inches

   4 inches

   4 inches

   A. 16 in²
   B. 128 in²
   C. 144 in²
   D. 160 in²

   Solution: C

   The surface area of a rectangular prism is found by finding the area of each of the faces of the prism and adding these areas together. The trick for this problem is recognizing that a wastepaper basket has no top, so there are only five faces.

   Surface Area of wastepaper basket: $(4 \cdot 4) + 2(4 \cdot 8) + 2(4 \cdot 8) = 16 + 64 + 64 = 144 \text{ in}^2$.

   Note: the first term is not multiplied by 2 because of the "missing" top.

Volume

Examples:

74. A fruit company ships 16 oranges in a crate. The radius of each orange is 1.5 inches, and the crate that the oranges are shipped in measures 12 inches by 12 inches by 3.5 inches. The space between the oranges is stuffed with crinkle cut paper filler. What is the volume of the box, to the nearest tenth, taken up by the crinkle cut paper filler?

   A. 202.6 in³
   B. 226.2 in³
   C. 277.8 in³
   D. 504.0 in³

Solution: C

To find the volume of the crate that the paper filler takes, find the volume of the crate and the volume of the oranges, then subtract the two values.

Volume of the crate: $V = lwh = 12 \cdot 12 \cdot 3.5 = 504 \text{ in}^3$

Volume of oranges (sphere): $V = 16 \cdot \left[\dfrac{4}{3} \pi r^3 \right] = 16 \cdot \left[\dfrac{4}{3} \pi (1.5)^3 \right] \approx 226.2 \text{ in}^3$

Volume of crinkle cut paper filler: $504 \text{ in}^3 - 226.2 \text{ in}^3 = 277.8 \text{ in}^3$

Therefore, the correct answer choice is C.

75. Which of the following cereal boxes could hold the most cereal?

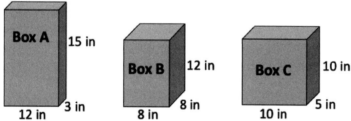

   A. Box A
   B. Box B
   C. Box C
   D. Both Boxes A and C

Solution: B

Find the volume of each box (rectangular solid).

Box A: $V = lwh = 12 \cdot 3 \cdot 15 = 540 \text{ in}^3$

Box B: $V = lwh = 8 \cdot 8 \cdot 12 = 768 \text{ in}^3$

Box C: $V = lwh = 10 \cdot 5 \cdot 10 = 500 \text{ in}^3$

Box B will hold the most cereal; therefore, the correct answer choice is B.

How a change in dimensions affects other measurements

When dimensions change by a given factor, area changes by the square of the factor, and volume changes by the cube of the factor. The example that follows shows why this happens.

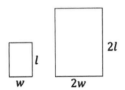

Area of a rectangle: $A = l \cdot w$

Area of a rectangle with sides doubled: $A = 2l \cdot 2w = 2^2 \left(l \cdot w \right)$

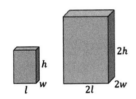

Volume of a rectangular solid: $V = l \cdot w \cdot h$

Volume of a rectangular solid with sides doubled: $V = 2l \cdot 2w \cdot 2h = 2^3 \left(l \cdot w \cdot h \right)$

Example:

76. Rhonda is having a small sign that measures 12 inches by 15 inches enlarged to create a poster. The dimensions will be increased by a scale factor of 4. What will be the area of the enlarged poster?

    A. 180 in²
    B. 720 in²
    C. 1,440 in²
    D. 2,880 in²

Solution: D

The area of the poster will increase by a factor of 4^2. Therefore, multiply the original area by 16, so the new area is $12 \cdot 15 \cdot 4^2 = 2,880$ in³. The correct answer choice is D.

> **Remember**
>
> When the sides of a figure change by a factor it means you are multiplying each side by the same number. Thus, the following rules apply:
>
> **The area is multiplied twice by that number.**
>
> **The volume is multiplied three times by that number.**

C. Knows the components of the coordinate plane and how to graph ordered pairs on the plane

The coordinate plane is made up of both a horizontal number line and a vertical number line, which split the coordinate plane into four quadrants. For the *Praxis®* exam, be able to identify the parts of the coordinate plane. Questions may reference any part of the coordinate plane with the definition being known by the test taker.

In addition to being able to identify parts of the coordinate plane, also be able to graph a point or identify in which quadrant a point lies. Knowing the signs of coordinates in each quadrant may help in answering test questions.

Parts of a Coordinate Plane

- *x*-axis
- *y*-axis
- Origin
- Quadrant I
- Quadrant II
- Quadrant III
- Quadrant IV

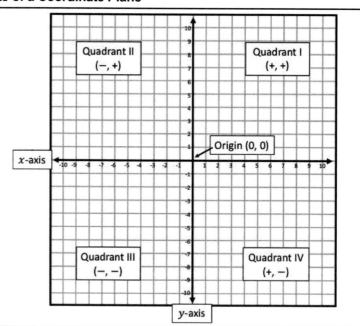

In addition to being able to identify parts of a coordinate plane and coordinates on the plane, you may be required to draw shapes and answer questions about shapes on a coordinate plane. This includes being able to find the perimeter or area of the figure.

Examples:

77. A triangle has the coordinates $(2,1), (2,6)$ and $(8,1)$. What is the area of the triangle?

    A. 15 square units
    B. 20 square units
    C. 25 square units
    D. 30 square units

Solution: A

It is useful to draw a quick sketch of the triangle to help find the lengths of the base and height (the two sides that form a right angle). The base and height of the triangle are 5 units and 6 units.

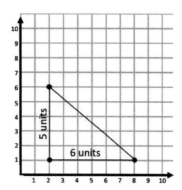

Thus, the area of the triangle is $A = \frac{1}{2}bh = \frac{1}{2} \cdot 6 \cdot 5 = 3 \cdot 5 = 15$ square units, answer choice A.

78. Given that the coordinates of a square are $(1,5)$, $(4,1)$, $(5,8)$, and $(8,4)$, find the perimeter of the square.

   A. 32 units
   B. 25 units
   C. 20 units
   D. 16 units

Solution: C

This question can be approached a few ways, but the fastest and easiest is to apply your knowledge of right triangles to quickly find the length of the sides of the square. First, quickly sketch the square on a coordinate plane.

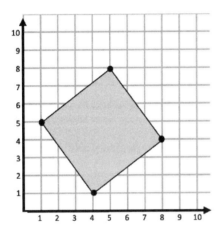

Because the square is drawn slightly rotated, we cannot count units from one point to the next to determine side lengths. What we can do, though, is see that we can sketch in a right triangle, with one of the sides of the square being the hypotenuse of the triangle. The triangle has two sides that are 3 units and 4 units, which makes the hypotenuse 5 units (recall Pythagorean triples in the previous triangle section).

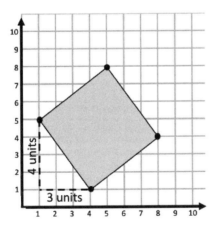

Because the hypotenuse of the triangle is also the side of the square, we can say that the sides of the square are each 5 units. Thus, the perimeter of the square is $P = 4s = 4 \cdot 5 = 20$ units.

D. Knows how to solve problems involving measurement

The measurement portion of the *Praxis*® exam includes conversions within the U.S. customary system, conversions within the metric system, and an understanding of the relative size of basic measurements. You may be asked what measurement would be used to measure the weight, length, or capacity of an object, so you should have an understanding of the relative size of each unit. The examples in the table should help you understand the size of the units and when each unit could be used in real-world scenarios.

U.S. Customary System	
Units	Realistic Use
Inches	Length of a pencil Length of a person's hand
Feet	Height of a door Length of a car
Yards	Length of a football field *About 1 meter*
Miles	Distance between buildings Distance between cities
Pint	Small glass School-sized milk carton
Quart	Measuring cup Bottle of automobile oil *About 1 liter*
Gallons	Large milk jug Gasoline
Ounces (weight)	Weight of a slice of bread Weight of a book
Pounds	Weight of a person Weight of a packed suitcase
Tons	Weight of a car Weight of a plane

Metric System	
Units	Realistic Use
Meter	Length around a track Length of a large swimming pool
Liter	Large bottle of soda Bottle of shampoo
Gram	Weight of a paperclip
Centimeter	Height of a person Length of a textbook
Kilometer	Driving distances
Milliliter	Liquid medications
Kilogram	Weight of a person Weight of a water bottle

Metric conversions

The metric system is based on units of 10. When converting within the metric system, you are only responsible for the basic units: kilo-, centi-, and milli-. The other units that are grayed out are to show the conversions by units of 10.

METRIC CONVERSIONS						
Prefixes						
Kilo-	Hecto-	Deca-	Basic Unit	Deci-	Centi-	Milli-
Abbreviations						
km	hm	dkm	meter (m)	dm	cm	mm
kL	hL	dkL	liter (L)	dL	cL	mL
kg	hg	dkg	gram (g)	dg	cg	mg
0.001	0.01	0.1	1	10	100	1,000

There are two different ways to approach metric conversions.

Convert by moving the decimal point:

If the conversion is from a **smaller unit to a larger unit**, move the decimal point LEFT the number of spaces between the two units.

If the conversion is from a **larger unit to a smaller unit**, move the decimal point RIGHT the number of spaces between the two units.

This method requires memorizing the abbreviations in order.

Examples:

79. 4.5L = _____ kL

    Solution:

    The conversion is going from a smaller unit to a larger unit. Therefore, the decimal point moves to the left. Liters is 3 units away from kiloliters, so the decimal point moves three places to the left.

    kiloliter   hectoliter   decaliter   liter

    4.5L = 0.0045 kL.

80. 4 km = _____ mm

    Solution:

    The conversion is going from a larger unit to a smaller unit. Therefore, the decimal point moves to the right. Kilometers and millimeters are six units apart, so the decimal point moves six places to the right.

    4 km = 4,000,000 mm

Convert using a proportion:

To use a proportion, create a ratio from the problem, and set up an equivalent ratio using the numbers in the table.

This method requires memorizing the abbreviations in order and knowing how to add in the numerical values.

Example:

81. 4L = _____ mL

    Solution:

    The ratio created from the problem is $\dfrac{4L}{x \text{ mL}}$, and the ratio created from the table would be $\dfrac{1 \text{ L}}{1000 \text{ mL}}$. Choose the units from the problem to determine the units for the second ratio. The proportion would be:

    $$\dfrac{4L}{x \text{ mL}} = \dfrac{1 \text{ L}}{1000 \text{ mL}}$$

    Cross-multiply and solve.
    $4000 = 1x$

Standard (U.S.) conversions

Standard conversions require quite a bit of straight memorization, which is not the purpose of the test items on the *Praxis®* exam. It is not likely (although anything is possible) that a question asks for conversions across multiple units, such as cups to gallons.

1 foot = 12 inches	1 cup = 8 fluid ounces
1 yard = 3 feet = 36 inches	1 pint = 2 cups
1 mile = 5,280 feet = 1,760 yards	1 quart = 2 pints
1 hour = 60 minutes	1 gallon = 4 quarts
1 minute = 60 seconds	1 pound = 16 ounces
	1 ton = 2,000 pounds

Standard conversions are often embedded in questions that contain measurements in two units but require only one unit to solve. For example, finding the area of a square that measures 8 inches by 2 feet.

E. Is familiar with basic statistical concepts

When conducting a survey, identifying an appropriate sample increases the validity of the survey results. Although characteristics of survey participants vary from survey to survey, some basic characteristics to consider include:

*   Sample size; the larger the sample, the more valid the results
*   Random selection of participants
*   Geographical location of survey participants
*   Biased participants based on survey topic

Example:

82. Suppose data from a recently conducted survey will decide whether or not dogs are allowed at the local beach. For valid results, which of the following would constitute a good sample of people to survey?

    A.   25 people at the dog park
    B.   A variety of 500 nearby business owners and beachgoers
    C.   100 people at the local mall
    D.   300 students at the elementary school

Solution: B

A large, random sample in a location related to the survey will provide the most valid results.

F. Knows how to represent and interpret data presented in various forms

Graphs that display trends, distribution of data, or measures of center and spread include:

1.   Venn diagram
2.   table
3.   bar graph
4.   pictograph
5.   frequency table
6.   histogram
7.   stem-and-leaf plot
8.   box-and-whisker plot (box plot)
9.   scatter plot
10. circle graph

Each of the following sections outlines how to create the statistical display, including special cases that require a more thorough understanding of what you may need to know to answer *Praxis®* exam questions.

Venn diagram

Data in a Venn diagram is categorical data, meaning that the data falls into specific categories. Venn diagrams are used to show relationships among sets using overlapping circles to depict relationships. Any relationships that overlap are counted in the region where the circles of the diagram also overlap (Overlapping data is when data falls in more than one category).

Data in Venn diagrams is often referred to using the terms union and intersection.

A **Union**, represented by the symbol ∪, is all the data in two or more sets put together.

An **Intersection**, represented by the symbol ∩, is only where two or more data sets overlap.

Example:

Data	Graph
Math only certification: 42 Science only certification: 28 Math & science certification: 8 *To graph, create a circle for each category. Data that does not overlap stays outside the overlap. Data that includes both categories should be in the overlap section.*	Math Certified / Science Certified 42　8　28

Sample Question:

83. The Venn diagram shows information about the math and science certifications of teachers in a small county in Florida. What is the probability that a randomly surveyed teacher is both math and science certified?

   A. $\dfrac{4}{21}$　　　B. $\dfrac{2}{7}$　　　C. $\dfrac{4}{35}$　　　D. $\dfrac{4}{39}$

   Solution: D

   To solve, find the total number of teachers: $42 + 28 + 8 = 78$. Make sure the 8 teachers who are certified in both are part of the total but be careful not to add the 8 in twice. Once the total number of teachers is found, write a fraction for certified in both out of the total, $\dfrac{8}{78}$, then reduce.

Tables

Tables are a quick and easy way to organize a set of data. Tables may contain any number of rows or columns of data; there is no limit on how small or how large a table can be. A table is best used to organize data, but tables do not typically provide a good visual for identifying trends, characteristics, or patterns in a data set.

Example:

Hours	1	2	3	4	5	6
Miles Traveled	60	120	180	240	300	360

Frequency table

A frequency table counts or tallies how many times a value falls within a defined range of values in a data set. Some frequency tables display the frequency of individual values while others display the frequency of a range of values occurring in a data set. An example of a range of values would be the number of students in a class scoring an A, scoring a B, scoring a C, or scoring a D on a quiz. Because an A may range from 90-100, the individual scores are unknown, but the number of scores falling within the A range are known.

Example frequency table:

SAT Math Score Range	Frequency
200-299	1
300-399	0
400-499	1
500-599	8
600-699	7
700-799	2

Bar Graph

A bar graph is typically used to track and compare change over time. The bars in a bar graph can be close together but should not touch. A bar graph may be used to compare the same data for more than one set of data on the same display. The following table compares Paul's sales to Ruben's sales and also compares their quarterly sales, providing data that can be compared over time and data that compares one person to another.

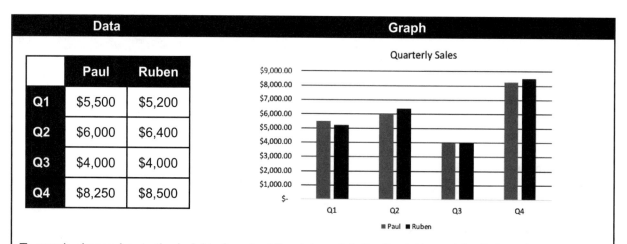

Data			Graph

	Paul	Ruben
Q1	$5,500	$5,200
Q2	$6,000	$6,400
Q3	$4,000	$4,000
Q4	$8,250	$8,500

To graph, draw a bar to the height of each of the data points for Paul. Repeat for Ruben, keeping bars in the same category grouped together.

Sample Question:

84. What type of graph would be best to display the data from the table above?

    A. Venn diagram
    B. Bar graph
    C. Stem-and-leaf plot
    D. Scatter plot

Solution: B

A bar graph is the best choice because the data is categorical and there are two data pieces for each category.

Pictograph

A pictograph is a graph that uses pictures to represent numerical data. The visual representation of data on a pictograph allows for quick identification of the mode and distribution of the data set. A key is important for a pictograph so that the reader of the graph knows what each picture represents.

Data	Graph

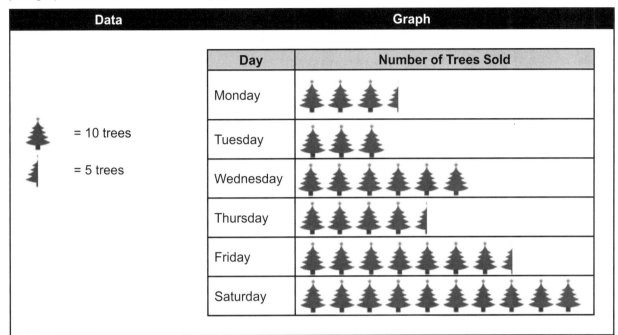

Day	Number of Trees Sold
Monday	
Tuesday	
Wednesday	
Thursday	
Friday	
Saturday	

= 10 trees

= 5 trees

Sample Question:

85. How many more people bought a tree on Friday than on Tuesday?

A. 5.5
B. 8.5
C. 45
D. 55

Solution: C

If each whole tree represents 10 trees sold and each half tree represents 5 trees sold, 75 trees were sold on Friday and 30 trees were sold on Tuesday. Thus, 45 more trees were sold on Friday than on Tuesday.

Histogram

A histogram is a display of information gathered in a frequency table. A histogram looks similar to a bar graph, but a histogram displays the frequency of data that falls within equally spaced ranges of values. An easy way to not confuse a histogram and a bar graph is to remember that the bars of a histogram touch each other, but the bars on a bar graph do not.

DATA	GRAPH
Class test grades: 91, 88, 100, 82, 73, 88, 52, 76, 95, 55, 85, 65, 99 87, 90, 65, 93, 75, 92, 66, 78, 80, 68, 84, 85, 91, 98	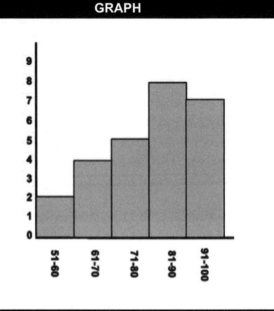

Grade Range	Frequency
51-60	2
61-70	4
71-80	5
81-90	8
91-100	7

Determine equally created ranges. Determine the number of data points that fall within each range. Create a bar chart, making sure that bars touch, to show the frequency within each range.

Sample Question:

86. Which of the following is a reason why a histogram would be used to compare data?

    A. To determine how frequently data falls within specified ranges
    B. To determine the mean of the data
    C. To compare categories of information
    D. To study bivariate data over time

    Solution: A

    A histogram is a visual way to display the frequency of data falling within specified ranges. Because individual values are not on a histogram, the mean cannot be found. The information is also numerical, not categorical, and is univariate, not bivariate.

Example:

87. Which of the following graphs would best display the results of students' favorite elective?

    A. Bar graph
    B. Histogram
    C. Venn diagram
    D. Table

    Solution: A

    A bar graph would best display the results because a bar graph compares data that is sorted by category. Option B is incorrect because the survey was not looking for the frequency of a data range. Option C is incorrect because the survey asked for one response (favorite elective), so there is no overlapping data. Option D is incorrect because the data could be written in a table, but the results of the data would not be as clear as with a bar graph.

Stem-and-Leaf Plot

A stem-and-leaf plot organizes numerical data in a way that allows the reader to quickly calculate the mode and range of a data set. The mean and median can also be found from a stem-and-leaf plot, but it may take more than a glance or quick calculation. A stem-and-leaf plot is best for data with stems that are no more than 10 numbers apart from one another. This is because the value of the stems must only increase by 1.

Data and Graph	How to Graph
Number of participants in a study group for the last 10 meetings: 20, 27, 22, 24, 28, 32, 35, 51, 22, 50 | Stem	Leaf | |---|---| | 2 | 0 2 2 4 7 8 | | 3 | 2 5 | | 4 | | | 5 | 0 1 | key 2 | 0 = 20	• Organize the data from least to greatest. • Create a table with two columns and label the first column stem and the second column leaf. • Each leaf can only contain a single digit. If all the numbers in a data set have two digits, the stem and leaf will both contain one digit. If the values contain three digits, like 341, then each stem will have two digits, and each leaf will still only have one digit. • Identify the smallest and largest stems in the data set. In the table, list the first stem and continue listing stems, going up by increments of 1 until reaching the largest stem. Do NOT skip any values in the list of stems. • List each leaf with its corresponding stem, in order, with no commas or decimal points. • Include a key to show how to read each value in the table.
Sample Question:	
88. Find the mode of the data set from the stem-and-leaf plot. A. 2 B. 20 C. 22 D. 28 **Solution: C** The number 22 is repeated twice, which can be seen in the row starting with the stem of 2.	

Line Graph

A line graph is a line connecting points plotted on a coordinate plane. **A line graph is often used to show change over time.** An example of change over time is the number of miles traveled after a certain number of hours. A line graph is used most often in middle and high school mathematics because many scenarios include a change over time and are graphed using a line graph on a coordinate plane.

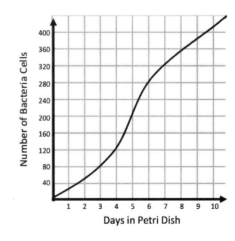

Scatter Plot

A scatter plot is a graph that contains bivariate data, or two data sets. An easy way to identify if data is univariate or bivariate is if the information is graphed on a single number line or a coordinate plane, which contains two number lines (one vertical and one horizontal). Points graphed on a scatter plot create a visual representation of the correlation between the two sets of data. Data on a scatter plot have a **positive correlation, negative correlation**, or **no correlation**.

A **trendline** is often drawn on a scatter plot to help visualize the relationship between the data and to make future predictions about the data.

Graphs		
Positive Correlation	Negative Correlation	No Correlation
A trendline with a positive slope can be drawn to model the direction of the data.	*A trendline with a negative slope can be drawn to model the direction of the data.*	*No trendline can be drawn to model the direction of the data.*
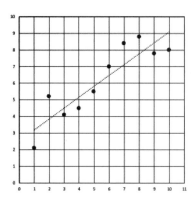	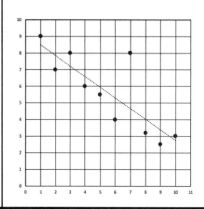	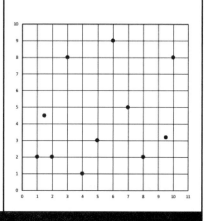

Sample Question:

89. Naomi surveyed 11 teachers in her school about the number of pets and the number of televisions each of them has at home. The graph of the data is shown below. What kind of correlation between these two data sets is most likely?

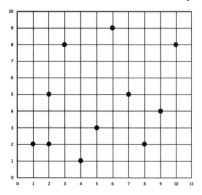

A. Positive correlation
B. Negative correlation
C. No correlation
D. Not enough information

Solution: C

There is no correlation between the number of pets a person has and the number of televisions they have in their home.

Example:

90. How do you know when the data in a scatter plot has no correlation?

    A. When a trendline can be drawn to show the data is increasing
    B. When a trendline can be drawn to show the data is decreasing
    C. When two trendlines can be drawn
    D. When no trend in the data is apparent enough to say that it is increasing or decreasing

    Solution: D

    If there is no apparent overall trend of the data increasing or decreasing, there is no correlation between the data.

Circle Graph

A circle graph, sometimes called a pie chart, is a visual representation that best shows proportional relationships. The data is presented in percentages and compares parts to a whole. What percent of a budget is used to pay various bills is an example of proportional data that could be displayed in a circle graph.

Data	Graph
A recent survey asked 500 high school students about the number of televisions in their house. The percents of students answering 1, 2, 3, or 4 or more are in the table below. 	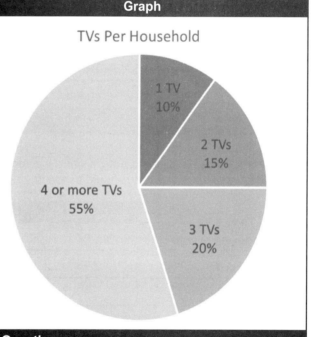

Number of TVs	Percent
1	10
2	15
3	20
4 or more	55

Once data is collected, find the percent of the total for each category. Use this percent to find the number of degrees out of the 360 degrees in a circle that each part of the survey represents (the size of each piece of the pie).

Sample Question:

91. Select TWO that could be found from a circle graph.

    A. Number of respondents that corresponds to each percent
    B. Change over time
    C. A fraction of the total
    D. A comparison of bivariate data

    Solution: A and C

    The first and third answer choices can be found from a circle graph. Circle graphs do not show change over time and do not compare bivariate data.

Praxis® exam questions asking for the appropriate graphical representation are probable because knowing the appropriate graph shows an understanding of its purpose. Although data can be displayed in more than one way, each display gives a visual of different characteristics that may make one graph better than another based on the situation.

The following table summarizes the information that each type of data display best represents.

Data Display	Purpose
Venn Diagram	Compare categories of data, including overlaps; likelihood of events
Bar Graph	Compare categories of data, sometimes over time
Pictograph	Uses visuals related to the data to compare categories
Table	Organize a list of data
Line Graph	Best to show change over time; two categories of data, e.g., time and distance
Stem-and-Leaf Plot	Useful for organizing set of data that are somewhat close together
Histogram	Determine the range or frequency where most data falls
Frequency Table	Organize data in a table by how frequently it occurs
Circle Graph	Comparison of parts to a whole
Scatterplot	Shows the correlation between two sets of data

Example:

92. A small business collected data on how customers are finding out about the business to determine where money for advertising should be focused. The number of contacts by method is listed in the table.

	June	July	August	September
Internet Search	42	50	78	63
Radio Advertisement	18	22	11	21
Friend Referral	10	15	25	32

Which of the following types of graphs would best display the data for comparison?

A. Triple bar graph
B. Frequency table
C. Pictograph
D. Stem-and-leaf plot

Solution: A

Because the data includes three methods of advertising, a triple bar graph would be best to compare the three methods.

Measures of center, or **measures of central tendency**, include mean, median, and mode. *Praxis*® exam questions that ask for the value of the mean, median, or mode may have data sets presented in a table, in a graph, or in a list, which may list data out of order.

Measures of Center/Central Tendency	
Mean	Find the average; add all the numbers and divide by how many numbers were added. *We think of the mean as "mean" because it's mean to make you do so much work to get an answer.*
Median	Place numbers in order; find the middle number. If there are two middle numbers, add them and divide by 2. *Remember, median is in the middle, just like the median in the road.*
Mode	The number or numbers that occur the most. *Mode and most both start with MO...__MO__DE __MO__ST.*

Examples:

93. On a quiz in Mrs. Fingal's class, 8 students scored 70%, 12 students scored 80%, and 4 students scored 95%. What is the mean score for the quiz? Round to the nearest whole number.

    A. 79
    B. 82
    C. 80
    D. 85

Solution: A

To find the mean of a list that groups values in sets, it is not necessary to list out all the numbers. Instead, find the sum of each like group of values, then add the sums together and divide by the total number of values.

Partial Sums:	Total sum:	Mean:
$8 \cdot 70 = 560$	$560 + 960 + 380 = 1,900$	$1,900 \div 24 = 79$
$12 \cdot 80 = 960$		
$4 \cdot 95 = 380$		

Therefore, the correct answer choice is A.

94. Find the mode of the data: $\{3, 3, 5, 6, 4, 5, 6, 2, 4, 5, 1, 10\}$

   A. 7
   B. 5
   C. 4
   D. 3

   Solution: B

   To find the mode, first put the numbers in order, then find the number that is repeated the most. $\{1, 2, 3, 3, 4, 4, 5, 5, 5, 6, 6, 10\}$ The number repeated the most is 5, so the correct answer choice is B.

Range

The range measures how far apart the values in a data set are spread. To find the range, arrange the numbers in the data set in order, then subtract the smallest value from the largest value.

Example:

95. Find the range of the data set: $\{6, 3, 1, 10, 12, 4, 9\}$

   A. 3
   B. 10
   C. 11
   D. 12

   Solution: C

   Place the values in order, $\{1, 3, 4, 6, 9, 10, 12\}$, then subtract the smallest from the largest, $12 - 1 = 11$. The correct answer is C.

G. Is familiar with how to interpret the probability of events

Probability is the likelihood of something happening and is generally written as a fraction or percent. To find probability, find the number of ways an event can happen and write as a fraction over the total number of events that can happen.

$$\text{Probability} = \frac{\text{number of ways event can happen}}{\text{total number of events that can happen}}$$

For example, to find the probability of rolling a 1 or 2 on a regular die, there are two numbers, 1 and 2, that are possibilities for the event we want to happen, and there are six numbers on the die, so six total possibilities that may happen when the die is rolled. Therefore, the probability of rolling a 1 or 2 is $\frac{2}{6} = \frac{1}{3}$.

Experimental probability is based on the outcomes of an actual experiment that was performed. Experimental probability is found after the experiment has taken place.

Theoretical probability is what is mathematically expected to happen based on the number of outcomes of an event. The theoretical probability can be found before an experiment has happened.

For example, when flipping a coin, we expect that it will land on heads 50% of the time. When a coin is flipped 10 times in an experiment, it actually lands on heads 6 times or 60% of the time. What we expected is the theoretical probability. What actually happened, landing on heads 6 times, is the experimental probability.

When an experiment is conducted with a limited number of trials, the results can be used to predict what will happen if a much larger experiment were conducted.

The same principle is true for theoretical probability. What is expected to happen in a small sampling can be used to predict what should happen in a much larger sample.

For either type of probability, proportions are used to make predictions.

Examples:

96. Mel and Thomas spun a spinner that was divided evenly into four colors: blue, red, green, and yellow. Find the number of times the spinner will theoretically land on green after 80 spins.

    A. 4
    B. 16
    C. 20
    D. 25

    Solution: C

    To make a prediction using theoretical probability, determine the probability of the spinner landing on green. Because there is one green section out of four total sections, the probability is $\frac{1}{4}$ Next, set up and solve a proportion to predict how many times the spinner lands on green after 80 spins.

    $$\frac{1}{4} = \frac{x}{80}$$
    $$4x = 80$$
    $$x = 20$$

97. After conducting the experiment in the previous problem, Mel and Thomas found the spinner landed on blue 18 times. Use this information to predict how many times the spinner will land on blue after 1,000 spins.

    A. 56
    B. 225
    C. 360
    D. 388

    Solution: B

    In the last problem, the spinner was spun 80 times. Set up and solve a proportion using the fact that the spinner landed on blue 18 out of 80 times.

    $$\frac{18}{80} = \frac{x}{1,000}$$
    $$80x = 18,000$$
    $$x = 225$$

98. A game contains a spinner with six different colors: red, blue, green, yellow, orange, and purple. You've spun the spinner three times, and each time it has landed on green. What is the probability that the spinner lands on green again for your fourth spin?

A. $\dfrac{1}{6}$

B. $\dfrac{1}{2}$

C. $\dfrac{2}{3}$

D. $\dfrac{4}{5}$

Solution: A

The information that the spinner landed on green three other times does not have any effect on the theoretical probability, which is what the question is asking for you to find. Therefore, the probability of landing on a green on the fourth spin is 1 out of 6, which is $\dfrac{1}{6}$, answer choice A.

Directions: Answer each question below.

1. Which of the following best depicts why $3 \times 5 = 15$?

A.

B.

C.

D.

2. A softball team is selling candles in boxes of 6. They make a profit of $2.75 for each candle they sell. If they want to make enough money to cover the $825 entry fee for a softball tournament, how many boxes of candles do they need to sell?

   A.   300

   B.   138

   C.   50

   D.   17

3. Which of the following pairs of numbers have the same prime factors?

   A.   10 and 12

   B.   18 and 24

   C.   16 and 28

   D.   15 and 30

4. Use the boxes below to write the numbers in order from least to greatest.

$$\frac{6}{9} \qquad \frac{5}{8} \qquad \frac{7}{11} \qquad \frac{3}{8}$$

5. Select ALL of the following that have a 2 in the thousands place and a 4 in the tens place.

   ☐ 37,241

   ☐ 32,741

   ☐ 32,645

   ☐ 24,340

   ☐ 82,403

   ☐ 62,148

6. Which of the following represents the largest value?

   A. 842 thousandths

   B. 82 hundredths

   C. 8 tenths

   D. 4 fifths

7. Which of the following expressions could be used to find 7% of $300?

   A. 300×0.7

   B. $300 \times \left(7 \div 100\right)$

   C. $300 \div \left(7 \times 100\right)$

   D. $300 \div \left(7 \times 10\right)$

8. Use the boxes below to write the numbers in order from greatest to least.

   $3\dfrac{2}{3}$ $\dfrac{10}{3}$ $3\dfrac{5}{9}$ 3.65

   ☐   ☐   ☐   ☐

9. Clive is painting a design in the middle of a museum floor. His design consists of three triangles, each with a height of 6 feet and a base of 10 feet and one rectangle with a height of $18\dfrac{1}{2}$ feet and a base of 10 feet. If each can of paint covers 250 square feet, what is the minimum number of cans of paint Clive will need to buy?

   A. 1

   B. 2

   C. 3

   D. 4

10. Mrs. Smith has 50 books to give away to 8 students. She wants to make sure each student gets the same number of books. How many books should she give to each student?

    A. 5

    B. 6

    C. 6.25

    D. 7

11. The cost of 4 notebooks is $5. Which expression below represents the cost of 7 notebooks?

    A. $7 \text{ notebooks} \times \dfrac{4 \text{ notebooks}}{\$5}$

    B. $4 \text{ notebooks} \times \dfrac{7 \text{ notebooks}}{\$5}$

    C. $7 \text{ notebooks} \div \dfrac{4 \text{ notebooks}}{\$5}$

    D. $7 \text{ notebooks} \times \dfrac{\$5}{4 \text{ notebooks}}$

12. Ryan works at a sandwich shop and can make 35 sandwiches in 50 minutes. At this rate, how many sandwiches can he make in a 4-hour shift?

    A. 168

    B. 170

    C. 280

    D. 342

13. Carlos got finished with soccer practice at 6:05 P.M. If practice lasted 2 hours and 20 minutes, what time did practice start?

    A. 2:45 P.M.

    B. 3:15 P.M.

    C. 3:20 P.M.

    D. 3:45 P.M.

14. Which of the following is the expanded form of 520,003,109?

    A. 500,000,000 + 20,000,000 + 3,000 + 100 + 9

    B. 520,000,000 + 3,000 + 100 + 9

    C. 500,000, + 20,000, + 3,000 + 100 + 9

    D. 500,000,000 + 20,000,000 + 30,000 + 100 + 9

15. Forrest is performing a magic trick and tells his friends to do the following:

    i.   Think of a number.

    ii.   Subtract seven from that number.

    iii. Divide your answer by five.

    iv. Cube the result.

    Which of the following could be used to represent these steps?

A. $\left(n-7\div5\right)^3$

B. $\left(7-n\right)\div5^3$

C. $\left(\dfrac{n-7}{5}\right)^3$

D. $\dfrac{\left(n-7\right)^3}{5}$

16. Which of the following is the function rule for the table given?

x	y
1	1
2	4
4	10
8	22

A. $y+3x=-2$

B. $y-3x=2$

C. $3x-y=-2$

D. $3x-y=2$

17. The parents of all the students in Mr. Harmon's class were invited to open house. 84% of the students' parents were in attendance. If there are 25 students in the class, what fraction represents the number of students' parents who were not in attendance?

A. $\dfrac{1}{25}$

B. $\dfrac{21}{25}$

C. $\dfrac{4}{25}$

D. $\dfrac{4}{21}$

18. If $\frac{2}{5}a + 3 = 11$, what is the value of $3a - 1$?

    A.   1.4

    B.   15.8

    C.   59

    D.   104

19. How many times larger is the first 6—underlined—than the second 6?

2$\underline{6}$3,461

    A.   1,000

    B.   600

    C.   100

    D.   60

20. Evaluate the expression for $b = -4$.

$-b^2 - 3b$

    A. -28

    B. -4

    C.   4

    D.   28

21. Four times the difference of twice a number and seven is subtracted from eight times a number. Which of the following represents this scenario?

    A. $4(7 - 2n) - 8n$

    B. $8n - 4(7 - 2n)$

    C. $8n - 4(2n - 7)$

    D. $4(2n - 7) - 8n$

22. Select all the options that represent an algebraic expression.

    ☐ $2x + 3 = 9$

    ☐ $5(x - 7)$

    ☐ $2a + 3b$

    ☐ $2x^2 = 4$

    ☐ $y - 8 + 2x$

23. The fraction of an hour it took 4 students to complete a test is listed in the table. What is the sum of the number of hours it took all four students to complete the test?

Student	Sara	Gary	Rudolph	Lorenzo
Time (hours)	$\dfrac{3}{5}$	$\dfrac{7}{10}$	$\dfrac{4}{5}$	$\dfrac{9}{10}$

A. $\dfrac{23}{10}$

B. $\dfrac{23}{15}$

C. $\dfrac{23}{30}$

D. $\dfrac{30}{10}$

24. Which of the following graphs the solutions of $(x+3)(x-4)=0$?

A.

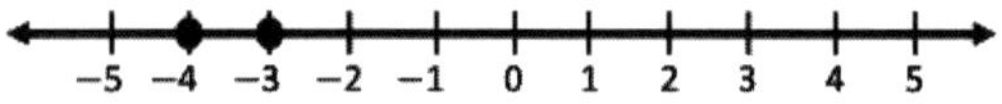

B.

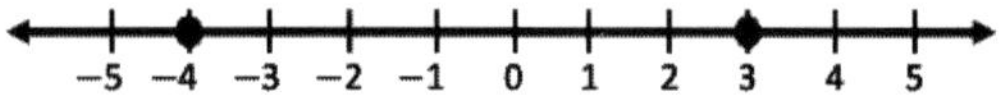

C.

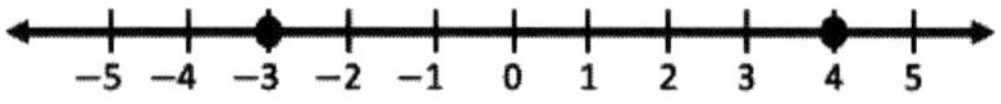

D.

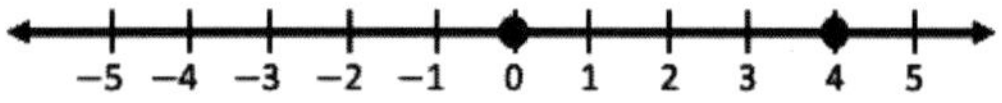

25. Jack's mom gave him $10 to spend at the school store for spiral notebooks that cost $1.25 and folders that cost $0.50. If he buys 3 spiral notebooks and the reset on folders, which option represents how much money he can spend if his mom asked him to spend under $10?

A. $0.5x + 3.75 < 10$

B. $1.25x + 1.5 > 10$

C. $0.5x + 3.75 \geq 10$

D. $1.25x + 1.5 \leq 10$

26. For the equation below, $y = 82$. Find the value of x.

$$y = \frac{2}{5}(x - 28) - 40$$

A. 375

B. 333

C. 280.5

D. 195.5

27. In which of the following choices was the distributive property of multiplication over subtraction applied to get $(4 \cdot 2a) - (4 \cdot 3b)$?

  A. $(2a - 3b)4$

  B. $4 - (2a \cdot 3b)$

  C. $4(2a + 3b)$

  D. $(4 \cdot 2a) - (4 \cdot 3b)$

28. In what quadrant is the point $(-2, 9)$?

  A. I

  B. II

  C. III

  D. IV

29. The point $(-8, -3)$ is reflected over the y-axis. What is the x-coordinate of the reflected point?

  A. -8

  B. -3

  C. 3

  D. 8

30. Given the equation $y = 3x + 1$, identify the dependent and independent variable.

  A. x is the dependent variable; y is the independent variable.

  B. y is the dependent variable; 3 is the independent variable.

  C. x is the dependent variable; 1 is the independent variable.

  D. y is the dependent variable; x is the independent variable.

31. The two figures below are similar. Choose TWO statements that are true about the figures.

  ☐ The ratio of x to y must be a $2:1$ ratio.

  ☐ If $x = 3a$, then $y = 1.5a$.

  ☐ $y:x$ is equivalent to a $2:1$ ratio.

  ☐ $\dfrac{4a}{2a} = \dfrac{y}{x}$

32. Goodie bag A has four fewer pieces of candy than goodie bag B. Together the bags have 48 pieces of candy. Which system of equations can be used to represent this scenario?

A. $A = B + 4$
$A + B = 48$

B. $A - B = 4$
$A + B = 48$

C. $B - 4 = A$
$A + B = 48$

D. $A + B = 4$
$A - B = 48$

33. There are four cookies in a jar: two chocolate chip and two oatmeal. Without looking, what is the probability of reaching into the jar and getting two oatmeal cookies in the same grab?

A. $\dfrac{1}{6}$

B. $\dfrac{1}{4}$

C. $\dfrac{1}{3}$

D. $\dfrac{1}{2}$

34. A six-sided cube has the numbers 1–6 on the sides. If the cube is rolled four times, and a 5 is rolled each time, what is the probability of the cube landing on a 5 on the fifth roll?

A. $\dfrac{2}{3}$

B. $\dfrac{1}{2}$

C. $\dfrac{1}{6}$

D. 0

35. Four students in Mr. Neal's class performed an experiment with a spinner containing four equal parts, each part a different color. The students spun the spinner 12 times and recorded the color it landed on in the table.

	1	2	3	4	5	6	7	8	9	10	11	12
Red	x			x		x		x		x		x
Blue		x	x									
Green					x				x			
Yellow							x				x	

What is the experimental probability of the spinner landing on red?

A. $\frac{1}{4}$

B. $\frac{1}{5}$

C. $\frac{4}{5}$

D. $\frac{1}{2}$

36. Lines a and b are perpendicular to one another, and line c is parallel to line a. What is the relationship between lines b and c?

    A. Parallel

    B. Perpendicular

    C. Intersecting but not at a right angle

    D. Parallel and intersecting

37. Using the figure below, choose all the rays that are shown.

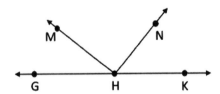

☐ $\overrightarrow{HG}$

☐ $\overrightarrow{MG}$

☐ $\overrightarrow{GK}$

☐ $\overrightarrow{HN}$

☐ $\overrightarrow{NH}$

☐ $\overrightarrow{KH}$

38. The steps to simplifying a problem are below. In which step was the distributive property used?

$$\text{Step 1: } 6x+3+4\left(2x+1\right)$$

$$\text{Step 2: } 3\left(2x+1\right)+4\left(2x+1\right)$$

$$\text{Step 3: } \left(2x+1\right)\left(3+4\right)$$

   A.   Step 1

   B.   Step 2

   C.   Step 3

   D.   The distributive property was never used.

39. The table below contains data to determine the relationship between the age of a driver and the farthest distance they are able to read a street sign.

Age (years)	16	20	40	65	80
Sign Reading Distance (ft)	530	500	450	330	290

Which of the following lines is the best fit for the data?

   A. $y = -\dfrac{15}{4}x+590$

   B. $y = -\dfrac{15}{4}x+530$

   C. $y = -\dfrac{15}{4}x+80$

   D. $y = -\dfrac{15}{4}x+290$

40. In a 7th grade survey, four students reported their favorite milkshake flavor was vanilla. How many students reported that caramel was their favorite flavor?

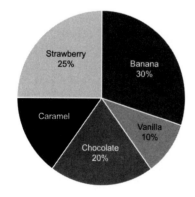

   A.   4

   B.   6

   C.   10

   D.   15

41. The net below is of which three-dimensional figure?

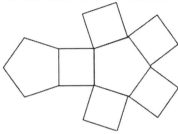

   A. Hexagonal prism
   B. Hexagonal pyramid
   C. Pentagonal prism
   D. Pentagonal pyramid

42. Drag and drop (write) the graph type in the square that would best display the data.

Line graph	Circle graph	Bar graph	Histogram

1.	2.	3.	4.
Number of students in grades 6–8	Frequency of answers in intervals of 10	Percent of families with 0, 1, or 2 children	Time and distance of a road trip

43. Which of the following could be the height of a front door to a residential home?
   A. 24 meters
   B. 244 mm
   C. 2 km
   D. 244 cm

44. Select all of the conversions that are correct.
   ☐ 2.8 g = 280 cg
   ☐ 0.4 kg = 40 g
   ☐ 400 g = 400,000 mg
   ☐ 10 g = 0.1 kg
   ☐ 12 cg = 1.2 mg

45. Find the area of the rectangle with the coordinates $(2, 0), (6, 3), (-4, 8),$ and $(0, 11)$.
   A. 25 square units
   B. 50 square units
   C. 75 square units
   D. 110 square units

46. Round 2,345.601 to the nearest tens.

    A.   2,340

    B.   2,346

    C.   2,345.6

    D.   2,350

47. Ellie's food truck currently serves four main dishes and three side dishes, and each meal consists of one main dish and one side. Next week, she is adding one main dish and two sides to the menu. How many more combinations of meals will her customers be able to get with the new additions?

    A.   2

    B.   12

    C.   13

    D.   25

48. What is the perimeter of a square with an area of 49 square inches?

    A.   7 inches

    B.   24.5 inches

    C.   28 inches

    D.   98 inches

49. Which of the following graphs is the best graph to use when graphing data over time?

    A.   Line graph

    B.   Venn diagram

    C.   Scatter plot

    D.   Histogram

50. Find the area of the figure.

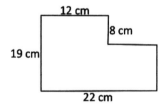

    A.   110 square cm

    B.   228 square cm

    C.   242 square cm

    D.   338 square cm

#	Answer	Category	Explanation
1.	A	I	The concrete representation of the multiplication problem 3×5 is a picture or array of 3 groups of 5 items. The array in option A contains 3 rows, each with 5 dots.
2.	C	I	First, find the profit for one box of candles. There are six candles in a box, and each candle sold makes a profit of $2.75. Therefore, the profit for a box is $6 \times \$2.75 = \$16.50$. Next, $16.50 times an unknown number of boxes has to equal the $825 tournament fee. Write as an equation and solve for x, the number of boxes needed. $16.50x = 825$ $$\frac{16.50x}{16.50} = \frac{825}{16.50}$$ $x = 50$ Therefore, 50 boxes of candles need to be sold to reach the $825 goal. **Note**: *If you recognize that you divide 825 and 16.50 without having to write an equation, just do that math. Save yourself as much time as possible on this test!*
3.	B	I	To answer this question efficiently, quickly evaluate the factors for each pair of numbers. 10 and 12: 10 has a factor of 5 and 12 does not, so eliminate answer choice A. 18 and 24: 18 has factors of 2 and 9 (which is 3 and 3). 24 has factors of 6 (2 and 3) and 4 (2 and 2). Therefore, both numbers have prime factors of 2 and 3 only, making answer choice B the correct answer. 16 and 28: 28 has a factor of 7 and 16 does not, so eliminate answer choice C. 15 and 30: 30 has a factor of 2 and 15 does not, so eliminate answer choice D.

#	Answer	Category	Explanation
4.	See explanation for drag and drop solution	I	**ANSWER:** $\boxed{\dfrac{3}{8}}$ $\boxed{\dfrac{5}{8}}$ $\boxed{\dfrac{7}{11}}$ $\boxed{\dfrac{6}{9}}$ To solve, write each fraction as a decimal by computing the top number (numerator) divided by the bottom number (denominator). Write each decimal out 3 places. $\dfrac{6}{9} = 0.667$ $\dfrac{5}{8} = 0.625$ $\dfrac{7}{11} = 0.636$ $\dfrac{3}{8} = 0.375$ In order from least to greatest is 0.375, 0.625, 0.636, 0.667
5.	32,741 32,645 62,148	I	First, look for all the answer choices that have a 2 in the thousands place, eliminating those that do not. ☐ ~~37,241~~ ☐ 32,741 ☐ 32,645 ☐ ~~24,340~~ ☐ 82,403 ☐ 62,148 Next, look for the numbers with a 4 in the tens place, and mark these as the correct answers. ☐ ~~37,241~~ ☐ 32,741 ☐ 32,645 ☐ ~~24,340~~ ☐ ~~82,403~~ ☐ 62,148
6.	A	I	Writing out each of the values to 3 decimal places allows for a quick comparison. A. 0.842 B. 0.820 C. 0.800 D. 0.800 Answer choice A is the largest value.
7.	B	I	First, pay attention to the language in the question. It asks you to find 7% **of** $300. The term *of* means to multiply. Therefore, you can eliminate answers C and D. Next convert 7% to a decimal by dividing 7 by 100 ($\dfrac{7}{100}$). This will also move the decimal point two places to the left (7 to 0.07). The answer choice that reflects this process is B.

#	Answer	Category	Explanation
8.	See explanation for drag and drop solution	I	ANSWER: $\boxed{3\dfrac{2}{3}}$ $\boxed{3.65}$ $\boxed{3\dfrac{5}{9}}$ $\boxed{\dfrac{10}{3}}$ Write out each number to 3 decimal places. $3\dfrac{2}{3} = 3.667$ $\dfrac{10}{3} = 3.333$ $3\dfrac{5}{9} = 3.556$ $3.65 = 3.650$ From greatest to least, $3.667, 3.650, 3.556, 3.333$.
9.	B	III	Find the area of the three triangles and the rectangle. Add the areas together to get the total square footage the design will cover. Next, divide the total area of the figure by 250 to get the number of paint cans needed. Round up to the next whole number, regardless of the decimal because a portion of a paint can cannot be purchased. Triangle Area: $3\dfrac{1}{2}bh = 3(0.5\cdot 6\cdot 10) = 90$ Rectangle Area: $bh = 18.5\cdot 10 = 185$ Total area: $90 + 185 = 275$ $275 \div 250 = 1.1$ This rounds to 2 paint cans, which is answer choice B.
10.	B	I	$50 \div 8 = 6.25$ Just as with the question before, the teacher cannot give 0.25 of a book to her students, so each student should get 6 books to make the distribution equal.
11.	D	I	Each of the answer choices multiplies a fraction by 7 notebooks. Therefore, the fraction must represent the cost per 1 notebook, which is found by dividing $\dfrac{\$5}{4\text{ notebooks}}$.

#	Answer	Category	Explanation
12.	A	I	The question gives a rate of 35 sandwiches in 50 minutes and asks for the number of sandwiches in 4 hours. Because there is a rate in the problem, and the question asks for another rate, this can be solved using a proportion. Before writing the proportion, convert 4 hours to minutes, $4 \cdot 60 = 240$ minutes, so that the units in each fraction are the same. Next, set up a proportion with the given rate and solve for x. $$\frac{35 \text{ sandwiches}}{50 \text{ minutes}} = \frac{x \text{ sandwiches}}{240 \text{ minutes}}$$ $$50x = 240\left(35\right)$$ $$50x = 8,400$$ $$x = 168 \text{ sandwiches}$$
13.	D	I	Work backward with the minutes first. Subtracting 20 minutes from 6:05 p.m. takes the time back to 5:45 p.m. Next, subtract the 2 hours to get 3:45 p.m.
14.	A	I	To write a number in expanded form, take each digit that is not zero and replace all numbers after the digit with zero. Write out an addition problem of each of these numbers to show that the sum is the original number. For 520,003,109, **5**20,003,109 = 500,000,000 5**2**0,003,109 = 20,000,000 520,00**3**,109 = 3,000 520,003,**1**09 = 100 520,003,10**9** = 9 Create an addition problem with each of the values for expanded form. 500,000,000 + 20,000,000 + 3,000 + 100 + 9
15.	C	II	The first step is to subtract 7 from n, or $n-7$. Eliminate answer choice B because this option subtracts incorrectly. Next, the result of $n-7$ is divided by 5, which means that $n-7$ needs to be computed before dividing by 5. This eliminates answer choice A, because with order of operations, the 7 would be divided by 5 before the subtraction. Last, both the subtraction and division must occur before being cubed, which means that answer choice D can be eliminated, leaving answer choice C as the correct response. **Note**: *Putting an expression inside parentheses ensures that what is in the parentheses gets completed before what is outside the parentheses.*

#	Answer	Category	Explanation
16.	D	II	To find the function rule that matches the table, first find the slope. Second, use the slope and any point to find $y = mx + b$. Last, rewrite the equation to match the form in the answer choices. To find the slope, use any 2 points from the table. $(2, 4)$ $(1, 1)$ Subtract the y-values and subtract the x values, writing their differences as a fraction $\dfrac{y_2 - y_1}{x_2 - x_1} = \dfrac{4 - 1}{2 - 1} = \dfrac{3}{1} = 3$. Next, pick any point. We are using $(1, 1)$ because it's easy to substitute into an equation. Substitute the values of the point along with the slope that was just found into $y = mx + b$ for $x, y,$ and m to find b. $y = mx + b$ $1 = 3 \cdot 1 + b$ $1 = 3 + b$ $-2 = b$ Next, use $m = 3$ and $b = -2$ to write an equation by substituting into $y = mx + b$. $y = 3x - 2$ Last, all the answers have x and y on the same side of the equation. Thus, we need to rearrange the equation to make sure the right answer choice is selected. Subtract $3x$ from both sides of the equal sign, then multiply all terms by -1 to get the correct answer in standard form. $y = 3x - 2$ $-3x + y = -2$ $-1(-3x + y = -2)$ $3x - y = 2$
17.	C	I	If 84% of the parents attended, then $100 - 84 = 16\%$ of the parents were not in attendance. To find the number of students' parents not in attendance, find 16% of 25. 16% of $25 = 0.16 \cdot 25 = 4$ 4 students' parents were not in attendance, which can be represented by the fraction $\dfrac{4}{25}$.

#	Answer	Category	Explanation
18.	C	II	Solve the first equation for a, then substitute a into the expression. $\dfrac{2}{5}a+3=11$ Subtracting 3 from both sides, we get: $\dfrac{2}{5}a+3-3=11-3$ $\dfrac{2}{5}a=8$ Change the fraction to a decimal. $0.4a=8$ Divide both sides by 0.4. $a=\dfrac{8}{0.4}=20$ Now, substitute 20 in for a in the expression $3a-1$. $3(20)-1=60-1=59$
19.	A	I	From the first 6 in the number to the second 6, there is a difference of three place values, 2**6**3,4**6**1. When moving from right to left (the question asks how many times larger is the second number than the first), each place value represents a factor of 10. Moving three place values is the same as multiplying by 10 three times or $10\cdot10\cdot10=1,000$. Thus, the first 6 is 1,000 times larger than the second 6.
20.	B	II	When evaluating, be very careful with all the negative signs. Any time there is a negative sign in front of a variable to the second power, the number will always be negative. This is because $-x^2=-1\cdot x^2$, and with order of operations, the exponent always gets simplified first. $-b^2-3b$ $=-(-4)^2-3(-4)$ $=-16-3(-4)$ $=-16-(-12)$ $=-16+12=-4$
21.	C	II	Four times the difference of twice a number and seven as an expression is $4(2n-7)$. Remember, *difference* represents the answer to a subtraction problem. This expression is subtracted from eight times a number or $8n$. This is written altogether as $8n-4(2n-7)$.

#	Answer	Category	Explanation
22.	$5(x-7)$ $2a+3b$ $y-8+2x$	II	An expression does not contain an equal sign, and an equation does. Therefore, any math sentence in the answer choices without an = is an expression.
23.	D	I	The sum is an answer to an addition problem, so add the values in the table. $$\frac{3}{5}+\frac{7}{10}+\frac{4}{5}+\frac{9}{10}$$ To save time, add the fractions with like denominators first, then find a common denominator for the remaining two fractions. $$\frac{3}{5}+\frac{4}{5}=\frac{7}{5} \text{ and } \frac{7}{10}+\frac{9}{10}=\frac{16}{10}$$ $$\frac{7}{5}+\frac{16}{10}=\frac{14}{10}+\frac{16}{10}=\frac{30}{10}=3$$
24.	C	II	To find the solutions of the equation, set each expression in parentheses equal to zero, and solve each for the variable. $x+3=0$ $x-4=0$ $x+3-3=0-3$ $x-4+4=0+4$ $x=-3$ $x=4$ There are two solutions to the equation, and each solution is a point. To graph on a number line, graph each point. (number line from −5 to 5 with points at −3 and 4)
25.	A	II	The total amount that Jack can spend is less than \$10, so the expression that represents the cost of the notebooks and folders is less than 10, or total cost < 10. Jack bought three spiral notebooks for \$1.25 each, so the notebooks cost $3 \cdot 1.25 = \$3.75$. He bought folders at \$0.50 each, so the folders cost $0.50x$. The inequality that represents the situation would then be: $0.50x+3.75<10$. * There is only one answer choice that is <. Because his mother asked him to spend LESS than \$10, you can eliminate answers B, C, and D right away.

#	Answer	Category	Explanation
26.	B	II	Substitute the value $y = 82$ into the equation and solve for x. $$y = \frac{2}{5}(x - 28) - 40$$ Substitute 82 for y. $$82 = \frac{2}{5}(x - 28) - 40$$ Add 40 to each side to isolate the variable. $$82 + 40 = \frac{2}{5}(x - 28) - 40 + 40$$ $$122 = \frac{2}{5}(x - 28)$$ Distribute $\frac{2}{5}$ (or 0.4). $$122 = 0.4x - 11.2$$ Add 11.2 to both sides. $$122 + 11.2 = 0.4x + 11.2 + 11.2$$ Divide both sides by 0.4. $$\frac{133.2}{0.4} = \frac{0.4x}{0.4}$$ $$x = 333$$
27.	A	I	Four is being multiplied in each of the parentheses, which means that a 4 was distributed to each term. The problem states distributive property of multiplication over subtraction, so the operation between the two terms should be subtraction. The correct answer is A, $(2a - 3b)4$ because if the 4 is distributed to each term, we would have the resulting expression in the question. If you aren't sure how to "undo" the distributive property, simplify each answer choice and compare it to the expression in the question.
28.	B	III	The quadrants make a C if you start at quadrant I and go around the coordinate plane in order to quadrant IV. Thus, the point is in quadrant II. The correct answer is B.

#	Answer	Category	Explanation
29.	D	III	When a point is reflected, or flipped, over the y-axis, the x-coordinate of the point changes signs. Therefore, $(-8, -3)$ becomes $(8, -3)$.
30.	D	II	The independent variable is x, and the dependent variable is y. The value of y depends on what the value of x is.
31.	See Explanation	III	**ANSWER:** The ratio of x to y must be a 2:1 ratio. If, $x = 3a$, then $y = 1.5a$. Check the validity of each statement by setting up a proportion. **Statement 1**: $\dfrac{x}{y} = \dfrac{4a}{2a}$; Simplifying the right side: $\dfrac{x}{y} = \dfrac{2}{1}$. Statement 1 is true. **Statement 2**: Use the ratio above and substitute in for x and y. $\dfrac{x}{y} = \dfrac{2}{1}$; $\dfrac{3a}{1.5a} = \dfrac{2}{1}$; Simplifying the left side, $\dfrac{2}{1} = \dfrac{2}{1}$. Statement 2 is true. **Statement 3**: This statement says that if we flip x and y, this is still equivalent to $\dfrac{2}{1}$, but it is not. Therefore, statement 3 is not true. **Statement 4**: is incorrect $\dfrac{4a}{2a} = \dfrac{x}{y}$ not $\dfrac{y}{x}$.
32.	C	II	If goodie bag A has four fewer pieces of candy, then the number of candies in A can be represented by the equation $A = B - 4$. If the total number of candies in both bags is 48, this can be represented by the equation, $A + B = 48$. Therefore, the correct answer choice is $\begin{cases} B - 4 = A \\ A + B = 48 \end{cases}$.

#	Answer	Category	Explanation
33.	A	III	To solve this problem, think of each cookie individually. There is chocolate chip 1, chocolate chip 2, oatmeal 1, and oatmeal 2. To make listing them easier, shorten the cookie names to c1, c2, o1, and o2. Next, list out all the possible combinations of cookies. c1, c2 / c1, o1 c1, o2 / c2, o1 c2, o2 / o1, o2 Therefore, the probability of getting two oatmeal cookies in one grab is 1 out of 6, or $\frac{1}{6}$.
34.	C	III	The first four rolls of the number cube do not affect the fifth roll. Therefore, the probability of rolling a 5 is 1 out of 6, or $\frac{1}{6}$
35.	D	III	To find the experimental probability, find the total number of events that you wanted to occur and the total number of events that occurred, and write these values as a fraction. $\dfrac{\text{\# of times landing on red}}{\text{total number of spins}} = \dfrac{6}{12} = \dfrac{1}{2}$
36.	B	III	A quick sketch of the lines shows that line b is perpendicular to line c.
37.	$\overrightarrow{HG}$ $\overrightarrow{GK}$ $\overrightarrow{HN}$ $\overrightarrow{KH}$	III	A ray has an endpoint on one end and then extends indefinitely on the other end, which is denoted by an arrow. The endpoint is always the first point named in the ray. $\overrightarrow{MG}$ is not a ray because it does not contain a line through the points. $\overrightarrow{NH}$ is not a ray because point H is an endpoint and thus $\overline{NH}$, in that order, cannot be a ray. $\overrightarrow{KH}$ is tricky because it may seem that it is a segment, but a ray can be named with any two points on the ray as long as the endpoint is the first letter used.

#	Answer	Category	Explanation
38.	B	II	In step 1, we cannot say if the distributive property was used or not because there are no previous steps. In step 2, the 3 is factored out, which is an application of the distributive property. In step 3, an expression with 2 terms is factored out. The distributive property refers to a single term being distributed or factored, so the distributive property does not apply in step 3.
39.	A	III	Notice that all the slopes for the equations, $-\dfrac{15}{4}$, are the same, so we only need to determine the y-intercept that would best match the data. The y-intercepts to choose from are 590, 530, 80, and 290. $$y = -\frac{15}{4}x + 590$$ $$y = -\frac{15}{4}x + 530$$ $$y = -\frac{15}{4}x + 80$$ $$y = -\frac{15}{4}x + 290$$ In a real-world application, the y-intercept is the starting point of the graph. In this situation, the table starts when a person is 16. If the pattern started earlier, for example, when a person is 10, would the distance from which they can read a sign be greater or less than when they are 16 based on the pattern in the table? Because the distances are decreasing as a person gets older, it would increase if we go backward in age. Thus, the y value that would be before the first point $\left(16, 530\right)$ in the table needs to be greater than 530. The only y-intercept that aligns with this is A.
40.	B	III	First, determine what percent of the circle graph is caramel. Subtract all the other percents from 100: $100 - 30 - 10 - 20 - 25 = 15\%$ Next, set up a proportion to find how many students responded to the survey by using the information about the vanilla milkshake. $\dfrac{4 \text{ students}}{x \text{ total students}} = \dfrac{10\% \text{ responded vanilla}}{100\% \text{ responded to survey}}$ Next, cross multiply to solve. $10x = 400$ $x = 40$, so 40 students responded to the survey. Last, find 15% of 40 because 15% of the total like caramel. $0.15 \cdot 40 = 6$

#	Answer	Category	Explanation
41.	C	III	The net has 2 bases that each have 5 sides. Thus, the figure is a pentagonal prism.
42.	Bar graph Histogram Circle graph Line graph	III	1. A bar graph compares a single data point among sets. 2. A histogram displays the frequency of data occurring. 3. A circle graph displays the percent of respondents. 4. A line graph is best for showing change over time.
43.	D	III	Answer choice D is most reasonable because 244 cm is 2.44 meters, which is about 2.5 yards, or 7.5 feet. That is a reasonable height of a door. Answer choice A is not reasonable because a meter is about a yard, so 24 meters would be way too tall. Answer choice B is not reasonable because it takes 1,000 mm to make 1 meter, making 244 less than a yard, which is way too short for a door. Answer choice C is not reasonable because 1 kilometer is almost a mile, so a door would not be measured in km.
44.	See Explanation	III	ANSWER: 2.8 g = 280 cg 400 g = 400,000 mg The other conversions should be the following: 0.4 kg = 400 grams 10g = 0.01 kg 12cg = 120 mg Because they are not, they are not part of the solution.

#	Answer	Category	Explanation
45.	B	III	This question can be approached a few ways, but the fastest and easiest is to apply your knowledge of right triangles to quickly find the length of the sides of the rectangle. First, quickly sketch the rectangle on a coordinate plane. Because the rectangle is drawn slightly rotated, we cannot count units from one point to the next to determine side lengths. What we can do is sketch in a right triangle, with one of the sides of the rectangle being the hypotenuse of the triangle, for both the base and height. The larger triangle has two sides that are 6 units and 8 units, which makes the hypotenuse 10 units (because it is a Pythagorean triple). The smaller triangle has two sides that are 3 units and 4 units, which makes the hypotenuse 5 units (because it is a Pythagorean triple). Thus, the sides of the rectangle are each 5 units and 10 units, and the area of the rectangle is $A = bh = 5 \cdot 10 = 50$ square units.
46.	D	I	The 4 is in the tens place, 2,3$\underline{4}$5.601, and the 5 to the right indicates that the 4 rounds up to a 5, making the new number 2,350.

#	Answer	Category	Explanation
47.	C	III	To find the number of combinations, multiply the number of choices for each category. Before the additional items: $4 \cdot 3 = 12$ After the additional items: $5 \cdot 5 = 25$. To find how many additional meal combinations can be made with the additions, subtract $25 - 12 = 13$.
48.	C	III	Because a square has equal side lengths, the square with an area of 49 will have side lengths of 7 inches because $7 \cdot 7 = 49$ (recall the area of a square is $A = s \cdot s$). Thus, the perimeter of the square, $P = 4s$, is $P = 4 \cdot 7 = 28$ inches.
49.	A	III	A line graph is always best for showing change over time.
50.	D	III	To solve composite area (area of basic figures joined together), separate the figure into two rectangles. This can be done two ways, so both are shown. Next, find the area of each rectangle. Add the two areas together to find the total area. $A = lw = 12 \cdot 8 = 96$ $A = lw = 11 \cdot 22 = 242$ $96 + 242 = 338$ square cm Next, find the area of each rectangle. Add the two areas together to find the total area. $= lw = 12 \cdot 19 = 228$ $A = lw = 11 \cdot 10 = 110$ $228 + 110 = 338$ square cm

Directions: Select the best answer choice for each question.

1. Select TWO fractions that are equivalent to 1.9.

    ☐ $\dfrac{19}{100}$

    ☐ $\dfrac{19}{10}$

    ☐ $\dfrac{1.9}{10}$

    ☐ $\dfrac{190}{100}$

2. How many times greater is 203.4 than 2.034?

    A. 10^1

    B. 10^2

    C. 10^3

    D. 10^4

3. Which of the following is a factor of 256?

    A. 16

    B. 28

    C. 125

    D. 512

4. What is the sum of the measures of the interior angles of an octagon?

    A. 1,800

    B. 1,440

    C. 1,260

    D. 1,080

5. The net would create which of the following 3-dimensional figures?

    A. Triangular prism

    B. Triangular pyramid

    C. Rectangular prism

    D. Trapezoidal pyramid

6. If $x = -4$, find the value of $-x^2 - 9x$.

    A. -52

    B. -20

    C. 52

    D. 20

7. Simplify the expression.
$-8 + 3 \cdot 6 \div 2$

    A. -17

    B. -15

    C. 1

    D. 5

8. Which of the following represents $1\frac{3}{4}$?

    A. $\frac{4}{4} + \frac{1}{4} + \frac{1}{2}$

    B. $\frac{4}{4} + \frac{1}{4} + \frac{1}{4}$

    C. $\frac{3}{4} + \frac{1}{4} + \frac{1}{4} + \frac{1}{4}$

    D. $\frac{4}{4} + \frac{3}{4} + \frac{2}{4} + \frac{1}{4}$

9. Kelly made 45 green bracelets, 30 black bracelets, and 20 brown and white bracelets. Which graph is best to depict this information?

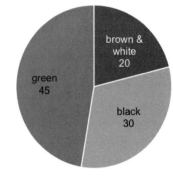

A.

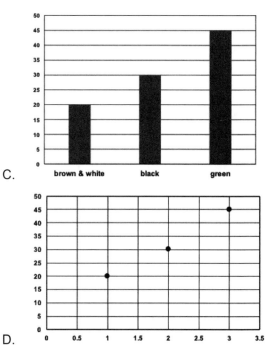

C.

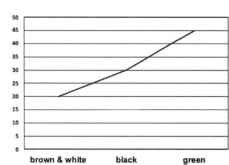

B.

D.

10. Select all the options that are equations.

- ☐ $3x - 7 = 2$
- ☐ $4x^2(x - 3)$
- ☐ $4x + 3 = 7x - 5$
- ☐ $(3 - y)(4 + y) = 0$
- ☐ $ab + bc$

11. Which of the following is an algebraic expression?

A. $2x = y + 7$

B. $ax^2 = bx + c$

C. $x^2 + 3x$

D. $2x + 3 = 4(x - 1)$

12. A canvas reproduction of a photograph costs $5 less than twice the price to print an 8" x 10" glossy photograph. Choose all options that represent this scenario.

- ☐ $5 - 2p$
- ☐ $2p - 5$
- ☐ $2(p - 1)5$
- ☐ $5(2p - 1)$
- ☐ $-5 + 2p$

13. Find the perimeter of a triangle with vertices $(2, 3), (2, 7), \text{and} (5, 3)$.

A. 6 units

B. 12 units

C. 13 units

D. 14 units

14. In which quadrant is the point $(-3, -6)$?

A. Quadrant I

B. Quadrant II

C. Quadrant III

D. Quadrant IV

15. Three noncollinear lines, a, b, and c all lie in the same plane. If lines a and b are perpendicular to c, which of the following must be true?

A. Line a is parallel to line b.

B. Line a is perpendicular to line b.

C. Lines a and b intersect at a point.

D. Line a is parallel to line c.

16. Use the boxes below to write the numbers in order from least to greatest.

$$\frac{5}{8} \qquad \frac{2}{3} \qquad \frac{7}{9} \qquad \frac{5}{9}$$

<table>
<tr><td> </td><td> </td><td> </td><td> </td></tr>
</table>

17. Simplify.

$$-5\left(2\right)+6-\left(-6\right)\left(-6\right)-8$$

   A.   −90

   B.   −48

   C.   12

   D.   24

18. Simplify.

$$\left(-4x^2+3x-8\right)-\left(3x^2-x+7\right)$$

   A. $-7x^2+2$

   B. $-7x^2+4x-15$

   C. $-x^2-5$

   D. $-7x^2+2x-1$

19. A box contains two red pens and one blue pen. What is the probability a red pen is selected from the box (without looking), and then without replacing the pen, that another red pen is selected?

   A. $\frac{1}{6}$

   B. $\frac{1}{3}$

   C. $\frac{1}{2}$

   D. $\frac{2}{3}$

20. Solve.

$$\frac{3}{4}\div\frac{1}{8}$$

   A. $\frac{1}{6}$

   B. $\frac{3}{2}$

   C.   2

   D.   6

21. Using the figure below, select the true statement.

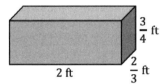

   A. The lateral area is twice as great as the surface area.

   B. The lateral area is 1 square unit greater than the surface area.

   C. The surface area is greater than the lateral area.

   D. The surface area is $5\frac{2}{3}$ square feet.

22. Mrs. Smith has a box of 72 pencils. She gives one-third of the box away to students during the first week of school. She then gives another 16 pencils away during the second week of school. On the third week, she gives away half of the remaining pencils. How many pencils does Mrs. Smith have after three weeks of school?

   A. 4

   B. 8

   C. 10

   D. 16

23. Which figure below depicts $2x+1$?

A.
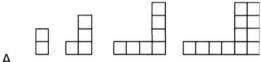

C.
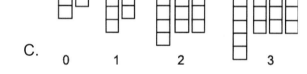

B.
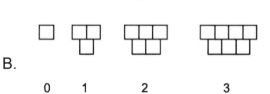

D.
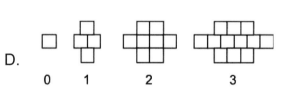

24. A meteor falls 12,000 feet in 24 seconds. It takes a total of 3 minutes and 15 seconds for the meteor to hit the earth. How many feet did the meteor fall?

   A. 12,000

   B. 36,000

   C. 75,200

   D. 97,500

25. Compare the 2 in 38,207 to the 2 in 2,451,039.

    A.   The first 2 is one one-hundredths times the second 2.

    B.   The first 2 is one one-thousandths times the second 2.

    C.   The first 2 is one ten-thousandths times the second 2.

    D.   The first 2 is one one-millionths times the second 2.

26. The expanded form $4 \times 100,000 + 3 \times 1,000 + 8 \times 100 + 6 \times 10,$ represents which of the answer choices?

    A.   430,860

    B.   403,860

    C.   403,086

    D.   438,060

27. Which of the following is an example of the distributive property?

    A. $\frac{3}{4}(2+a) = \frac{3}{4}(2) + \frac{3}{4}(a)$

    B. $2(3 \cdot a) = (2 \cdot 3)(a)$

    C. $(2x+1)(x) + (2x+1)(7) = (2x+1)(x+7)$

    D. $\frac{1}{2}x \cdot 1 = \frac{1}{2}x$

28. Which of the following probabilities has the highest likelihood of occurring?

    A.   10%

    B.   24%

    C.   60%

    D.   100%

29. Which of the graphs represents the solution set of $3 - 4x \geq -13$?

30. The weight of a man is 70 metric units. Which metric unit is most appropriate for this measurement?

    A.   milligrams

    B.   kilograms

    C.   grams

    D.   centigrams

31. Select TWO conversions that are true.

   ☐   4 g = 400 cg

   ☐   0.5 km = 5 m

   ☐   78 L = 7,800 mL

   ☐   45 m = 0.045 km

32. Choose all that are equivalent to 0.4.

   ☐   40%

   ☐ $\dfrac{2}{5}$

   ☐ $\dfrac{4}{100}$

   ☐ $\dfrac{8}{12}$

33. The total sales for $12 scarves can be represented by the equation $T = 12n$, where T is the total sales and n is the number of scarves sold. Which of the following represents the independent variable for this scenario?

   A.   The number of scarves sold

   B.   The $12 cost of the scarves

   C.   The total sales

   D.   The cost of n scarves

34. Which of the tables can be represented by the equation $y = 3x + 1$?

A.

x	y
0	1
1	3
2	6
5	15

C.

x	y
1	4
3	10
7	22
8	25

B.

x	y
0	1
3	7
5	9
7	11

D.

x	y
1	4
2	6
3	8
4	10

35. Solve $6y > 4y + 7$

    A. $y > \dfrac{7}{2}$

    B. $y < \dfrac{7}{2}$

    C. $y > -\dfrac{7}{2}$

    D. $y < -\dfrac{7}{2}$

36. Use the formula $F = \dfrac{9}{5}C + 32$ to convert 45 degrees Celsius to Fahrenheit.

    A. $33°F$

    B. $113°F$

    C. $1°F$

    D. $104°F$

37. Choose all the statements that are true about the number below.

    3,214.89

    ☐ The place value of the 2 is 100 times larger than the place value of the 4.

    ☐ The 9 is in the thousandths place.

    ☐ The place value of the 8 is one-tenth the place value of the 4.

    ☐ The place value of the 1 is 1,000 times larger than the place value of the 9.

38. A rectangular backyard is fenced in using 224 feet of fencing. All sides are fenced except the side against the house. If the length of the house is 80 feet, how wide is the backyard?

    A. 144 feet

    B. 72 feet

    C. 64 feet

    D. 8 feet

39. Given the formula $I = prt$, identify the dependent variable.

    A. I

    B. p

    C. r

    D. t

40. Which problem is depicted by the array below?

   A. 4×8

   B. 4×7

   C. 6×5

   D. 6×4

41. The football team is selling coupon cards for $20 each. For each card they sell, they make $10. Which answer choice represents how many cards they need to sell in order to raise at least $1,400?

   A. $10x < 1,400$

   B. $20x \geq 1,400$

   C. $10x \geq 1,400$

   D. $20x > 1,400$

42. Which number has the same prime factors as 15?

   A.   20

   B.   25

   C.   30

   D.   45

43. An ice cream shop has 12 flavors of ice cream and four toppings when they open. By 4:00 p.m., they ran out of two ice cream flavors and one topping. How many more combinations of one ice cream flavor and one topping could they offer before running out of two ice cream flavors and one topping?

   A.   12

   B.   18

   C.   30

   D.   48

44. East Middle School students were surveyed, and 252 of the students surveyed said they would like school uniforms. Given the pie chart of the survey results, how many students are undecided about school uniforms?

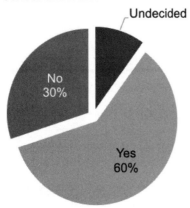

A. 10

B. 30

C. 60

D. 42

45. Mrs. Patter's science class conducted an experiment rolling a number cube with the numbers 1–6 on the faces. The cube was rolled 50 times with the following results.

Number Rolled	Number of Times Rolled
1	7
2	8
3	9
4	5
5	11
6	10

What is the experimental probability of rolling a 6?

A. $\frac{1}{5}$

B. $\frac{1}{6}$

C. $\frac{6}{50}$

D. $\frac{3}{5}$

46. Which of the graphs is best to show a correlation, if any, between two sets of data?

    A.   Histogram

    B.   Bar graph

    C.   Scatter plot

    D.   Pictograph

47. What is the y-coordinate of the point $(1, -5)$ after a reflection over the x-axis?

    A.   1

    B.   −1

    C.   5

    D.   −5

48. If $a = 24$, find the value of b for the equation $a = \frac{2}{3}b + 10$.

    A.   16

    B.   21

    C.   23

    D.   51

49. The list below shows the amounts of various ingredients in a recipe.

    · $\frac{1}{2}$ cup of brown sugar

    · $\frac{3}{4}$ cup of white sugar

    · $\frac{2}{3}$ cup of milk

    · $\frac{1}{3}$ cup of cream cheese

How many cups of ingredients are listed?

    A. $1\frac{1}{2}$

    B. $2\frac{1}{2}$

    C. $2\frac{1}{4}$

    D. $2\frac{3}{4}$

50. If $\frac{2}{7}x + 4 = 10$, find $2x - 4$.

    A.   37

    B.   38

    C.   20

    D.   21

This page intentionally left blank.

#	Answer	Category	Explanation
1.	$\frac{19}{10}$ and $\frac{190}{100}$	I	To solve, convert each fraction to a decimal by dividing the numerator (top number) by the denominator (bottom number). $\frac{19}{100} = 0.19$ $\frac{19}{10} = 1.9$ $\frac{1.9}{10} = 0.19$ $\frac{190}{100} = 1.9$
2.	B	I	To get 203.4 from 2.034, move the decimal point two places to the right. This means 203.4 is 10×10 greater or 10^2 greater, than 2.034.
3.	A	I	A factor is a number that divides evenly into another number. The only answer choice that divides evenly into 256 is 16.
4.	D	III	To find the sum of the measures of the interior angles in a polygon, use the formula, $(n-2)180$, where n represents the number of sides the polygon has. An octagon has 8 sides, so substituting 8 for n, $(8-2)180$ $6 \cdot 180 = 1,080$
5.	B	III	There is only one base, which is in the shape of a triangle. One base instead of two means the figure is a pyramid. Because the pyramid base is a triangle, it is a triangular pyramid.
6.	D	I	Substituting -4 in for x, $-x^2 - 9x$ $-(-4)^2 - 9(-4)$ $-(16) - 9(-4)$ $-16 - (-36)$ $-16 + 36 = 20$
7.	C	I	Following order of operations, $-8 + 3 \times 6 \div 2$ $-8 + 18 \div 2$ $-8 + 9 = 1$
8.	A	I	A is the correct answer. Answer choice B adds to $1\frac{1}{2}$. Answer choice C adds to $\frac{6}{4}$. Answer choice D adds to $2\frac{1}{2}$.

#	Answer	Category	Explanation
9.	C	III	When comparing different values in a category of data, like bracelets, a bar graph is best. A circle graph compares percents of numbers, a line graph is best for measuring change over time, and a scatter plot compares two different sets of data.
10.	$3x - 7 = 2$ $4x + 3 = 7x - 5$ $(3 - y)(4 + y) = 0$	II	Any math sentence that contains an equal sign (=) is an equation.
11.	C	II	Expressions do NOT contain an equal sign. The only answer choice without an equal sign is C.
12.	$2p - 5$ $-5 + 2p$	II	Five dollars less than twice the price means that we are taking 5 away from 2 times the photograph price or $2p - 5$. If the terms are switched around in the expression, you could also have $-5 + 2p$.
13.	B	III	First sketch the triangle on the coordinate plane. Notice that the two legs, or the sides that make the right angle, are 3 units and 4 units long. (Count squares on the grid to find vertical and horizontal lengths.) When two legs are 3 and 4 units, the hypotenuse is always 5. (Recall this is a 3-4-5 Pythagorean triple.) To find the perimeter, add all of the sides. $P = 3 + 4 + 5 = 12$ units
14.	C	III	The quadrants make a C if you start at quadrant I and go around the coordinate plane in order to quadrant IV. Thus, the point $(-3, -6)$ is in quadrant III.

#	Answer	Category	Explanation
15.	A	III	Draw a quick sketch of the scenario. For both a and b to be perpendicular to c, a and b must be parallel to each other.
16.	See answer explanation for drag and drop solution	I	ANSWER: Change each fraction to a decimal by dividing the numerator (top number) by the denominator (bottom number). Write out each number to 3 decimal places. $\dfrac{5}{8} = 0.625$ $\dfrac{2}{3} = 0.667$ $\dfrac{7}{9} = 0.778$ $\dfrac{5}{9} = 0.556$ From least to greatest, $0.556, 0.625, 0.667, 0.778$.
17.	B	I	Follow order of operations while being very careful of signs. $-5\left(2\right)+6-\left(-6\right)\left(-6\right)-8$ $-10+6-\left(-6\right)\left(-6\right)-8$ $-10+6-36-8$ $-4-36-8$ $-40-8 = -48$

#	Answer	Category	Explanation
18.	B	II	The easiest step to take when simplifying two expressions that are being subtracted is to change the sign to addition AND change every sign in the second expression. $$\left(-4x^2 + 3x - 8\right) - \left(3x^2 - x + 7\right)$$ $$= \left(-4x^2 + 3x - 8\right) + \left(-3x^2 + x - 7\right)$$ Next, add like terms. $$\left(-4x^2 + 3x - 8\right)$$ $$+\left(-3x^2 + x - 7\right)$$ $$\overline{\quad -7x^2 + 4x - 15}$$
19.	B	III	Probability is the total number of desirable outcomes over the total possible outcomes. For the first pick, there are two red pens out of three total pens, which is $\frac{2}{3}$. For the second pick, because the first pen is not replaced, there is now one red pen out of two total pens, which is $\frac{1}{2}$. When there are two separate events, multiply each probability together to get the probability of both events happening. The probability of picking two red pens is $\frac{2}{3} \times \frac{1}{2} = \frac{2}{6} = \frac{1}{3}$..
20.	D	I	To solve a division of fractions problem, multiply by the reciprocal. This is sometimes referred to in elementary classes as keep, change, flip (keep the first fraction the same, change the operation from division to multiplication, and flip the second fraction). $$\frac{3}{4} \div \frac{1}{8} = \frac{3}{4} \times \frac{8}{1} = \frac{24}{4} = 6$$
21.	C	III	Lateral area is the surface area of the faces; it excludes the areas of the bases. Therefore, the surface area will always be greater than the lateral area. This eliminates answer choices A and B and makes answer choice C correct. The surface area of the box is $6\frac{2}{3}$, making answer choice D incorrect.
22.	D	I	First, find one-third of the 72 pencils by dividing 72 by 3, which equals 24. Therefore, after giving away 24 pencils, she has 48 pencils left because $72 - 24 = 48$. Then she gives away another 16 pencils, leaving her with 32 pencils because $48 - 16 = 32$. Finally, she gives away half of the 32 pencils, leaving her with 16 pencils because $32 \div 2 = 16$.

#	Answer	Category	Explanation
23.	B	II	The easiest way to find the correct pattern is to make a table of values, using 0, 1, 2, 3 for x values (the number under the figures) and find the results using $2x+1$ in the y column.

x	$2x+1$
0	
1	
2	
3	

Next, fill out the y column of the table by substituting the x values into $2x+1$.

x	$2x+1$
0	1
1	3
2	5
3	7

The resulting numbers in the y column should be the number of squares in each of the corresponding patterns.
For this question, the number of squares that matches the values in the table is answer choice B.

#	Answer	Category	Explanation
24.	D	I	First, use the rate 12,000 feet in 24 seconds to find how many feet the meteor drops in 1 second.

$$\frac{12{,}000 \text{ ft}}{24 \text{ sec}} = 500 \text{ feet per second.}$$

Next, convert 3 minutes 15 seconds to seconds.
$3 \cdot 60 = 180$ and $180 + 15 = 195$ seconds. The meteor took 195 seconds to hit the earth. If it drops 500 feet per second, set up a proportion and solve.

$$\frac{500 \text{ ft}}{1 \text{ sec}} = \frac{x \text{ ft}}{195 \text{ sec}}$$
$$1x = 500(195)$$
$$x = 97{,}500$$

Note: *If you saw that you could multiply 500 and 195 without setting up the proportion, that works too.*

#	Answer	Category	Explanation
25.	C	I	The first 2 is in the hundreds place, and the second 2 is in the millions place, making them 4 place values away from one another. Because the first 2 is smaller, it is one-ten thousandths times smaller than the second 2.

As a number, this would be $\dfrac{1}{10{,}000} = \dfrac{1}{10^4} = \dfrac{1}{10 \times 10 \times 10 \times 10}$.

#	Answer	Category	Explanation
26.	B	I	To simplify standard form, look at each product: $4 \times 100,000$: 4 hundred thousand $3 \times 1,000$: 3 thousand 8×100: 8 hundred 6×10: 60 Writing that number out results in 403,860, which is answer choice B.
27.	A	I	Answer choice A is an example of the distributive property because a single value, $\frac{3}{4}$, is being "distributed" or multiplied to all terms added together inside parentheses. Answer choice B is an example of the associative property of multiplication. Answer choice C is an example of factoring out a binomial, and answer choice D is an example of the multiplicative identity of 1.
28.	D	III	The highest likelihood that an event will occur is 1 or 100% Therefore, D is the correct answer.
29.	C	II	Because the inequality symbol includes the "or equal to," the point will be filled in. This eliminates answer choices B and D. Next, solve the inequality for x. $3 - 4x \geq -13$ $3 - 3 - 4x \geq -13 - 3$ Subtract 3 from both sides. $\dfrac{-4x}{-4} \geq \dfrac{-16}{-4}$ Divide both sides by -4. $x \leq 4$ Flip the inequality symbol since dividing by a negative. Numbers less than or equal to 4 are to the left, or smaller than, 4, so C is the correct answer choice.
30.	B	III	Kilograms is the most appropriate measure for a man. A kilogram is about 2.2 pounds, so a 70 kg man would weigh about 154 pounds.
31.	See answer explanation for solution.	III	ANSWER: 4 g = 400 cg 45 m = 0.045 km For the other answer choices, the correct conversions would be 0.5 km = 500 m and 78 L = 78,000 mL.

#	Answer	Category	Explanation
32.	40% and $\frac{2}{5}$	I	To change 40% to a decimal, move the decimal point two places to the left. So, 40% = 0.40. To change a fraction to a decimal, divide the numerator by the denominator. $$\frac{2}{5} = 0.40$$ $$\frac{4}{100} = 0.04$$ $$\frac{8}{12} = 0.\overline{6}$$ Only the first two options are equivalent to 0.4.
33.	A	III	The independent variable is n, the number of scarves. The total sales depend on the number of scarves sold, so the total, T, is the dependent variable. The other answer choices are not variables and therefore not possible answer choices.
34.	C	II	To determine which table matches the equation, make sure to substitute 2 or 3 values of x into the equation to be sure you found the correct answer. Often the first number works, but the rest do not. The table that represents the equation is answer choice C. $$y = 3(1) + 1 = 4$$ $$y = 3(3) + 1 = 10$$ $$y = 3(7) + 1 = 22$$ $$y = 3(8) + 1 = 25$$ All values of x in the table match with their corresponding y when substituted into the equation.
35.	A	II	Move all the variables to the same side of the inequality. Then divide to get the solution. $6y > 4y + 7$ $6y - 4y > 4y - 4y + 7$ Subtract $4y$ from both sides. $2y > 7$ Simplify. $\frac{2y}{2} > \frac{7}{2}$ Divide both sides by 2. $y > \frac{7}{2}$ Solution.
36.	B	II	To solve, substitute 45 in for C and follow order of operations. $$F = \frac{9}{5} \cdot \frac{45}{1} + 32$$ $$F = 81 + 32 = 113$$

#	Answer	Category	Explanation
37.	See answer explanation for solution.	I	ANSWER: The place value of the 2 is 100 times larger than the place value of the 4. The place value of the 8 is one-tenth the place value of the 4. The place value of the 1 is 10^3 times larger than the place value of the 9. The option with 9 in the thousandths place is incorrect; it is in the hundredths place.
38.	B	III	To find the perimeter of a rectangle, add all the sides. In this case, one of the sides measuring 80 is not included because no fencing is needed against the house. x feet $P = 224$ feet x feet 80 feet $224 = 80 + x + x$ (Remember not to include the 2nd 80.) $224 = 80 + 2x$ $144 = 2x$ $72 = x$
39.	A	II	The dependent variable is the one that depends on all the other variables, typically the one alone on one side of an equation or formula. In this case, I is the dependent variable because the amount of interest earned depends on the principal amount invested, the rate, and the time of investment.
40.	D	I	The array has 6 rows and 4 columns, which represents the multiplication problem 6×4.
41.	C	II	The $20 is extra information. If the team makes $10 per card, or $10x$, and they want to earn $1,400 or more, then the correct inequality is C, $10x \geq 1,400$. **Note**: *Eliminate answers A and D right away because they do not have the correct inequality sign,* $\geq$.
42.	D	I	Answer choices A and C can be eliminated because they are even, which means that 2 is one of their prime factors. Answer choice B can also be eliminated because the only prime factor of 25 is 5. Therefore 15 and 45 have the same prime factors, 3 and 5.
43.	B	I	To find the total number of combinations of one ice cream flavor and one topping multiply how many of each there are together. Before running out of supplies: $12 \times 4 = 48$. After running short on supplies: $10 \times 3 = 30$. Therefore, they could offer $48 - 30 = 18$ more options before running out of supplies than they could after.

#	Answer	Category	Explanation
44.	D	III	First, find the percentage of students who are undecided. The circle graph represents 100% of the population, so subtract the given percentages from 100 to get the percent of students undecided. Undecided: $100 - 30 - 60 = 10\%$ Next, set up a proportion using the 252 students who want school uniforms, which is 60% on the circle graph, to find the total number of students surveyed. $$\frac{60\%}{100\%} = \frac{252 \text{ students}}{x \text{ students}}$$ $$60x = 100(252)$$ $$\frac{60x}{60} = \frac{25,200}{60}$$ $$x = 420$$ Last, find 10% of 420 students to find the number of students who are undecided. To find the percent of a number, change the percent to a decimal and multiply the two numbers. $0.10 \times 420 = 42$ students
45.	A	III	The experimental probability is how many times the event actually occurred over how many times the experiment was conducted. In this case, a 6 was rolled 10 times out of 50 total rolls for a probability of $\frac{10}{50} = \frac{1}{5}$.
46.	C	III	A scatter plot is the only graph that displays bivariate data, which is two different data sets, such as hours spent studying and grades on a test.
47.	C	III	When a point is reflected, or flipped, over the x-axis, the y-coordinate of the point changes signs. Therefore, $(1, -5)$ becomes $(1, 5)$.

#	Answer	Category	Explanation
48.	B	II	Substitute 24 for a in the equation and solve for b. $24 = \dfrac{2}{3}b + 10$ $\underline{-10 \qquad -10}$ $14 = \dfrac{2}{3}b$ You cannot change $\dfrac{2}{3}$ into a terminating decimal, so it is best to multiply both sides of the equation by its reciprocal, $\dfrac{3}{2}$. $\dfrac{3}{2} \cdot 14 = \dfrac{3}{2} \cdot \dfrac{2}{3}b$ $\dfrac{42}{2} = \dfrac{6}{6}b$ $21 = b$
49.	C	I	Add the fractions to get the sum of the cups of ingredients. Notice that you can add the last two fractions together to get one, so a common denominator is only needed for the first two fractions. $\dfrac{1}{2} + \dfrac{3}{4} + \dfrac{2}{3} + \dfrac{1}{3}$ $\dfrac{2}{4} + \dfrac{3}{4} + (1)$ $\dfrac{5}{4} + 1 = 1\dfrac{1}{4} + 1 = 2\dfrac{1}{4}$
50.	B	II	First, solve the equation for x. Then substitute the value found for x into the expression $2x - 4$. $\dfrac{2}{7}x + 4 = 10$ $\dfrac{7}{2} \cdot \dfrac{2}{7}x = 6 \cdot \dfrac{7}{2}$ $1x = \dfrac{42}{2}$ $x = 21$ Next, $2(21) - 4 = 42 - 4 = 38$

Social Studies Subtest

This page intentionally left blank.

The social studies subtest of the Praxis Elementary Education exam is designed to test your knowledge of social studies topics at both the elementary and middle school levels. The assessment is not aligned to a particular grade or course but is closely aligned to national social studies standards for both elementary and middle grades.

Test at a Glance	
Test Name	*Praxis*® Elementary Education Social Studies Subtest 5004
Format	Computer-based test (CBT)
Time	60 minutes; 1 minute per question
Number of Questions	Approximately 60 (field testing items may be added)
Passing Score	A scaled score of at least 155 for most states
Items Provided	Scratch paper and pencils
Format of Questions	Multiple choice (A, B, C, D)

Test Competency Breakdown			
	COMPETENCY	**Approximate Percentage of Total Test Questions**	**Approximate Number of Total Test Questions**
	I. United States History, Government, and Citizenship	45%	27
	II. Geography, Anthropology, and Sociology	30%	18
	III. World History and Economics	25%	15
	TOTAL	100%	60

I. United States History, Government, and Citizenship

Section I, United States history, government, and citizenship, tests your knowledge of the founding of the United States and important historical documents, figures, and developments leading to the establishment of the current system of government. You will be expected to identify laws, documents, historical figures, and parts of government. There will not be any questions that address the history of individual states.

The skills you need to know in this section include the following:

A. Knows European exploration and colonization in United States history and growth and expansion of the United States

B. Knows about the American Revolution and the founding of the nation in United States history

C. Knows the major events and developments in United States history from founding to present (e.g., westward expansion, industrialization, Great Depression)

D. Knows about twentieth-century developments and transformations in the United States (e.g., assembly line, space age)

E. Understands connections between causes and effects of events

F. Understands the nature, purpose, and forms (e.g., federal, state, local) of government

G. Knows key documents and speeches in the history of the United States (e.g., United States Constitution, Declaration of Independence, Gettysburg Address)

H. Knows the rights and responsibilities of citizenship in democracy

A. European exploration and colonization

The European colonization of the Americas was the invasion, settlement, and establishment of control of the continents of the Americas by various European powers: Spain, France, and England. The motives ranged from finding riches to spreading religion. The main motive was to find the Northwest Passage, which was believed to be a direct and efficient route to the Orient, where the European powers could claim spices, silks, and wealth.

Key Motives

- **Spanish** – Gold, Northwest Passage

- **French** – Spread Christianity, Northwest Passage

- **England** – Colonize, Northwest Passage

Explorers to Know

- **Christopher Columbus** – Made one of the most famous voyages of exploration in 1492 when he sailed from Palos, Spain in search of a route to Asia and the Indies. Instead, Columbus found the New World—the Americas.

- **Hernán Cortés** – In 1519, Cortés landed in Mexico with 600 men and fewer than 200 horses. Upon discovering the vast Aztec wealth, Cortés' motivations quickly changed from colonization and Christianity to acquiring gold. Cortés began the first phase of the Spanish colonization of the Americas and conquered the Aztec empire.

Exploration of the Americas Timeline

- **1000** – Leif Erikson discovers Vinland (New England).

- **1492** – Christopher Columbus discovers the New World (Hispaniola, San Salvador).

- **1497** – John Cabot discovers continental North America.

- **1507** – New World named after Amerigo Vespucci.

- **1513** – Vasco Nuñez de Balboa discovers the Pacific Ocean.

- **1519** – Hernán Cortés conquers Mexico by defeating the Aztecs and their leader Montezuma. The victory gave Spain a stronghold over Central American land and gold for years to come.

- **1521** – Ferdinand Magellan sails around the world.

First American Settlements

St. Augustine – The oldest city in the United States is St. Augustine, founded in 1565 by the Spanish. Ponce de León, a Spanish conquistador, explored St. Augustine looking for gold and other resources.

Jamestown – Jamestown, Virginia was the first permanent English colony in the Americas and was established in 1607.

Plymouth Colony – Plymouth Colony, America's first permanent Puritan settlement, was established by English Separatist Puritans in December 1620. The Pilgrims left England to seek religious freedom.

Rhode Island Colony – Founded in 1636 by Roger Williams, an English Puritan who advocated for religious freedom and the fair treatment of Native Americans (The Editors of Encyclopedia Britannica, n.d.).

The First Colonies

1st – Jamestown, Virginia (1607)

2nd – Plymouth, Massachusetts (1620)

The House of Burgesses

The House of Burgesses at Jamestown, Virginia, was the first legislative assembly in the colonies. The main player or name associated with the House of Burgesses is George Yeardley, who was Governor of the Virginia Colony.

Key Players and Events of American Colonization

- **The Pilgrims** – English Puritan separatists seeking religious freedom.

The 13 Colonies

- **New England Colonies**
  1. New Hampshire Colony
  2. Massachusetts Bay Colony
  3. Rhode Island Colony
  4. Connecticut Colony

- **Middle Colonies**
  5. New York Colony
  6. New Jersey Colony
  7. Pennsylvania Colony
  8. Delaware Colony

- **Southern Colonies**
  9. Maryland Colony
  10. Virginia Colony
  11. North Carolina Colony
  12. South Carolina Colony
  13. Georgia Colony

- **The Mayflower** – An English ship that transported the Puritans from England to the New World. The ship has become a cultural icon in the history of the United States.

- **The Mayflower Compact** – The first document of self-governance signed by the passengers of the Mayflower on September 16, 1620.

B. American Revolution

The American Revolution was the colonists' revolt against Great Britain from about 1765 to 1783. It began with a series of British taxes imposed on the colonists, which led to a clash of political ideologies, protests, and war. With the help of the French, the American colonists fought the British and won their independence. The 13 colonies formed the United States of America.

Main Players of the Revolutionary War

George Washington – Military general and 1st U.S. president

John Adams – Lawyer and diplomat, 2nd U.S. president

Sam Adams – Founding father, politician

Paul Revere – Patriot, midnight ride, "The British are coming…"

Thomas Jefferson – Founding father, 3rd U.S. president, principal author of the Declaration of Independence

Alexander Hamilton – Founding father, Federalist.

John Locke – Philosopher of the social contract theory, impacted the Declaration of Independence

Causes of the American Revolution

- **Stamp Act** – The Stamp Act was a tax put on the American colonies by the British in 1765.

- **Townshend Acts** – A series of laws passed by the British Parliament in 1767. The laws taxed goods (paper, paint, lead, glass, and tea) imported to the American colonies and established the following (History.com Editors, 2018):

  – American Customs Board in Boston to collect taxes

  – Courts in America to prosecute smugglers (without using a local jury)

  – The right of British officials to search colonists' houses and businesses

- **Boston Massacre** – Confrontation where a British soldier shot and killed several people in Boston. Leading patriots like Paul Revere and Samuel Adams used this as propaganda for the Revolutionary War (Antal, 2013).

- **Boston Tea Party** – A protest by the American Colonists against the British government. It occurred on December 16, 1773.

  – A result of the Tea Tax of 1773

  – Dumped 90,000 pounds of tea into Boston Harbor

  – Perpetrated by the Sons of Liberty

- **Sons of Liberty** – The Sons of Liberty was a secret organization created in the 13 American Colonies to advance the rights of the colonists and to fight taxation by the British government.

- **Samuel Adams** – Political writer, founder of the Sons of Liberty

- **Benedict Arnold** – Businessman, future general in the Continental Army, traitor, and coward

- **John Hancock** – Merchant, smuggler, fire warden

- **Patrick Henry** – Lawyer from Virginia, served as Virginia's first governor, leader of the Anti-Federalists who opposed the ratification of the 1787 U.S. Constitution

- **Paul Revere** – Silversmith from Boston, charged with notifying colonial militia of British troop movements prior to the Battle of Lexington and Concord

- **John Brown** – Businessman from Rhode Island First Political Parties

Political Parties

First Political Parties	
Federalist Party	Created by Alexander Hamilton; considered the "big government party"
Democratic-Republican Party	Created by Thomas Jefferson and James Madison; considered the "small government party"
Second Political Parties (The Democratic-Republican Party splits.)	
Republican Party	Henry Clay faction
Democratic Party	Andrew Jackson faction
Whig Party	An opposition to Jackson Transitioned into the Republican party

C. Major events and developments in the United States

Constitutional Era and Early Republic

- **Articles of Confederation** – First U.S. Constitution, weak central government, inability to levy taxes, inability to regulate interstate and international trade, each state was represented by one vote regardless of its size.

- **Constitutional Convention** – Meeting with delegates to establish a stronger constitution. The opposition felt the Constitution increased the power of the executive branch but failed to provide protection of individual rights. Eventually, the Bill of Rights was added to appease the anti-federalists and ratify the Constitution in 1787 (Rosen and Rubenstein, n.d.).

Magna Carta

English common law signed in 1212, which established that individuals have natural rights of security, liberty, and property. Samuel Adams believed the colonists were entitled to these same rights and referenced the Magna Carta when he wrote The Rights of Colonists (Smithsonian, n.d.).

Presidents of the Early Republic under the U.S. Constitution

- **George Washington (1789–1797)** – No political party affiliation; former military general; served two terms.

- **John Adams (1797–1801)** – Federalist; favored a strong central government; served one term.

- **Thomas Jefferson (1801–1809)** – Democratic-Republican; brokered the Louisiana Purchase; served two terms.

- **James Madison (1809–1817)** – Democratic-Republican; president during the War of 1812 and the burning of the national capital; served two terms.

The Adams Family

Samuel Adams – Patriot, founder of the Sons of Liberty

John Adams – 2nd president and 2nd cousin of Samuel Adams

John Quincy Adams – 6th president and son of John Adams

Charles Francis Adams – Key U.S. diplomat during the American Civil War, son of John Quincy Adams

---

Westward Expansion

Many factors contributed to the westward expansion, which was the movement of settlers into the American West from about 1840 to 1850. The primary factors for the expansion were population growth and search for new land for economic benefit. The westward expansion was fueled by the *Gold Rush*, the *Oregon Trail*, and the belief in *Manifest Destiny* (History.com Editors, 2019).

- **Gold Rush** – When gold was discovered in California in 1848, people from California were the first to rush to the goldfields. News quickly spread to Oregon and Latin America and eventually throughout the world.

- **Oregon Trail** – A major route from Missouri to Oregon that pioneers used to migrate west.

- **Manifest Destiny** – Belief that the United States was destined by God to expand control and spread democracy across the continent.

- **The Louisiana Purchase (1803)** – The Louisiana Purchase was a land deal between the United States and France in which the United States acquired approximately 827,000 square miles of land west of the Mississippi River for $15 million. The Louisiana Purchase occurred during Thomas Jefferson's term as president.

  Eventually, 15 states were added to the Union because of the Louisiana Purchase: Louisiana, Missouri, Arkansas, Iowa, Minnesota, Nebraska, Kansas, Colorado, North Dakota, South Dakota, Wyoming, Oklahoma, Texas, Montana, and New Mexico.

- **Lewis and Clark Expedition (1804)** – President Thomas Jefferson instructed Meriwether Lewis and William Clark to explore the area gained from the recent Louisiana Purchase. During the 8,000-mile expedition, Lewis and Clark endured dangerous terrain, extreme weather, injuries, and disease. They encountered friendly and hostile Native American tribes. From the experience, they were able to provide a detailed description of the geographic, ecological, and social features of the new region (History.com Editor, 2009).

- **The Erie Canal (1825)** – The Erie Canal is a man-made waterway that connects the Atlantic Ocean— through New York City—to the Great Lakes. The completion of the Erie Canal was significant because it allowed people and freight to travel between the eastern seaboard and the Michigan port (Klein, 2018), allowing for cheaper transportation.

- **The Fort Laramie Treaty of 1851** – This treaty between the United States and representatives of several Native American tribes assigned each tribe a defined territory, where they were to remain (reservations). The Fort Laramie Treaty was later broken by the U.S. government when gold was discovered on the land that was assigned to the Native American tribes. The United States seized back the land and pushed Native Americans farther into isolated territories.

War of 1812

There were several catalysts to the War of 1812:

- A series of trade restrictions introduced by Britain to impede American trade with France

- The British support for Native Americans, who were offering armed resistance to the expansion of the American frontier to the Northwest

- A refusal by the British to give up lands in the western part of America

- Seizure of American ships

During the War of 1812, several Native American tribes fought for the British to stop the westward expansion into their homeland.

Neither the British nor the United States had a substantial victory in the War of 1812. Both sides wanted the war to end and agreed to restore the status quo antebellum (before the war) with the Treaty of Ghent.

Antebellum Period

The Antebellum Period in American history is considered to be the period after the War of 1812 and before the Civil War. It was characterized by an unstable political environment, including the rise of abolition and the gradual polarization of the country between abolitionists and supporters of slavery. This eventually led to the Civil War (History.net, 2019).

Presidents During the Antebellum Period

- **James Monroe (1817–1825)** – Democratic-Republican; signed the Missouri Compromise making Maine a free state and Missouri a slave state; gave the famous "Monroe Doctrine" speech to warn Europeans against further colonization; served two terms.

- **John Quincy Adams (1825–1829)** – National Republican; defeated Andrew Jackson for the presidency, which split the Democratic-Republican party into two political parties; oversaw the completion of the Erie Canal; served one term.

- **Andrew Jackson (1829–1837)** – Democrat; supported state's rights to expand slavery; implemented the Indian Removal Act, which allowed the government to forcibly move Native Americans west of the Mississippi River (also known as the Trail of Tears); implemented poor economic policies that created the financial crisis of 1837; served two terms.

- **Martin Van Buren (1837–1841)** – Democrat; president during the economic Panic of 1837; served one term.

- **William Henry Harrison (1841)** – Whig Party; died 32 days after taking office; known for the shortest presidency in U.S. history; served less than one term.

- **John Tyler (1841–1845)** – Whig Party; vice president to William Henry Harrison and successor after Harrison's death; vetoed several bills, which led his own party to attempt to impeach him; served one term.

- **James K. Polk (1845–1849)** – Democrat; significantly expanded the country with the annexation of Texas, Oregon Compromise with Great Britain, and Mexican Cession after the Mexican-American War; supported Jacksonian democracy and slavery; served one term.

- **Zachary Taylor (1849–1850)** – Whig Party; opposed new slave states; supported statehood of California as a free state; negotiated the Compromise of 1850 (finalized two months after his death); died of cholera while in office.

- **Millard Fillmore (1850–1853)** – Whig Party; vice president to Zachary Taylor and successor after Taylor's death; served one term.

- **Franklin Pierce (1853–1857)** – Democrat; signed the Kansas-Nebraska Act, which allowed people of these territories to choose to become a free or slave state (also known as "popular sovereignty"); exacerbated the rift within the Democratic Party and increased tension over slavery; served one term.

- **James Buchanan (1857–1861)** – Democrat; supported the Supreme Court decision in Dred Scott v. Sanford, which stated that black people, "were not and could never become citizens of the United States (Eschner, 2017)"; fanned the fury between abolitionists and pro-slavery supporters; served one term.

The Civil War (1861–1865)

As the United States moved closer to a civil war, sectionalism became a problem as the country became increasingly divided. People no longer had loyalty to the entire nation. Rather, their loyalty was only to a part of the nation. The Civil War was the war between the Union (north) and the Confederacy (south), and it resulted in roughly 700,000 deaths. There were many positive effects of the Civil War:

Quick Tip

Conscription was the compulsory enlistment of people in a <u>national service</u>, most often a <u>military service</u>. It was similar to the U.S. draft during the Vietnam War.

- Dissolution of the Confederacy

- Re-uniting the country

- Abolished slavery

- Beginning of the Reconstruction era, which aimed to rebuild the Union after the Civil War

- Passing of the Thirteenth, Fourteenth, and Fifteenth Amendments or the "Reconstruction Amendments"

  - Thirteenth Amendment – Abolished slavery

  - Fourteenth Amendment – Granted equal civil and legal rights to freed slaves

  - Fifteenth Amendment – Prohibits federal or state government from denying a citizen the right to vote based on color

President During the Civil War

- **Abraham Lincoln (1861–1865)** – Republican; ordered Union naval blockade of the South; delivered landmark Gettysburg Address; preserved the Union during the worst political and moral crisis in U.S. history; abolished slavery; assassinated while in office; served one term.

Key Players of the Civil War

- **Ulysses S. Grant** – Top Union general after General George B. McClellan's termination; waged total war against the South starting in 1863, including major victory at Vicksburg

- **Robert E. Lee** – General who turned down Lincoln's offer to command Union forces in favor of commanding the Army of Northern Virginia for the Confederacy

- **Stonewall Jackson** – Confederate general during the Civil War

- **Jefferson Davis** – Elected president of the Confederate States of America

- **Charles Francis Adams** – U.S. diplomat for Abraham Lincoln who effectively kept France and Great Britain out of the war (Burlingame, n.d.)

Immigration and Migration During the Late 19th and Early 20th Centuries

In the late 1800s, many people from various parts of the world immigrated to the United States because it was perceived as the land of economic opportunity.

When people migrate to another country, it is usually because something pushes them away from their native country and pulls them toward a new place. This idea is called the push-pull factor.

- **Agrarianism** – A social and political philosophy that values rural society as superior to urban society. Property ownership and family farming, which is a way of life that can shape the ideal social values, are central to agrarianism.

- **Industrialization** – The process by which an economy is transformed from primarily agricultural to one based on the manufacturing of goods.

- **Urbanization** – Refers to the population shift from rural areas to urban areas.

Industrial Revolution

The Industrial Revolution, which began in the middle of the 18th century (approximately 1750), was the transition from an agrarian (farming) economy to an industrialized economy (Encyclopedia Britannica, 1998).

Players of the Industrial Revolution

Andrew Carnegie – Steel

John D. Rockefeller – Oil

Karl Marx – Worker revolution

Eli Whitney – Cotton gin

Key Features of the Industrial Revolution (Pettinger, 2016)

- Population shifted; people moved from rural areas and agriculture work to cities and factory work.

- Goods were mass-produced.

- Increased efficiency, increased production, and lower costs.

- Wages increased.

- Technology developments increased.

- Many wealthy industrialists became philanthropists.

- Government regulations increased, leading to standards in health care and education.

Impacts of the Industrial Revolution (Pettinger, 2016)

- **Child labor** – Children were exploited by manufacturers. They received extremely low pay and were often involved in accidents resulting in dismemberment or death.

- **Poor sanitation** – People were living in areas of higher concentration. Poor sanitation caused outbreaks of infectious diseases.

- **The Slave Trade** – The textile industry was still reliant on slave labor.

Key Events of the Industrial Revolution (Pettinger, 2016)

- **Marxism** – Karl Marx wrote *Das Capital* and *The Communist Manifesto*. Marx argued capitalism exploited the workers (the Proletariat) and anticipated an overthrow of capitalism.

- **Trade unions and working-class movements** – Workers organized to demand better conditions.

- **Suffragette movement** – Women's groups organized to gain political rights. Suffrage was granted in 1920 with the ratification of the 19th amendment, which granted women the right to vote.

- **Nationalist movements** – Industrialism created a stronger sense of collective society.

- **Chinese Exclusion Act of 1882** – The Chinese Exclusion Act of 1882 prohibited immigration of Chinese laborers.

- **The Sherman Antitrust Act of 1890** – The Sherman Antitrust Act of 1890 was the first federal law that outlawed monopolistic business practices.

- **The Federal Reserve Act of 1913** – The Federal Reserve Act established the Federal Reserve System and Central Bank to oversee monetary policy.

Presidents During the Late 19th and Early 20th Centuries

- **Andrew Johnson (1865–1869)** – Democrat; assumed office after the assassination of Abraham Lincoln during the reconstruction era of the Union; vetoed the Freedmen's Bureau bill and the Civil Rights bill; first American president to be impeached; served one term.

- **Ulysses S. Grant (1869–1877)** – Republican; commanded the Union army during the Civil War; assumed office in the middle of the Reconstruction era; worked to reconcile the North and South; protected the civil rights of freed slaves; signed legislation that limited the activities of white terrorist groups like the Ku Klux Klan; negotiated the 1871 Treaty of Washington; served two terms.

- **Rutherford B. Hayes (1877–1881)** – Republican; withdrew troops from the Reconstruction states and ended the Reconstruction era; led the way to civil service reform; appointed Southerners to federal positions; made financial appropriations for Southern improvements; served one term.

- **James A. Garfield (1881)** – Republican; addressed civil service reform; initiated reform of the Post Office Department; assassinated; served one term.

- **Chester A. Arthur (1881–1885)** – Republican; advocated for civil service reform; signed the Pendleton Civil Service Act; signed the Chinese Exclusion Act of 1882; encouraged modernization of the U.S. Navy; served one term.

- **Grover Cleveland (1885–1889)** – Democrat; attempted to reduce government spending; fought to have protective tariffs lowered; credited for the Interstate Commerce Act and the Dawes General Allotment Act; served one term.

- **Benjamin Harrison (1889–1893)** – Republican; supported the passage of the McKinley Tariff Act of 1890; signed the Sherman Antitrust Act; advocated for veterans' benefits, forest conservation, and the expansion of the U.S. Navy; served one term.

- **Grover Cleveland (1893–1897)** – Democrat; worked to alleviate the Treasury crisis; repealed the Sherman Silver Purchase Act of 1890; served one term.

- **William McKinley (1897–1901)** – Republican; raised customs duties; resulting in the Dingley Tariff Act; intervened in the conflict between Cuba and Spain, resulting in the Spanish American War; supported the Treaty of Paris, which officially ended the Spanish American War; supported the Open Door policy; assassinated; served one term.

- **Theodore Roosevelt (1901–1909)** – Republican; advocated for conservation for 200 million acres for national forests, reserves, and wildlife refuges; supported the National Reclamation Act; facilitated the start of construction on the Panama Canal; negotiated an end to the Russo-Japanese War; served two terms.

- **William Howard Taft (1909–1913)** – Republican; supported the Payne-Aldrich Tariff; encouraged nationwide commerce and trade by forming a parcel post service; set railroad rates through the Interstate Commerce Commission; supported the Sixteenth Amendment that called for a federal income tax and the Seventeenth Amendment for the direct election of senators by the people; served one term.

D. Twentieth-century developments and transformations

World War I

World War I (WWI) was also known as the Great War. The assassination of Archduke Franz Ferdinand of Austria, heir to the Austro-Hungarian throne, and his wife Sophie, Duchess of Hohenberg, occurred on June 28, 1914 in Sarajevo. This was the catalyst to World War I.

The world powers aligned into two groups:

Allied Powers	Central Powers
France	Austria-Hungary
Britain	Germany
Russia	Ottoman Empire
United States	Bulgaria

President During World War I

- **Woodrow Wilson (1913–1921)** – Democrat, founder public administration theories, resisted pressure to enter World War I until it could no longer be avoided, served two terms.

Key Events During World War I

- **Espionage Act** – Congress passed the Espionage Act, which made it illegal to interfere with the operation of the military. This included obstructing the recruitment of servicemen into the military.

- **Schenck v. United States** – Charles Schenck is arrested for distributing leaflets urging men to resist the military draft and convicted of violating the Espionage Act. He appealed to the Supreme Court, claiming the federal government was infringing on his First Amendment right of free speech. The court determined speech (written or spoken) that created a clear and present danger to society was not protected by the First Amendment (Encyclopedia Britannica Editors, n.d.).

World War I Timeline

1914

- Archduke Franz Ferdinand of Austria-Hungary is assassinated in Sarajevo by Serbian, Gavrilo Princip.
- Austria-Hungary declares war on Serbia.
- Germany declares war on Russia.
- December 24 – Christmas Truce.

Arrest of the Archduke's assasin

1915

- The Allies launch offensive against the Ottoman Empire at the Battle of Gallipoli. The Ottomans defeated the Allies after an 8-month battle.
- Germans torpedo the British-owned steamship Lusitania, setting off a chain of events that led to the U.S. entering WWI.

British ship Lusitania

1917

- The Zimmerman Telegram (a secret communication between Germany and Mexico, describing their possible alliance) was intercepted and decoded by British intelligence.
- The Zimmerman Telegram is considered one of the main reasons the U.S. entered WWI.

1918

- January 8 – President Woodrow Wilson issues his Fourteen Points plan to end the war.
- March 21 – Germany launches the Spring Offensive hoping to defeat the Allies before the United States military can be deployed.
- Germany agrees to an armistice and fighting comes to an end at 11am on 11/11/1918 (11-11-11).

Woodrow Wilson

Treaty of Versailles signing

1919

- June 28 – The Treaty of Versailles, a peace treaty, is signed, officially ending the war.
- The United States did not sign the treaty because the Senate did not want to join the League of Nations.

Interwar Period

The Interwar Period refers to the time between the end of World War I and the beginning of World War II.

U.S. Presidents During the Interwar Period

- **Warren G. Harding (1921–1923)** – Republican; reduced taxes for corporations and the wealthy; supported high protective tariffs; limited immigration; signed the Budget and Accounting Act of 1921; died of a heart attack; served one term.

- **Calvin Coolidge (1923–1929)** – Republican; finished Harding's term; cut taxes; limited government spending; supported small government; set high tariffs on imported goods; refused U.S. membership in the League of Nations; served two terms.

> **Quick Tip**
>
> During the Roaring 20s, both President Harding and President Coolidge adopted a *laissez-faire* approach to the economy, where the government did not interfere with business. This approach left the market unregulated and was a contributing factor to the stock market crash of 1929.

The Roaring 20s

The Roaring 20s was an age of dramatic social and political change and the beginning of modern America. Most Americans moved to the cities during this period. The nation's total wealth more than doubled between 1920 and 1929, making way for the *consumer society* (History.com Editors, 2019).

- **F. Scott Fitzgerald** – Author of *The Great Gatsby*

- **Andrew Mellon** – Treasury secretary; tax breaks for the wealthy

- **Henry Ford** – Assembly line

The Harlem Renaissance

The Harlem Renaissance refers to the development of the Harlem neighborhood in New York City as a cultural mecca for African Americans in the early 20th century. The Harlem Renaissance is considered a golden age in African-American culture, manifesting in literature, music, stage performance, and art (History.com Editors, 2019).

- **Langston Hughes** – Poet and activist

- **Zora Neale Hurston** – Author

- **Louis Armstrong** – Jazz musician

The Great Depression (1929–1939)

The Great Depression was the worst economic downturn in the history of the industrialized world. When the Great Depression reached its lowest point, approximately 15 million Americans were unemployed and nearly half the country's banks had failed (History.com Editors, 2019).

- **Stock Market Crash of October 1929** – Millions of shares of stocks were traded after a wave of economic panic, causing their value to plummet.

- **The Dust Bowl 1930s** – A drought-stricken area in the Southern Plains of the United States. The Dust Bowl intensified the economic impacts of the Great Depression. Because of the Dust Bowl, many farming families set off on a migration across the United States in search of work and better living conditions (History.com Editors, 2017).

- **New Deal (1933–1939)** – A series of programs, public work projects, financial reforms, and regulations enacted by President Franklin D. Roosevelt in the United States between 1933 and 1936. The New Deal included new constraints and safeguards on the banking industry and efforts to re-inflate the economy after prices had fallen sharply.

- **The Securities and Exchange Act of 1934** – The Securities Exchange Act of 1934 is sweeping legislation enacted after the stock market crash in 1929 to regulate transactions on the secondary market and ensure financial transparency of publicly traded companies.

Presidents During the Great Depression

- **Herbert Hoover (1929–1933)** – Republican; took much of the blame for the stock market crash of 1929; served one term.

- **Franklin Delano Roosevelt (1933–1945)** – Democrat; led the nation through the Great Depression by implementing the New Deal; led the country during World War II; elected three times; served 12 years.

World War II

World War II (WWII) was a global conflict that lasted from 1939 to 1945. The conflict involved the vast majority of the world's nations, including all the superpowers.

The superpowers formed two opposing military alliances:

Allied Powers	Axis Powers
Great Britain – Winston Churchill	Germany – Adolph Hitler
Soviet Union – Joseph Stalin	Italy – Benito Mussolini
United States – Franklin Delano Roosevelt, Harry S. Truman	Japan – Emperor Hirohito
China – Chiang Kai-shek	

After World War I, the American public felt foreign affairs should be avoided and advocated for peace through isolation (Link, 2019). The United States was reluctant to enter the war because of the economic crisis happening at home.

Roosevelt implemented a central management system of resources in order to supply the war. This included rations on civilians for food and essential products. As men went to war, women and minorities took jobs in factories and assembly lines manufacturing the products used in the war. This helped end discriminatory employment practices by federal contractors (Link, 2019).

Presidents During World War II

- **Franklin Delano Roosevelt (1933–1945)** – Democrat; led the nation through the Great Depression by implementing the New Deal; led the country during World War II; elected three times; served 12 years.

- **Harry S. Truman (1945–1953)** – Democrat; vice president to Franklin Delano Roosevelt and successor after Roosevelt's death; staunch anti-communist who did not trust Stalin; authored the Truman Doctrine; served two terms.

World War II Timeline

Events Leading to WWII

- **1933** – Adolf Hitler, head of the Nazi Party (the Third Reich) becomes Chancellor of Germany.

- **1936** – Nazi Germany and Fascist Italy form the Rome-Berlin Axis Treaty.

- **1937** – Japan invades China.

- **1939** – Germany invades Poland, marking the official beginning of WWI.

During WWII

- **1940** – Winston Churchill becomes Prime Minister of England.

- **1940** – Italy enters the war as a member of the Axis Powers.

The Catalyst

Many scholars assert one of the major catalysts to World War II was the Treaty of Versailles, an agreement signed between Germany and the Allied Powers, marking the end World War I. Germany was required to take responsibility for the war, pay retributions, and make territorial concessions to certain countries. This is often cited as the reason many Germans were bitter over the deal and why they voted for the Nazi Party.

- **1941** – The Axis Powers launch a massive attack on the Soviet Union consisting of over four million troops.

- **1941** – The Japanese attack Pearl Harbor and destroy nearly 20 American naval vessels, including eight battleships and over 300 airplanes. More than 2,400 Americans died in the attack, including civilians, and another 1,000 people were wounded. This event pulled the United States into WWII.

- **1944** – D-Day and the Normandy invasion. Allied forces invade France, forcing the Germans back.

- **1945** – United States Marines invade Iwo Jima. Each side suffered heavy losses before the Marines finally took the island.

- **1945** – Franklin D. Roosevelt (FDR) dies and is succeeded by Harry S. Truman.

- **1945** – Adolf Hitler commits suicide.

- **1945** – Germany surrenders to the Allies ending the European conflict of World War II.

- **1945** – Truman orders a nuclear attack on Hiroshima and Nagasaki, Japan. Over 200,000 people were killed.

- **1945** – Japan surrenders to the Allies, ending the war.

The Manhattan Project (1942–1946)

The Manhattan project was the research and development of the nuclear bomb. The project was top secret and took place in Oakridge, Tennessee. It was led by the U.S. with the support of Canada and United Kingdom.

The Cold War (1945–1990)

The Cold War was a post-World War II period of geopolitical tension between the United States and its allies and the Soviet Union and its satellite states. The conflict is referred to as a "cold war" because there was no large-scale fighting directly between the two sides; however, there were minor proxy-wars, military build-ups, and political posturing, which brought the world dangerously close to another major conflict.

Key Terms of the Cold War

- **Superpowers** – A powerful, influential nation with a bloc of allies; specifically, the United States and the Soviet Union during the Cold War.

- **Containment** – A United States policy using numerous strategies to prevent the spread of communism abroad. A component of the Cold War, this policy was a response to a series of moves by the Soviet Union to enlarge its communist sphere of influence in Eastern Europe, China, Korea, and Vietnam.

- **Domino Theory** – The theory that a political event in one country will cause similar events in neighboring countries, like a falling domino causing an entire row of upended dominoes to fall.

Key Events of the Cold War

- **Truman Doctrine (1947)** – With the Truman Doctrine, President Harry S. Truman established that the United States would provide political, military, and economic assistance to all democratic nations under threat from external or internal authoritarian forces.

- **Marshall Plan (1948)** – Also known as the European Recovery Program, this was a United States program providing aid to Western Europe following the devastation of World War II. In addition to economic redevelopment, one of the stated goals of the Marshall Plan was to halt the spread of communism on the European continent. The plan was a major proponent of Containment.

- **Berlin Airlift (1948)** – In response to the Soviet blockade of land routes into West Berlin, the United States conducted a massive airlift of food, water, and medicine to the citizens of the besieged city.

- **North Atlantic Treaty Organization (NATO) (1949)** – NATO is a formal alliance between the territories of North America and Europe. NATO's main purpose was to defend each other from the possibility of communist Soviet Union taking control of their nation.

- **The Arms Race (1949)** – Competition between the United States and the Soviet Union to develop the first nuclear weapons program.

- **Warsaw Pact (1955)** – Soviet response to NATO. Formed the Eastern Bloc of nations led by the Soviet Union. The Warshaw Pact included the Soviet Union, Albania, Poland, Czechoslovakia, Hungary, Bulgaria, Romania, and the German Democratic Republic.

- **The Space Race (1957)** – Competition between the United States and the Soviet Union to develop the first space program.

  - Russians launch Sputnik into space in 1957.

  - United States amps up its space program.

  - Kennedy wants to beat Russia to the moon.

  - United States is the first to land men on the moon in 1969.

- **Bay of Pigs Invasion (1961)** – A failed attempt to overthrow Fidel Castro (president of Cuba). Cuban exiles trained and financed by the CIA launched an ill-fated invasion of Cuba from the sea in the Bay of Pigs. It was one of President Kennedy's biggest failures.

- **Cuban Missile Crisis (1962)** – The Cuban Missile Crisis of October 1962 was a direct and dangerous confrontation between the United States and the Soviet Union during the Cold War and was the moment when the two superpowers came closest to nuclear conflict.

- **Anti-Ballistic Missile Treaty (1972)** – Agreement between the United States and the Soviet Union to limit the use of ballistic missiles to defend other countries.

- **Perestroika (1979)** – The Soviet Union's restructuring of its economic and political system. Perestroika was intended to improve social and working conditions for the masses. First proposed by Leonid Brezhnev in 1979 and actively promoted by Mikhail Gorbachev, perestroika originally referred to increased automation and labor efficiency but came to entail greater awareness of economic markets and the ending of central planning. The policy was seen as an attempt to democratize the communist Soviet Union.

- **Intermediate-Range Nuclear Forces (INF) Treaty (1987)** – Agreement between the United States and the Soviet Union to decrease nuclear arsenals signed by Ronald Reagan and Mikhail Gorbachev.

Key Individuals of the Cold War

1. **Joseph Stalin** – Communist dictator of the Soviet Union from 1924–1953. He turned against the United States and Britain after World War II.

2. **Leonid Brezhnev** – General Secretary of the Soviet Union's Communist Party from 1964–1982. He expanded the Soviet military.

3. **Nikita Khrushchev** – In 1954, he became the first secretary of the Soviet Union's Communist Party. He denounced Stalin and lessened government control over citizens.

4. **Mikhail Gorbachev** – General Secretary of the Communist Party of the Soviet Union from 1985–1991. He reformed the Soviet Union, effectively ending the Cold War.

Presidents During the Cold War

- **Harry S. Truman (1945–1953)** – Democrat; vice president to Franklin Delano Roosevelt and successor after Roosevelt's death; staunch anti-communist who did not trust Stalin; authored the Truman Doctrine; served two terms.

- **Dwight Eisenhower (1953–1961)** – Republican; served as the supreme commander of the Allied forces in WWII prior to his presidency; managed tensions during the Cold War; ended the Korean War; implemented covert Central Intelligence Agency operations throughout the world to stop communism; served two terms.

- **John F. Kennedy (1961–1963)** – Democrat; successfully got Soviet nuclear weapons out of Cuba during the Cuban Missile Crisis; instrumental leader in the Civil Rights Movement; assassinated in Texas in 1963; served less than one term.

- **Lyndon B. Johnson (1963–1969)** – Democrat; vice president to John F. Kennedy and successor after Kennedy's assassination; served one term.

- **Richard Nixon (1969–1974)** – Republican; expanded United States involvement in the Vietnam War; initiated the Anti-Ballistic Treaty with the Soviet Union; resigned from office in his second term after impeachment hearings for cheating in the election; served less than two terms.

- **Gerald Ford (1974–1977)** – Republican; vice president to Richard Nixon and successor after Nixon's resignation; served one term.

- **Jimmy Carter (1977–1981)** – Democrat; struggled to manage the energy crisis and unemployment in the late 1970s; failed to free Americans in the Iran hostage crisis; served one term.

- **Ronald Reagan (1981–1989)** – Republican; instrumental in diplomacy with the Soviet Union to end the Cold War; implemented "trickle-down economics" and "The War on Drugs"; served two terms.

> **United States v. Richard Nixon**
>
> During an ongoing impeachment process for Richard Nixon, the Supreme Court ordered Nixon to hand over tape recordings of his conversations with those involved with Watergate—a scandal involving a break in at the Democratic National Committee headquarters. The Watergate scandal led to an uncovering of a number of abuses of powers by the Nixon administration. The United States v. Richard Nixon is considered the most crucial Supreme Court case limiting executive privilege.

The Civil Rights Movement

The Civil Rights Movement began in the late 1940s. The movement was initiated by African Americans as an effort to end racial discrimination. By the 1960s, laws were passed to help protect the civil rights of every American citizen.

Civil Rights Movement Timeline

- **1948** – President Truman issues an executive order to end segregation in the armed services.

- **1954** – Brown v. The Topeka Board of Education is a landmark U.S. Supreme Court case ruling that declared racial segregation in public schools unconstitutional.

- **1955** – Rosa Parks refuses to give up her seat on a bus to a white man in Montgomery, Alabama. This incident sparks a yearlong boycott of city buses in Montgomery.

- **1957** – President Eisenhower is forced to send federal troops to Arkansas to protect nine African-American students while they integrated into high school. These African-American students are known as the Little Rock Nine.

- **1957** – Eisenhower signs the Civil Rights Act of 1957. The law protects voter rights.

- **1960** – A series of "sit-ins" take place around the country inspired by four black youths refusing to leave a "whites only" lunch counter inside a Woolworth store in Greensboro, North Carolina.

> **Jim Crow Laws**
>
> Jim Crow Laws were used to enforce racial segregation in public areas and facilities. Beginning in the 1870s and 1880s, Jim Crow Laws were upheld by the Supreme Court under the separate but equal legal doctrine, established with the court case Plessy v. Ferguson. These laws were enforced until 1965.

- **1963** – 250,000 people march on Washington, D.C. for jobs and freedom. Dr. Martin Luther King Jr. gives his "I Have a Dream" speech on the steps of the Lincoln Memorial.

- **1963** – A bomb kills four young girls at the 16th Street Baptist Church in Birmingham, Alabama, sparking protests around the country.

- **1963** – President John F. Kennedy is assassinated, and Lyndon B. Johnson is sworn in as president of the United States.

- **1964** – President Johnson signs the Civil Rights Act of 1964. The law prevents employment discrimination based on race, color, creed, religion, or nationality.

- **1965** – Malcom X is assassinated.

- **1965** – March from Selma, Alabama, to Montgomery, Alabama, in protest of voter suppression.

- **1965** – President Johnson signs the Voting Rights Act of 1965. The law prevents the use of literacy tests as a voting requirement.

- **1968** – Dr. Martin Luther King Jr. is assassinated by James Earl Ray. King was shot on the balcony of his hotel room in Memphis, Tennessee.

- **1968** – President Johnson signs the Civil Rights Act of 1968, also known as the Fair Housing Act. The law requires equal housing rights for individuals regardless of race, religion, or nationality.

Presidents During the Late 20th and Early 21st Centuries

- **George Bush (1989–1993)** – Republican; led successful military operations during the Persian Gulf War; struggled to manage economic recession in the early 1990s; served one term.

- **Bill Clinton (1993–2001)** – Democrat; successfully led the country during peacetime and economic stability; appointed a number of women and minorities to prominent positions, including Janet Reno (first female U.S. attorney general) and Madeline Albright (first female U.S. secretary of state); impeached by the U.S. House of Representatives for sexual misconduct; acquitted of charges by the U.S. Senate; served two terms.

- **George W. Bush (2001–2009)** – Republican; narrowly defeated democrat Al Gore, which triggered a vote recount in Florida and was ultimately decided by the U.S. Supreme Court; led the controversial War on Terror in Afghanistan and Iraq after the terrorist attacks on September 11, 2001; served two terms.

- **Barack Obama (2009–2017)** – Democrat; first Black U.S. president; prioritized the expansion of health care for Americans through the Affordable Care Act; led the covert military operation to kill Osama Bin Laden, who was the mastermind behind the terrorist attacks on September 11, 2001; served two terms.

E. Causes and effects of events

It is important to recognize the circumstances that led to major social movements and political conflicts in U.S. history.

Social Movements and Political Conflicts in U.S. History

Event	Causes and Effects
World War I (WWI)	• 1914–1918 • Began after the assassination of Austrian Archduke Franz Ferdinand. • Central Powers (Germany, Austria-Hungary & Turkey) against Allies (France, Great Britain, Russia, Italy, Japan, and from 1917, the United States). • Also called the Great War. • Allies were victorious. • Treaty of Versailles ended WWI and set the stage for WWII.
First Wave of Feminism	• 1848–1920 • The goal of the movement was equal rights for women with an emphasis on suffrage. In 1848, 300 men and women met at Seneca Falls to outline women's political strategies (Rampton, n.d.). • The Industrial Revolution played a large role in equality for women. Women worked in factories while men went to war. After WWI, women wanted the same freedoms and rights as men. • In 1920, the Nineteenth Amendment was ratified giving women the right to vote.
World War II (WWII)	• 1939–1945 • Began on September 1, 1939, when Germany invaded Poland. Britain and France declared war on Germany on September 3. • The German invasion of Poland marks the official start of WWII. • Deadliest war in history. • Axis Powers (Germany, Italy, and Japan) and Allies (France, Great Britain, the United States, the Soviet Union, and China). • Involved more than 30 countries. • Allied Powers Leaders: Winston Churchill – United Kingdom, Joseph Stalin – Soviet Union, Charles de Gaulle – France, and Franklin D. Roosevelt and Harry S. Truman – United States. • Axis Power Leaders: Adolf Hitler – Germany, Benito Mussolini – Italy, Hideki Tojo – Japan. • Pearl Harbor attack – December 7, 1941. • Bombing of Hiroshima – August 6, 1945.
Containment	• 1950s • Strategic foreign policy pursued by the United States in the late 1940s and the early 1950s in order to check the expansionist policy of the Soviet Union (Encyclopedia Britannica, 2019).

Event	Causes and Effects
Partition of India	• 1947 • The British Empire agreed to give India its independence after World War II. When the British withdrew, India split into two independent dominions based on religion. • The two dominions formed were India (Hindu) and Pakistan (Islam).
The Cold War	• 1945–1990 • Rivalry that developed after WWII between the United States and the Soviet Union and their allies. • Warsaw Pact – Soviet response to NATO. Formed the Eastern Bloc of nations led by the Soviet Union. • The Berlin Wall – Was a guarded concrete barrier that physically and ideologically divided Berlin from 1961 to 1989. The German communist regime built the wall to separate the Communist East from the Democratic West. East Germany saw the west as fascists and a threat to socialism (History.com Editors, 2019). • Ended with the collapse of the Soviet Union.
The Korean War	• 1950–1953 • War between North Korea and South Korea. • Korea had been split into two sovereign states in 1948 as a result of the Cold War.
The Vietnam War	• 1955–1975 • Conflict between communist government of North Vietnam against South Vietnam and its ally, the United States. • U.S. military Operation Ranch Hand used the herbicide known as Agent Orange to destroy plants in order to expose the trails, roads, and camps used by the Viet Cong. • President Richard Nixon ordered withdrawal of forces in 1973.
Second Wave of Feminism	• During the 1960s, women's advocacy groups focused on women's issues in politics, work, family, and sexuality. • The National Organization of Women (NOW) pressured Congress to pass legislation to ensure equal rights regardless of sex and demanded greater access to contraception and abortion services (Burkett, n.d.).
The Six-Day War	• 1967 • War between the Israelis and Arabs. • The cause of the war was attacks conducted against Israel by Palestinian guerrilla groups based in Syria, Lebanon, and Jordan. • The Six-Day War ended with significant friction still existing between Israelis and Arabs over ownership of what is now the Gaza Strip.

Event	Causes and Effects
Energy Crisis of 1970	• 1973 • During the Yom Kippur War in 1973, the United States provided military support to Israel. • The surrounding Arab nations did not recognize Israel as a legitimate nation-state. • The United States' support of Israel triggered the Organization of Petroleum Exporting Countries (OPEC) to dramatically reduced their petroleum production and establish an embargo on oil to the United States (History.com Editors, 2010).
Persian Gulf War	• 1990–1991 • Two-phase war: Operation Desert Shield and Operation Desert Storm. • President George H.W. Bush. • Iraq's leader, Saddam Hussein, invades Kuwait. Iraq occupies Kuwait for 7 months. United States retaliates. • August 6 – Council imposed worldwide ban on trade with Iraq.
Iraq War	• 2003–2011 • Second Persian Gulf War. • President George W. Bush went to war because of suspicion of weapons of mass destruction. Later, it was discovered there were never weapons of mass destruction. • United States and Great Britain invaded Iraq.

F. Nature, purpose, and forms of government

The United States is a republic, which means it is governed by elected representatives and by an elected leader (such as a president) rather than by a king or queen. The structure of the government and division of its power and the laws by which the nation is governed are outlined in the United States Constitution.

The United States Constitution, which was ratified in 1788, is a document outlining the overarching laws and division of powers among governmental organizations.

Separation of Power

Separation of power is outlined in the United States Constitution, where the federal government is divided into three branches:

• Article I outlines the legislative branch (House of Representatives and the Senate).

• Article II outlines the executive branch (the president).

• Article III outlines the judicial branch (the Supreme Court).

Federalism

Federalism refers to a type of government where powers are divided between the federal government and state governments.

- **States' rights** – Political powers held for state governments rather than the federal government. The following fall under the umbrella of state powers:

  - Issue licenses (e.g., marriage, drivers, business).

  - Create local governments.

  - Regulate industry.

  - Ratify amendments to the State Constitution.

  - Regulate commerce within state lines.

Branches of Government

The United States government is composed of three branches: legislative, judicial, and executive. This separation of powers is intended to create a system of checks and balances to ensure no one branch is more powerful than another.

Quick Tip

Section 10 of Article I prohibits states from printing money, granting Title of Nobility, and declaring war.

Article I – Legislative Branch

The legislative branch includes the two chambers of Congress: the **House of Representatives** and the **Senate**.

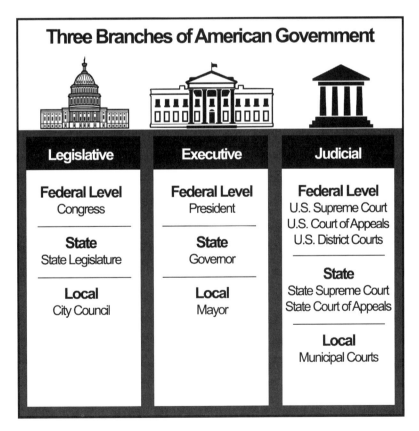

Three Branches of American Government

Legislative	Executive	Judicial
Federal Level Congress	**Federal Level** President	**Federal Level** U.S. Supreme Court U.S. Court of Appeals U.S. District Courts
State State Legislature	**State** Governor	**State** State Supreme Court State Court of Appeals
Local City Council	**Local** Mayor	**Local** Municipal Courts

The **House of Representatives**, as outlined in the Constitution, is responsible for making and passing federal laws. There is a fixed number of voting representatives; since 1911, the number has been fixed at 435. The Constitution states that seats in the House of Representatives are to be distributed among the states by population. The population of each state is determined by the census conducted every 10 years. Elections for the House of Representatives are held every two years (U.S. House of Representatives, n.d.).

The **Senate** includes 100 members, who are elected for a six-year term in dual-seat constituencies (two from each state), with one-third of the total number of seats being renewed every two years. The group of the Senate seats that is up for election during a given year is known as a "class"; the three classes are staggered so that only one of the three groups is renewed every two years.

Quick Tip

While many people are interested in the federal government—who's running for president and who won the Senate seat—local government has the most impact on people's daily lives. Local governments impose taxes, issue licenses (driver's, business, occupational), and handle community needs.

Article II – Executive Branch

The **President of the United States** (or POTUS) is the head of state of the United States, the chief executive of the federal government, and commander-in-chief of the armed forces. According to Article II of the United States Constitution, the president must be a natural-born citizen of the United States, be at least 35 years old, and must have been a resident of the United States for 14 years (The White House, n.d.).

Article III – Judicial Branch

The **Supreme Court of the United States** (or SCOTUS) is the highest federal court in the country and the head of the judicial branch of government. The court is made up of nine justices and has the power to check the actions of the other two branches of government: the executive branch and the legislative branch. Supreme Court justices are nominated by the president of the United States and confirmed (or denied) by the United States Senate (The Supreme Court of the United States, n.d.).

Supreme Court powers and structure:

- Officially created by the Judiciary Act of 1789.
- The Supreme Court is made up of nine justices (judges): one chief justice and eight associate justices.
- A Supreme Court appointment is a lifelong position held until death or retirement.
- Article III, Section II of the Constitution outlines the Supreme Court's jurisdiction:
  - Lawsuits between/among two or more states
  - Cases involving ambassadors or other public ministers
  - Appellate (appeals) jurisdiction over any case involving constitutional and/or federal law
  - Cases involving treaties or maritime law—navigable international and domestic waterways

Quick Tip

The United States v. Nixon Supreme Court case resulted in a unanimous decision to subpoena Nixon, who cited "executive privilege" as a basis for withholding information and audio recordings from government agencies.

This case was a catalyst for President Nixon's resignation (Hohmann, 2018).

Judicial Review is the best-known Supreme Court power. Judicial Review is the Supreme Court's ability to declare a legislative (House of Representatives or Senate) or executive (President) act to be in violation of the United States Constitution.

Checks and Balances

The term **checks and balances** refers to a system that ensures that one branch does not exceed its bounds. This is what guards against fraud or errors. The definition states, "A system that allows each branch of a government to amend or veto acts of another branch to prevent any one branch from exerting too much power" (Merriam-Webster, 2019).

Examples:

- The legislative branch can pass a law. The executive branch can check that power by either agreeing with the law or vetoing the law (voting it down).

- The judicial branch upholds the laws. The executive branch checks that power by appointing justices to the court.

- The executive branch can veto a bill. The legislative branch checks that power by evaluating the law again and possibly overriding the veto by two-thirds vote in the Senate and House of Representatives.

U.S. Presidential Electoral Process

The presidential election process can be consolidated into five steps shown in the following table.

Presidential Election Process

Presidential Elections
Step 1: Primary and Caucus • **Primary:** A primary is a state-level election where party members vote for the candidate who will represent them in the general election. • **Caucus:** A closed meeting of a group of persons belonging to the same political party or faction, usually to select candidates or to decide on policy (Merriam-Webster, 2019).
Step 2: National Conventions • The elected delegates cast their vote for a party candidate, and the candidate with the most delegates receives the party's nomination. The end of the convention marks the beginning of the general election process. • Each party holds a national convention to finalize the selection of one presidential nominee. At each convention, the presidential candidate chooses a running mate (vice presidential candidate).
Step 3: Election Campaigning • General election campaigning begins after a single nominee is chosen from each political party via primaries, caucuses, and national conventions. • These candidates travel the country, explaining their views and plans to the general population and trying to win the support of potential voters. Rallies, debates, and advertising are a big part of general election campaigning.
Step 4: General Election • Usually held in November. • Takes place every four years. • On election day, the voters of each state and the District of Columbia vote for one presidential "ticket" that includes candidates for president and vice president. • One must be at least 18 years of age to vote in the presidential election. • Only citizens of the United States can vote in a United States election. • To win the election, a candidate must secure more than 270 electoral votes.
Step 5: Electoral College • Each state has a certain number of electors based on the state's total number of representatives in Congress. • Each of the 50 states and Washington D.C. (a district that does not belong to any state) has a set number of electors that reflects their population. California is the most populated (over 38 million people) and has 55 electoral votes—more than any other state. On the other hand, a state such as Montana, which is geographically large but has a relatively small population (just over 1 million people), only has three electors. • There are 538 electoral votes. • The candidate who receives more than half of the electoral votes (270) wins the election.

(US.gov, n.d.)

Electoral College

Many modern voters might be surprised to learn that when they step into a ballot box to vote, they are actually casting a vote for a group of people known as electors. An elector is a member of the Electoral College, which consists of 538 electors. These electors, appointed by the states, formally elect the president and vice president of the United States. They are pledged to support the presidential candidate the voters have supported.

Even if the majority of people in the United States vote for a candidate, that does not mean that the candidate will win the presidential election. There are instances where the candidate who won the popular vote lost the election.

Voter Turnout in the United States

- More Americans vote when there is a highly competitive election.

- More Americans vote in presidential elections than in off-year elections.

- More Americans vote in general elections than in primary elections.

- Older, white Americans vote more than other demographics.

- Women vote more than men.

- Voting laws impact voter turnout.

(FairVote.org, n.d.)

State and Local Branches of Government

- Executive Branch

  - State – Governor
  - Local – Mayor
- Legislative Branch

  - State – State Senate and State House Representatives
  - Local – City Council
- Judicial Branch

  - State – District Court, Appeals Court, State Supreme Court
  - Local – Municipal Courts

State Government

State government is modeled after the federal government's three branches: executive, legislative, and judicial. Each state has its own constitution. State constitutions are much more detailed than their federal counterpart. State and local governments are required to uphold a republican form of government, although the three-branch structure is not a requirement (The White House, n.d.).

State governments typically control the following:

- Driver licenses and business licenses

- Vehicle registration

- Birth certificates

- Death certificates

- Unemployment compensation

- Licensing for professionals, such as attorneys, pharmacists, chiropractors, etc.

- Agriculture

- Veterans affairs

- Education

- Energy

- Human services

Local Government

Local government is the public administration of towns, cities, counties, and districts. This type of government includes both county and municipal government structures. Citizens have much more contact with local governments than they do with the federal government (The White House, n.d.).

Common local government structures:

- Libraries

- Fire and emergency management

- Public parks and recreation

- Local law enforcement

- Public works and engineering

- Water and environmental services

- Roads, bridges, and traffic control

Local government boundary setting:

- **Boundary Delimitation** – Process of drawing electoral district boundaries.

- **Constituency** – A group of voters who elect representatives to legislative bodies.

- **Gerrymandering** – Drawing political boundaries to gain an advantage over opponents.

Political Systems

- **Direct Democracy** – Also known as "pure democracy". In a direct democracy, the people decide on policies directly.

- **Representative Democracy** – In a representative democracy, people elect representatives to decide on policies on their behalf. For example, in the United States, the president is not elected directly by the people; representatives called "electors" make the decision (Budge, 2001).

- **Republic** – A republic is a government with a chief of state who is usually a president, not a monarch. Power ultimately resides with the citizens, who elect representatives to govern on their behalf and according to rule of law (Merriam-Webster, 2019).

- **Absolute Monarchy** – Undivided rule or absolute sovereignty by a single person (Merriam-Webster, 2019). The monarch comes into power by marriage or offspring. Saudi Arabia is an example of absolute monarchy.

- **Constitutional Monarchy** – This type of monarchy is known as the "limited monarchy" because the monarch's power is limited, and the power to alter legislation resides with the Parliament (Merriam-Webster, 2019). Britain is an example of constitutional monarchy.

> **Cult of Personality**
>
> When dictators use propaganda to present themselves as saviors and heroes to be admired and loved by the people of their country (Plamper, 2012).

- **Communist State** – Single political party, based on the ideology of Marxism-Leninism. Communist states call themselves "socialist states" because they aimed to establish a socialist society (Busky, 2000).

- **Dictatorship** – An authoritarian form of government that has a single leader or group of leaders (Ezrow, 2011). A dictatorship is the opposite of a democracy.

Examples of Types of Political Systems			
Dictatorship (Iraq)	**Democracy (India)**	**Theocracy (Iran)**	**Monarchy (Jordan)**
Rule by a single leader who has not been elected but who took power through violence or force.	In a democracy, the government is elected by the people. All the people who are eligible to vote—which is a majority of the population—have a chance to have their say about who runs the country.	A form of government where the rulers claim to be ruling based on religious beliefs and ideals. Leaders believe they are ruling by the word of God.	A monarchy has a king or queen, who often has absolute power. Power is passed along through the family.
Parliamentary (Israel)	**Republic (USA)**	**Anarchy (Afghanistan)**	**Oligarchy/Plutocracy (Pakistan)**
A parliamentary system is led by representatives of the people. Each is chosen as a member of a political party and remains in power as long as his/her party does.	A republic is led by representatives of the voters.	Anarchy is a situation where there is no government. This can happen after a civil war in a country.	A form of government that consists of rule by an elite group who rules in its own interests, especially when it comes to the economy and lifestyle.

G. Key documents and speeches in the history of the United States

There are several historical documents that have shaped the United States. It is important to understand the distinctions among these documents.

Founding Documents of the United States

Document	What It Outlines	Authors
Declaration of Independence	Government is no more powerful than man. If government is tyrannical, people have the right to rebel and start over.	Thomas Jefferson, John Adams, Benjamin Franklin, Roger Sherman, Robert R. Livingston
Federalist Papers	Made the case for checks and balances and separation of powers.	Alexander Hamilton, James Madison, and John Jay
Articles of Confederation	Functioned as the first constitution of the United States. Officially established the government that united the 13 colonies as one union.	A committee of 13 men from the Second Continental Congress; primary author was John Dickinson
Constitution	Articles I–III outlined: I. Legislative Branch II. Executive Branch III. Judicial Branch (in that order!)	Thomas Jefferson, John Adams, James Madison, Alexander Hamilton
The Bill of Rights	The first 10 amendments to the U.S. Constitution. Provides unalienable rights of citizens.	James Madison

The Bill of Rights to the U.S. Constitution

Number	Amendment	Description
1	Freedom of Religion, Speech, and the Press	The First Amendment provides several protections, including the right to express ideas through speech and the press, the right to assemble or gather with a group to protest or for other reasons, and the right to ask the government to fix problems. It also protects the right to religious beliefs and practices. It prevents the government from creating or favoring a religion.
2	The Right to Bear Arms	The Second Amendment provides the right to own a firearm.
3	The Housing of Soldiers	The Third Amendment prevents the government from forcing homeowners to allow soldiers to use their homes. Before the Revolutionary War, laws gave British soldiers the right to take over private homes—the Quartering Act.
4	Protection from Unreasonable Searches and Seizures	The Fourth Amendment states that the government cannot search or seize a person or their property without just cause.
5	Protection of Rights to Life, Liberty, and Property	The Fifth Amendment provides several protections for people accused of crimes. It states that serious criminal charges must be started by a grand jury. A person cannot be tried twice for the same offense (double jeopardy) or have property taken away without just compensation. People have the right against self-incrimination and cannot be imprisoned without due process of law (fair procedures and trials).
6	Rights of Accused Persons in Criminal Cases	The Sixth Amendment provides additional protections to people accused of crimes, such as the right to a speedy and public trial, trial by an impartial jury in criminal cases, and to be informed of criminal charges. Witnesses must face the accused, and the accused is allowed his or her own witnesses and to be represented by a lawyer.
7	Rights in Civil Cases	The Seventh Amendment extends the right to a jury trial in federal civil cases.
8	Excessive Bail, Fines, and Punishments	The Eighth Amendment bars excessive bail and fines and cruel and unusual punishment.
9	Other Rights Kept by the People	The Ninth Amendment states that listing specific rights in the Constitution does not mean that people do not have other rights that have not been spelled out.
10	States' Rights	The Tenth Amendment says that the Federal Government only has those powers delegated in the Constitution. If it is not listed, it belongs to the states or to the people.

(U.S. Senate, n.d.)

Item	Description	Author
Monroe Doctrine (1823)	The Monroe Doctrine was an isolation policy that stated in order for America to develop, Europe and the United States must stay out of each other's affairs. This policy of isolationism would last until World War I.	President James Monroe
Truman Doctrine (1947)	The Truman Doctrine effectively reoriented the United States' foreign policy by establishing that the United States would provide political, military, and economic assistance to all democratic nations (Encyclopedia Britannica, 2019).	President Harry S. Truman
Marshall Plan (1949)	Officially called the European Recovery Program, this was an American initiative to help Western Europe to rebuild the European economic system after World War II (Office of the U.S. Historian, n.d.).	Secretary of State George Marshall
North Atlantic Treaty Organization (NATO) (1949)	NATO is a military alliance, also called the Washington Treaty. NATO was sought to create a counterweight to Soviet armies stationed in Central and Eastern Europe (Haglund, n.d.). The Soviet Union created the Warsaw Pact in response to NATO.	The original members were Belgium, Canada, Denmark, France, Ireland, Italy, Luxembourg, the Netherlands, Norway, Portugal, the United Kingdom, and the United States.
Containment (1940s and early 1950s)	Foreign policy to counter the expansionist policy of the Soviet Union (Encyclopedia Britannica, 2019).	Diplomat George F. Kennan
Domino Theory (1954)	A theory or position in United States foreign policy that the fall of a noncommunist state to communism would cause the fall of noncommunist governments in neighboring states. If one state goes communist, there is a threat that communism will spread (Nolen, n.d.).	President Dwight D. Eisenhower
Foreign Assistance Act and USAID (1961)	Policy of implementing diplomacy through foreign aid (USAID.gov, 2019).	President John F. Kennedy

Famous Speeches and Quotes in U.S. History

Speech/Quote	Speaker	Significance
Gettysburg Address	President Abraham Lincoln	Speech delivered at the dedication of the National Cemetery of Gettysburg in Pennsylvania. Addressed the principles of human equality that are outlined in the Declaration of Independence. A call to the people to preserve the Union and its ideals.
I Have a Dream	Martin Luther King, Jr.	This speech was delivered during the March on Washington for Jobs and Freedom in 1963. It was a call to end racial inequality and discrimination on the basis of race. Dr. Martin Luther King, Jr. encouraged a society that supported civil and economic rights for all.
"Ask not what your country can do for you; ask what you can do for your country."	President John F. Kennedy	President Kennedy's inauguration speech in 1961 addressed the importance of civic action and public service. He encouraged every American to contribute to the public good.
"Tear down this wall."	President Ronald Reagan	President Reagan gave a speech in West Berlin in 1987 with a message to Mikhail Gorbachev to open the Berlin Wall. In 1989, Gorbachev ordered the removal of the wall between East and West Germany.
"The only thing we have to fear is fear itself."	President Franklin D. Roosevelt	President Roosevelt's first inauguration speech in 1933 addressed the economic crisis and described the plan to declare war on the Great Depression. To do this, he would have to utilize the power of the executive branch.

H. Rights and responsibilities of American citizens

The Fourteenth Amendment states that all persons born or naturalized in the United States, and subject to the jurisdiction thereof, are citizens of the United States and of the state where they reside.

Rights of American Citizens

Every American citizen is guaranteed certain rights. These rights are outlined by the United States Constitution.

- Freedom of expression

- Freedom to practice any religion

- Right to a prompt, fair trial by jury

- Right to vote in elections for public officials

- Right to apply for federal employment (requires United States citizenship)

- Right to run for elected office

- Freedom to pursue life, liberty, and the pursuit of happiness

Responsibilities of American Citizens

Along with the guaranteed rights enjoyed by American citizens, there are also specific duties that are required of each American citizen.

- Support and defend the Constitution

- Stay informed of the issues affecting one's community

- Participate in the democratic process (vote)

- Respect and obey federal, state, and local laws

- Respect the rights, beliefs, and opinion of others

- Participate in your local community

- Pay income taxes honestly and on time to federal, state, and local authorities

- Defend the country if the need should arise

(United States Citizen and Immigration Services, 2016)

II. Geography, Anthropology, and Sociology

Section II may be intertwined with questions from section I and from section III. Questions may include questions regarding maps, populations, settlement patterns, how environment affects society, and geography's role on important historical periods, such as the Industrial Revolution.

The skills you need to know in this section include the following:

A. Knows world and regional geography (e.g., spatial terms, places, regions)

B. Understands the interaction of physical and human systems (e.g., how humans change the environment, how the environment changes humans, importance of natural and human resources)

C. Knows the uses of geography (e.g., apply geography to interpret past, to present, to plan for future)

D. Knows how people of different cultural backgrounds interact with their environment, family, neighborhoods, and communities

A. World and regional geography

Geography is the study of the physical features of the Earth's surface and atmosphere, including how humans affect the physical features of the Earth and the ways these physical features affect humans (National Geographic, n.d.).

There are six essential elements of geography:

1. The world in spatial terms

2. Places and regions

3. Physical systems

4. Human systems

5. Environment and society

6. Uses of geography

This section focuses on world and regional geography, which includes the world in spatial terms and places and regions. The other elements are discussed in the sections that follow.

World in Spatial Terms

The world in spatial terms refers to location on the Earth.

- **Absolute location** – Exact location of a point using latitude and longitude or an address

- **Relative location** – Location of a point in relation to another point

Absolute vs. Relative Location

- Absolute: 37N, 63W or "I live at 6570 Irish Rd."

- Relative: New York City is about 90 minutes from Philadelphia.

International Date Line

The International Date Line (IDL) is an imaginary line of navigation on the surface of the Earth that runs from the North Pole to the South Pole and indicates the change of one calendar day to the next. It passes through the middle of the Pacific Ocean, roughly following the 180° line of longitude, but deviates to pass around some territories and island groups. The IDL detours around political boundaries (Heim, 2018).

International Date Line

Hemispheres

The Earth is divided into four hemispheres: Northern, Southern, Eastern, and Western. The Equator divides the Earth into the Northern and Southern Hemispheres. The Prime Meridian (0° longitude) divides the Earth into the Eastern and Western Hemispheres. The Eastern Hemisphere is east of the Prime Meridian and west of the IDL. The Western Hemisphere is west of the Prime Meridian and east of the IDL (National Geographic, n.d.).

According to an international agreement, the official Prime Meridian runs through Greenwich, England. Most of Asia and Africa are a part of the Eastern Hemisphere. The Americas and northwestern Africa are a part of the Western Hemisphere.

Equator and Prime Meridian

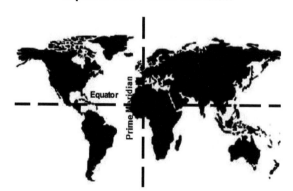

Geographic Coordinate System

Latitude is the angle between the equatorial plane and the straight line that passes through that point and through the center of the Earth. Latitudinal lines run horizontally across the Earth (University of Hawaii, n.d.).

Longitude is the angle east or west of a reference meridian to another meridian that passes through that point. Longitudinal lines run vertically across the Earth (University of Hawaii, n.d.).

Quick Tip

The distance on the Earth's surface for one degree of latitude or longitude is just over 69 miles.

Places and Regions

Places are defined by both physical and human characteristics, including uses of the area.

Regions are areas broadly divided by physical characteristics, human impact characteristics, and the interaction of humanity and the environment (Bailey, 1996). The Pacific Northwest, Southwest Florida, and the Sunbelt are all examples of regions.

Examples

- **Nation** – Nation refers to a community of people who share similar history, culture, and traditions and reside in the same area or territory (Merriam-Webster, 2019).

- **Sovereign State** – A sovereign state is a self-governing geopolitical entity that has defined borders and controls its internal sovereignty over its existence and affairs (Philpott, 2003).

- **Country** – A nation with its own government and economy that occupies a defined territory. A country may be an independent sovereign state or one that is occupied by another state (Merriam-Webster, 2019).

The Sun Belt

The Sun Belt is a region of the United States generally considered to stretch across the Southeast and Southwest. It is called the Sun Belt because of its mild winter, frequent sunny skies, and growing economic opportunities.

- **Continent** – A continent is one of the world's seven main continuous expanses of land: Africa, Antarctica, Asia, Australia, Europe, North America, and South America.

Maps

Maps provide a representation of the elements of geography.

Political maps show locations of cities, towns, and counties and might show some physical features such as rivers, streams, and lakes.

Physical maps illustrate the physical features of an area, such as the mountains, rivers, and lakes. The water is usually shown in blue. Colors are used to show relief, i.e., differences in land elevations. Green is typically used to indicate lower elevations. Orange and brown indicate higher elevations.

Road maps show major (and some minor) highways and roads, airports, railroad tracks, cities, and other points of interest in an area. People use road maps to plan trips and for driving directions.

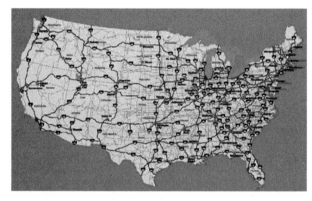

Special purpose maps focus on details such as topography, climate, or district. Special purpose maps can be useful for finding more information about population, tourism, elevation, etc.

Other Types of Maps

- **Climate maps** provide general information about the climate and precipitation (rain and snow) of a region. Climate of an area is determined by the amount of rainfall, temperature, and wind in the area. Cartographers, or mapmakers, use colors to show different climate or precipitation zones.

- **Economic or resource maps** feature the type of natural resources or economic activity that dominates an area. Cartographers use symbols to show the locations of natural resources or economic activities. For example, oranges on a map of Florida tell you that oranges are grown there.

- **Topographical maps** are similar to physical maps in that they show streams, valleys, rivers, mountains, hills, and more. Unlike physical maps, topographical maps use contour lines instead of colors to illustrate different feature of the land. Topographical maps also display important landmarks and roads. Topographical maps can indicate how people migrated and settled the land. This type of map can also provide information about ancestral properties, buildings, local cemeteries, and other important buildings and features.

B. Physical and human systems

Physical Systems

Physical systems and processes shape the Earth's surface. This field of geography includes the study of how these systems and processes interact with plant and animal life to create, sustain, and modify ecosystems. There are four physical systems, and geographers study how the physical processes interact with the physical systems.

- **Atmosphere** – The envelope of gases surrounding the Earth or another planet.

- **Biosphere** – Includes all life on the planet.

- **Hydrosphere** – Includes all water—liquid, ice, and vapor—on the planet.

- **Lithosphere** – The outer region of the Earth. Includes the crust and upper mantle.

Quick Tip

Because the hydrosphere includes all the water in all its forms, scientists study the hydrosphere to understand the Earth's climate.

Geographic Features

Geographic Feature	Definition	Example
Archipelago	An archipelago is a group of islands or island chains	Hawaiian Islands
Atoll	A coral island that surrounds a lagoon	Maldives
Barrier island	A band of beach parallel to the mainland that protects the shore from the effects of the ocean	Clearwater Beach, Florida
Bays	An inlet of the sea or other body of water--usually smaller than a gulf	Chesapeake Bay, Ha Long Bay

Geographic Feature	Definition	Example
Continent	One of the seven great divisions of land on the globe	Africa, North America
Deciduous forest	A forest of trees, which lose their leaves seasonally	Eastern Deciduous Forrest, United States
Delta	A landform that forms from deposition of sediment carried by a river as the flow leaves its mouth and enters slower-moving or standing water	Mississippi Delta, Louisiana; Nile River Delta, Egypt
Desert	A barren area of landscape where little precipitation occurs and, consequently, living conditions are hostile for plant and animal life; can be hot or cold	Sahara, Antarctica
Fjord	A long, narrow, deep inlet of the sea between high cliffs	Skelton Inlet, Antarctica
Forest	A dense growth of trees and underbrush covering a large tract	Tongass National Forest, Alaska
Grassland	Land on which the natural dominant plant forms are grasses and herbs	North American prairies, Argentine pampas
Ice caps	A glacier forming on an extensive area of relatively level land and flowing outward from its center	Greenland Ice Sheet, Svartissen Ice Cap in Norway
Island	A tract of land surrounded by water and smaller than a continent	Ireland, Long Island
Isthmus	Narrow strip of land connecting two large land areas otherwise separated by bodies of water	Isthmus of Panama, connecting North and South America; Isthmus of Suez, connecting Africa and Asia
Mountain	A large area of raised land formed through tectonic movement or volcanic activity	Mt. St. Helens
Mountain ranges	A series of mountains or mountain ridges closely related in position and direction	Andes, Rocky Mountains
Oceans	The whole body of saltwater that covers nearly three-fourths of the surface of Earth	Atlantic, Pacific
Peninsula	A land mass mostly surrounded by water and connected to a larger area of land	Indochina Peninsula
Plains	An extensive area of level or rolling, treeless country	The Great Plains
Plateaus	A usually extensive land area having a relatively level surface raised sharply above adjacent land on at least one side	Antarctic Plateau

Geographic Feature	Definition	Example
Rain forest	A woodland with annual rainfall of 100 inches and heavy tree canopy	Amazon Rainforest, Daintree Rainforest
Rivers	A large system of natural flowing water	Amazon River
Seas	A body of saltwater that is partially enclosed by land	Baltic Sea, Mediterranean Sea
Taiga	A moist, subarctic forest of conifers that begins where the tundra ends	Alaska, Canada
Tundra	A level or rolling, treeless plain that is characteristic of arctic and subarctic regions, consists of black mucky soil with a permanently frozen subsoil, and has a dominant vegetation of mosses, lichens, herbs, and dwarf shrubs	Arctic tundra, alpine tundra
Valleys	An elongated depression of Earth's surface usually between ranges of hills or mountains	Hunza Valley, Yosemite Valley, Grand Canyon

(Definitions from Merriam-Webster online dictionary)

Human Systems

Humans, through their daily activities, shape and reshape the Earth. This aspect of geography explores how people and the environment change each other.

- Settlement

- Population

- Literacy

- Healthcare

- Technology

- Trade

- Tourism

- Agriculture

- Production and consumption patterns

- Waste management

- Human-caused land degradation

- Human-induced pollution

- Anthropogenic global warming and climate change

Another example of human impact on the environment is through migration. In the 15th and 16th centuries, Europeans brought disease to the Americas when they were exploring the New World. These diseases killed millions of Native Americans, who had no previous exposure and no immunity to the diseases of the European continent.

Population Density

Population density is the number of people in relation to the square miles (U.S. Census, 2010). According to the Table 1.1 below:

- Which country has the highest population density?
- Which country has the lowest population density?

Example Population Density

Country	Population	Square Miles
A	11,382,820	428 square miles
B	24,500,265	640 square miles
C	24,000,000	473 square miles
D	8,409,572	288 square miles

In this example, Country C has the highest population density because it has the highest number of people per square mile. Country A has the lowest population density because it has the fewest people per square mile.

$$Population\ density = \frac{Population}{Square\ Miles}$$

Ecological Catastrophes of the 20th Century

Throughout history, humans have played a significant role in changing the shape of the physical environment. With the advent of industry and technology, these changes have become more severe in recent years.

- **Desertification of the Sahel (1900s)** – The Sahel is a region along the southern border of the Sahara Desert that was once supported a prosperous community of farming and agriculture. Overpopulation, overgrazing, and agriculture led to the deforestation of the area and ultimately caused the desertification of the Sahel (Brough, 2004).

- **Castle Bravo Nuclear Test (1954)** – The United States detonated a hydrogen bomb on Bikini Atoll in the Marshall Islands, which led to the largest radiological contamination in U.S. history.

- **Desertifi cation of the Aral Sea (1960)** – The Soviet water management system was created for irrigation and has caused the 4th largest inland water body in the world to dry up (Howard, 2014).

- **Three Mile Island Nuclear Meltdown (1979)** – A partial nuclear meltdown at a U.S. nuclear power plant in Dauphin County, Pennsylvania resulted in the release of radioactive material into the environment.

- **Chernobyl (1986)** – The Soviet nuclear power plant explosion and fi res caused a nuclear meltdown and released radioactive material into the environment. The accident caused countless deaths of humans and animals.

Interaction of Human and Physical Systems

Humans have altered the environment throughout the world. For example, the construction of the City of Dubai changed the desert to an urban environment.

The environment can also have a significant impact on human habitats. For example, Hurricane Katrina displaced thousands of people who never returned to their home.

- **Exxon-Valdez Oil Spill (1989)** – An Exxon-Valdez oil tanker ran into a reef off the coast of Alaska and spilled approximately 250,000-750,000 barrels of crude oil in Prince William Sound killing hundreds of thousands of birds, fish, and sea animals.

- **Kuwait Oil Fires (1991)** – As the Iraqi military forces retreated Kuwait during the Persian Gulf War, they set fire to 600 oil wells.

- **Deep Water Horizon BP Oil Spill (2010)** – The explosion and sinking of the Deep Water Horizon oil rig spilled 4.9 million barrels of crude oil into the Gulf of Mexico.

(Dimdam, 2013)

C. Uses of geography

Geography is used in many ways to understand the Earth and its inhabitants.

- Geography is used to interpret the past.

    - Understanding how farmers in the 1800s used land in different ways
    - Understanding why civilizations inhabited certain areas

- Geography is used to understand the present and plan for the future.

    - Studying hurricane patterns to plan for future storms and keep society safe
    - Understanding how changes in landmasses can affect quality of life in the future

Agriculture

Agriculture is the practice of farming and has evolved since the Neolithic era. Some techniques of farming used by the ancient civilizations are still utilized today (bbc.com, n.d.).

Terms associated with agriculture include:

- **Arable** – Producing crops

    - **Terrace farming** – Invented by the Inca; steps are built on hilly or mountainous areas (World Atlas, n.d.)
    - **Crop rotation** – Planting different crops sequentially to maximize the nutrients in the soil

- **Pastoral** – Producing animals

- **Sustenance** – Producing what is needed for self and family

- **Commercial** – Producing to sell

- **Intensive** – Small areas of land; high inputs of resources

- **Extensive** – Large areas of land; low inputs of resources

- **Irrigation** – The supply of water to land and crops to promote growth (Centers for Disease Control and Prevention, 2016)

    - **Rain fed** – Natural application of water to crops form direct rainfall

    - **Surface irrigation** – Using gravity to move water across land; no mechanical system

    - **Localized irrigation** – Using a network of pipes and low pressure to distribute water

    - **Center pivot irrigation** – Using a system of sprinklers that move in a circular pattern often used in flat areas

    - **Sub-irrigation** – Using pumping stations, canals, dams, gates, and ditches

    - **Manual irrigation** – Using manual labor and watering cans to distribute water

> **Quick Tip**
>
> Aqueducts (a method of surface irrigation) were first used in the Neolithic period around 2,000 BC in Mesopotamia. The aqueducts were used to move water through a series of bridges and canals in order to cultivate crops. However, it was the ***Romans who perfected the engineering of aqueduct building*** and who are the most famous for their successful and complex irrigation systems (Cartwright, 2012).

During the Western Expansion, early settlers in the western United States suffered tremendous loss because of the lack of water available for life and farming. The western United States does not have many natural water resources and rain is relatively infrequent. In order to migrate to the western frontier, the government invested in large irrigation projects to help cultivate the land for farming and agriculture (Berkes, 2003).

Energy

Energy resources play a critical role in everyday human life. We use energy to power everything from a coffee machine to the space shuttle. Our energy resources come from the Earth in a variety of forms. Some energy resources cannot be renewed as quickly as they are being consumed (nonrenewable); some energy resources can be renewed quickly by the Earth's physical processes (renewable).

- **Clean energy** – energy from wind, solar, wind, water, geothermal, biomass, and nuclear

- **Fossil energy** – energy from coal, oil, and natural gas

- **Electric power** – energy from charged particles

Renewable and Nonrenewable Resources

Renewable	Nonrenewable
solar	fossil fuels
wind	coal
hydro power	natural gas

Technology

Technology refers to methods, systems, and devices that are the result of scientific knowledge being used for practical purposes (Merriam-Webster, 2019). There are several types of technology:

- **Transportation** – cars, buses, trains, airplanes

- **Communication** – telephones, computers, Internet

- **Construction** – bulldozers, cranes, machines

- **Energy and power** – wind turbines, dams, solar panels

- **Chemical and biological** – vaccines, antibiotics

- **Manufacturing** – factories, assembly lines, machines

D. Culture, environment, and society

- **Anthropology** – The study of human beings, their culture, origins, environment, and social norms (Merriam-Webster, 2019).

  - **Physical anthropology** – The study of physical characteristics of human groups through measurement and observation (Merriam-Webster, 2019).

- **Cultural anthropology** – The study of cognitive and social organization of human groups, including folklore, linguistics, religion, politics, and ethnology (Merriam-Webster, 2019).

- **Assimilation** – The process of individuals absorbing the dominant culture of a group different from their own heritage (Encyclopedia Britannica Editors, n.d.).

- **Socialization** – The process of understanding oneself and societal expectations through social interactions with others (Encyclopedia Britannica Editors, n.d.).

Sociology Theories and Classroom Implementation

Sociologist	Theory	Classroom Implementation
Dewey (1910–1930)	Learning by exploring and doing (experiential learning)	• After a lesson about Naturalism in American literature, the class goes to an outdoor classroom to observe a particular aspect of their natural surroundings and then write a short story or poem about their observations. • As part of a seed germination unit, students plant seeds in clear containers and observe/note changes at regular intervals. • Before reading about rocks, collect and categorize different rocks.
Skinner (1930s)	Behaviorism	• Positive reinforcement; increasing positive behaviors through incentives (token economy) or positive feedback • Negative reinforcement; increasing positive behaviors through the removal of an undesired stimulus • Reinforcement of positive behavior preferred to punishment
Piaget (1940s)	Stages of Cognitive Development; prior knowledge (schema); discovery learning	• Providing students with pre-cut letters to form words • Allowing opportunities for students to participate in age-appropriate experiments • Using small group discussions to brainstorm ideas surrounding a current political issue • Connecting new concepts to previously learned concepts
Maslow (1960s)	Hierarchy of Needs	• Meeting students' needs before moving on to high-level assignments/activities • Considering students' situations at home before assigning work
Vygotsky (1960s)	Zone of Proximal Development (ZPD)	• Cooperative learning activities • Scaffolded activities • Peer and teacher support

Community

A community is an interacting population of various kinds of individuals (as species) in a common location (Merriam-Webster, 2019). Generally, communities can be broken down into three types:

- **Urban** – Cities

- **Suburban** – Residential areas surrounding urban centers

- **Rural** – Farmland

Ethnic enclave – Subsection of a community where the population is ethnically distinguished from the surrounding area. For example, Little Havana is an ethnic enclave of Cuban Americans living in Miami, Florida.

Language

Language is a method of human communication, either spoken or written, consisting of the use of words in a structured and conventional way (Merriam-Webster, 2019).

- There are roughly 6,500 languages spoken around the world.

- Though English is the most widely spoken language in the United States, the United States does not have an official language.

In addition to differences in language and dialect, cultural differences can also have an impact on communication. Sometimes the intended meaning is lost or misunderstood because of context. Organizations can improve their international business relations by understanding other cultures and implementing appropriate communication strategies (Communicaid Group, 2019).

- **High-context culture** – Relies heavily on gestures, eye contact, relationships, and other non-verbal communication.

  - Indirect and implicit messages

  - Multiple tasks are managed at once; frequent disruptions; low emphasis on timelines

  - High use of non-verbal communication

  - Low use of written communication

  - Decisions are made on intuition and emotions

  - Emphasis on long-term relationships

  - Exclusive

  - Prefer in-person communication to technology

- **Low context cultures** – Relies heavily on explicit written or verbal communication.

  - Direct, clear messages

  - Tasks are performed linearly; high emphasis on timelines

  - Low use of non-verbal communication

- High use of written communication

- Decisions are made based on facts and information

- Short-term relationships

- Inclusive

- High use of technology with communication

Religions and Ideologies

Religions and ideologies are both systems of belief. Religion examines the afterlife and other aspects that are not in the materialistic world, whereas ideologies focus on materiality of human nature (Claval, 2016).

Religions

Religion	Origin	Countries	Foundations	Sacred Text
Christianity	Originated in 1st century AD. Christianity is the most widely practiced religion worldwide.	United States, Brazil, Mexico, Russia, Philippines, Nigeria, Germany, France	Based on the life and teachings of Jesus of Nazareth. Christians believe Jesus is the son of God and savior of all people. The cross is the symbol of Christianity.	Bible
Islam	Originated at the start of the 7th century in Mecca, Arabia. It is the second most widely practiced religion worldwide.	Indonesia, India, Pakistan, Nigeria, Egypt, Iran, Turkey, Algeria, Iraq, Saudi Arabia, Jordan, Morocco	Muslims worship one all-knowing God who is known as Allah in Arabic. The word "Islam" means "submission to the will of God". Five pillars of Islam are: declaration of faith, prayer, giving money to charity, fasting, and pilgrimage to Mecca.	Koran
Catholicism	Originated circa 30–95 AD.	Brazil, Mexico, Philippines, United States, Italy, France, Colombia, Argentina	Belief that the Roman Catholic church is the one true church. Belief in purgatory. Mass is vital to Catholic worship. Belief in Seven Sacraments: baptism, confirmation, the Eucharist, penance, extreme unction, marriage, holy orders.	Bible

Religion	Origin	Countries	Foundations	Sacred Text
Buddhism	Originated in northeastern India in 6th century BC.	China, Japan, Thailand, Myanmar, Sri Lanka, Cambodia, Mongolia, Japan, Vietnam	Buddhism is based on the teachings of the Buddha, or the "Awakened One". Buddha's teachings were based on human suffering and dissatisfaction. Nirvana is the ultimate spiritual goal of Buddhism. Four Noble truths: life involves suffering; the cause of suffering is craving for pleasure; this craving and suffering can be eliminated; elimination of craving is the result of following a path that involves living ethically, meditating, and developing wisdom.	Pali Canon
Hinduism	Originated around the Indus Valley near the River Indus in modern-day Pakistan between 2300 BC and 1500 BC.	India, Nepal, Malaysia, Bangladesh, Indonesia, Pakistan	Hinduism is not a single religion but a compilation of different beliefs and has no one founder. Hindus worship Brahman, a single supreme God force present in all things, and they recognize other gods and goddesses. Hindus believe in karma and that all life is sacred.	The Vedas
Judaism	Originated in the Middle East over 3500 years ago and founded by Moses.	Israel, United States	Belief in one God with whom they have a covenant (a special agreement) Jews seek to bring holiness into every aspect of life. Belief that Messiah has not arrived yet.	Torah

(history.com/topics/religion)

Section III questions will intertwine with questions from the previous sections. Questions may include identifying ancient civilizations from Egypt, Greece, and Rome and their contributions, and 20th century developments. In addition, it is important to be able to define basic economic terminology and economic systems and know technology's role in economical developments.

The skills you need to know in this section include the following:

A. Knows the major contributions of classical civilizations (e.g., Egypt, Greece, Rome)

B. Understands twentieth-century developments and transformations in world history

C. Understands the role of cross-cultural comparisons in world history instruction

D. Knows key terms and basic concepts of economics (e.g., supply and demand, scarcity and choice, money and resources)

E. Understands how economics affects population, resources, and technology

F. Understands the government's role in economics and the impact of economics on government

A. Contributions of classical civilizations

Neolithic (Agricultural) Revolution

The Neolithic Revolution was the turning point in human history from the hunter-gatherer model for sustenance to an agrarian lifestyle. Loosely formed groups of people went from foraging and hunting to farming and developing communities.

As the Ice Age ended, people could grow plants and domesticate animals, which helped civilizations to form. Farming could support a larger population and allow people to focus on activities that were not directly related to finding food. This was a major development for humans and quickly spread to India, Europe, and other areas (Mann, 2011).

Quick Tip

Scientists believe the Agricultural Revolution happened in Mesopotamia around 9000 BC because of a gradual warming pattern of the Earth.

The Neolithic Revolution sparked the formation of tools, writing, art, technology, and religion. Groups became more densely populated settlements. This led to specialization, division of labor, and increased trade (Violatti, 2018).

- **Hunter-gatherer societies** – Loosely formed; followed animal migratory patterns; no governmental organization

- **Agriculture-based societies** – Beginning of modern civilization; stationary civilizations that grew crops and domesticated animals; formed government, laws, and economic systems

The four main regions responsible for the advancements of the Neolithic Revolution are referred to as "riverine civilizations" due to their reliance on their corresponding rivers to succeed:

- **Mesopotamia** – Tigris-Euphrates river system

- **Egypt** – Nile River Valley

- **Indus Valley Civilization** – Indus River (Pakistan)

- **China** – Yellow River

Mesopotamia

Civilizations of Mesopotamia (The Fertile Crescent) – Mesopotamia is the site of the earliest developments of the Neolithic Revolution starting around 10,000 BC. Mesopotamia has been identified as having inspired some of the most important developments in human history:

- Tools and weapons (wheeled vehicles, sailing boats, potter's wheel)

- Cereal crops (wheat, flax)

- Cuneiform writing

- Agriculture

- Irrigation (dams, aqueducts)

- Pottery, polished stone tools

- Domestication of animals

- Domestication of plants

- Deforestation

- Food surpluses

- Rectangular houses

- Wooden plows

Game Changers

Throughout history, advancements in literature and the capability to disseminate information have created significant turning points in human history. For example:

- **Cuneiform writing** in Mesopotamia triggered the recording of history.

- **The printing press**, created by Johannes Gutenberg in Germany, sparked the Age of Enlightenment.

- **The telegraph** allowed people to communicate over long distances and paved the way for modern electronic communication (Andrews, n.d.).

Mesopotamia is located in western Asia, situated within the Tigris-Euphrates river system. In modern days, the location covers a variety of Middle Eastern countries: Iraq, Kuwait, northern Saudi Arabia, eastern Syria, southeastern Turkey, and regions along the Turkish–Syrian and Iran–Iraq borders.

Map of Mesopotamia

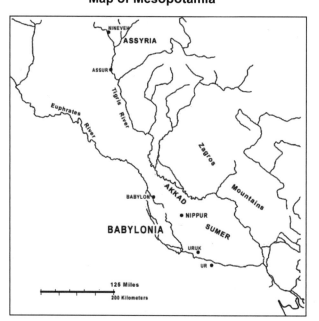

Mesopotamia was surrounded by a complex system of rivers. The two main rivers include the Euphrates and the Tigris. Mesopotamia experienced annual flooding, which made dams and aqueducts extremely important. There were also drier areas of land between the rivers, which required irrigation systems (History. com Editors, 2017).

- **Sumerians (5000 BC–1750 BC)** – The southern civilization of Sumer lived in cities, created writings, and spoke complex languages. The Sumerians had specialized labor, commerce, business, government, and a system of writing. They built mud-brick homes, made public art, and created the written language called cuneiform (History.com Editors, 2017).

- **Assyrians (2000 BC–900 BC)** – The Assyrians were a complex civilization in Mesopotamia. The Assyrians built businesses, formed religions, and waged wars. The Assyrians evolved through the Bronze Age and into the Iron Age.

- **Babylonians (1895 BC–539 BC)** – Babylonia was a state in Mesopotamia, and Babylon was the capital. Babylon was one of the largest ancient civilizations. The Babylonians created large, complex buildings. They also created the Code of Hammurabi, which was a system of law and order (History.com Editors, 2018).

Mesopotamian Advancements

- **Writing** – One of the greatest outcomes of the civilizations of Mesopotamia was a sophisticated method of writing called cuneiform. Cuneiform is a form of script on clay tablets. This was a significant contribution to the development of civilizations because information could be recorded (Mesopotamia.co.uk, n.d.).

- **Mathematics** – The Babylonian Numerals were a series of symbols used to indicate ones, tens, and hundreds similar to a decimal system. Because Babylonians had the capability of writing, they could then record and compute numbers. The Babylonians could process large numbers using this numerical system. The Sumerians used a sexagesimal (base 60) numerical system. This system is still used today as is evident when dividing a circle into 360 degrees and an hour into 60 minutes (Shuttleworth, 2010).

- **Government** – The Sumer, Assyrian, and Babylon civilizations used sophisticated systems of government and rule of law.

- **Literature and Religion** – Modern-day religions can be attributed to the civilizations of Mesopotamia. The Epic of Gilgamesh is considered the most significant piece of literature during this time period and influenced some of the writings in the Bible. Gilgamesh is believed to have been born in the city of Uruk in Mesopotamia around 2700 BC.

Egyptian Advancements

- **Writing** – Egyptians were the first to develop their language into a codified form of writing; ancient Egyptian writing is known as hieroglyphics. Egyptians expressed ideas through pictures using hieroglyphs. Ancient Egyptians believed that when something was written, it would actually happen by means of magic. Therefore, the central purpose of writing was to bring certain concepts or events into existence (David, 2003).

- **Literature** – Egyptian literature represented the people's life, culture, and beliefs. The first forms of Egyptian literature were the autobiography and the prayer. The early literature encompassed a wide array of narrative and poetic forms, religious writings, philosophical works, and more. The literature was of high literary merit and was mainly concerned with astrology, weaving, cooking, and production and purification of metal (DeYoung, 2014).

- **Art** – Ancient Egyptian art was influential and served a practical and a functional purpose. For example, the statues held the spirits of the deceased, and charms protected one from harm. Art included various types of pottery, sculpture, and paintings. The paintings were created with the intent of leading the dead into the afterlife, and the sculptures often represented Egyptian gods.

- **Architecture** – One of the most famous architects and builders during that time was Pharaoh Ramesses the Great. He engineered the corbelled arch, which helped in the construction of pyramids. The Egyptians are well-known for the pyramids they built; the Great Pyramid at Giza is Egypt's most famous landmark.

- **Mathematics and Geometry** – Ancient Egyptians were skilled in math and geometry. They introduced the earliest base-10 number system of hieroglyphs (decimal system). The ancient pyramids are also a testament to Ancient Egyptians' mathematical abilities.

- **Science** – Ancient Egyptians were great inventors and are credited for inventing paper (papyrus sheet) and ink, the calendar, clocks, household goods, cosmetic makeup, and basic machines such as the lever. They were also renowned for being great astronomers. They could easily predict lunar and solar eclipses.

Indus Valley Advancements

The Indus Valley Civilization was located in the northwest region of India and lasted from 3300 BC to 1300 BC. The Indus Valley Civilization is known for the following contributions (Write, 2009):

- Urban planning

- Brick houses

- Innovative drainage system

- Water supply systems

- Copper, bronze, metal, and tin works (metallurgy)

- Large buildings

Yellow River Advancements

The Yellow River Civilization is the ancient Chinese civilization that existed from the Neolithic period through the Bronze Age. Early Chinese settlers established communities in the basin of the Yellow River. As with other early civilizations, the Yellow River Civilization was able to manage the flood plain for agriculture. This allowed the civilization to create art, build buildings, and redistribute crops (Wertz, 2007).

- 10,000 BC–3100 BC: Neolithic Period

  - Farming
  - Carvings and art
  - Religion and pictographs
  - Crops and craftsmen

- 3100 BC–1600 BC: Bronze Age (Charles, 1996)

  - Weapons
  - Tools
  - Art

- 2070 BC–1600 BC: Ancient China (Chinese Civilisation Center, 2007)

  - Xia dynasty
  - Shang dynasty

Ancient Civilizations

Civilization	Dates	Major Contributions
Ancient Greece	2000 BC–100 BC	<ul><li>Minoans and Mycenaean were first occupants of Greece</li><li>The *Polis* (city-state)</li><li>Democracy</li><li>Philosophy, science and math, art, architecture, literature, and theater</li><li>Olympic games</li><li>Athens: center for ideas and thought</li><li>Sparta: center for military</li><li>Gods, myths</li><li>Homer: Iliad, Odyssey</li><li>Alexander the Great defeats Persians, and the Hellenistic period begins</li></ul>
Roman Empire	800 BC–500 AD	<ul><li>Architecture, arches, concrete, plumbing</li><li>Re-engineered and redesigned aqueducts</li><li>*The Republic* (representative democracy)</li><li>*Twelve Tables* (equality under law)</li><li>Julius Caesar, Brutus, and Spartacus</li><li>Games, gladiators, and chariots</li><li>Spain, Gaul, Italy, Macedonia, Asia Minor, Egypt, North Africa</li><li>Romans conquer the Greeks</li><li>Julius Caesar proposes the 365.25-day calendar in 46 BC</li></ul>
Indian	2500 BC–1600 BC	<ul><li>Hinduism<ul><li>Considered oldest religion in the world</li><li>Karma, dharma, reincarnation</li></ul></li><li>Buddhism<ul><li>Purpose within the universe</li><li>Siddhartha and enlightenment</li></ul></li><li>Caste system (hereditary social class)</li><li>Gupta period of art, literature, and intellectuals</li></ul>
Chinese	1600 BC–1912 AD	<ul><li>Dynasties (rulers from the same family)<ul><li>Shang Dynasty (1600 BC–1046 BC)</li><li>Han Dynasty (206 BC–220 AD)</li><li>Tang Dynasty (618–907 AD)</li></ul></li><li>Philosophies:<ul><li>Confucianism – social responsibilities</li><li>Taoism (sometimes Daoism) – the meaning of life</li></ul></li></ul>

Civilization	Dates	Major Contributions
Byzantine Empire	330 AD–1453 AD	• Athens, Constantinople, Southern Italy • Art, literature, and education • Diversity • Epicenter for trade • Connection between Europe and India • Orthodox Church • Conquered by the Ottoman Empire in 1453
Ottoman Empire	1200 AD–1922	• Founded in 1200 AD • Conquered and ended the Byzantine Empire in 1453 • Controlled much of Western Europe • Known as the Turkish Empire • Replaced by the Turkish Republic in 1922

Africa	1000 BC–1500 AD	• African Kush
		  – Gold
		  – Extreme wealth
		• Resources:
		  – Iron, incense, ivory, wheat, barley, cotton
		• Trans-Sahara trade
		• Societies had different systems of government
		• Ghana, Mali, and Benin Kingdoms
		• Trade with Portuguese mariners
		• European colonization and slave trade

Central and South American Empires	9000 BC–1500 AD	• Resources
		  – Corn, beans, squash, paper
		• Mathematics and astronomy
		• Compass, writing, water management
		• Medicines
		• Pyramids (History.com Editors, 2009)
		  – Olmec – La Venta in Tabasco Mexico
		  – Teotihuacán – Pyramid of the Sun in Teotihuacán, Mexico
		  – Mayan – Yucatan, Guatemala
		  – Aztec – Tenochtitlan
		  – Moche and Inca – South America

B. 20th Century developments

Major developments in technology, communication, energy, and society occurred in the 20th century. There was a rapid use of natural resources and exploitation of labor. The combination created 100 years of innovation and advancements.

Advancement	Significance
Assembly line	Henry Ford invented the first moving assembly line, which dramatically reduced the time it took to build an automobile. The assembly line had applications across many industries and allowed for mass production of consumer products (History.com, 2009).
Light bulb	Thomas Edison created the incandescent lightbulb for commercial use in the late 1800s. This invention was significant in the factories during World War I and World War II because people could work longer hours. Industrial plants could work 24 hours a day with rotating shifts (Smithsonian, n.d.).
Bessemer steel	The Bessemer steel process was created in the late 1800s and allowed steel to be mass-produced. Andrew Carnegie saw how the steel was being developed and implemented the process in the United States to create railroad tracks.
Atomic energy	Albert Einstein and others created the first fission bomb (hydrogen bomb), which drastically changed the impacts of war and diplomacy worldwide.
Sputnik	First satellite launched into space by the Russians. This triggered the space race between the Soviet Union and the United States.

C. Cross-cultural comparisons

Throughout history, similar cultural and social events occur in different areas of the world.

Age of Reason and the Enlightenment

The Age of Reason and the Enlightenment (approximately 1600 AD–1800 AD) took place between the medieval and contemporary eras. The main outcome of this time period is that philosophers began exploring based on facts and reason rather than religion. This occurred in several places throughout the world around the same time.

The Age of Reason and the Enlightenment

Movement	Time frame	Major Players and Contributions
The Age of Reason Transition from faith-based reasoning of the Medieval era to rational reasoning	17th Century	• **Thomas Hobbes** – English philosopher, wrote *Leviathan*, a book about the structure of society and legitimate government. • **René Descartes** – French philosopher, generally considered to be the father of modern philosophy. He was the first major figure in the philosophical movement known as *rationalism*, a view that our actions should be based on reason and knowledge. • **John Locke** – Political scientist, wrote *Two Treaties of Government* and advocated for the social contract theory. Locke had a profound influence on Thomas Jefferson and Jefferson's framing of the Declaration of Independence. • **Thomas Paine** – Author of the famous anti-church texts: *Common Sense, The Age of Reason*, and *Rights of Man*. His writing had a profound influence on the framing of American government, specifically the separation of church and state.
The Enlightenment Intellectual movement for freedom, democracy, and reason	18th Century	• **Bishop George Berkeley** – Irish philosopher of immaterialism. Wrote *A Treatise Concerning the Principles of Human Knowledge.* • **Voltaire** – French writer and philosopher. Criticized the Christianity. Wrote *Candide*. • **Jean-Jacques Rousseau** – French philosopher and influencer. Wrote *The Social Contract.* • **Adam Smith** – Economist. Wrote *The Wealth of Nations.* • **Immanuel Kant** – German philosopher. Wrote *Critique of Pure Reason.* • **Edmund Burke** – Irish statesman. Criticized British colonialism. Wrote *A Vindication of Natural Society.*

Age of Exploration, Colonialism, and Imperialism

The Age of Exploration began in the early 15th century and lasted through the 20th century. Europeans began exploring trade routes to avoid the Ottoman Empire (Briney, 2019). Nations were searching for more resources, including crops, gold, silk, and spices. The Ottoman Empire blocked European access to the east when it took over Constantinople. The Age of Exploration led to the discovery and conquer of the Americas (Briney, 2019). European nations explored and conquered lands throughout the world.

Results of the Age of Exploration

- More knowledge about Americas.

- Increased European wealth because of new trade in goods, spices, and precious metals.

- Decline of the Ottoman Empire.

- Mapping improved with the use of the first nautical maps and the invention of the compass.

- New food, plants, and animals were exchanged between the Americas and Europe.

- The Europeans decimated the indigenous population with disease and massacres.

- The massive amount of work led to the 300-year slave trade.

Triangular Salve Trade

The Triangular Slave Trade (or Trade Triangle) refers to the routes European Colonials used to transport slaves from Africa to the Americas and Europe.

Map of Triangular Slave Trade

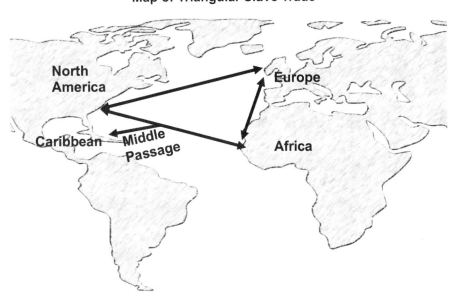

During the period from 1500–1900 in Africa, European mariners began capturing African people and selling them as slaves in Europe and the Americas. This had devastating effects on African civilizations.

The Middle Passage

The part of the slave trade where African captives were packed into ships and sent from Africa to the West Indies (part of the Caribbean).

Age of Revolution

The Age of Revolution is the period of time between 1760–1830, when significant social uprisings occurred in response to tyrannical government control. During this time, the American Revolution and the French Revolution took place, and absolute monarchies were overthrown for democracies (Encyclopedia Britannica, 2019).

American Revolution

The Revolutionary War (1775–1783) was between the British and the 13 American colonies. The colonists did not like the way the British were treating them, especially when it came to taxes. Eventually, small arguments turned into larger fights, and the colonists decided to fight for their independence from Britain. (See Competency 5). In 1781, the battle of Yorktown, led by George Washington and French General Comte de Rochambeau, resulted in the final surrender of the British forces (History.com Editors, 2019).

French Revolution

Prior to the French Revolution, France had experienced years of expensive wars, one of which was the Seven Years' War fought between France and its Native American allies and Great Britain. This war, along with economic and financial crisis France was facing, contributed to the French Revolution (Office of the historian, n.d.). The French Revolution (1789–1799) was a time of social and political upheaval in France and its colonies. Historians widely regard the Revolution as one of the most important events in human history (Palmer & Colton, 1978).

Quick Tip

One of the major contributions to the French Revolution was the leadership of King Louis the 16th. He was only 20 when he took the throne, and many of his decisions caused civil unrest and upheaval.

Key Events (Encyclopedia Britannica, 2019)

- Political conflict – Conflict between the monarchy and the nobility over the tax system led to economic paralysis and bankruptcy. The storming of the political prison known as the Bastille signaled the start of the French Revolution.

- The Enlightenment – The political philosophies of the Enlightenment were spreading with the advent of the printing press. People were not satisfied with monarchical rule and wanted independence.

- Social disruptions among social classes – The aristocracy was the traditional group of elite landowners who were born into the ruling class over centuries. During the French Revolution, another group of middle to upper class merchants and factory workers called the bourgeoisie gained power and influence in economics and politics. The aristocracy and the bourgeoisie often clashed but found common ground to stamp out peasant uprisings.

- Ineffective leadership – King Louis XVI's excessive spending and support for the American Revolutionary War left France on the verge of bankruptcy.

- Economic hardship – The agrarian crisis of 1788–1789 led to discontent and food shortages.

Key Figures

- Jean-Jacques Rousseau – Philosopher, writer, lawyer, politician. He authored *The Social Contract*, which helped inspire political reform (Duignan & Cranston, 2019).

- Maximilien Robespierre – Lawyer, politician, and advocate of democratic reforms. He was the architect of the Reign of Terror and a prominent member of the Committee of Public Safety, which had dictatorial control over the French government (Bouloiseau, 2019).

Latin American Revolution

The **Latin American Wars of Independence** were the revolutions, or a revolutionary wave, that took place during the late 18th and early 19th centuries and resulted in the creation of a number of independent countries in Latin America. During the Latin American Revolution, countries in South and Central America broke from Spanish control.

Key Events

- Hispaniola becomes the first state to break from Spanish rule and become independent.

- Revolt in Latin America – After Hispaniola becomes independent, more countries follow.

- Mexico's Independence – Mexico becomes independent in 1810.

- Battle at Ayacucho – A battle led by Simón Bolívar, which resulted in Peru's independence from Spain.

Key Figures

- Simón Bolívar (aka El Libertador) – Venezuelan military and political leader who led the secession of Venezuela, Bolivia, Colombia, Ecuador, Peru, and Panama from the Spanish Empire (Bushnell, 2003).

- Benito Juárez – The president of Mexico (1861–1872), who fought against foreign occupation.

Scramble for Africa

In the late 19th century, European nations realized the advantages of seizing land in the interior of Africa. 14 countries, including the United States, met in Belgium to map out the region and divide the continent into colonies. From the 1800s to the early 1900s, these countries engaged in conflicts with existing African communities and seized their land. By 1914, Liberia and Ethiopia were the only independent countries on the African continent (University of Cambridge, n.d.).

Decolonization in Asia and Africa

After World War I, African and Asian colonies began to revolt against European rule. During World War II, European countries were unable to hold on to their colonies from the Central Powers. Japan invaded and seized British territory in Asia, including Malaya, Singapore, and Burma. By the end of the war, the Allied Powers wanted to discontinue colonialism and imperialism and foster the principles of sovereignty and self-determination (Klose, 2014).

Anticolonial Leaders:

- **Mahatma Gandhi** – India

- **Ho Chi Minh** – Indochina

- **Messali Hadj** – Algeria

Exploration, Imperialism, and Decolonization Timeline

Time frame	Events
15th Century European Exploration	• Advent of better navigation technology, including maps and the compass, makes exploration possible. • Portugal and Spain began exploring new trade routes. • Portugal discovered the Cape of Good Hope and route around the tip of Africa. • Spanish explorer Christopher Columbus discovered San Salvador and Hispaniola in 1492. • Italian explorer John Cabot discovered continental North America in 1497.
16th Century and 17th Century European colonization of the Americas	• New World is named after Italian explorer Amerigo Vespucci in 1513. • Spanish explorer Vasco Nuñez de Balboa discovers the Pacific Ocean. • Netherlands, England, and France began exploring the New World.
18th Century American colonies revolt	• The colonies in North America declare independence from Britain, initiating the Revolutionary War. • Beginning in the late 18th century and ending in the early 19th century, nearly all of the Latin American colonies gained independence from Spain and Portugal.
19th Century European colonization of Africa and Asia	• French Indochina was formed in 1887 after the Sihno-French War. • Imperialism and trade trigger the Scramble for Africa. • The Berlin Conference in 1884 is held with European nations to partition Africa. • European counties invade and conquer areas with existing African civilizations.
20th Century African and Asian colonies revolt	• 1947 – The British Empire agreed to give India its independence after World War II. When the British withdrew, India split into two independent dominions based on religion. The two dominions formed were India (Hindu) and Pakistan (Islam). Bangladesh gained independence from Pakistan in 1971 (Asrar, 2017). • 1945–1950 – Indonesia fought for independence from the Netherlands. • 1945–1954 – Vietnamese fought for independence from the French. • 35 developing nations were admitted to the United Nations. The United States tried to influence these new governments toward democracy while the Soviet Union tried to influence them toward the communist bloc (Office of the Historian, n.d.). • By 1975, nearly all of the colonial empires were removed from the global system.

D. Basic concepts of economics

It is important to understand basic principles of economics and the global market. Economics is the study of rational human behavior as it relates to production, consumption, and transfer of wealth. Apply your experiences as a consumer when answering exam questions related to economics. Below are some terms and definitions related to economics.

- **Economy** – The wealth and resources of a country or region, especially in terms of the production and consumption of goods and services.

- **Depression** – A long and severe recession in an economy or market.

- **Recession** – A period of temporary economic decline during which trade and industrial activity are reduced, generally identified by a fall in Gross Domestic Product (GDP) in two successive quarters.

- **Market** – A venue where producers and sellers can come together to buy and sell goods.

- **Gross Domestic Product (GDP)** – The value of all the goods and services a country produces in a year.

- **Capitalism** – An economic system where business owners produce goods and provide services for sale in order to make a profit, not for personal consumption.

- **Socialism** – An economic system where there are no private business owners; there is a system of collective or government ownership and administration of production and distribution of goods.

- **Communism** – An economic system where no private property exists and there is centralized production and distribution.

- **Perfect competition** – A perfect market structure where all producers sell an identical product (homogeneous), producers cannot manipulate the price of the product, market share does not influence the price, and buyers have complete information. A perfect competition is the opposite of a monopoly.

- **Monopolistic competition** – A market structure where producers sell similar goods and services, barriers to enter the market are low, and decisions made by one producer do not affect its competitors.

- **Monopoly** – A market structure where there is only one producer/seller. The monopoly has control over the price of its goods and services. The market is restricted due to economic, political, or social barriers.

- **Oligopoly** – A market structure where only a few producer/sellers make up the industry. An oligopoly has control over prices and maintains barriers from others entering the market.

Consumer Spending

Consumer spending is the exchange of money for goods and services by private purchases (Kenton, 2018). Consumer spending is the demand side of supply and demand principles.

- Budgeting – A budget is a plan for spending and saving money. The main reason for making a budget and sticking to it is to save for future goals while meeting present needs.

  - **Planning** – A budget ensures a person's total income meets total expenditures and helps to manage cash flow so income and expenditures coincide.

  - **Communication** – A budget is a concrete communication of personal goals and monetary plans.

  - **Motivation** – A budget can help motivate individuals to reach goals by setting achievable intermediate objectives.

  - **Control** – A budget allows control of finances because it shows what actually occurred versus what was planned.

Types of Accounts

Account	Description
Checking Account	A bank account where the account holder can make deposits and withdrawals, and access is unlimited.
Savings Account	A bank account where the account holder can make deposits and withdrawals, and the account earns interest. This type of account is commonly used to store money for longer periods of time. The money is readily accessible.
Money Market Accounts	A bank account with a higher interest rate than a savings account but with limited withdrawals per statement cycle. This type of account usually requires a minimum balance.
Certificates of Deposit (CD)	A bank account with a higher interest rate than a money market account but from which the money cannot be withdrawn for a set period of time.
Individual Retirement Account (IRA)	A retirement account that offers tax advantages but cannot be withdrawn until retirement (age 59.5) without penalty.
U.S. Savings Bonds	A government bond that is exempt from state and local taxes and is used to fund capital projects. The bond has a fixed interest rate for a fixed period of time, usually 15–30 years. Federal taxes are applied at the time the bond matures.

Credit Management

Credit leads to an increase in spending, thus increasing income levels in the economy. This leads to higher GDP and thereby faster productivity growth. If credit is used to purchase productive resources, credit helps in economic growth and adds to income.

- **Consumer Credit** – The portion of credit consumers use to buy non-investment services. These are goods that depreciate quickly (automobiles, TVs, recreational vehicles, boats, etc.). One form of consumer credit is a credit card.

  - **Advantage** – Consumers can purchase goods and services and pay for them later over an extended period of time.

  - **Disadvantage** – If consumers fail to repay a loan or a credit card balance, this impacts their credit scores, affects terms and conditions, and results in late fees and penalties.

Types of Consumer Credit:

- **Non-Installment Credit** – Short-term borrowing that ends with the borrower making one payment by the end of the credit period.

- **Close-End Credit** – A specific amount of money is lent to the borrower—the total purchase price of the good or service. This type of credit is typically used by car dealerships.

- **Revolving Open-End Credit** – This type of consumer credit is found with most credit cards. With this kind of credit, the lender extends credit for use by the consumer with an outside limit that depends on the debtor's credit history and ability to manage the debt repayment.

Supply and Demand

Supply and demand theory is one of the basic concepts of a market economy. Demand is how much product consumers want; supply is how much product the market can provide. The quantity supplied refers to the price suppliers are willing to receive for a specific good.

- **Law of Demand** – When prices increase, demand decreases. Demand is centered on the consumer's behavior. Consumers will purchase fewer products if the price is high.

- **Law of Supply** – When prices increase, supply increases. Supply is centered on the supplier's behavior. Suppliers will sell more products if the price is high.

- **Equilibrium** – Supply and demand equilibrium occurs at the intersection of the demand curve and the supply curve. Equilibrium is a balance between supply and demand, also called *allocation efficiency*. This can only be reached in theory because supply and demand are constantly changing with the fluctuations of the market.

Supply and Demand

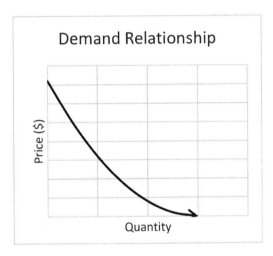

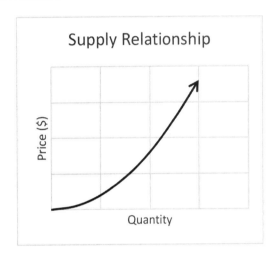

Supply and Demand Equilibrium

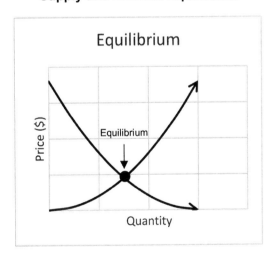

- **Disequilibrium** – This occurs when the price or the quantity are not equal to the equilibrium.

  - **Excess supply (economic surplus)** – The quantity of goods supplied is more than the quantity demanded.

  - **Excess demand (economic shortage)** – The quantity demanded for a good is higher than what can be supplied.

  - **Elasticity** – The degree in which consumers change their demand and producers change their supply in response to changes in price or income.

    ○ **Elastic** – The quantity demand of a good or service changes significantly when its price changes.

    ○ **Inelastic** – The quantity demand of a good or service only changes modestly when its price changes.

$$Elasticity = \frac{\%\ Change\ in\ Quantity}{\%\ Change\ in\ Price}$$

If the elasticity is greater than or equal to 1, the good or service is elastic. If the elasticity is less than 1, the good or service is inelastic.

Simultaneous Changes in Supply and Demand

It is important to understand what happens to the equilibrium price and quantity when there are simultaneous changes in supply and demand. The table below provides the information you need to know for this exam.

Simultaneous Changes in Supply and Demand

	Demand Increases	Demand Decreases
Supply Increases	Equilibrium price cannot be determined Quantity increases	Equilibrium price decreases Quantity cannot be determined
Supply Decreases	Equilibrium price increases Quantity cannot be determined	Equilibrium price cannot be determined Quantity decreases

For example, a coffee mug company decides to reduce the number of porcelain mugs it produces because fewer people are buying them. There is a decrease in demand and a decrease in supply. What happens to the equilibrium price and the quantity when both demand and supply are decreased?

A. Price increases, quantity increases

B. Price is indeterminate, quantity decreases

C. Price increases, quantity decreases

D. Price decreases, quantity decreases

The correct answer is B. From the table, you know that at least one element of the answer must be indeterminate (cannot be determined). Answer choice B is the only option with an indeterminate component. But let's look at a graph to see what is happening.

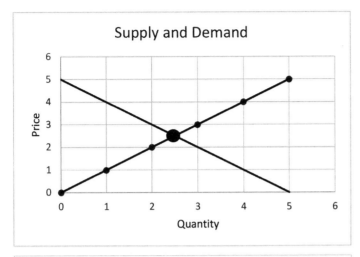

This graph is showing the supply and demand relationship before any changes are made. The equilibrium price is about 2.5 and the quantity is about 2.5.

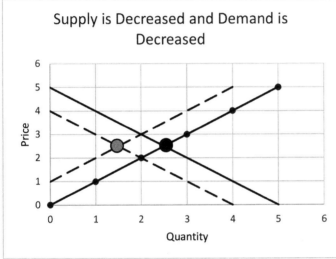

This graph is showing what happens when both supply and demand are decreased. The graph moves to the left because it is a decrease. The equilibrium price stayed about 2.5 and but the quantity decreased to about 1.5. The price stayed the same, but the quantity decreased.

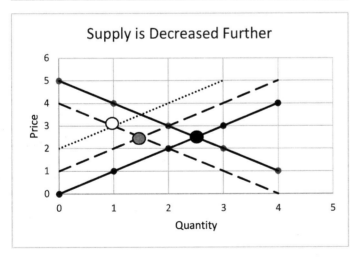

This graph is showing the supply and demand relationship when both supply and demand are decreased, but supply is decreased even further. The equilibrium price is about 3 and the quantity is about 1. In this case, the price actually increased, and the quantity decreased.

The graphs are provided for perspective. It is not important for you to be able to graph these shifts, but you should be able to recite the information in the table. Remember, when there are simultaneous shifts in supply and demand, one of the elements cannot be determined.

Scarcity and Opportunity

Cost scarcity refers to a limited availability of goods and services. It occurs when people cannot obtain much of something they need. Scarcity often involves a trade-off because people must sacrifice resources or goods they have in order to obtain more of the scarce resources they need or want (Siddiqui, 2010).

> **Think About It**
>
> When things are scarce, they cost more. For example, if there were only 100,000 iPhones available in the United States, the price of iPhones would be very high. However, if Apple overproduced more iPhones than people wanted, Apple would have to put them on sale or reduce the price so people would buy.

Key Idea: Scarcity influences market prices.

Example:

- The gasoline shortage in the 1970s resulted in soaring gas prices and long lines at the pumps.

Opportunity Cost – The loss of potential gain from other alternatives when one alternative is chosen.

Examples:

- A business is considering adding to its parking lot so it can serve more customers. The construction will cause a temporary reduction in parking space; therefore, the business will lose some revenue while adding to the parking lot. However, when construction is completed, the parking lot will hold two times as many cars as the original parking lot; therefore, revenue will increase. In this case, the *opportunity cost* is the money the business will lose during the construction of the new parking spaces. The *opportunity* is the chance to earn more money by serving more customers after the parking lot expansion is complete.

- An employer is hiring new personnel to grow the business. The *opportunity cost* is the additional payroll cost (salary and taxes). The *opportunity* is the chance to earn higher profit by growing the new business with the additional personnel.

Investments – The action or process of investing money for profit or material result (U.S. Securities and Exchange Commission, 2019).

Higher returns come from higher interest rates.

Example:

- 7% annual interest on $100 = $107 at the end of the year.
- 3% annual interest on $100 = $103 at the end of the year.

Quarterly Return/Compound Interest Example

Quarter	Start	Interest	End of Quarter Return
Quarter 1	$100.00	7%	$107.00
Quarter 2	$107.00	7%	$114.49
Quarter 3	$114.49	7%	$122.50
Quarter 4	$122.50	7%	$131.08
Total for the year			**$131.08**

Investments can be made for short-term or long-term gain. Long-term investments are typically held for more than one year. Short-term investments are held for a year or less (U.S. Securities and Exchange Commission, 2019).

Examples of short-term investment:

- Buying and renovating a home to re-sell

- Buying Certificates of Deposit (CDs)

- Enrolling in an interest-bearing savings account

Examples of long-term investments:

- Investing in stocks (i.e., 401K)

- Investing in IRAs (i.e., Traditional, Roth, SEP)

- Investing in bonds

E. Economics and its effects

Economics impacts where people live. People move toward economic opportunities. In the 18th and 19th centuries, millions of Europeans moved to the New World for a better life with more economic freedom. In the late 19th and early 20th centuries, Americans moved to cities to get jobs in factories.

When people migrate to another country, it is usually because something pushes them away from their native country and pulls them toward a new place. This idea is called the push-pull factor.

- **Push factors** are the circumstances that make a person want to leave. For example, lack of employment or education opportunities, a tyrannical government, famine, or war.

- **Pull factors** are the advantages a country has that make a person want to live there. America has pull factors for many people around the world whose native countries have unstable governments, limited job opportunities, or no reliable security.

Quick Tip

A **PUSH factor** on an Irish family leaving Ireland during the Potato Famine would be the lack of food in the old country. A **PULL factor** would be food and opportunity to buy more food in a more prosperous country.

The Great Famine of Ireland (The Potato Famine)

Beginning in 1845 and lasting for six years, the potato famine killed nearly 1 million men, women, and children in Ireland and caused another 2 million to flee the country. The crisis started with a natural event that infected potato crops. The situation was further exacerbated by the government's laissez-faire economic policies and its continuation of exporting of food to Great Britain. The potato famine in Ireland resulted in Irish immigrants coming to the United States, causing a large increase in the Irish population in U.S. cities (Mokyr, 2019).

F. Government and economics

Government influence in economics has played a huge role in American history. In the 17th and 18th century, economic opportunity brought people to the American colonies and the New World. Trade restrictions, taxes, and tariffs caused the American colonists to revolt against the British government. Proposed restrictions on slave labor caused the southern states to secede from the Union and ignited the American Civil War. The laissez-faire economic policies of the 1920s allowed the economy to swell too fast and contributed to the Great Depression. The government's deregulation of banks in the early 2000s led to the housing market crash of 2008. Government action and inaction influence the economy.

- **Embargo** – An official ban on trade or other commercial activity with a particular country.

- **Eminent domain** – The right of a government or its agent to expropriate private property for public use, with payment of compensation.

- **Sanctions** – A threatened penalty for disobeying a law or rule.

- **Trade regulation** – Monitoring including government regulation of unfair methods of competition and unfair or deceptive business acts or practices.

The Federal Reserve

The Federal Reserve (sometimes called "the Fed") is the central banking system of the United States. It was established in 1913 to gain control of the economy and alleviate financial crisis. The Federal Reserve also lends money to smaller banks and determines interest rates (The Board of Governors of the Federal Reserve System, 2019).

When the economy grows too fast, the Federal Reserve increases interest rates to counteract borrowing. When the economy slows down, the Federal Reserve lowers interest rates to encourage borrowing.

The Federal Reserve has several primary functions (Federal Reserve System, 2016):

- Promote the health and stability of the U.S. economy and financial system

- Conduct monetary policy

    - Expansionary monetary policy – Policy intended to stimulate the economy

    - Contractionary monetary policy – Policy intended to abate the economy

- Supervise and regulate financial institutions and activities

- Promote a safe, efficient, and accessible settlement system for transactions

- Promote consumer protection and community development

Department of the Treasury

The Department of the Treasury manages federal finances by collecting taxes, paying bills, and managing currency, government accounts, and public debt. The Department of the Treasury also enforces finance and tax laws (U.S. Department of Treasury, 2019).

The Department of the Treasury is responsible for:

- producing all currency and coinage of the United States.

- collecting taxes, duties, and money paid to and due to the United States.

- paying all bills of the United States.

- managing the federal finances.

- managing government accounts and the United States public debt.

- supervising national banks and thrift institutions.

- advising on domestic and international financial, monetary, economic, trade, and tax policy (fiscal policy being the sum of these).

- enforcing federal finance and tax laws.

- investigating and prosecuting tax evaders.

- publishing statistical reports.

Terms of Trade

A *tariff* is a tax or duty to be paid on a particular class of imports or exports. The result of a tariff is often higher prices on goods for the consumers (Gleckman, 2018).

Examples:

- Tariffs (taxes) on cars imported from Japan

- Tariffs (taxes) on coffee imported from South America

An *embargo* is an official ban on trade with a specific country or commodity. Typically, embargoes are implemented as a form of punishment or for diplomatic leverage.

In the Real World

President Trump imposed tariffs of 10% on $200 billion worth of Chinese imports in September 2018. Walmart and other retailers announced that the tariffs would result in some combination of higher prices and lower profits.

Example:

- In 2006, the U.N. Security Council (UNSC) imposed an embargo on North Korea in response to North Korea's first nuclear test. The embargo prohibited the supply of heavy weapons and select luxury goods.

Comparative Advantage

Comparative advantage is when a country produces a good or service for a lower opportunity cost than other countries. The country may not be the best at producing something, but the good or service has a low opportunity cost for other countries to import (Amadeo, 2018).

Example:

- Companies in the United States use call center services from India because the services are less expensive than locating the call center in the United States. Indian call centers are not necessarily better than United States call centers; however, India's services are inexpensive, making the trade-off worthwhile.

Absolute Advantage

Absolute advantage is when a country produces greater quantity of a good, product, or service than competitors using the same amount of resources.

Example:

- Saudi Arabia can produce more oil than many other countries. Saudi Arabia does not have to spend as many resources to produce oil as many other countries do. Therefore, Saudi Arabia has an absolute advantage over other non-oil producing countries.

Economic Systems

- **Traditional Economic System** – The original economic system in which traditions, customs, and beliefs shape the goods and the services the economy produces.

- **Command Economic System** – The government determines what goods should be produced, how much should be produced, and the price at which the goods are offered for sale. This is also referred to as Communism.

  - **Centralized Control** – A feature of a command economy is that a large part of the economic system is controlled by a centralized power, most often the federal government.

- **Market Economic System** – Decisions regarding investment, production, and distribution are based on market, supply, and demand. Prices of goods and services are determined in a free price system.

- **Capitalism** – Capitalism affords economic freedom, consumer choice, and economic growth.

- **Socialism** – The means of production, distribution, and exchange are owned or regulated by the community as a whole.

- **Mixed Economic System** – Features characteristics of both capitalism and socialism.

Macroeconomics

Macroeconomics is a branch of economics dealing with the performance, structure, behavior, and decision-making of regional, national, and global economies (O'Sullivan & Sheffrin, 2003).

National income refers to the total value of a country's output of all new goods and services produced in a year, both domestically and internationally. It is important to measure the level of national income in order to understand economic growth, living standards, and income distribution.

Gross domestic product (GDP) is the value of the goods and services produced domestically in a year. The percentage that GDP increases or decreases from one period to another is an important way for the people of a country to measure the health of the economy. The GDP measures income of anyone in the country, including foreign businesses (U.S. Bureau of Economic Analysis, 2019).

Think About It

The broadest and most widely used measure of national income is GDP. The GDP is the value of expenditures on final goods and services at market prices produced by domestic factors of production (labor, capital, materials) during the year (Ott, n.d.).

Labor is the amount of physical, mental, and social effort used to produce goods and services in an economy. It supplies the expertise, manpower, and service needed to turn raw materials into finished products and services (Amadeo, 2018).

Full employment is a stable rate of unemployment—1 to 2 percent of the total workforce.

Underemployment is when skilled workers are working fewer hours than they would like to work or when the workers take lower paying jobs that do not require the skills or education the workers hold (Beveridge, 1944; O'Sullivan & Sheffrin, 2003).

Unemployment is when people who are actively seeking work cannot find employment. There are three types of unemployment:

- **Frictional unemployment** – Refers to difficulty in matching qualified workers with jobs. For example, a college graduate who is actively looking for work cannot find a job that matches her skills.

- **Cyclical unemployment** – Refers to unemployment that is a product of the business cycle (Simpson, n.d.). For example, when tourist season ends in Florida, people lose their jobs or have difficulty finding work.

- **Structural unemployment** – Refers to unemployment that occurs when workers are not qualified for the jobs that are available (Simpson, n.d.). An example of this is when manufacturing jobs and trade jobs go unfilled because workers do not have the necessary skills. The job skills such workers possess become obsolete, and the workers need to be retrained.

Price stability indicates that the economy's price level does not fluctuate much over a period of time, and there are no long periods of inflation or deflation (Poole & Wheelock, 2008).

- **Inflation** – A rise in the general price level of goods and services in an economy over time, resulting in a decline in the value of money and purchasing power.

  - Inflation complicates economic decision-making.

  - Rapid inflation slows economic growth.

  - Inflation diminishes the value of savings.

- **Deflation** – A decrease in the general price level of goods and services over a longer period of time.

  - Deflation slows economic growth.

  - People stop buying, so companies stop producing.

  - Loans are not repaid, which poses a threat to the stability of financial institutions.

Exchange Rates and the International Price of Goods

In finance, an exchange rate is the rate at which one currency will be exchanged for another. It is also regarded as the value of one country's currency in relation to another country's currency (O'Sullivan & Sheffrin, 2003).

Movements in exchange rates alter the international price of goods and services.

If the U.S. dollar depreciates, the exchange rate falls, and:

- the relative price of domestic goods and services decreases.

- the relative price of foreign goods and services increases.

- the change in relative prices will increase U.S. exports and decrease its imports.

If the dollar appreciates, the exchange rate increases:

- the relative price of domestic goods and services increases.

- the relative price of foreign goods and services falls.

- the change in relative prices will decrease U.S. exports and increase its imports.

This page intentionally left blank.

1. Which of the following early colonial leaders advocated for religious freedom?

    A.   Roger Williams

    B.   John Adams

    C.   John Locke

    D.   James Madison

2. Which of the following is the belief that people have the right to disobey the government if the government fails to protect their natural rights?

    A.   Manifest destiny

    B.   Social contract

    C.   Conservatism

    D.   Civil rights

3. Which of the following best describes the similarity between 16th century Latin America and 19th century Africa?

    A.   Industrialization

    B.   European colonialism

    C.   Revolution

    D.   Renaissance

4. Pakistan and Bangladesh were formed from which British colony after it gained independence following World War II?

    A.   India

    B.   Cambodia

    C.   Malaysia

    D.   Kazakhstan

5. Which of the following describes the trade routes of raw materials, manufactured goods, and slaves among Europe, Africa, and the United States?

    A.   Intrastate trade

    B.   Silk Road

    C.   NAFTA

    D.   Trade triangle

6. Which of the following regions was once a prosperous civilization but has become a barren desert due to deforestation?

    A.   Siberia

    B.   Sahel

    C.   Saskatchewan

    D.   Sahara

7. Which of the following is the process of cultivating crops on the sides of hills to maximize land area?

    A. Crop rotation

    B. Sustenance farming

    C. Terrace farming

    D. Commercial farming

8. Which of the following inventions of the Industrial Revolution made it possible for factory workers to work longer hours?

    A. Henry Ford's assembly line

    B. Thomas Edison's lightbulb

    C. Eli Whitney's cotton gin

    D. Henry Bessemer's steel process

9. Which of the following amendments to the U.S. Constitution abolished slavery?

    A. The First Amendment

    B. The Fourth Amendment

    C. The Thirteenth Amendment

    D. The Nineteenth Amendment

10. What purpose did the Articles of Confederation serve?

    A. To establish the first constitution of the United States

    B. To declare independence from Great Britain

    C. For the southern states to secede from the Union

    D. To strengthen the central government

11. The United States and Great Britain signed which of the following documents to end the War of 1812?

    A. The Treaty of Versailles

    B. The Treaty of Ghent

    C. The Treaty of Paris

    D. Oregon Treaty

12. Which of the following triggered the Space Race?

    A. Sputnik satellite

    B. First woman in space

    C. First moon landing

    D. International space station

13. Which of the following nations built the irrigation system that caused the desertification of the Aral Sea?

    A. Egypt

    B. Japan

    C. United States

    D. Soviet Union

14. Which of the following refers to the social movement in the late 19th and early 20th centuries that focused on women's suffrage?

    A. First-wave of feminism

    B. Second-wave of feminism

    C. Militant feminism

    D. Third-wave of feminism

15. Which of the following was a catalyst for the energy crisis in the 1970s?

    A. United States support to Israel

    B. Soviet Union support to the United States

    C. Decreased consumption of fossil fuels

    D. Increased trade with OPEC

16. Prior to the end of the War of 1812, which of the following is true?

    A. Native American tribes did not support British troops in fighting the American colonists.

    B. France refused to trade with Britain and the American colonists.

    C. Russia dominated trade while the French, British, and American colonists were fighting wars with each other.

    D. The British provided protection for Native Americans in resisting the American colonists from settling in present-day Indiana.

17. Which of the following is the most significant development in ancient Mesopotamia?

    A. Farming

    B. Transportation

    C. Writing

    D. Irrigation

18. Which of the following civilizations was best known for its complex aqueduct systems?

    A. Egypt

    B. Mesopotamia

    C. Pangea

    D. Ancient Rome

19. Which Mesoamerican civilization built the Pyramid of the Sun?

    A. Inca

    B. Teotihuacán

    C. Aztec

    D. Olmec

20. Which of the following types of economies supports advances in technology?

    A. Market

    B. Mixed

    C. Command

    D. Traditional

21. Which of the following consists of a group of people that has a prominent ethnicity different from the surrounding community?

    A. An embassy

    B. An ethnic enclave

    C. A religious community

    D. A linguistic community

22. Which of the following is an example of an archipelago?

    A. Himalayas

    B. Great Lakes

    C. Great Plains

    D. Hawaiian Islands

23. Anti-Federalists opposed the ratification of the U.S. Constitution because of which of the following reasons?

    A. It lacked a bill of rights.

    B. It lacked the ability to trade independently with other nations.

    C. It gave too much power to the states.

    D. It did not include an executive branch.

24. Following the Louisiana Purchase, Thomas Jefferson ordered which of the following tasks to be completed?

    A. Implementation of the Indian removal process

    B. Reconstitution of the southern states

    C. Exploration of the new territory

    D. Initiation of the first U.S. census

25. Using the map below, which country is at 60°N, 120°E?

    A. Russia

    B. South Africa

    C. Australia

    D. Canada

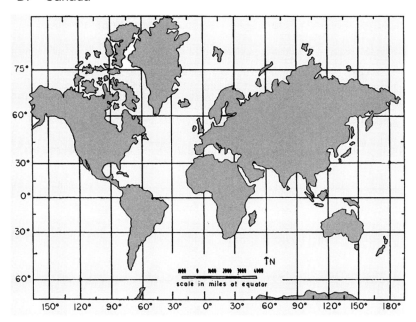

26. Which of the following is an example of absolute advantage?

    A. When a country produces goods at a lower opportunity cost than its competitors

    B. When a country specializes in the product they are most efficient at producing

    C. When a country has an economic surplus and its trading partner has an economic shortage

    D. When a country only exports products and does not import products

27. Which of the following was established to restrict monopolies?

    A. Sherman Anti-Trust Act

    B. Chinese Exclusion Act

    C. Federal Reserve Act

    D. Securities Exchange Act

28. Which of the following restricted the First Amendment, specifically the freedom of speech?

    A. Plessy v. Ferguson

    B. Schenck v. United States

    C. Dred Scott v. Sandford

    D. Miranda v. Arizona

29. Which of the following terms refers to a sense of identity and perception of societal norms?

    A. Assimilation

    B. Competition

    C. Cooperation

    D. Socialization

30. Which of the following developments helped increase agriculture during the western expansion?

    A. Irrigation from dams

    B. Crop rotation

    C. Terrace farming

    D. Desalination of seawater

31. Which of the following is true of voter turnout in the United States?

    A. Fewer people vote in general elections than in primary elections.

    B. More people vote in presidential elections than in midterm elections.

    C. More people vote in local elections than in presidential elections.

    D. More independents vote in presidential elections than democrats and republicans combined.

32. Demand for a product sharply decreases. As a result, companies produce less of the product. What happens to the equilibrium price and quantity?

    A. Quantity increases; price increases.

    B. Quantity increases; price is indeterminate.

    C. Quantity increases; price decreases.

    D. Quantity decreases; price is indeterminate.

33. Which of the following is attributed to Henry Ford's assembly line?

    A. Increased wages

    B. Reduced migrant workers

    C. Increased production

    D. Reduced workplace accidents

34. Which of the following is a characteristic of the Industrial Revolution?

    A. People moved away from urban areas to rural and suburban areas.

    B. Immigrant workforce increased in factories.

    C. Government regulators provided protection for workers.

    D. Environmental activists pushed big business toward conservation.

35. Which of the following is a characteristic of early 18th century America?

    A. Dependence on trade with France and Great Britain

    B. Dependence on trade with Italy and Germany

    C. Independent from trade with Europe

    D. Dependence on trade within the colonies

36. Which of the following states would be most affected by the Mississippi River flooding?

    A. Utah

    B. Texas

    C. Washington

    D. Louisiana

37. What is Thomas Jefferson advocating for in the following quote?
    It is more dangerous that even a guilty person should be punished without the forms of law than that he should escape.

    A. Due process

    B. Crime and punishment

    C. Civic duty to understand the law

    D. Extradition

38. What did Andrew Carnegie use the Bessemer steel process for?

    A. Railroads

    B. Canals

    C. Irrigation systems

    D. Assembly line

39. Which of the following characteristics best describes President Coolidge's approach to economics in the 1920s?

    A. Authoritarian

    B. Laissez-faire

    C. Democratic

    D. Collaborative

40. Which of the following describes the duty of the judicial branch of U.S. government?

    A. Makes laws

    B. Enforces laws

    C. Interprets laws

    D. Implements policy

41. Which entity of U.S. government has the power to declare war?

    A. Supreme Court

    B. Congress

    C. House of Representatives

    D. The President

42. Which term is used to describe the study of folklore, linguistics, and ethnology?

    A.   Physical anthropology

    B.   Biology

    C.   Cultural anthropology

    D.   Civics

43. Which region of the world had the highest population at the beginning of the 21st century?

    A.   North and South America

    B.   Africa

    C.   Europe

    D.   Asia

44. How did the U.S. government ensure resources were available during WWII?

    A.   Central planning

    B.   Eminent domain

    C.   Market economy

    D.   Mix economy

45. Which of the following best describes the similarities between 18th Century America and 20th Century Africa?

    A.   Industrialization

    B.   European colonialism

    C.   Revolution

    D.   Renaissance

46. Which of the following strategies was used during the Cold War to stop the spread of communism?

    A.   Colonialism

    B.   Containment

    C.   Imperialism

    D.   Proliferation

47. Which of the following terms is used to describe agriculture where large parcels of land are cultivated using machinery rather than manual labor?

    A.   Extensive farming

    B.   Intensive farming

    C.   Sustenance farming

    D.   Pastoral farming

48. Which of the following types of power generation creates the most greenhouse gasses?

    A.   Nuclear

    B.   Wind

    C.   Hydro

    D.   Coal

49. Which of the following is the type of economic policy where the government regulates the price of goods and services?

    A. Capitalism

    B. Mix-market

    C. Socialism

    D. Competition

50. Which of the following best exemplifies the concept of manifest destiny?

    A. Westward expansion in the United States

    B. Scramble for Africa

    C. Internment camps of Japanese-Americans

    D. Decolonization of India

51. The idea that students can reach higher-level goals if their basic human needs are realized describes which of the following theories?

    A. Piaget's stages of cognitive development

    B. Erikson's stages of psychosocial development

    C. Maslow's hierarchy of needs

    D. Vygotsky's zone of proximal development

52. Which of the following mountain ranges passes through Argentina and Chile?

    A. Himalayas

    B. Andes

    C. Alps

    D. Rockies

53. Why would the Federal Reserve increase interest rates?

    A. To boost the economy out of a recession

    B. To increase lending by banks

    C. To mitigate a rapid expansion of the economy

    D. To increase inflation

54. Which of the following concepts describes a government structure that is a mixed or compound mode of government that combines a general government with regional (state) governments in a single political system, dividing the powers between the two?

    A. Federalism

    B. Separation of power

    C. Representative democracy

    D. Liberalism

55. Which of the following religions is practiced in East Asia and focuses on the Four Noble Truths?

    A. Islam

    B. Catholicism

    C. Hinduism

    D. Buddhism

This page intentionally left blank.

#	Answer	Category	Explanation
1.	A	I	Roger Williams was a political and religious leader who strongly advocated for religious freedom and the separation of church and state.
2.	B	I	Social contract is the belief that there are political and moral obligations between a government and its people. Thomas Hobbes, John Locke, and Jean-Jacques Rousseau are well-known advocates of social contract theory. John Locke proposed that when the government fails in its moral obligations to its people, the people have the right to revolt.
3.	B	III	Spanish and Portuguese colonists established settlements in Latin America in the 16th century during the Age of Exploration. A second wave of European colonialism hit Africa in the 19th century with massive military invasions throughout the continent led by Britain, France, Germany, Belgium, Italy, Portugal, and Spain.
4.	A	III	Following its independence, India was partitioned into Hindu-majority India and Muslim-majority Pakistan. Bangladesh gained independence from Pakistan in 1971.
5.	D	III	The trade triangle, also known as the triangle slave trade, is a system of trade where Europe brought manufactured goods to Africa in exchange for slaves. European traders brought the slaves to the Americas in exchange for raw materials.
6.	B	II	The Sahel is a region along the southern border of the Sahara Desert that was once supported a prosperous community of farming and agriculture. Overpopulation, overgrazing, and agriculture led to the deforestation of the area and ultimately caused the desertification of the Sahel.
7.	C	II	Terrace farming was used by the ancient Incas to maximize land area on the sides of hills and mountains. Terrace farming is still used today, especially in rice farming.
8.	B	III	Thomas Edison's invention of the light bulb had a significant impact on the Industrial Revolution because it allowed workers to continue working at night. This increased manufacturing production.
9.	C	I	The Thirteenth Amendment to the U.S. Constitution was ratified in 1865 after the Civil War. The Thirteenth Amendment abolished slavery and involuntary servitude.

#	Answer	Category	Explanation
10.	A	I	The Articles of Confederation was the original constitution of the United States. However, it lacked the ability for the central government to implement taxes and regulate trade. This and other issues led to the Constitutional Convention in 1787 and the end of the Articles of Confederation.
11.	B	I	Neither Britian nor the United States had a substantial victory in the War of 1812. Both sides wanted the war to end and agreed to restore the status quo antebellum with the Treaty of Ghent.
12.	A	III	The Soviet Union launched the first satellite, Sputnik, into space. This event was the beginning of the Space Race between the Soviet Union and the United States.
13.	D	II	The Aral Sea was once a freshwater lake where civilizations thrived. In the 1960s, the Soviet Union built an irrigation system of canals, reservoirs, and dams to provide fresh water to cotton and wheat fields in Kazakhstan and Uzbekistan.
14.	A	I	The first-wave feminist movement began in Seneca Falls in 1848, when 300 people rallied for women's equality with a focus on women's right to vote.
15.	A	I	During the Yom Kippur War in 1973, the United States provided military support to Israel. This triggered the Organization of Petroleum Exporting Countries (OPEC) to dramatically reduce its petroleum production and establish an embargo on oil to the United States.
16.	D	I	The British provided protection for Native American tribes in exchange for their support in fighting with the British against the Americans in the War of 1812.
17.	C	III	While farming, transportation, and irrigation were all important developments in ancient Mesopotamia, the invention of writing (Cuneiform) marks the beginning of written history and is the most significant development during this time period.
18.	D	III	Aqueducts were first used in Mesopotamia to move water through a series of bridges and canals to cultivate crops. However, the Ancient Romans are the most famous for their complex aqueducts and irrigation systems.
19.	B	III	The Pyramid of the Sun, which is the most famous single pyramid in Latin America, was built by the Teotihuacán. The Aztecs discovered the ancient pyramid centuries after it was constructed and named it the Pyramid of the Sun.
20.	A	III	A market economy supports innovation and competition, which drive entrepreneurs to create new technology.

Social Studies - 344

#	Answer	Category	Explanation
21.	B	II	An ethnic enclave is subsection of a community where the population is ethnically distinguished from the surrounding area. For example, a barrio is a Spanish-speaking area or neighborhood in a city.
22.	D	II	An archipelago is a group of islands or island chains. Hawaii is an archipelago formed from volcanic eruptions.
23.	A	I	The Anti-Federalists feared that the original draft of the U.S. Constitution gave too much power to the central government. Without a bill of rights, the individual could easily be oppressed.
24.	C	I	Thomas Jefferson instructed Meriwether Lewis and William Clark to explore the area from the recent Louisiana Purchase, also known as the Lewis and Clark Expedition.
25.	A	II	The point at 60 degrees north of the Equator and 120 degrees east of the Prime Meridian is in Russia.
26.	B	III	Absolute advantage describes how countries can increase their wealth by specializing in producing and exporting goods they produce most efficiently.
27.	A	I	The Sherman Anti-Trust Act of 1890 was the first federal law that outlawed monopolistic business practices.
28.	B	I	Schenck v United States established that speech (written or spoken) that creates a clear and present danger to society is not protected under the First Amendment.
29.	D	II	Socialization is the process of understanding oneself and societal expectations through social interactions with others.
30.	A	II	Early settlers in the American west suffered tremendous loss because of the lack of water available for life and farming. In order to increase migration to the western frontier, the U.S. government invested in large irrigation projects to help cultivate the land for farming and agriculture.
31.	B	I	More people vote in the presidential elections than they do in midterm or local elections. Low voter turnout occurs in primary, midterm, and local elections. Voter turnout is influenced by electoral competitiveness, election type, voting laws, and demographics.
32.	D	III	When both supply and demand decrease simultaneously, the equilibrium quantity decreases but the change in price is unknown. The price could go up, down, or remain the same depending on the degree of shift in demand and the degree of shift in supply.
33.	C	I	The assembly line allowed mass manufacturing, which increased production. Henry Ford's assembly line made it possible to manufacture cars at a much faster rate than before.

#	Answer	Category	Explanation
34.	B	I	Immigration to the United States increased significantly during the Industrial Revolution. The United States was seen throughout the world as a place of opportunities. Within the United States, people moved from rural areas to urban areas for factory jobs. At the time, there were very few government regulations to protect workers and the environment.
35.	A	I	In the 17th century, Great Britain established restrictions on American trade where the colonies could only trade with Great Britain. By the 18th century, colonists were ignoring the law and trading fur, cotton, and timber with the French West Indies for molasses.
36.	D	II	The Mississippi River borders the eastern part of Louisiana and has caused historic floods throughout the state.
37.	A	I	Thomas Jefferson is advocating for due process of law. He is saying that it is more dangerous to society to punish someone without a fair legal process than for the person to escape punishment.
38.	A	I	The Bessemer steel process was invented by British inventor Henry Bessemer and was instrumental in the American Industrial Revolution, especially in the railroad industry. Carnegie saw the process while visiting Europe and used the process in the United States to mass-produce steel for railroads.
39.	B	I	Laissez-faire is an economic philosophy that the government should not interfere with economics. This philosophy was exercised by President Harding and President Coolidge in the 1920s, when there was very little government oversight of the market or industry.
40.	C	I	The judicial branch is responsible for interpreting laws and setting precedence. The legislative branch makes laws, and the executive branch enforces laws.
41.	B	I	While the president is the commander in chief of the U.S. armed forces, Article 1, Section 8 of the Constitution gives the legislative branch the power to decide when the United States goes to war.
42.	C	II	Cultural anthropology is the study of human cultures and societies. Folklore, linguistics, and ethnology are all characteristics of a human culture.
43.	D	II	Asia had the highest population in 2000 with over 3 billion of the world's 6 billion people residing there.

#	Answer	Category	Explanation
44.	A	I	Franklin D. Roosevelt used central planning economics to ration supplies for the war effort. He established the War Protection Board, which created and implemented the Controlled Materials Plan. This plan allocated steel, aluminum, and copper to the branches of the military and civilian agencies and reduced conflict over supplies.
45.	C	III	During the late 1700s, the American colonies began to revolt against British rule and won independence. A similar movement called "decolonization" occurred in Africa and Asia after World War II.
46.	B	I	A component of the Cold War, containment was a response to a series of moves by the Soviet Union to enlarge its communist sphere of influence in Eastern Europe, China, Korea, and Vietnam.
47.	A	II	Extensive farming is where large land areas are farmed using low inputs of resources.
48.	D	II	One of the biggest drawbacks to coal power generation is the significant amount of greenhouse gasses generated in the process. Nuclear, wind, and hydropower generation have low greenhouse gas emissions.
49.	C	III	In a socialist economy, the government controls production and sets the price for goods and services. This can adversely impact the balance of supply and demand and lead to supply shortages.
50.	A	I	Manifest destiny is the belief that the expansion of the United States was preordained and justified.
51.	C	II	Maslow's theory of hierarchy of needs explains that people must achieve basic humans needs (i.e., shelter, food, safety) before they can achieve higher-level needs (i.e., self-esteem, love, self-actualization).
52.	B	II	The Andes is the longest continental mountain range in the world, stretching 4,300 miles along the western part of South America through Venezuela, Colombia, Ecuador, Peru, Bolivia, Chile, and Argentina.
53.	C	III	The Federal Reserve increases interest rates when the economy is rapidly growing to slow things down and prevent inflation. When interest rates increase, banks increase their interest rates, which results in less borrowing and less spending.

#	Answer	Category	Explanation
54.	A	I	Federalism is a type of government that advocates for states' rights, and powers are divided between the federal government and state governments.
55.	D	II	Buddhism originated in northeast India and is practiced in China, Japan, Thailand, Sri Lanka, Mongolia, and Vietnam. Buddha's teachings are based on the Four Noble Truths of suffering and achieving nirvana.

1. Which of the following mountain ranges crosses through southern Asia?

    A.   The Appalachians

    B.   The Alps

    C.   The Himalayas

    D.   The Cascades

2. What type of map would show land structure?

    A.   Thematic

    B.   Topographic

    C.   Political

    D.   Meteorological

3. Which of the following is true about the U.S. House of Representatives?

    A.   The number of seats each state gets in the U.S. House of Representatives is based on the size of the state.

    B.   The number of seats each state gets in the U.S. House of Representatives is based on the number of senators for the state.

    C.   The number of seats each state gets in the U.S. House of Representatives is based on the population of the state.

    D.   The number of seats each state gets in the U.S. House of Representatives is based on the number of the voters in the state.

4. Where is the highest mountain located?

    A.   Asia

    B.   North America

    C.   Italy

    D.   Africa

5. Which civilization had the most influence on the U.S. government?

    A.   Greek

    B.   Roman

    C.   Indian

    D.   Chinese

6. What percentage of seats in the U.S. House of Representatives is up for election every two years?

    A.   100%

    B.   70%

    C.   50%

    D.   20%

© 2022 Kathleen Jasper

7. Which of the following refers to the arrangement of powers that prevents one branch of the government from becoming too powerful?

   A. Senate

   B. Federalism

   C. Transparent government

   D. Checks and balances

8. Which is not a monotheistic religion?

   A. Islam

   B. Christianity

   C. Taoism

   D. Judaism

9. Which of the following is true about the U.S. Senate?

   A. Every state in the U.S. elects 2 senators.

   B. The number of senators is based on the population of the state.

   C. Senators are the only elected officials in the Congress.

   D. Senators conduct judicial review.

10. An influential person in the development of the U.S. Constitution who emphasized life, liberty, and property is:

   A. John Hobbes

   B. Andrew Jackson

   C. John Locke

   D. George Washington

11. The Bill of Rights comprises:

   A. Amendments 1–10

   B. Amendments 1–5

   C. Amendments 1–6

   D. Amendments 1–3

12. Plymouth was colonized because colonists were seeking:

   A. Political freedom

   B. Religious freedom

   C. Freedom from taxation

   D. Freedom from illegal search and seizure

13. The ___ Amendment addresses unlawful search and seizure.

   A. First

   B. Second

   C. Third

   D. Fourth

14. In Iran, the government rules based on Islamic doctrine. This type of government is called a:

    A. Theocracy

    B. Monarchy

    C. Democracy

    D. Oligarchy

15. Congress is part of the _____ branch of government.

    A. Legislative

    B. Executive

    C. Judicial

    D. All of the above

16. An official ban on trade or other commercial activity with a particular country is called a(n):

    A. Boycott

    B. Litigation

    C. Veto

    D. Embargo

17. What are the Seven Wonders of the Ancient World?

    A. Great Pyramid at Giza, Egypt; Hanging Gardens of Babylon; Statue of Zeus at Olympia, Greece; Temple of Artemis at Ephesus; Mausoleum at Halicarnassus; Colossus of Rhodes; Eiffel Tower

    B. Great Pyramid at Giza, Egypt; Hanging Gardens of Babylon; Statue of Zeus at Olympia, Greece; Temple of Artemis at Ephesus; Mausoleum at Halicarnassus; Colossus of Rhodes; Lighthouse at Alexandria, Egypt

    C. Grand Canyon; Hanging Gardens of Babylon; Statue of Zeus at Olympia, Greece; Temple of Artemis at Ephesus; Mausoleum at Halicarnassus; Colossus of Rhodes; Lighthouse at Alexandria, Egypt

    D. Great Pyramid at Giza, Egypt; Niagara Falls; Statue of Zeus at Olympia, Greece; Temple of Artemis at Ephesus; Mausoleum at Halicarnassus; Colossus of Rhodes; Lighthouse at Alexandria, Egypt

18. The Cold War was a state of political and military tension between:

    A. United States and Germany.

    B. United States and Soviet Union.

    C. United States and Iraq.

    D. United States and Afghanistan.

19. Which article of the U.S. Constitution established the legislative branch of the United States of America?

    A. Article I

    B. Article II

    C. Article III

    D. Article IV

20. A _____ is prolonged period of high inflation, high unemployment, and increased public fear.

  A. Depression

  B. Stagnation

  C. Recession

  D. Inflation

21. Who conducts impeachment trials in the United States?

  A. Supreme Court

  B. House of Representatives

  C. Senate

  D. President

22. The _____ is a line that runs between Russia and Alaska and goes around political boundaries in the Pacific Ocean.

  A. Prime Meridian

  B. International Date Line

  C. Equator

  D. Latitude and longitude

23. Which of the following authorities are delegated to state governments?

  A. Regulate foreign commerce

  B. Regulate intrastate trade

  C. Oversee national defense

  D. Establish postal service

24. Which country was NOT part of the Axis Powers during World War II?

  A. Germany

  B. Japan

  C. France

  D. Italy

25. The source of the Amazon River can be found close to which mountain range?

  A. Himalayas

  B. Andes

  C. Rockies

  D. Cascades

26. Which of the following best exemplifies direct human-environment interaction?

  A. A man builds a house on the beach.

  B. People shop at a mall.

  C. A family takes a road trip.

  D. Senate votes on an environmental protection bill.

27. Referring to Topographical Map: What is this map showing?

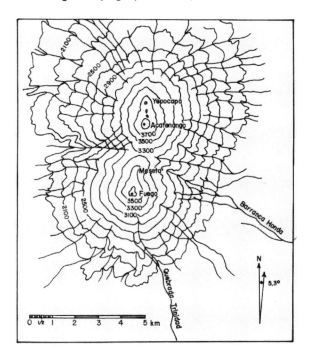

A. Mountain

B. River valley

C. Ocean

D. Plains

28. Which of the following maps would best represent population density in the United States?

A. Typographical map

B. Special purpose map

C. Political map

D. Climate map

29. Which of the following is the longest river in the world?

A. Amazon

B. Congo

C. Nile

D. Yellow

30. Which of the following is considered to be the riskiest investment?

A. Government bonds

B. Stocks

C. Mutual funds

D. Land

31. A newspaper publishing an interview with a major political figure during a time of national crisis is an example of the rights established by which constitutional amendment?

    A. First Amendment

    B. Second Amendment

    C. Tenth Amendment

    D. Nineteenth Amendment

32. The president of the United States has the power to do all the following EXCEPT:

    A. Issue executive order

    B. Pardon criminals

    C. Nominate Supreme Court judges

    D. Appoint state representatives

33. Which of the following would be considered an example of checks and balances?

    A. The president pardons a convicted criminal.

    B. The U.S. Senate votes on new environmental regulations.

    C. The Supreme Court rules a law passed by Congress unconstitutional.

    D. The government taxes large corporations.

34. Which of the following are major contributions from the Ancient Greeks?

    A. Philosophy, mathematics, and drama

    B. Music, art, and mathematics

    C. Irrigation, art, and architecture

    D. Cuneiform, architecture, and music

35. What was the reason for the sudden growth of Western European exploration in the 15th and 16th centuries?

    A. Colonization of the New World

    B. Finding a passage to Africa

    C. The establishment of new trade routes with Asia

    D. The understanding of other cultures

36. Which two countries fought for control of North America in the early 1700s?

    A. France and Britain

    B. France and Germany

    C. Britain and America

    D. France and Spain

37. Which of the following was significant for being the first self-governing document in the American Colonies?

    A. The Mayflower Compact

    B. The Virginia House of Burgesses

    C. The Declaration of Independence

    D. The Bill of Rights

38. Who delivered the Gettysburg Address on November 19, 1863?

    A. Thomas Jefferson

    B. John F. Kennedy

    C. Martin Luther King, Jr.

    D. Abraham Lincoln

39. What was the reason for the United States declining to sign the Treaty of Versailles?

    A. Its punishment of Germany was too harsh.

    B. The Senate did not want to join the League of Nations.

    C. President Wilson rejected the treaty.

    D. The United States wanted to write its own treaty.

40. Which of the following is the main reason for westward expansion in America?

    A. Agriculture

    B. Land ownership and financial opportunity

    C. New hunting grounds

    D. Business opportunities with Native Americans

41. Which president was in office during the Louisiana Purchase?

    A. Andrew Jackson

    B. Ulysses S. Grant

    C. Thomas Jefferson

    D. William Henry Harrison

42. This is the imaginary horizontal line that divides Earth into the Northern Hemisphere and the Southern Hemisphere:

    A. International Date Line

    B. Equator

    C. Prime Meridian

    D. Latitude

43. Deflation is the:

    A. decrease in the general price level of goods and services over a shorter period of time.

    B. decrease in the general price level of goods and services over a longer period of time.

    C. increase in the general price level of goods and services over a longer period of time.

    D. increase in the general price level of goods and services over a shorter period of time.

44. Which of the following was not a cause, leading up to World War II?

    A. German invasion of Poland

    B. Russian invasion of Poland

    C. The Treaty of Versailles

    D. Attack on Pearl Harbor

45. Which of the following was the direct cause of World War I?

    A.   The Ottoman Empire's defeat of the Allies

    B.   Woodrow Wilson's Fourteen Points

    C.   The assassination of Archduke Franz Ferdinand

    D.   The Zimmerman Telegram

46. The Senate holds all the following powers EXCEPT:

    A.   Confirm or reject treaties

    B.   Confirm or reject presidential appointments to office

    C.   Conduct judicial review of cases against the executive branch

    D.   Try a government official who commits a crime against the United States

47. Supreme Court justices are nominated by the:

    A.   President

    B.   House of Representatives

    C.   Senate

    D.   Electoral College

48. In order to become the President of the United States, the candidate must:

    A.   be a natural-born citizen.

    B.   be at least 21 years of age.

    C.   have served in the military.

    D.   pass a citizenship test.

49. Which of the following political systems is based on socialism?

    A.   Communism

    B.   Republic

    C.   Democracy

    D.   Parliament

50. A person cannot be tried twice for the same offense (double jeopardy). This constitutional right falls under which amendment?

    A.   First Amendment

    B.   Third Amendment

    C.   Fifth Amendment

    D.   Ninth Amendment

51. Why would the government raise price floors in agricultural markets?

    A.   To protect farmers

    B.   To protect consumers

    C.   To keep interest rates stable

    D.   To inspire competition

52. The government established rent control in some cities to regulate the maximum price for housing. This action by the government to protect consumers is an example of what?

    A.   Price floor

    B.   Price ceiling

    C.   Employee protection

    D.   Opportunity cost

53. In 1492, Italian explorer Christopher Columbus discovered San Salvador and Hispaniola while searching for trade routes for which country?

    A.   Italy

    B.   Spain

    C.   France

    D.   Portugal

54. What was the first legislative assembly in the American colonies called?

    A.   The Continental Congress

    B.   The Virginia House of Burgesses

    C.   The Plymouth Colony Assembly

    D.   The Jamestown Congress

55. The first federal tax on a domestically produced product resulted in which event?

    A.   The Whiskey Rebellion

    B.   The War of 1812

    C.   Nat Turner's Rebellion

    D.   The Missouri Compromise

This page intentionally left blank.

#	Answer	Category	Explanation
1.	C	II	The Himalayas run through southern Asia.
2.	B	II	Topographic maps show land structure, bodies of water, and some man-made features.
3.	C	I	The Constitution states that seats in the U.S. House of Representatives are to be distributed among the states by population. The population of each state is determined by the census conducted every 10 years. There are currently 435 representatives in the U.S. House of Representatives. You may be tempted to choose D; however, representatives are assigned to states based on number of people, whether those people vote or not.
4.	A	II	The highest mountain is Mount Everest, which is a part of the Himalayas that run through Asia.
5.	B	III	The Romans established a representative type of government instead of a monarchy. This representative government was copied for centuries by many, including the U.S. government. (ushistory.org).
6.	A	I	Every two years, all 435 seats in the U.S. House of Representatives are up for election.
7.	D	I	Checks and balances is a fundamental principle of American government. This principle is outlined in the U.S. Constitution.
8.	C	II	Monotheistic means to have belief in one god. All the religions listed believe in one God except for Taoism.
9.	A	I	The U.S. Senate includes 100 members, who are elected for a six-year term in dual-seat constituencies (two from each state), with one-third of the total number of seats being renewed every two years. You can eliminate answer B because representatives, not senators, are based on population. Answer C is incorrect because Congress is made up of members who are elected to the U.S. Senate and the U.S. House of Representatives. Finally, the judicial branch conducts judicial review, eliminating answer D.
10.	C	I	Commonly known as the "father of liberalism," John Locke was a philosopher and physician. He was widely regarded as one of the most influential of the Enlightenment thinkers. Locke's philosophy on liberty and the social contract influenced the written works of Alexander Hamilton, James Madison, Thomas Jefferson, and other Founding Fathers of the United States.
11.	A	I	The first 10 amendments to the U.S. Constitution are the Bill of Rights. The Bill of Rights was ratified in 1791.

#	Answer	Category	Explanation
12.	B	I	The Pilgrims left England to seek religious freedom and find a better life.
13.	D	I	The Fourth Amendment of the U.S. Constitution provides, "[t]he right of the people to be secure in their persons, houses, papers, and effects, against unreasonable searches and seizures, shall not be violated…"
14.	A	III	A theocracy is a system of government in which leaders rule by religious doctrine.
15.	A	I	The legislative branch is made up of the two houses of Congress: the Senate and the House of Representatives. It is the duty of the legislative branch to make laws.
16.	D	III	An embargo is when one country refuses to do business with another country. A boycott is when private citizens refuse to buy products from a company. Litigation is the process of taking legal action. A veto is a constitutional right to reject a decision or proposal made by a law-making body.
17.	B	II	Niagara Falls, the Grand Canyon, and the Eiffel Tower are not part of the Ancient Wonders of the World.
18.	B	I	The term "cold" is used because there was no large-scale fighting directly between the two sides (United States and Soviet Union). The Cold War was very contentious, and both sides feared a nuclear invasion.
19.	A	I	Article I states, "All legislative Powers herein granted shall be vested in a Congress of the United States, which shall consist of a Senate and House of Representatives."
20.	A	III	A depression is a severe and prolonged downturn in economic activity.
21.	C	I	The Constitution requires a two-thirds vote of the Senate to convict, and the penalty for an impeached official is removal from office.
22.	B	II	The International Date Line separates two consecutive calendar dates.
23.	B	I	The U.S. Constitution allows states to regulate trade that occurs within the state borders. The other three choices in this item (post office, foreign commerce, national defense) are part of the federal government's domain.
24.	C	III	Axis Powers included Japan, Germany, and Italy.
25.	B	II	The Andes, like the Amazon River, are located in South America. The Amazon River meets the Andes mountain range near Peru. The Himalayas are in Asia. The Rockies and Cascades are in the United States.

#	Answer	Category	Explanation
26.	A	II	Although all the choices have some impact on the environment, building a house on the beach has the most **direct** impact on the environment.
27.	A	II	The topographical map is showing a mountain and its different elevations. The elevations increase toward the peak or center of the map.
28.	B	II	A population density map is a special purpose map. A typographical map shows physical features of an area. A political map shows political boundaries (like state lines). A climate map shows climate.
29.	C	II	The Nile River is the world's longest river at 4,132 miles. In close second is the Amazon River.
30.	B	III	Stocks are the riskiest investment due to the amount of volatility that affects their value.
31.	A	I	The First Amendment establishes the freedom of the press.
32.	D	I	State representatives are elected by the citizens of each state. The president has the authority to issue executive orders, issue pardons, and nominate judges to the U.S. Supreme Court.
33.	C	I	Laws can be passed by Congress (legislative branch), but the laws can be challenged by the other branches (executive and judicial branches).
34.	A	III	Ancient Greece is famous for contributing to philosophy, math, and the dramatic arts.
35.	C	I	During the 15th and 16th centuries, European explorers were seeking to establish trade with the Orient.
36.	A	I	France and Britain fought in the Seven Years' War for control of colonial America from 1754–1763.
37.	A	I	The Mayflower Compact was a set of rules and guidelines for self-governance in the New World.
38.	D	I	Abraham Lincoln gave his address on the battlefield of Gettysburg.
39.	B	I	The United States never ratified the treaty and did not want to join the League of Nations.
40.	B	I	Economic and land opportunities drove the westward expansion. Many Americans believed that the United States was destined by God to expand its control into the west (Manifest Destiny).

#	Answer	Category	Explanation
41.	C	I	Thomas Jefferson was the president who negotiated the Louisiana Purchase from France.
42.	B	II	The Equator divides Earth into the Northern Hemisphere and the Southern Hemisphere. The Prime Meridian (0° longitude) and the International Date Line divide Earth into the Eastern Hemisphere and the Western Hemisphere.
43.	B	III	Deflation is a decrease in the general price level of goods and services over a longer period of time. It slows economic growth and production.
44.	D	III	The Treaty of Versailles was signed at the end of World War I, but it is often cited as one of the reasons Germans voted for the Nazi Party. German invasion of Poland in 1939 sparked World War II. Russia invaded Poland a few days after Germany invaded. Shortly after, France and Great Britain declared war on Germany. Pearl Harbor happened during World War II and is one of the reasons the United States joined the war, but it was not a cause of World War II.
45.	C	III	The assassination of Archduke Franz Ferdinand in 1914 by Gavrilo Princip started World War I. Tensions in the Balkans (Bosnia, Serbia, Herzegovina) threatened existing alliances between European powers, the Ottoman Empire, and Russia, and eventually led to the assassination. The Zimmerman Telegram happened during World War I. The Ottoman Empire's defeat of the Allies also happened during World War I.
46.	C	I	The Senate does not hold the power of judicial review against the executive branch. The Supreme Court is responsible for judicial review.
47.	A	I	According to Article III, Supreme Court justices are nominated by the President of the United States.
48.	A	I	To be elected president, the candidate must be a natural born citizen, at least 35 years old, and a U.S. resident for 14 years.
49.	A	III	Communist states call themselves socialist states because they aim to establish a socialist society.
50.	C	I	The Fifth Amendment (protection of rights to life, liberty, and property) addresses criminal procedure and other aspects of the U.S. Constitution.
51.	A	III	Price floors are mandated minimum price a seller is required to pay. Governments often seek to assist farmers by setting price floors in agricultural markets.

#	Answer	Category	Explanation
52.	B	III	Price ceiling is a mandated maximum price a seller is allowed to charge for a good or service. A rent control district in New York City is an example of a price ceiling intended to increase the availability of affordable housing.
53.	B	III	Christopher Columbus made one of the most famous voyages of exploration in 1492, when he sailed from Palos, Spain, in search of a route to Asia and the Indies. Instead, Columbus found the New World—the Americas.
54.	B	I	At Jamestown, Virginia, this was the first legislative assembly in the colonies. The main name associated with the House of Burgesses is George Yeardley, who was the governor of the Virginia Colony at the time.
55.	A	I	The Whiskey Rebellion was a protest against the "whiskey tax." It was not only the first tax imposed on a domestic product by the newly formed federal government, but was also a tax on one of the most popular beverages in the country.

This page intentionally left blank.

Bibliography

Amadeo, K. (2018). *Comparative advantage: Theory and examples*. Economic Theory The Balance. Retrieved from https://www.thebalance.com/comparative-advantage-3305915

Amadeo, K. (2018). Labor, one of four factors of production. Retrieved from https://www.thebalance.com/labor-definition-types-and-how-it-affects-the-economy-3305859

Andrews, E. (n.d.). *11 innovations that changed history*. Retrieved from: https://www.history.com/news/11-innovations-that-changed-history

Asrar, Shakeeb (2017). *How India, Pakistan and Bangladesh were formed*. Retrieved from: https://www.aljazeera.com/indepth/interactive/2017/08/india-pakistan-bangladesh-formed-170807142655673.html

Bailey, R. G. (1996) *Ecosystem Geography*. New York: Springer-Verlag

Beveridge, W. (1944). *Full employment in a free society*: UK: Allen & Unwin

Board of Governors of the Federal Reserve System. 2019 *About the fed.* Retrieved from: https://www.federalreserve.gov/aboutthefed.htm

Briney, A. (2019). *A brief history of the age of exploration*. ThoughtCo. Retrieved from https://www.thoughtco.com/age-of-exploration-1435006

Brough, W. and Kimenyi, M. (2004). *Desertification of the Sahel*. Retrieved from: https://www.perc.org/2004/06/01/desertification-of-the-sahel/

Berkes, H. (2003). *The vision of John Wesley Powell: Explorer foresaw water issues that would plague the West.* Retrieved from: https://www.npr.org/programs/atc/features/2003/aug/water/part1.html

Burkett, E. (n.d.). *Women's rights movement: Political and social movement.* Retrieved from: https://www.britannica.com/topic/womens-movement

Burlingame, M. (n.d.). *Abraham Lincoln: foreign affairs.* Retrieved from: https://millercenter.org/president/lincoln/foreign-affairs

Bushnell, D. (2003). El Libertador: Writings of Simón Bolívar. New York: Oxford University Press

Cartwright, M. (2012). *Aqueduct*. Ancient History Encyclopedia. Retrieved from: https://www.ancient.eu/aqueduct/

Centers for Disease Control and Prevention (2016). *Types of agricultural water use*. Retrieved from: https://www.cdc.gov/healthywater/other/agricultural/types.html

Centers for Disease Control and Prevention (2019). *1918 pandemic (H1N1virus)*. Retrieved from: https://www.cdc.gov/flu/pandemic-resources/1918-pandemic-h1n1.html

Chinese Civilisation Center. (2007). *China: Five thousand years of history and civilization.* City University of Hong Kong Press

Claval, P. (2015). Religions and ideologies. In S. Brunn (Ed.), *The changing world religion map* (349-362). Dordrecht: Springer.

David, R. (2003). *Religion and magic in ancient Egypt.* London: Penguin Books.

DeYoung, G. (2014). Metallurgy in Egypt. In *Encyclopedia of the History of Science, Technology, and Medicine in Non-Western Cultures.* Springer-Verlag. Retrieved from https://link.springer.com/referenceworkentry/10.1007%2F978-1-4020-4425-0_9274

Dimdam, E. (2013). *25 biggest man made environmental disasters in history.* Retrieved from: https://list25.com/25-biggest-man-made-environmental-disasters-in-history/

Duignan, B., & Cranston, M. (2019). Jean-Jacques Rousseau. In *Encyclopedia Britannica.* Retrieved from https://www.britannica.com/biography/Jean-Jacques-Rousseau

Encyclopedia Britannica Editors. (n.d.). Command economy. Encyclopedia Britannica. Retrieved from https://www.britannica.com/topic/command-economy

Encyclopedia Britannica Editors. n.d. *Rodgers Williams: American religious leader.* Retrieved from: https://www.britannica.com/biography/Roger-Williams-American-religious-leader

Encyclopedia Britannica Editors. (n.d.). *Schneck v. United States.* Encyclopedia Britannica. Retrieved from: https://www.britannica.com/event/Schenck-v-United-States

Encyclopedia Britannica Editors. (1998). *Industrial revolution.* Retrieved from https://www.britannica.com/event/Industrial-Revolution

Encyclopedia Britannica Editors. (1998). *Ming dynasty: Chinese history.* Retrieved from https://www.britannica.com/topic/Ming-dynasty-Chinese-history

Encyclopedia Britannica Editors. (1998). *Qing dynasty: Chinese history.* Retrieved from https://www.britannica.com/topic/Qing-dynasty

Encyclopedia Britannica Editors. (1998). *South African War.* Retrieved from: https://www.britannica.com/event/South-African-War

Encyclopedia Britannica Editors. (2019). *The age of revolution.* Retrieved from https://www.britannica.com/topic/history-of-Europe/The-age-of-revolution

Eschner, K. (2017). *President James Buchanan directly influenced the outcome of the Dred Scott decision.* Retrieved from: https://www.smithsonianmag.com/smart-news/president-james-buchanan-directly-influenced-outcome-dred-scott-decision-180962329/#Zqpfkotgkhgl9qyy.99

Ezrow, N. (2011). Dictators and dictatorships: Understanding authoritarian regimes and their leaders. Frantz, Erica. New York: Continuum.

FairVote.org (n.d.). *Voter turnout.* Retrieved from: https://www.fairvote.org/voter_turnout#what_affects_voter_turnout_rates

Federal Reserve System. (2016). *The Federal Reserve System purpose & functions.* Retrieved from https://www.federalreserve.gov/aboutthefed/pf.htm.

Friend, Celest (n.d.), *Social contract theory.* Retrieved from: https://www.iep.utm.edu/soc-cont/

Gleckman, H. (2018). *What is a tariff and who pays it?* Tax Policy Center. Retrieved from https://www.taxpolicycenter.org/taxvox/what-tariff-and-who-pays-it

Heim, D. (2018). *The international dateline, explained.* LifeScience. Retrieved from https://www.livescience.com/44292-international-date-line-explained.html

History.com Editors. (n.d.). *Religion.* Retrieved from: http://history.com/topics/religion

History.com Editors. (2009). *Ford's assembly line starts rolling.* Retrieved from: https://www.history.com/this-day-in-history/fords-assembly-line-starts-rolling

History.com Editors. (2009). *Lewis and Clark.* Retrieved from: https://www.history.com/topics/westward-expansion/lewis-and-clark

History.com Editors. (2009) *Pyramids in Latin America.* Retrieved from: https://www.history.com/topics/ancient-history/pyramids-in-latin-america

History.com Editors. (2010). *Energy crisis (1970's).* Retrieved from: https://www.history.com/topics/1970s/energy-crisis

History.com Editors. (2017). *Church of England.* Retrieved from: https://www.history.com/topics/british-history/church-of-england

History.com Editors. (2017). *The Dust Bowl.* Retrieved from https://www.history.com/topics/great-depression/dust-bowl

History.com Editors. (2017). *Mesopotamia.* Retrieved from https://www.history.com/topics/ancient-middle-east/mesopotamia

History.com Editors. (2018). *The 13 Colonies.* Retrieved from https://www.history.com/topics/colonial-america/thirteen-colonies

History.com Editors. (2018). *Townshend Acts.* Retrieved from https://www.history.com/topics/american-revolution/townshend-acts

History.com Editors. (2019). *Battle of Yorktown.* Retrieved from https://www.history.com/topics/americanrevolution/siege-of-yorktown

History.com Editors. (2019). *Berlin Wall.* Retrieved from https://www.history.com/topics/cold-war/berlin-wall.

History.com Editors. (2019). *Great Depression history.* Retrieved from https://www.history.com/topics/great-depression/great-depression-history

History.com Editors. (2019). *Harlem renaissance.* Retrieved from https://www.history.com/topics/roaring-twenties/harlem-renaissance

History.com Editors. (2019). *The roaring twenties history.* Retrieved from https://www.history.com/topics/roaring-twenties/roaring-twenties-history

History.com Editors. (2019). *Westward expansion.* Retrieved from https://www.history.com/topics/westward-expansion

History.com Editors. (2019). *Who was Vladimir Lenin?* Retrieved from https://www.history.com/topics/russia/vladimir-lenin

History.net. (2019). *Antebellum Period.* Retrieved from https://www.historynet.com/antebellum-period

Howard, B. C., (2014), *First time in 600 years: Once thriving, the vast Asian lake was drained for irrigation.* National Geographic. Retrieved from: https://news.nationalgeographic.com/news/2014/10/141001-aral-sea-shrinking-drought-water-environment/

Iweriebor, Ehiedu E. G. (n.d.), The colonization of Africa. Retrieved from: http://exhibitions.nypl.org/africanaage/essay-colonization-of-africa.html

Klein, C. (2018). 8 ways the Erie Canal changed America. History.com Retrieved from https://www.history.com/news/8-ways-the-erie-canal-changed-america

Lewis, T. (2015). *Transatlantic slave trade: Slavery*. Encyclopedia Britannica. Retrieved from https://www.britannica.com/topic/transatlantic-slave-trade

Link, A. S. (2019). *The United States from 1920-1945: The postwar Republican administrations*. Retrieved from: https://www.britannica.com/place/United-States

Mann, C. C. (2011). *The birth of religion.* National Geographic Magazine 219(6), 34-59. Retrieved from http://www2.nau.edu/~gaud/bio301/content/neolth.htm.

McNamara, R. (2019). *The Bessemer steel process.* Retrieved from: https://www.thoughtco.com/bessemer-steel-process-definition-1773300

Merriam Webster (2019). Anthropology - Definition. Retrieved from https://www.merriam-webster.com/dictionary/anthropology

Merriam Webster (2019). Caucus - Definition. Retrieved from https://www.merriam-webster.com/dictionary/caucus

Merriam Webster (2019). Checks and Balances - Definition. Retrieved from https://www.merriam-webster.com/dictionary/checks%20and%20balancesy

Merriam Webster (2019). Community - Definition. Retrieved from https://www.merriam-webster.com/dictionary/community

Merriam Webster (2019). Cultural Anthropology - Definition. Retrieved from https://www.merriam-webster.com/dictionary/cultural%20anthropology

Merriam Webster (2019). Language - Definition. Retrieved from https://www.merriam-webster.com/dictionary/community

Merriam Webster (2019). Monarchy - Definition. Retrieved from https://www.merriam-webster.com/dictionary/monarchy

Merriam Webster (2019). Nation - Definition. Retrieved from https://www.merriam-webster.com/dictionary/nation

Merriam Webster (2019). Physical Anthropology - Definition. Retrieved from https://www.merriam-webster.com/dictionary/physical%20anthropology

Merriam Webster (2019). Republic - Definition. Retrieved from https://www.merriam-webster.com/dictionary/republic

Merriam Webster (2019). Technology - Definition. Retrieved from https://www.merriam-webster.com/dictionary/community

Mesopotamia.co.uk. (n.d.). Ancient civilizations: Mesopotamia. Retrieved from http://www.mesopotamia.co.uk/

Mokyr, J. (2019). *Great famine.* Retrieved from: https://www.britannica.com/event/Great-Famine-Irish-history

National Geographic (n.d.). *Geography*. National Geographic: Resource Library. Retrieved from https://www.nationalgeographic.org/encyclopedia/geography/

National Geographic (n.d.). *Hemisphere*. National Geographic: Resource Library. Retrieved from https://www.nationalgeographic.org/encyclopedia/hemisphere/

Nolen, J. (n.d.). Domino Theory. Britannica Online. Retrieved from https://www.britannica.com/topic/domino-theory

O'Sullivan, A., Sheffrin, S, M. (2003), Economics: Principles in Action, Upper Saddle River, New Jersey 07458: Pearson Prentice Hall, p. 57

Office of the Historian (n.d.). French and Indian War/ Seven Years' War. Retrieved from https://history.state.gov/milestones/1750-1775/french-indian-war

Office of the Historian (n.d.). The Truman Doctrine, 1947. Retrieved from https://history.state.gov/milestones/1945-1952/truman-doctrine

Office of the Historian (n.d.). *The decolonization of Asia and Africa: 1945-1960*. Retrieved from: https://history.state.gov/milestones/1945-1952/asia-and-africa

Office of the Historian (n.d.). The development of foreign policy. Retrieved from https://history.state.gov/departmenthistory/short-history/development

Ott, M. (n.d.). National Income accounts. In *The Library of Economics and Library.* Retrieved from http://www.econlib.org/library/Enc/NationalIncomeAccounts.html

Palmer, R. & Colton, J. (1978) *A History of the Modern World* (5th ed)

Pettinger, T. (2016). *Facts about the Industrial Revolution*. Oxford. Retrieved from https://www.biographyonline.net/facts-about-the-industrial-revolution/

Philpott, D. (2003). Sovereignty. In *Stanford Encyclopedia of Philosophy.* Retrieved from https://plato.stanford.edu/entries/sovereignty/

Plamper, J. (2012). *The Stalin Cult: A Study in the Alchemy of Power*. (The Yale-Hoover Series on Stalin, Stalinism, and the Cold War.) New Haven: Yale University Press.

Poole, W. & Wheelock, D. C. (2008). Stable prices, stable economy: Keeping inflation in check must be No. 1 goal of monetary policymakers. The Regional Economist. Retrieved from https://www.stlouisfed.org/publications/regional-economist/january-2008/stable-prices-stable-economy-keeping-inflation-in-check-must-be-no-1-goal-of-monetary-policymakers

Rampton, M. (n.d.). *Four Waves of Feminism.* Pacific University Oregon. Retrieved from: https://www.pacificu.edu/about/media/four-waves-feminism

Rosen, J. and Rubenstein, D. (n.d.). *The Declaration, the Constitution, and the Bill of Rights.* Retrieved from: https://constitutioncenter.org/interactive-constitution/white-pages/the-declaration-the-constitution-and-the-bill-of-rights

Shuttleworth, M. (2010). *Babylonian mathematics and Babylonian numerals*. Retrieved from Explorable. com: https://explorable.com/babylonian-mathematics

Siddiqui, A. S. (2011). Comprehensive Economics XII. Laxmi Publications Pvt Limited.

Simpson, S. (n.d.). Macroeconomics: Unemployment. Investopedia. Retrieved from https://www.investopedia.com/university/macroeconomics/macroeconomics8.asp

Smithsonian. (n.d.). Lighting a revolution: Consequences of Edison's lamp. Retrieved from: https://americanhistory.si.edu/lighting/19thcent/consq19.htm

Tassava, C.(2008). *The American economy during World War II*. EH.Net Encyclopedia, edited by Robert Whaples. Retrieved from: http://eh.net/encyclopedia/the-american-economy-during-world-war-ii/

The History Channel (2018). The Boston Massacre. Retrieved from https://www.history.com/topics/american-revolution/boston-massacre

The History Channel (2019). The Vietnam War. Retrieved from: https://www.history.com/topics/vietnam-war/vietnam-war-history#section_1

The U.S. Department of Treasury (2019). *U.S. Department of Treasury: Agency details.* Retrieved from https://www.usa.gov/federal-agencies/u-s-department-of-the-treasury

The White House (n.d.). State and local government. Retrieved from: https://www.whitehouse.gov/about-the-white-house/state-local-government/

University of Cambridge (n.d.). *The scramble for Africa*. Retrieved from: https://www.joh.cam.ac.uk/library/library_exhibitions/schoolresources/exploration/scramble_for_africa

U.S. Bureau of Economic Analysis. (2019). Gross domestic product. BEA. Retrieved from https://www.bea.gov/resources/learning-center/what-to-know-gdp

U.S. Census (2010). Population density. Data. Retrieved from https://www.census.gov/data/tables/2010/dec/density-data-text.html

U.S. Geological Survey (2019). *West Africa: Land use and land cover dynamics*. Bioclimatic Regions Map. Retrieved from https://eros.usgs.gov/westafrica/node/147

USAGov (2018). Presidential Election Process. Retrieved from: https://www.usa.gov/election

USAID.gov. 2019. USAID history: Celebrating fifty years of progress. Retrieved from: https://www.usaid.gov/who-we-are/usaid-history

U.S. Securities and Exchange Commission. (2019). Introduction to Investing. Retrieved from https://www.investor.gov/introduction-investing

U.S. Senate (n.d.) *The Constitution: The Bill of Rights*. Retrieved from https://www.senate.gov/civics/constitution_item/constitution.htm

Violatti, C. (2018). Neolithic period. In *Ancient History Encyclopedia*. Retrieved from https://www.ancient.eu/Neolithic/

Wertz, R. R. (2007). Neolithic and Bronze Age cultures: Exploring Chinese history. Retrieved 10 February 2008.

World Atlas (n.s.). *What is terrace farming?* Retrieved from: https://www.worldatlas.com/articles/what-is-terrace-farming.html

Science Subtest

This page intentionally left blank.

The science subtest of the *Praxis®* Elementary Education exam is designed to test your knowledge of science topics at both the elementary and middle school levels. The assessment is not aligned to a particular grade or course but is closely aligned to national science standards for both elementary and middle grades.

Test at a Glance	
Test Name	*Praxis®* Elementary Education Science Subtest 5005
Format	Computer-based test (CBT)
Time	60 minutes; 1 minute 6 seconds per question
Number of Questions	Approximately 55 (field testing items may be added)
Passing Score	A scaled score of at least 159 for most states
Items Provided	On-screen scientific calculator (TI-30XS Multiview), scratch paper, and pencils
Format of Questions	Multiple choice (A, B, C, D)

Test Competency Breakdown			
	COMPETENCY	**Approximate Percentage of Total Test Questions**	**Approximate Number of Total Test Questions**
	I. Earth Science	33% – 34%	17–18
	II. Life Science	33% – 34%	18–19
	III. Physical Science	33% – 34%	18–19
	TOTAL	100%	55

You are not provided a hand-held calculator, but the online calculator is the same as a handheld TI-30XS Multiview. ETS® (Educational Testing Service, writers of Praxis exams) does provide training through Texas Instruments for the calculator (visit https://ibt2calc.ets.org/practicetest for calculator training access). We strongly suggest you access and complete their training. Some questions will require the use of a calculator, and there are certain functions this calculator can perform that will save you time.

I. Earth Science

Section I, Earth Science, tests your knowledge of the history, structure, composition, environment, and atmosphere of the Earth. Skills include identifying and defining layers of the Earth, processes of the atmosphere, the oceans, and solid Earth, Earth's history, and the solar system.

The skills you need to know in this section include the following:

A. Understand the structure of the Earth system (e.g., structure and properties of solid Earth, the hydrosphere, the atmosphere).

B. Understand processes of the Earth system (e.g., processes of solid Earth, the hydrosphere, the atmosphere).

C. Understand Earth's history (e.g., origin of the Earth, paleontology, the rock record).

D. Understand Earth and the universe (e.g., starts and galaxies; the solar system and planets; Earth, Sun, and Moon relationships).

E. Understand Earth's patterns, cycles, and change.

F. Understand science as a human endeavor, a process and career.

G. Understand science as inquiry (e.g., questioning, gathering data, drawing reasonable conclusions).

H. Understand how to use resources and research material in science.

I. Understand the unifying processes of science (e.g., systems, order, organization).

A. Structure of Earth

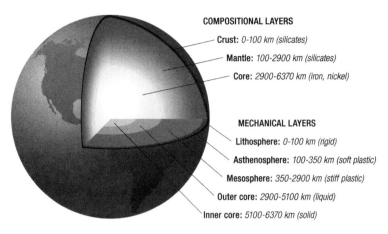

COMPOSITIONAL LAYERS

Crust: *0-100 km (silicates)*

Mantle: *100-2900 km (silicates)*

Core: *2900-6370 km (iron, nickel)*

MECHANICAL LAYERS

Lithosphere: *0-100 km (rigid)*

Asthenosphere: *100-350 km (soft plastic)*

Mesosphere: *350-2900 km (stiff plastic)*

Outer core: *2900-5100 km (liquid)*

Inner core: *5100-6370 km (solid)*

Solid Earth

The Earth is made up of several layers: crust/lithosphere, mantle, and core.

The Earth gets denser toward the center.

The temperature of the Earth increases as you move closer to the center of the Earth. For example, the mantle is 1900°K, the outer core is 3000°K, and the inner ore is 5000–7000°K.

Composition Layers		
Layer	**Definition**	**Depth**
Crust	The outermost solid layer of Earth.	0–100 km
Mantle	The mantle is not liquid; it is ductile or plastic, which means that some parts of the mantle can flow under certain conditions and changes in pressure. The mantle is mainly composed of aluminum and silicates.	100–2900 km
Core	The innermost layers of Earth. Earth has an outer core (liquid) and an inner core (solid). The core is mainly composed of nickel and iron.	2900–6370 km

Mechanical Layers		
Layer	**Definition**	**Depth**
Litho-sphere	The outermost and most rigid mechanical layer of Earth. The lithosphere includes the crust and the top of the mantle.	0–100 km
Meso-sphere	Beneath the asthenosphere. It encompasses the lower mantle, where material still flows but at a much slower rate than in the asthenosphere.	350–2900 km
Outer Core	A layer of liquid iron and nickel (and other elements) beneath the mesosphere. This is the only layer of Earth that is a true liquid.	2900–5100 km
Inner Core	The Earth's inner core is a solid ball. However, scientists now say that it is neither solid nor liquid; the Earth's inner core is considered super ionic.	5100–6370 km

Adapted from Penn State University (2019)

Earth's Spheres – Above the Crust

Earth is made up of different types of spheres.

- **Lithosphere** – The outermost shell of Earth. Earth's crust is the lithosphere.

- **Hydrosphere** – All the water on Earth in liquid form. For example, lakes, rivers, and oceans are all part of the hydrosphere.

- **Biosphere** – The global sum of all ecosystems and living organisms.

- **Cryosphere** – The masses of frozen water. For example, frozen lakes, frozen rivers, frozen oceans, and glaciers are part of the cryosphere.

- **Atmosphere** – The layer of gases that surround the planet.

Earth's atmosphere is a layer of gases surrounding the planet. The gases present in Earth's atmosphere are:

- **Nitrogen** – 78%
- **Oxygen** – 21%
- **Argon** – .09%
- **Carbon dioxide** – .01%
- **Helium** – small traces
- **Neon** – small traces
- **Other gases** – small traces

Earth's atmosphere also contains multiple layers:

- **Troposphere** – 0–12 km above Earth.
  *Most of Earth's weather occurs here.
- **Stratosphere** – 12–50 km above Earth.
  *Contains the ozone layer.
- **Mesosphere** – 50–80 km above Earth.
- **Thermosphere** – 80–700 km above Earth.
- **Exosphere** – 700–1000 km above Earth.

The ozone layer absorbs 97%-99% of the sun's ultraviolet light and is contained in the stratosphere. This layer contains high levels of ozone (O_3). Two decades of scientific research has shown that human-produced chemicals are responsible for the observed depletions of the ozone layer. (NOAA, n.d.).

> **Did You Know?**
>
> Glaciers contain 69% of Earth's fresh water. Ice and glaciers are part of the water cycle.

> **Quick Tip**
>
> Nitrogen and oxygen make up 99% of the gases in Earth's atmosphere, with nitrogen being the most prevalent.
>
> Researchers assert Earth's atmosphere was formed from volcanic eruptions that happened early in Earth's history.

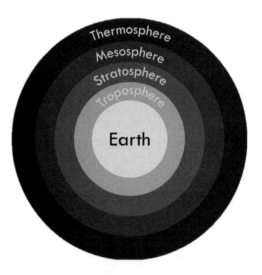

> **Quick Tip**
>
> When we drive cars, carbon dioxide (CO_2) is released into the atmosphere. The CO_2 is trapped inside the ozone layer and prevents the sun's rays from escaping, which contributes to Earth's increase in temperature.

The Processes of the Lithosphere (Crust)

Geologic formations are formations made from rocks that exist on the lithosphere. Examples include volcanoes, mountains, and canyons.

Mountains are formed as a result of Earth's tectonic plates smashing together.

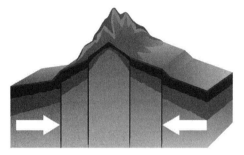

Volcanoes are formed when magma from within Earth's upper mantle erupts through the surface.

Canyons are formed by weathering and erosion caused by the movement of rivers. Canyons are also formed by tectonic activity.

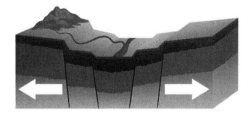

Earthquakes

Earthquakes are usually caused when plates rub against each other in an opposite motion, and rock underground suddenly breaks along a fault. This sudden release of energy causes seismic waves that make the ground shake.

Scientists assign a magnitude rating to earthquakes based on the strength and duration of their seismic waves. A quake measuring 3 to 4.9 is considered minor or light; 5 to 6.9 is moderate to strong; 7 to 7.9 is major; and 8 or more is great.

Ring of Fire

The Ring of Fire is a ring of volcanoes around the outer edge of the Pacific Ocean. These volcanoes are a result of subduction of oceanic plates beneath lighter continental plates. In fact, most of Earth's volcanoes and earthquakes happen along the Ring of Fire.

(National Geographic, n.d.).

Seismic Waves

A seismic wave is an elastic wave caused by an earthquake. There are three types of seismic waves:

1. **Primary (P waves)** – These are the fastest waves (5 kilometers per second or approximately 3 miles per second) and can travel through solid, liquids, and gases.

2. **Secondary (S waves)** – Secondary waves travel through Earth's interior at about half the speed of primary waves. Secondary waves can travel through rock, but unlike primary waves, they cannot travel through liquids or gases.

3. **Surface** – Surface waves are seismic waves that move along Earth's surface, not through its interior. Surface waves are the slowest of the three seismic waves.

Tsunamis

Tsunamis are giant waves caused by earthquakes or volcanic eruptions under the sea. Out in the depths of the ocean, tsunami waves do not dramatically increase in height. However, as the waves travel inland, they build up to higher and higher heights as the depth of the ocean decreases. The speed of tsunami waves depends on ocean depth. Tsunamis may travel as fast as jet planes over deep waters, only slowing down when they reach shallow waters (NOAA, 2019).

Plate tectonics is the theory that Earth's outer shell is divided into several plates that glide over the mantle or the rocky inner layer above the core. The plates move and separate, causing Earth to separate and change.

Divergent – Pulling apart

Convergent – Coming together

Subduction – Sideways and downward movement of the edge of a plate into the mantle beneath another plate

Soil

Soil is a mixture of minerals, organic matter, gases, liquids, and many organisms that together support life on Earth.

The Water Cycle

The water cycle, also called the hydrologic cycle, is a continuous circulation of water throughout Earth and Earth's atmosphere.

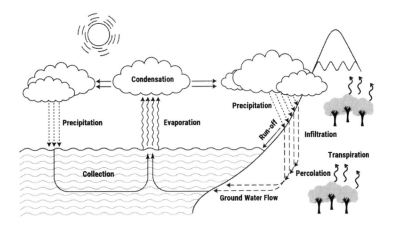

- **Precipitation** is rain and snow.
- **Evaporation** is when water turns from a liquid to a gas (water vapor).
- **Condensation** is when water vapor turns back into liquid—water collects as droplets on a cold surface when humid air is in contact with it, forming clouds.
- **Transpiration** is when plants suck water from roots to the small pores in leaves, releasing the water vapor into the atmosphere.

Quick Tip

The main stages of the water cycle are:
- Evaporation
- Condensation
- Precipitation
- Transpiration

C. Earth's history

Scientists believe Earth is 4.5 billion years old. Earth has a central core, a rocky mantle, and a solid crust. Scientists estimate that life began on Earth 3.8 billion years ago (NASA, n.d.).

Eon	Time	Description
Hadean	4.5 billion	Earth is formed out of debris around the solar protoplanetary disk. There is no life. Temperatures are extremely hot with frequent volcanic activity. The Moon is formed around this time.
Archean	2.5 billion	Prokaryote life, the first form of life, emerges. The atmosphere is composed of volcanic and greenhouse gases.
Proterozoic	541 million	Eukaryotes, a more complex form of life, emerge, including some forms of multicellular organisms. Bacteria begin producing oxygen, shaping the third and current of Earth's atmospheres. Plants, animals (later in this time period), and possibly earlier forms of fungi form around this time.
Phanerozoic	541 million–present	Complex life, including vertebrates, begin to dominate Earth's ocean. Gradually, life expands to land, and familiar forms of plants, animals, and fungi begin appearing. Animals—including humans—evolve at the most recent phases of this eon.

U.S. Geological Survey, 1997

Rocks

A rock is any naturally occurring solid mass or aggregate of minerals or mineraloid matter. Rocks are categorized by the minerals they include, their chemical composition, and their formation (origin). Rocks are usually grouped into three main categories: igneous, metamorphic, and sedimentary. Rocks form the Earth's outer solid layer: the lithosphere.

Type	Igneous	Metamorphic	Sedimentary
Made from…	lava, magma	heat pressure	deposition, cementation
Looks like…	glassy, smooth surface, gas bubble holes, random arrangement of minerals	sparkly crystals, ribbon-like layers	sand grains or visible pebbles; fossils may be visible
Examples	granite, pumice, obsidian	marble, slate, gneiss	conglomerate, sandstone, limestone, shale

D. Earth and the Universe

Earth is the third planet from the sun. Earth is the densest planet in the solar system, the largest of the solar system's four terrestrial planets, and the only astronomical object known to harbor life.

The sun is the star at the center of the solar system. It is the most important source of energy for life on Earth.

The moon is Earth's only natural satellite. The moon is thought to have formed approximately 4.5 billion years ago, not long after Earth.

The Solar System

The solar system is a planetary system that orbits the sun. The solar system consists of the sun and everything that orbits around it. This includes the eight planets and their natural satellites (such as our moon), dwarf planets (Pluto) and their satellites, as well as asteroids, comets, and countless particles of smaller debris (NASA, n.d.).

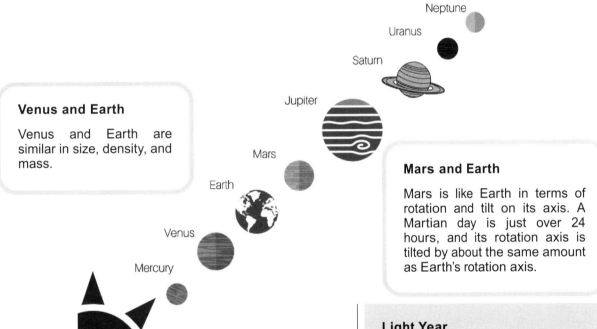

Venus and Earth

Venus and Earth are similar in size, density, and mass.

Mars and Earth

Mars is like Earth in terms of rotation and tilt on its axis. A Martian day is just over 24 hours, and its rotation axis is tilted by about the same amount as Earth's rotation axis.

Light Year

A light year is a unit of astronomical distance equal to the distance light travels in one year. For example, if an event occurs 13 light years away, it will take 13 years to observe the event from Earth.

Speed of Light

The speed of light in a vacuum is approximately 300,000 km/sec. In a vacuum is where speed of light is fastest. Traveling through any other medium, the speed of light is slower.

Other Components of the Solar System

- **Comets** – A chunk of ice and rock originating outside of the solar system.

- **Asteroids** – A chunk of rock and metal in orbit in between Mars and Jupiter.

- **Meteorite** – A small asteroid.

Earth's Tilt

Seasons are a result of Earth's **tilt on its axis.** When Earth is tilted toward the sun, it is warmer (summer). When Earth is tilted away from the sun, it is colder (winter). During spring and fall, Earth is tilted on its side. See diagram below.

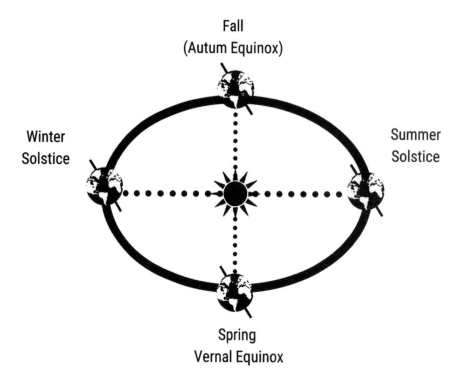

Season	Description
Fall – Autumn Equinox	Date in the fall when Earth experiences 12 hours of daylight and 12 hours of darkness. This occurs around September 23.
Summer – Solstice	Earth's maximum tilt is toward the sun, causing the longest period of daylight in the Northern Hemisphere. This occurs around June 22.
Spring – Vernal Equinox	Date in the spring when Earth experiences 12 hours of daylight and 12 hours of darkness. This occurs around March 21.
Winter – Solstice	The North Pole is tilted furthest away from the sun, causing the shortest period of daylight in the Northern Hemisphere. This occurs around December 21.

Heliocentric vs. Geocentric

The Scientific Revolution began as the Renaissance was coming to an end. The Scientific Revolution marked the emergence of modern science and the heliocentric model regarding the universe. The heliocentric theory, introduced by Nicolaus Copernicus, positioned the sun at the center of the universe. Copernicus also asserted Earth rotates on its axis while revolving around the sun. Up until that point, it was believed Earth sat stationary at the center of the universe (the geocentric theory). In his book, *On the Revolutions of Heavenly Spheres*, Copernicus' heliocentric model replaced the geocentric model.

The Moon

The moon affects the tides. When the part of the moon that is illuminated is increasing, the moon phase is waxing. When the part of the moon that is illuminated is decreasing, the moon phase is waning. A waxing moon is illuminated on the right side; a waning moon is illuminated on the left side.

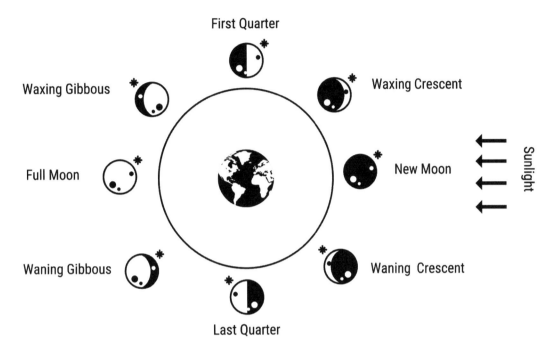

Stars

A star is a luminous ball of gas, mostly hydrogen and helium, held together by its own gravity. A star's color relies on its temperature. Hotter stars emit blue light; cooler stars emit red light (Temming 2014).

Type	Color	Temperature
O	Blue	Over 25,000 Kelvin
B	Blue	11,000–20,000 Kelvin
A	Blue	7,500–11,000 Kelvin
F	Blue to White	6,000–7,500 Kelvin
G	White to Yellow	5,000–6,000 Kelvin
K	Orange to Red	3,500–5,000 Kelvin
M	Red	Under 3,500 Kelvin

Lunar Eclipse – Positions

A **lunar eclipse** occurs when the moon passes directly behind Earth into its umbra (shadow).

Moon

Earth

Sun

Solar Eclipse – Positions

A **solar eclipse** happens when the moon moves in front of the sun.

Earth

Moon

Sun

A Bit of History

The Space Race refers to a time when the U.S. was competing with Russia to be the first to put a man on the moon. The competition began in 1957 when the Russians launched Sputnik, the very first artificial satellite. After that, the U.S. committed to getting to the moon before Russia and called on all scientists, technology specialists, engineers, and mathematicians to work toward the common goal.

E. Earth's patterns, cycles, and change

Earth goes through several patterns, cycles, and changes.

- **Patterns** – Earth spins on its axis. It makes one full rotation on its axis every 24 hours. Earth also revolves around the sun. It takes 365 days for Earth to make one full revolution around the sun.

- **Cycles** – Earth's rotation on its axis and revolution around the sun causes cycles on Earth: day, night, seasons, weather. Other cycles include the phases of the moon, water cycle, and life cycles (covered in Category 2 – Life Sciences).

- **Changes** – Earth goes through various changes. Some changes happen quickly; for example, an earthquake or a storm can change Earth rapidly. Other changes happen slowly; for example, the North American and Eurasian tectonic plates are separated by the Mid-Atlantic Ridge, and the two continents are moving away from each other at the rate of about 2.5 centimeters (1 inch) per year (National Geographic, n.d.).

Continental Drift

First proposed by Alfred Wegener, continental drift suggests the Earth's continents were once one big landmass that separated or drifted apart over time because of plate tectonics.

The Earth's plates are still constantly moving. Plate tectonics causes earthquakes, volcanic eruptions, and rift valleys.

Earth's Magnetic Poles

Earth has a magnetic field that extends from its interior to outer space. A compass is calibrated based on Earth's magnetic field. Over time, Earth's poles reverse—every 200,000 to 300,000 years. Magnetic fields morph, push, and pull at one another, with multiple poles emerging at odd latitudes throughout the process. Scientists estimate reversals have happened at least hundreds of times over the past 3 billion years.

On Earth, the magnetic field S pole is near Earth's geographic North Pole. The magnetic field N pole is near Earth's geographic South Pole.

F. Science as a human endeavor

Science is a result of human endeavors, imagination, and creativity. According to the Next Generation Science Standards (NGSS), the practice of science should outline the following skills:

- Asking questions and defining problems
- Developing and using models
- Planning and carrying out investigations
- Analyzing and interpreting data
- Using mathematics and computational thinking
- Constructing explanations and designing solutions
- Engaging in arguments based on evidence
- Obtaining, evaluating, and communicating information

Think About It

Notice that all the skills listed in the NGSS are inquiry-based, higher-order skills. We call these **good words** because you will find them in the correct answer choices on the test.

Once you know the **good words**, you'll be able to identify correct answer choices easily because they will stand out from the other choices.

For the category of Earth Science, teachers would apply the practice of science in various activities. For example, teachers may have students evaluate the impact climate change has on human society. Students may look at data to evaluate increases in CO_2 emissions. Students could design solutions to the emissions problem. They may also engage in a debate with their classmates while citing evidence and research they have explored.

G. Science inquiry

First things first, science is inquiry-based, meaning students must be given the opportunity to interact with the concepts they are studying. For example, talking about living and nonliving things is one thing. However, going outside and **observing** living and nonliving things is quite another. Students must have the opportunity to touch, observe, and interact with the environment they are studying.

According to the National Science Teacher Association (NSTA) (2009), effective science instruction includes:

- having pedagogical knowledge;

- providing learning opportunities that meet the individual needs of students, placing the learner at the center of instruction; and

- facilitating learning opportunities that develop students' conceptual understanding.

Teachers must know the science content, empower the students to learn, differentiate to meet the needs of a diverse population, and foster inquiry-based learning activities. Students must touch, feel, and observe to understand science.

Scenario: If the teacher wants her students to understand the structure of the solar system, having students touch a model of the solar system is a good way to engage them. Reading about the solar system is ok. However, allowing students to manipulate a model brings an abstract concept, like the solar system, into a concrete, inquiry-based activity.

H. Using resources and research material in science

For teachers to be effective in the science classroom, they must have a current and relevant understanding of the research governing the profession. There are several ways to do this:

1. Teachers can join reputable science organizations. These organizations often publish research teachers can use to guide their decisions in the classroom. Organizations like the NSTA, Association for Science Teacher Education, and the National Earth Science Teacher Association focus on developing effective science teachers through research and professional development.

2. Teachers can attend professional development that focuses on researched-based strategies in science.

3. Teachers can be data-driven in their decision making.

4. Teachers can engage in lifelong learning practices.

I. Unifying processes of science

There are five main ideas under the unifying concepts and processes of science.

Main Idea	Earth Science Example
1. Systems, order, and organizations	Parts are related to the whole. For example, the atmosphere affects the entire climate of Earth. That climate impacts humans. Humans impact the environment.
2. Evidence, models, and explanations	Students use a model of the solar system to discuss the relationship among planets and the sun.
3. Change, constancy, and measurement	Because of Earth's tilt on its axis, we experience changes in seasons as the we move through the year.
4. Evolution and equilibrium	Phases of matter and changes in Earth's sky are examples of evolution and equilibrium.
5. Form and function	Earth's features like its mass and shape impact functions such as gravity and rotation.

II. Life Science

Section II, Life Science, tests your knowledge of living things, including the structure of living things, life processes, life cycles, reproduction, heredity, adaptation, and classification.

The skills you need to know in this section include the following:

A. Understands the structure and function of living systems (e.g., living characteristics and cells, tissues and organs, life processes).

B. Understands reproduction and heredity (e.g., growth and development, patterns of inheritance of traits, molecular basis of heredity).

C. Understands change over time in living things (e.g., life cycles, mutations, adaptation, and natural selection).

D. Understands regulation and behavior (e.g., life cycles, responses to external stimuli, controlling the environment).

E. Understands unity and diversity of life, adaptation, and classification.

F. Understands the interdependence of organisms (e.g., ecosystems, populations, communities).

G. Knows about personal health (e.g., nutrition, communicable diseases, substance abuse).

H. Understands science as a human endeavor, a process, and a career.

I. Understands science as inquiry (e.g., questioning, gathering data, drawing reasonable conclusions).

J. Understands how to use resources and research material in science.

K. Understands the unifying processes of science (e.g., systems, order, organization).

A. Structure and function of living systems

Living things have physical entities and biological processes, such as homeostasis, cell division, cellular respiration, and photosynthesis. Nonliving things do not have these processes and are classified as **inanimate**.

Cell theory made up of three components:

1. All living things are composed of cells.

2. The cell is the smallest unit of life.

3. All cells come from pre-existing cells.

The organization of life is as follows:

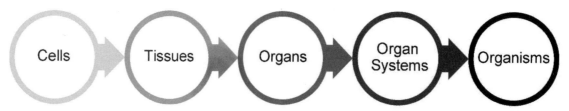

© 2022 Kathleen Jasper

Prokaryote vs. Eukaryote

A **prokaryote** is a unicellular organism that lacks a nucleus, mitochondria, or any other membrane-bound organelle (NC State University, n.d.). In a prokaryotic cell, the Deoxyribose Nucleic Acid (DNA) floats freely throughout the cell. Prokaryotes are divided into two domains: archaea and bacteria.

A **eukaryote** is a multicellular organism that contains a nucleus, mitochondria, and membrane-bound organelles.

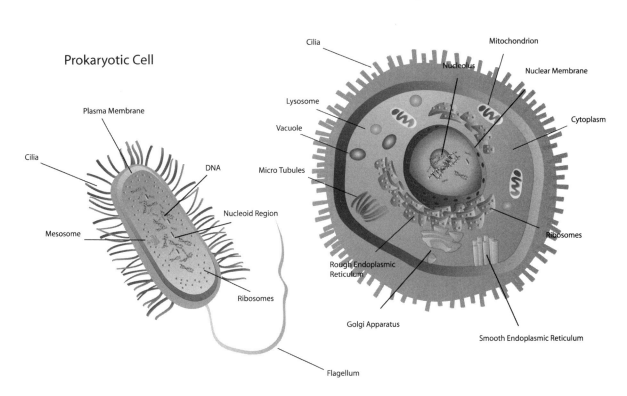

Eukaryotic Cell

Prokaryotic Cell

> ### Quick Tip
>
> The structures within the cell membrane or cell wall are called **organelles**. The main structures of the cell are:
> - **Cellular membrane** – Fluid, permeable outside covering of the cell. In a plant cell, this is a cell wall and it is rigid.
> - **Nucleus** – Command center of the cell. The nucleus controls the rest of the cell. This is where the DNA lives in eukaryotic cells.
> - **Mitochondria** – Powerhouse (energy source) of the cell.
> - **Cytoplasm** – Water-like substance in the cell.

Bacteria vs. Virus

Both bacteria and viruses are prokaryotic cells and can only be seen under a microscope. Bacteria are usually harmless while viruses cause diseases.

Animal Cells vs. Plant Cells

Animal and plant cells are both eukaryotic. However, there are differences between an animal cell and a plant cell.

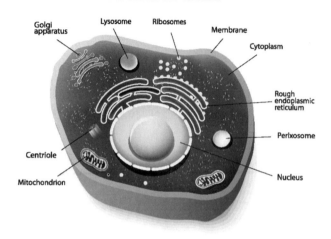

ANIMAL CELL

Cellular Respiration

Animal cells go through a process of cellular respiration. This is the process of taking in food in the form of carbohydrates, making energy in the form of ATP, and removing waste. The equation for this process is:

Glucose (sugar) + Oxygen →

Carbon dioxide + Water + Energy (as ATP)

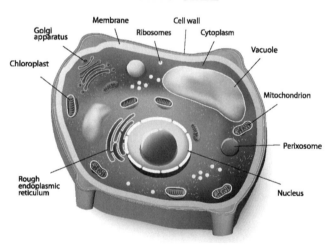

PLANT CELL

Photosynthesis

Plant cells make their own food through photosynthesis. This is the process of using carbon dioxide, water, and sunlight, and turning them into carbohydrates. The equation for this process is:

Carbon dioxide + Water + Sunlight →

Glucose (sugar) + Oxygen

Notice the waste of animal cells becomes the nutrients plants use to go through photosynthesis, and the waste of plant cells becomes the nutrients animals use to go through cellular respiration. It is a symbiotic relationship.

Plant Cells	Animal Cells
Cell wall	Plasma membrane
Chloroplast	No chloroplast
Photosynthesis (CO_2 + H_2O + light = Carbohydrates)	Cellular respiration (Carbohydrates + O_2 = CO_2 and H_2O

B. Reproduction and heredity

There are two main types of reproduction in living things: **sexual** and **asexual**.

Sexual reproduction – Involves two parents. Each parent contributes a gamete to the process of reproduction. Gametes are sex cells. In males, the gametes are sperm. In females, the gametes are ova (or eggs). Sexual reproduction occurs in plant and animal cells.

Quick Tip

Prokaryotic cells reproduce asexually, typically through binary fission. While prokaryotes do not go through mitosis, the cell does split into identical copies.

Asexual reproduction – Involves only one parent. There are four main types of asexual reproduction.

1. **Binary fission** is when a single parent cell doubles its DNA, then divides into two cells. This usually occurs in bacteria.

2. **Budding** is when a small growth on the surface of parent breaks off to continue growing into adulthood. This typically occurs in yeast and some animals.

3. **Fragmentation** is when a piece of an organism breaks off, and those pieces develop into a new organism. This happens with starfish. If a piece of a starfish leg breaks off, the fragment will form a new starfish.

4. **Parthenogenesis** is when an embryo develops from an unfertilized cell. This occurs in invertebrates as well as in some fish, amphibians, and reptiles.

Benefits of Sexual Reproduction over Asexual Reproduction

In sexual reproduction, offspring are genetically different; in asexual reproduction, offspring are identical. Genetic diversity is advantageous because it allows populations to adapt and evolve.

Cellular Replication – Mitosis

According to cell theory, all cells come from pre-existing cells. For that to happen, cells must reproduce, and they must reproduce rapidly. Cells reproduce by going through mitosis—a series of steps in creating an identical cell from another cell. Although there are many complicated nuances to mitosis, elementary teachers will most likely focus on interphase (not actually part of mitosis) and the four main phases of mitosis that follow: prophase, metaphase, anaphase, and telophase.

Interphase (technically not part of mitosis, but it is important to know) – The cell prepares for division. It plumps up and replicates its DNA within its nucleus.

Prophase – The DNA tightly coils into chromosomes to make splitting efficient. The nuclear membrane dissolves. The microtubes or spindle fibers move to opposites sides of the cell.

Metaphase – The chromosomes (tightly coiled DNA) move to the middle of the cell. The spindle fibers attach to each chromosome.

Anaphase – The spindle fibers begin to pull apart the chromosomes, bringing them to opposites sides of the cell for efficient splitting.

Telophase – With the chromosomes at either side of the cell, the two new cells pinch off, forming two identical sister cells of the original cells. **Cytokinesis** is when the cell separates into two cells during the final stage of mitosis.

Stages of Mitosis

INTERPHASE
(Technically NOT
Part of Mitosis)

The cell prepares for
division by replicating
the DNA.

Organelles also double.

The DNA is *uncoiled*.
This is called
chromatin.

1.
PROPHASE

The nuclear membrane starts to disappear.

Mitotic spindle fibers begin to appear (these will split the cell).

The DNA begins to coil into *chromosomes*, making it easier for them to be pulled apart.

2.
METAPHASE

Distinct chromosomes line up in the middle of the cell.

Spindle fibers attach to the centromeres (center) of the chromosomes.

3.
ANAPHASE

Spindle fibers begin to pull chromosomes apart.

The halves of the chromosomes pull toward opposite sides of the cell.

4.
TELOPHASE

The cell splits into two identical cells.

The nucleus in both cells begins to appear and surround the DNA.

Cytokinesis cuts the cell in two.

Sexual Reproduction – Meiosis

The other type of cell division, meiosis, ensures that humans have the same number of chromosomes in each generation. It is a two-step process that reduces the chromosome number by half—from 46 to 23—to form sperm and egg cells. When the sperm and egg cells unite at conception, each contributes 23 chromosomes so the resulting embryo will have the usual 46 (U.S. National Library of Medicine, 2019).

This is necessary so that the sex cells contain only half the chromosomes (23).

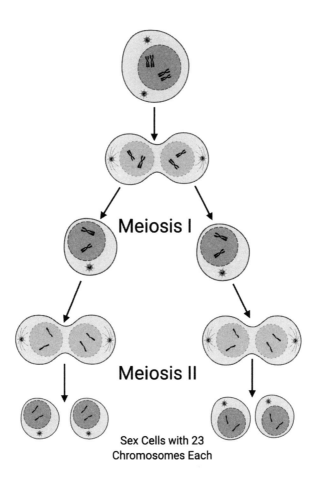

Sex Cells with 23
Chromosomes Each

Trisomy

Sometimes abnormalities happen during cell division, and cells do not split chromosomes evenly. This results in extra chromosomes in the cell. Perhaps the most widely known instance of this is Trisomy 21, also known as Down syndrome. Trisomy 21 means that each cell in the body has three copies (tri) of chromosome 21 instead of the usual two copies (U.S. National Library of Medicine, 2019).

DNA

DNA is the hereditary material in living organisms. In eukaryotic cells, DNA is mainly located in the cell's nucleus; there is DNA in the mitochondria too. The DNA contains a code with four nitrogen bases: adenine, thymine, guanine, and cytosine. These bases pair up with each other—adenine with thymine, cytosine with guanine. These four bases make up approximately 3.1 billion genetic combinations running down the human DNA molecule. Most of the combinations are identical in all humans. The sequence of the combinations determines the traits of a person (U.S. National Library of Medicine, 2019).

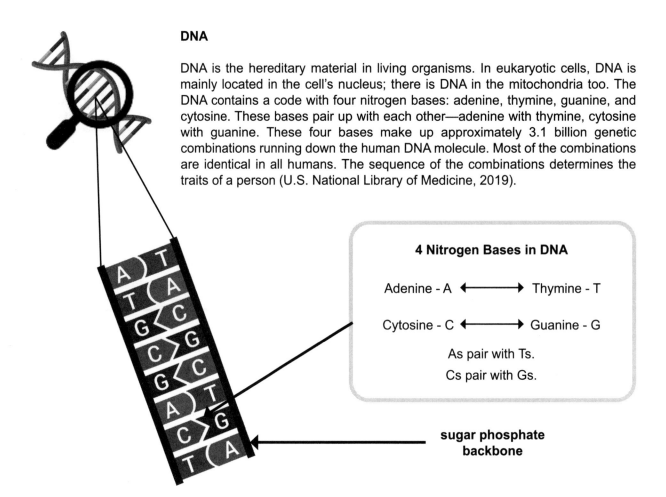

4 Nitrogen Bases in DNA

Adenine - A ⟷ Thymine - T

Cytosine - C ⟷ Guanine - G

As pair with Ts.

Cs pair with Gs.

sugar phosphate backbone

Amino Acids

Amino acids are organic compounds that form proteins. The four nitrogen bases on the DNA molecule code for the 20 different amino acids. Chains of amino acids make proteins. Those proteins make cell structures, cells, tissues, organs, organ systems, and the organism.

DNA Replication

Mitosis is when the cell divides resulting in two identical cells. To do this, the DNA must replicate. DNA replication is necessary in the survival of an organism. The process of DNA replication is as follows:

1. The DNA unzips.

2. Free-flowing nucleotides (As, Ts, Gs, and Cs) bind to the unzipped portion of the DNA.

3. Two identical DNA strands are the result.

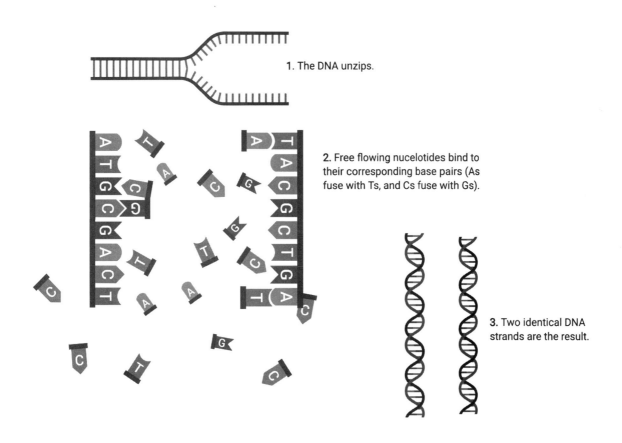

1. The DNA unzips.

2. Free flowing nucelotides bind to their corresponding base pairs (As fuse with Ts, and Cs fuse with Gs).

3. Two identical DNA strands are the result.

Genes and Heredity

A gene is the basic physical and functional unit of heredity. Genes are made up of DNA. Genes act as instructions to make molecules called proteins. These proteins make cells, which make tissues, which make organs, which make organ systems. Every person has two copies of each gene, one inherited from each parent. Most genes are the same in all people, but a small number of genes (less than 1 percent of the total) are slightly different among people. These small differences contribute to each person's unique physical features (U.S. National Library of Medicine, 2019).

Alleles are forms of the same gene with slight differences in their sequence of DNA bases. **Dominance** is when the effect of one phenotype of one allele masks the contribution of a second allele at the same locus. The first allele is dominant, and the second allele is recessive. For example, in humans, brown eye color is dominant over blue eye color. For a person to display blue eyes, she must have both recessive alleles.

Gregor Mendel - The Father of Genetics

Gregor Mendel is known as the Father of Genetics for his work with pea plants in the 1850s and 1860s. Mendel showed that when a true-breeding yellow pea (YY) and a true-breeding green pea (yy) were cross-bred, their offspring always produced yellow seeds. However, in the next generation, the green peas reappeared. To explain this phenomenon, Mendel coined the terms recessive and dominant in reference to certain traits.

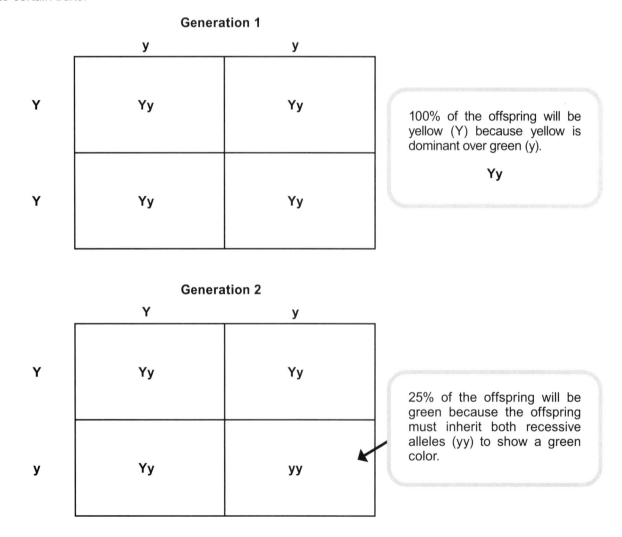

Generation 1

	y	y
Y	Yy	Yy
Y	Yy	Yy

100% of the offspring will be yellow (Y) because yellow is dominant over green (y).

Yy

Generation 2

	Y	y
Y	Yy	Yy
y	Yy	yy

25% of the offspring will be green because the offspring must inherit both recessive alleles (yy) to show a green color.

C. Change over time in living things

Organisms and populations change over time. Some of these changes take short periods of time, such as a caterpillar changing into a butterfly; other changes can take thousands of years, such as evolution of populations.

An organism's life cycle consists of an organism changing over time.

Metamorphosis is the process of transformation from an immature form to an adult form in two or more distinct stages. There are two types of metamorphosis:

1. **Complete metamorphosis** – The insect goes through four stages: egg, larva, pupa, imago.

   Example: A caterpillar changes completely into something else: a butterfly.

2. **Incomplete metamorphosis** – The insect hatches from an egg and then goes through several nymphal stages.

   Example: Grasshoppers gradually get bigger, but they do not change into something else. Each stage of growth looks like a bigger version of the original stage.

Evolution is a type of change that happens over thousands of years. It is important to note that organisms do not evolve; populations evolve. For example, a bird will not suddenly go through evolution during its lifetime. However, through genetic mutations over lengthy periods of time, populations of birds will evolve and change to adapt to their environment.

Adaptation is the distribution of traits in the population that can change with environmental conditions. For example, over time, frogs inherited genetic variations that resulted in camouflage—ability to blend in with its surroundings. This allowed the frog to survive and reproduce.

> **Natural Selection**
>
> Charles Darwin and Alfred Russel Wallace developed the theory of evolution: traits can be passed down to offspring that allow organisms to adapt to the environment better than other organisms of the same species. This enables better survival and reproduction compared with other members of the species, leading to evolution.

Variation of genetically determined traits in a population may give some members a reproductive advantage in a given environment. This is often random and a result of a mutation on the DNA molecule. This natural selection can lead to adaptation. Such adaptations can eventually lead to the development of separate species in separated populations (National Research Council, 2012).

Mutations are changes in the DNA molecule caused by mistakes during cell division or exposure to environmental factors (such as ultraviolet [UV] light and cigarette smoke). Sometimes these mutations are beneficial to species because they help species evolve. For example, in the 19th century, smog from the factories in England turned many trees in the area black. This made the white moths living in the area easily seen by predators. The white moths were picked off as food. The black moths, who had inherited a certain gene sequence to make them black, were camouflaged against the black trees. More black moths were able to survive and reproduce. The black moths ended up dominating in the area.

D. Regulation and behavior

All organisms must be able to grow, reproduce, and maintain stable internal conditions even when the world and environment around them change. Regulation of the organism's internal body allows the organism to survive conditions. Organisms differ in how they regulate their bodies.

The behavior of individual organisms is influenced by internal cues (hunger and internal temperature) and external cues (changes in the environment). Humans and other organisms have senses that help them detect internal and external cues (National Research Council, 2012).

Homeostasis

The tendency to maintain a stable, relatively constant internal environment is called homeostasis. For example, no matter how hot or cold it is outside, the human body will maintain a temp of $98.6\,°F$ on average, unless there is sickness or infection.

Organism Type	Definition	Types of Animals
Cold-blooded	Animals that have a body temperature varying with that of the environment.	amphibians, reptiles, fish, insects
Warm-blooded	Animals that maintain a constant body temperature, regardless of the temperature in the environment. For example, humans will sweat when they are hot and shiver when they are cold.	Mammals, birds

Vertebrates vs. Invertebrates

The main distinction between vertebrates and invertebrates is the presence of a backbone. Vertebrates do have a backbone; invertebrates do not have a backbone. Both vertebrates and invertebrates are animals or come from the Kingdom Animalia.

Circulatory System	Definition	Animal Types
Open	The blood is pumped into the body cavity and is not enclosed in blood vessels.	Most invertebrates - insects, crustaceans, most mollusks
Closed	The blood is pumped by the heart and is enclosed in blood vessels.	Most vertebrates – mammals, reptiles, fish, birds

Main Human Systems

Circulatory & Respiratory System – This system is responsible for the flow of blood, nutrients, oxygen and other gases, and hormones to and from cells.

- heart (cardiovascular)
- lungs (pulmonary)
- arteries, veins, coronary and portal vessels (systemic)

Digestive & Excretory System – This system is responsible taking in food and breaking it up into nutrients the body will use for fuel. It is also responsible for removing the waste left over after the food is processed for nutrients.

- gastrointestinal tract (stomach and intestines)
- bladder
- colon
- kidneys (filter the blood)

Nervous, Endocrine & Immune System – This system is the master control system.

- brain – hypothalamus, thalamus, and pituitary gland
- spinal cord
- neurons
- hormones

E. Unity and diversity of life, adaptation, and classification

Unity and Diversity

With the national standards in mind, Core Idea LS4: Biological Evolution: Unity and Diversity states that students should understand this concept in elementary school.

According to the National Research Council (2012):

- **By the end of grade 2,** students should understand that some kinds of plants and animals that once lived on Earth (e.g., dinosaurs) are no longer found anywhere. They should also understand that some living organisms resemble species no longer found on Earth (e.g., lizards and birds resemble dinosaurs).

- **By the end of grade 5,** students should understand that fossils provide evidence about the types of organisms (both visible and microscopic) that lived long ago and also about the nature of their environments. Fossils can be compared with one another and to living organisms according to their similarities and differences.

Adaptation

The special characteristics that allow plants and animals to be successful in a particular environment are called adaptations. These special characteristics happen over time because of genetic variation.

Variation of genetically determined traits in a population may give some members a reproductive advantage in a given environment. This is often random and a result of a mutation on the DNA molecule. This natural selection can lead to adaptation or a distribution of traits in the population that is matched to and can change with environmental conditions. Such adaptations can eventually lead to the development of separate species in separated populations (National Research Council, 2012).

Classification

The **classification of living things** was first done by Carl Linnaeus, as set forth in his Systema Naturae (1735).

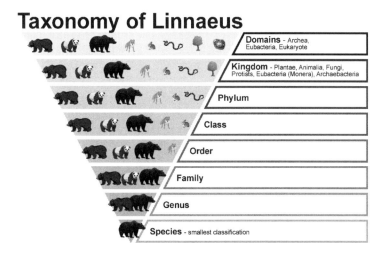

F. The interdependence of organisms

Scientists recognize that life can be organized into several different levels of function and complexity. These functional levels are: species, populations, communities, and ecosystems (Pidwirny, 2006).

Level	Description	Examples
Species	A group of interbreeding organisms that do not ordinarily breed with members of other groups.	The polar bear (Ursus maritimus) is a hypercarnivorous bear whose native range lies largely within the Arctic Circle.
Populations	Comprises all the individuals of a given species in a specific area or region at a certain time. Populations can evolve over time because of genetic variation.	The population includes all the polar bears in the Arctic Circle. Within the population, the polar bear species can reflect genetic variance.
Communities	All the populations in a specific area or region at a certain time. There are many interactions among species in a community (food webs).	The polar bears, the penguins, the fish, and the plants make up the community. These all interact when it comes to food and survival.
Ecosystems	The dynamic entities composed of the biological (living) community and the abiotic (nonliving) environment.	The Arctic ecosystem is made up of the water/ice, the animals, and the atmosphere in that area.

Food/Energy Pyramid

Within ecosystems there is an interdependence among organisms of the same or different species. There is also interdependence between living and nonliving elements in the environment. For example, organisms in an ecosystem interact with one another in complex feeding hierarchies, which together represent a food web.

Producers (plants) – These organisms produce their own food from sunlight, carbon dioxide, and water. These are usually the bottom tier of the food web/energy pyramid.

Consumers – These organisms eat their food. Categorized into four main groups:

1. **Primary** consumers are herbivores; they eat plants. In the energy pyramid, the bunny is the primary consumer.

2. **Secondary** consumers eat the primary consumer. In the energy pyramid, the snake is the secondary consumer.

3. **Tertiary** consumers eat the secondary consumers and are usually carnivores (meat-eaters). In the energy pyramid, the bird is the tertiary consumer.

4. **Quaternary** consumers eat the tertiary consumers and are carnivores. In the energy pyramid, the quaternary consumer is the hawk. This food chain ends with the hawk, which would be considered the top carnivore.

> **Quick Tip**
>
> All energy comes from the sun. The sun provides the electrons necessary for plants to go through photosynthesis. That process results in carbohydrates animals need to survive.

Decomposers – These organisms turn dead material, such as an animal carcass or a dead tree, into soil by recycling nutrients as food. Decomposers are not shown below, but they live underground. Decomposers include earthworms, small soil beetles, fungi, and bacteria.

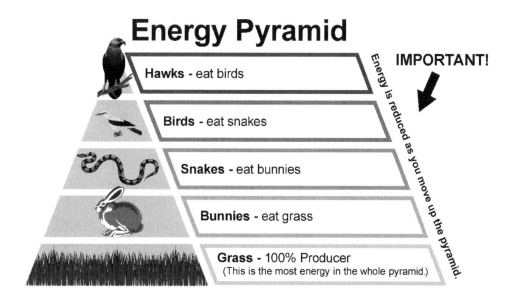

Energy Pyramid

Hawks - eat birds

Birds - eat snakes

Snakes - eat bunnies

Bunnies - eat grass

Grass - 100% Producer
(This is the most energy in the whole pyramid.)

Energy is reduced as you move up the pyramid.

IMPORTANT!

Interaction of Organisms

Interactions among organisms may be predatory, competitive, or mutually beneficial. These are referred to as ecological relationships (National Geographic, n.d.).

Relationship	Definition	Example
Competition	When two or more organisms rely on the same environmental resource	Because they eat the same type of food, cheetahs and lions compete within their ecosystem.
Predation	Behavior of one animal feeding on another	The lion eats the zebra. The lion is the predator; the zebra is the prey.
Symbiosis	The close relationship of two dissimilar organisms	There are three type of symbiosis: mutualism, commensalism, and parasitism.
Mutualism	A symbiotic relationship where both organisms benefit	Humans have a mutualistic relationship with micro-organisms. Bacteria in the digestive tract keeps humans healthy while the bacteria are fed by what the human eats.
Commensalism	A symbiotic relationship where one organism benefits and one does not benefit but is unharmed	The cattle egret sits on top of the cattle and eats the bugs that land on the cattle.
Parasitism	A symbiotic relationship where one organism benefits and one is harmed	A tick living on a dog benefits while the dog is harmed.

Carrying Capacity

Carrying capacity is the maximum population of a particular organism that a given environment can support without detrimental effects. Individual survival and population sizes depend on such factors as predation, disease, availability of resources, and parameters of the physical environment. Earth's varied combinations of these factors provide the physical environments in which its ecosystems (e.g., deserts, grasslands, rain forests, and coral reefs) develop and in which the diverse species of the planet live (National Research Council, 2012).

According to the National Research Council (2012):

- **By the end of grade 2,** students should understand that animals depend on their surroundings to get what they need: food, water, shelter, and favorable temperature.

- **By the end of grade 5,** students should understand that the food of almost any kind of animal can be traced back to plants, according to the food web or energy pyramid.

G. Personal health

The Centers for Disease Control and Prevention (CDC) has outlined performance indicators for the National Health Education Standards (NHES). These performance indicators were developed to establish, promote, and support health-enhancing behaviors for students in all grade levels, from pre-Kindergarten through grade 12. The NHES provide a framework for teachers, administrators, and policymakers in designing or selecting curricula, allocating instructional resources, and assessing student achievement and progress. Importantly, the standards provide students, families, and communities with concrete expectations for health education (Centers for Disease Control and Prevention, 2019).

Standard	Indicator	k-6 Application
1	Students will comprehend concepts related to health promotion and disease prevention to enhance health.	• Describe ways to prevent common childhood injuries and health problems. • Describe when it is important to seek healthcare.
2	Students will analyze the influence of family, peers, culture, media, technology, and other factors on health behaviors.	• Identify how peers can influence healthy and unhealthy behaviors. • Describe how the school and community can support personal health practices and behaviors.
3	Students will demonstrate the ability to access valid information, products, and services to enhance health.	• Identify trusted adults and professionals who can help promote health. • Identify ways to locate school and community health helpers.
4	Students will demonstrate the ability to use interpersonal communication skills to enhance health and avoid or reduce health risks.	• Demonstrate refusal skills that avoid or reduce health risks. • Demonstrate nonviolent strategies to manage or resolve conflict.
5	Students will demonstrate the ability to use decision-making skills to enhance health.	• Differentiate between situations when a health-related decision can be made individually or when assistance is needed.
6	Students will demonstrate the ability to use goal-setting skills to enhance health.	• Set a personal health goal and track progress toward its achievement. • Identify resources to assist in achieving a personal health goal.
7	Students will demonstrate the ability to practice health-enhancing behaviors and avoid or reduce health risks.	• Demonstrate healthy practices and behaviors to maintain or improve personal health. • Demonstrate behaviors that avoid or reduce health risks.
8	Students will demonstrate the ability to advocate for personal, family, and community health.	• Express opinions and give accurate information about health issues. • Encourage others to make positive health choices.

H. Science as a human endeavor

According to the Next Generation Science Standards (NGSS), the practice of science should outline the following skills:

- Asking questions and defining problems

- Developing and using models

- Planning and carrying out investigations

- Analyzing and interpreting data

- Using mathematics and computational thinking

- Constructing explanations and designing solutions

- Engaging in arguments based on evidence

- Obtaining, evaluating, and communicating information

I. Science inquiry

According to the National Science Teacher Association or NSTA (2009), effective science instruction includes:

- having pedagogical knowledge;

- providing learning opportunities that meet the individual needs of students;

- placing the learner at the center of instruction; and

- facilitating learning opportunities that develop students' conceptual understanding.

Teachers must know the science content, empower the students to learn, differentiate to meet the needs of diverse population, and foster inquiry-based learning activities. Students must touch, feel, and observe to understand science.

Scenario:

If the teacher wants her students to understand the diet of an owl, she should give them an opportunity to dissect owl pellets (a mass of undigested parts of a bird's food that some bird species occasionally regurgitate). Reading about owl diets is ok, but dissecting owl pellets is much better.

J. Using resources and research material in science

Teachers in the area of life science must find reputable research to drive their decisions in the classroom. Resources that are helpful for elementary science instructors include:

- National Science Teacher Association press

- National Science Teacher Association journals

- Any academic journal with peer-reviewed research.

The main thing to consider when choosing material for the science classroom is the standards. Standards outline what skills students should be able to master based on grade level. For more on the national science standards visit the Next Generation Science Standards at https://www.nextgenscience.org/.

K. Unifying processes of science

A unifying principle of life science is that all organisms are related by evolution and that evolutionary processes have led to the diversity of the biosphere. There is diversity within species as well as among species, and the function of a gene, cell, organ system, or organism is relevant to other organisms because of their ecological interactions and evolutionary relatedness (National Research Council, 2012).

According to the National Research Council (2012), there are four core ideas that encompass life science.

Core and Component Ideas in Life Science
Core Idea LS1: From Molecules to Organisms: Structures and Processes
• LS1.A: Structure and Function   • LS1.B: Growth and Development of Organisms   • LS1.C: Organization for Matter and Energy Flow in Organisms   • LS1.D: Information Processing
Core Idea LS2: Ecosystems: Interactions, Energy, and Dynamics
• LS2.A: Interdependent Relationships in Ecosystems   • LS2.B: Cycles of Matter and Energy Transfer in Ecosystems   • LS2.C: Ecosystem Dynamics, Functioning, and Resilience   • LS2.D: Social Interactions and Group Behavior
Core Idea LS3: Heredity: Inheritance and Variation of Traits
• LS3.A: Inheritance of Traits   • LS3.B: Variation of Traits
Core Idea LS4: Biological Evolution: Unity and Diversity
• LS4.A: Evidence of Common Ancestry and Diversity   • LS4.B: Natural Selection   • LS4.C: Adaptation   • LS4.D: Biodiversity and Humans

III. Physical Science

Section III, Physical Science, tests your knowledge of matter and energy. Topics include the foundational skills of chemistry and physics such as properties of matter, forces and motion, forms of energy, and sound.

The skills you need to know in this section include the following:

A. Understands the physical and chemical properties and structure of matter (e.g., changes of states, mixtures and solutions, atoms, and elements).

B. Understands forces of motion (e.g., types of motion, laws of motion, forces, and equilibrium).

C. Understands energy (e.g., forms of energy, transfer and conservation of energy, simple machines).

D. Understands interaction of energy and matter (e.g., electricity, magnetism, sound).

E. Understands science as a human endeavor, a process, and a career.

F. Understands science as inquiry (e.g., questioning, gathering data, drawing reasonable conclusions).

G. Understands how to use resources and research material in science.

H. Understands the unifying processes of science (e.g., systems, order, organization).

A. Physical and chemical properties and structure of matter

- **Solid** – Particles are very close together.
- **Liquid** – Particles are closer together than a gas but farther apart than a solid.
- **Gas** – Particles are very far apart.

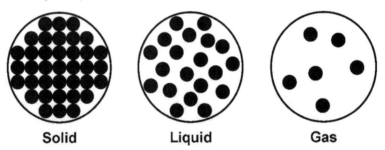

Physical – Results in change in the size and shape by:	Chemical – Results in any change that forms new substances at the molecular level by:
tearing	rotting
folding	burning
melting	cooking
freezing	rusting
evaporating	
cutting	

Phase Changes in Matter

Changes in matter can happen by removing or adding energy in the form of boiling, condensation, and evaporation.

- **Boiling** – Rapid vaporization of a liquid (liquid to gas).

- **Condensation** – Water that collects as droplets on a cold surface when humid air is in contact with it (gas to liquid).

- **Evaporation** – Vaporization of a liquid that occurs from the surface of a liquid into a gaseous phase (liquid to gas).

Quick Tip

Have you ever walked into a grocery store after your workout, and you become chilly? That's because when water evaporates, it leaves behind cooler air. It's called *temperature moderation*, and it's an amazing property of water that is essential for life on Earth.

Mixtures

A mixture is a material system made up of two or more different substances that are mixed but are not combined chemically. The identities of the mixed elements are retained in a mixture. There are two types of mixtures: **homogeneous** and **heterogeneous**.

Homogeneous Mixture	Heterogeneous Mixture	Colloid	Suspension	Solutions
homo = same	hetero = different	homogeneous mixture	heterogeneous mixture	homogeneous mixture
You cannot see different parts of the mixture.	You can see different parts of the mixture.	One substance of microscopically dispersed insoluble particles is suspended throughout another substance. Particles do not settle and cannot be separated out by ordinary filtering.	Contains solid particles that are sufficiently large for sedimentation.	The dissolving agent is the solvent.
coffee, creamy peanut butter, Kool-Aid	chicken noodle soup, cereal	gels, emulsions	orange juice, salad dressing	salt water, sugar water

pH Scale

The pH scale is a measure of acidity or alkalinity of water-soluble substances (pH stands for "potential of Hydrogen"). A pH value is a number from 1 to 14, with 7 as the middle (neutral) point. Values less than 7 have acidity. Values above 7 have alkalinity.

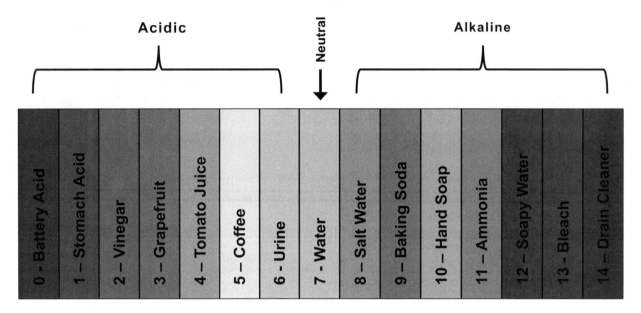

Atoms

Atoms are the smallest part of an element that retains its chemical properties. More than 99.94% of an atom's mass is in the nucleus.

- **Electrons** – Negatively charged subatomic particles that circle around the atom's nucleus.

- **Neutrons** – Neutrally charged subatomic particles that are located in the atom's nucleus.

- **Protons** – Positively charged subatomic particles that are located in the atom's nucleus.

Elements

Elements – More than 100 substances that cannot be chemically interconverted or broken down into simpler substances and are primary constituents of matter.

Atomic number – How an element is identified. It is also the number of protons in the nuclei of its atoms.

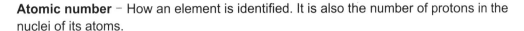

The Periodic Table of the Elements

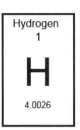

The periodic table can be used a variety of ways and is broken up several ways.

- **Groups** – Vertical/columns

- **Periods** – Horizontal/rows

- **Metals** – Shiny, good conductors of electricity

- **Nonmetals** – Dull, poor conductors of electricity

- **Metalloids** – Dull or shiny, good semiconductors

- **Noble gases** – Last column on the right of the periodic table

Reactivity

In metals, reactivity increases as you move down and to the left to the periodic table. For example, potassium (K) is more reactive than magnesium (Mg). In nonmetals, reactivity increases up and to the right of the periodic table. For example, fluorine (F) is more reactive than iodine (I).

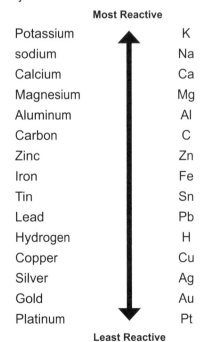

Most Reactive

Potassium	K
sodium	Na
Calcium	Ca
Magnesium	Mg
Aluminum	Al
Carbon	C
Zinc	Zn
Iron	Fe
Tin	Sn
Lead	Pb
Hydrogen	H
Copper	Cu
Silver	Ag
Gold	Au
Platinum	Pt

Least Reactive

Molecules

Molecules are the smallest particle in a chemical element or compound that has the chemical properties of that element or compound. Molecules are made up of atoms that are held together by chemical bonds.

 H_2O

> **Water** is the molecule H_2O. This amazing molecule is composed of two hydrogen elements and one oxygen element.

Characteristics of Water

Water is a polar molecule, which causes it to have properties that make it necessary for life on Earth. Water has the following properties:

- **Cohesion** – Water is attracted to other molecules. When you put a drop of water close to another drop of water, they combine quickly because they are attracted to each other.

- **Adhesion** – Water is attracted to other molecules. This allows water to stick to roots—capillary action in a plant.

- **High-specific heat** – This allows water to moderate temperature.

- **High heat of evaporation** – This gives off a cooling affect, like when humans sweat. That evaporation of water cools off the body.

- **Lower density of ice** – Water is less dense than ice, causing ice to float in water.

- **High polarity** – This makes water a powerful solvent.

Compounds

Compounds are composed of two or more elements bonded together. All compounds are molecules, but not all molecules are compounds.

> Molecules *can* be made up of multiples of a single element like oxygen (O_2), while compounds *must* be made up of two different molecules (CO_2).

Compounds/ Molecules	Only Molecules
CO_2	O_2
H_2O	H_2
CH_4	N_2

Ions are charged elements or molecules that have lost or gained one or more electrons.

Isotopes are two or more forms of the same element that have the same number of protons but a different number of neutrons.

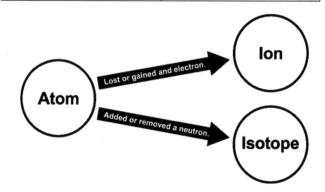

B. Forces of motion

A **force** is any interaction that, when unopposed, will change the motion of an object. A force can cause an object with mass to change its velocity (including beginning motion from a state of rest).

Friction is the force resisting the relative motion of solid surfaces, fluid layers, and material elements sliding against each other.

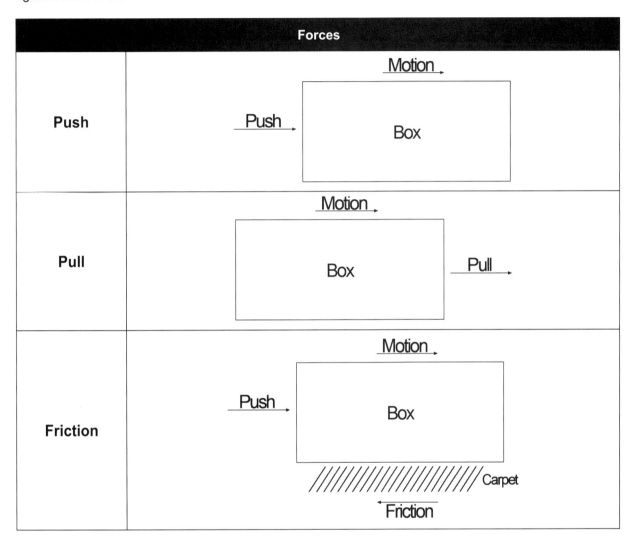

Forces	
Push	Motion → Push → Box
Pull	Motion → Box Pull →
Friction	Motion → Push → Box /////// Carpet ← Friction

Newton's Laws of Motion

1. An object either remains at rest or continues to move at a constant velocity unless acted upon by a force.

2. Force is equal to the change in motion (mV) per change in time. For a constant mass, force equals mass times acceleration ($F = m \times a$)..

3. For every action, there is an equal and opposite reaction.

(NASA, n.d.)

Equilibrium:

A state in which opposing forces or influences are balanced.

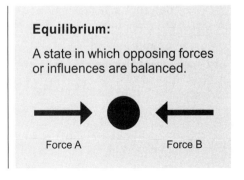

Force A   Force B

Magnetism

Magnetism is the force exerted by magnets when they attract or repel each other. Magnetism is caused by the motion of electric charges (National Geographic, n.d.).

Opposite poles attract – N & S

Same poles repel – S & S and N & N

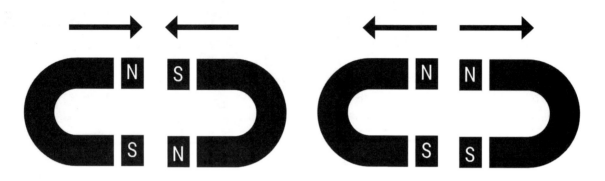

Common Units of Measure in Physics

Unit	Symbol	Measure
hertz	Hz	frequency
newton	N	force, weight
density	p	density
joule	J	energy, work
watt	W	power
volt	V	electrical voltage
degree Celsius	°C	temperature
gram/kilogram	g/kg	mass

Density

Density is the amount of matter an object has to its volume. An object with a lot of matter in a certain volume has high density. An object with little matter in the same amount of volume has a low density.

One way to measure density is to put the object in water. If it floats, it is less dense than the water; if it sinks, it is denser than the water. For example, ice is less dense than water because ice cubes float in water.

Density is found by dividing the mass of an object by its volume.

(p is density in this equation)

The best way to measure density is to use water displacement in a graduated cylinder.

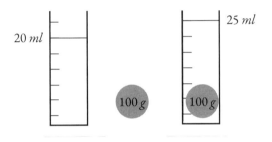

Because the mass of the weight is 100 g and the water displaced is 5 ml (25 - 20 = 5), the volume is 5 ml.

d the water dis

$$p = \frac{100}{5}$$

$$p = 20$$

The density of the weight is 20.

Remember: p represents density in the equation.

Energy

Energy is a property that can be transferred in between and among objects. Energy can also be converted into different forms.

Kinetic energy – Object is in motion; the actual movement of an object. For example, a rock rolling down a hill or a swing swinging in the air both have kinetic energy. Because the objects are in motion, they have kinetic energy.

Potential energy – The energy possessed by an object or individual by virtue of its position relative to others, stresses within itself, electric charge, and other factors. For example, a rock on the top of the hill has potential to roll down; therefore, the rock has potential energy. A swing being pulled to the top before it is released has potential energy.

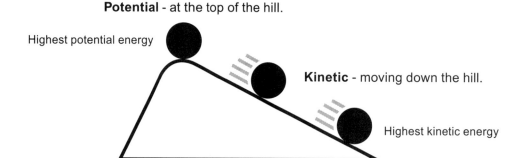

Potential - at the top of the hill.

Highest potential energy

Kinetic - moving down the hill.

Highest kinetic energy

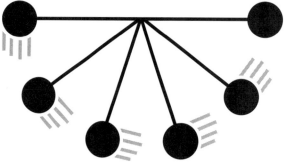

Potential - at the top of the pendulum.

Kinetic - moving through the pendulum.

Types of Energy

Type	What It Does...	Examples
mechanical	objects in motion	a swing
electrical	moving through the wire	light bulb
chemical	rearrangement of molecular structure	photosynthesis, lighting a match, rusting
thermal	moving particles	boiling water

Heat Transfer

Heat transfer is the exchange of thermal energy between physical systems.

- **Convection** – The transfer of heat by the actual movement of the warmed matter. For example, in a convection oven, air is moved by a fan around the food.

- **Conduction** – The transfer of heat from particle to particle. For example, if a cold spoon is placed in hot soup, the spoon will get hotter until the soup and the spoon become the same temperature.

- **Radiation** – The transfer of heat from electromagnetic waves through space. Sunlight is a form of radiation.

Quick Tip

We use wooden spoons when cooking because wood is a bad conductor of heat. The handle of a wooden spoon stays cool even when submerged in hot water. A metal spoon will eventually become as hot as the water because metal is a good conductor of heat.

Convection

In a convection oven, a fan swirls heat around the food.

Conduction

The spoon handle will get hot because it is touching the hot water.

Radiation

The heat coming off the fire is a form of radiation.

D. Interaction of energy and matter

Electricity can be defined as the flow of an electric charge. The most familiar electricity is the type used in homes and businesses to power lights and appliances. Electrical circuits allow electricity to flow in a loop and power different things.

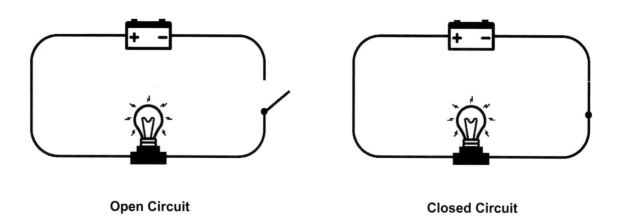

Open Circuit   **Closed Circuit**

Types of Circuits

Series circuits – The components are arranged end to end. The electric current flows through the first component, then through the next component, and so on until it reaches the battery again.

Parallel circuits – A circuit with branches that allows multiple applications to happen at once.

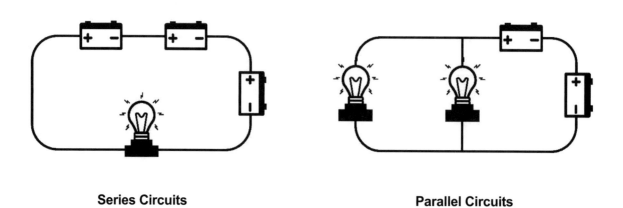

Series Circuits   **Parallel Circuits**

Conductors and Insulators

Conductors – Good for Electricity	Insulators – Bad for Electricity
Wire	Rubber
Metal	Cloth
Water	Polystyrene (Styrofoam)

Lightning

Lightning is a giant spark of electricity in the atmosphere between clouds, the air, or the ground. As lightning starts, air acts as an insulator between the positive and negative charges in the cloud and between the cloud and the ground. When the opposite charges build up enough, this insulating capacity of the air breaks down, and there is a rapid discharge of electricity (NSSL, 2019).

Cloud-to-ground lightning occurs between opposite charges within the thunderstorm cloud (intra-cloud lightning) or between opposite charges in the cloud and on the ground (cloud-to-ground lightning).

E. Science as a human endeavor

Through science, humans seek to improve their understanding and explanations of the natural world. Science involves the construction of explanations based on evidence and science knowledge can be changed as new evidence becomes available. Like scientists, students use the scientific method to guide their exploration of physical science. For example, when engaging in science students make observations, form hypotheses, conduct experiments, and evaluate results. Teachers can help students understand the world around them by using models. Models help students understand abstract concepts like atoms and molecules.

F. Scientific method

Scientists use **models** to communicate ideas and to represent abstract phenomena. For example, the solar system is impossible to see in a classroom or lab; however, a model of the solar system is easily accessible in a classroom or lab. Scientific **theories** are based on a body of evidence and many experiments, trials, and tests. Theories are explanations for observable phenomena. Scientific theories are based on a body of evidence developed over time. Scientific **explanations** describe the mechanisms for natural events. Scientific **laws** are regularities or mathematical descriptions of natural phenomena. A **hypothesis** is used by scientists as an idea that may contribute important new knowledge for the evaluation of a scientific theory.

Steps to the Scientific Method
1. Make an observation.
2. Ask a question.
3. Form a hypothesis.
4. Conduct an experiment.
5. Analyze the data and draw a conclusion.

Students in science:

- **Observe** – Employ the five senses to interact with phenomena and recording findings.

- **Classify** – Arrange living and nonliving things based on attributes.

- **Predict** – Make assumptions based on evidence.

- **Hypothesize** – State a prediction based on evidence.

- **Investigate** – Conduct experiments.

Scientific method – The scientific method is a body of techniques for investigating phenomena, acquiring new knowledge, or correcting and integrating previous knowledge. To be termed scientific, a method of inquiry is commonly based on empirical or measurable evidence subject to specific principles of reasoning.

An **experiment** is a procedure carried out to refute or validate a hypothesis. Experiments help students understand cause-and-effect relationships by demonstrating what outcome occurs when a particular factor is manipulated.

An experiment usually has three kinds of variables: independent, dependent, and control. The independent variable is the one that is changed by the scientist.

- Independent variable is the element manipulated in the experiment.

- Dependent variable is what the scientist is measuring during the experiment.

- Control variables are the elements of the experiment that a scientist wants to remain constant, so the scientist can observe them as carefully as the dependent variables.

Example:

If a scientist wants to test the effectiveness of a fertilizer, she might make a hypothesis, "Fertilizer A will increase the growth of the plant by 15% over fertilizer B."

To test the hypothesis, she would place two plant bulbs of the same plant and same size in two different pots. The pots are the same size. She uses the same amount of water, allows the plants to receive the same amount of light, and ensures both plants have the same environment. The only thing that is different is the **independent variable**, which is fertilizer A versus fertilizer B.

To make the experiment stronger, the scientist adds a third pot that contains no fertilizer. This allows for a baseline measure and will help the scientist determine if the change in growth is significant.

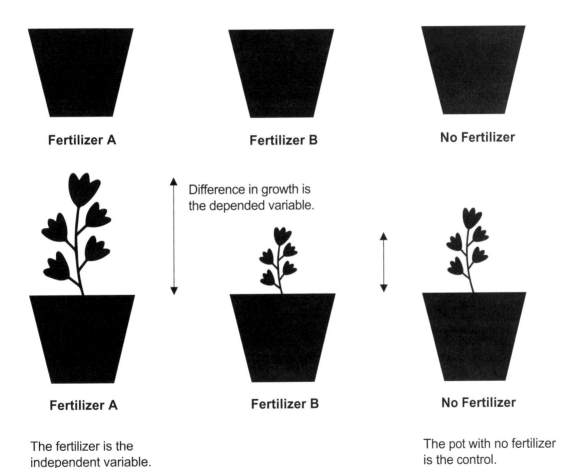

Fertilizer A   Fertilizer B   No Fertilizer

Difference in growth is the depended variable.

Fertilizer A   Fertilizer B   No Fertilizer

The fertilizer is the independent variable.

The pot with no fertilizer is the control.

Types of Graphs Used in Science

Graph	How It Is Used	Example
Line	Line charts, or line graphs, are powerful visual tools that illustrate trends in data over a period of time or a particular correlation. This line graph shows population growth in certain species over time. There are three different lines representing three different species.	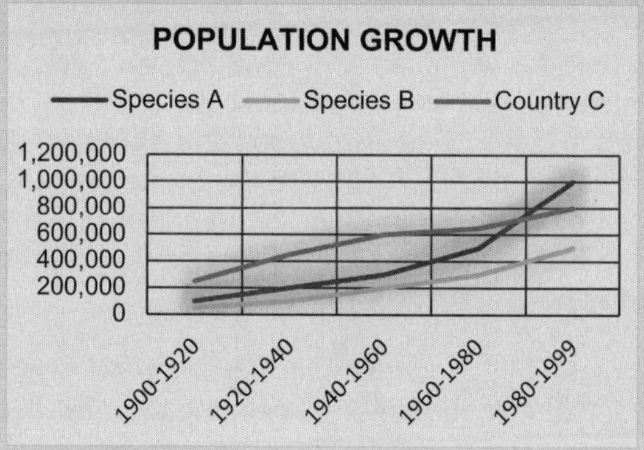
Bar	One can easily compare two or more variables when using a bar graph. Each bar represents a variable. When the bars are stacked next to each other, it is easy to compare data. This bar graph is comparing carrying capacity of several species in different ecosystems.	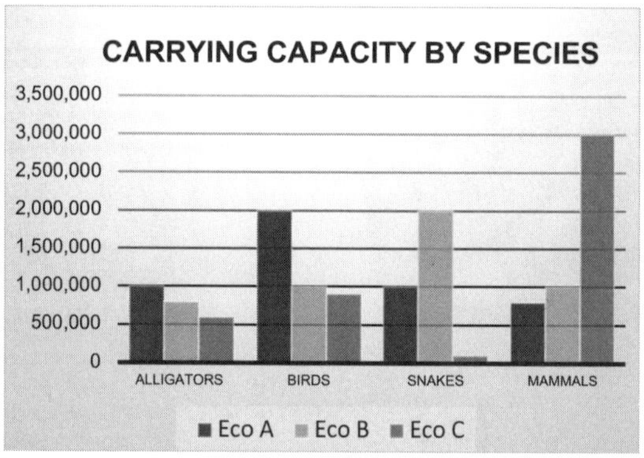
Pie	Pie charts are generally used to show percentage or proportional data. The percentage represented by each category is provided next to the corresponding slice of pie. In this example, the percentages of substances in the atmosphere are broken down.	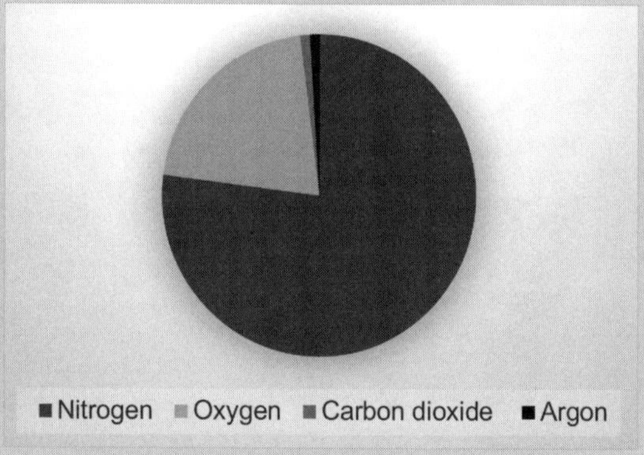

Teaching Methods for Science

While teaching methods for science are not explicitly stated in the specs, it is important to understand best practices in science. Science is inquiry-based, meaning students must be given the opportunity to interact with science. Along with this, teachers must keep students safe in the science classroom.

Safety

Safety is important when providing students the opportunity to learn in science classrooms. Teachers must communicate procedures and guidelines repeatedly so students understand what is expected in terms of safety and security.

Here are some do's and don'ts when it comes to science classroom safety:

Remember Developmentally Appropriate Practices (DAP):

Match the students' age to the appropriate task. For example, 4–6 graders might have to interact with chemicals during labs, while K–3 graders might not.

Do	Don't
Communicate procedures repeatedly and provide plenty of practice with students to engage in procedures and emergency operations. Practice makes perfect. Send procedures home for parents to read and sign, indicating they received the procedures and understood them.	Post procedures on the wall and expect students review them on their own.
Lock up chemicals, sharp tools, and other hazardous materials used in labs.	Leave chemicals, sharp tools, and other hazardous materials near your desk.
Leave the chemical safety manual out where students can access it in case there is an emergency with chemicals.	Lock up the chemical manual with the chemicals so only the person with a key can access it.
Predetermine student lab groups to maximize time on task and minimize student misbehavior, accidents, or mishaps.	Let students get into groups on their own before the lab.
Keep your principal and administration informed when you are doing a lab or controversial science unit.	Administer complex or dangerous labs without informing administration.

ELLs and Science Instruction

Science is an effective way to engage with ELL students. Science, in many ways, transcends language because every student has a sense of wonder and inquiry.

To maximize ELL participation and mastery of science concepts:

- Provide ELL students with science materials in their native language.

- Use translators or paraprofessionals to help you explain complex science concepts in students' native language.

If you give students a writing assignment in science, you are also assessing writing in English. Therefore, if you want to measure ELL students' understanding of science concepts, a science diagnostic test in the student's native language is the best way to do that. That way, you are assessing science skills and not English language skills.

This page intentionally left blank.

1. How long does it take for Earth to go around the sun?

    A. 24 hours

    B. 30 days

    C. 180 days

    D. 365 days

2. Where are aquifers located?

    A. beneath Earth's crust

    B. beneath the bedrock

    C. in Earth's mantle

    D. in Earth's core

3. What happens during a solar eclipse?

    A. Earth casts a shadow on the moon.

    B. Earth and the moon are on opposite sides of the sun.

    C. The moon moves in front of the sun relative to Earth.

    D. Earth and the sun align.

4. On which day is there approximately 12 hours of daylight and 12 hours of night?

    A. summer solstice

    B. winter solstice

    C. New Year's Day

    D. fall equinox

5. Which planet is closest in size and density to Earth?

    A. Venus

    B. Uranus

    C. Saturn

    D. Mercury

6. Gravity is responsible for:

    A. rotation of Earth on its axis.

    B. phases of the moon.

    C. Earth's orbit.

    D. Earth's seasons.

7. The picture below is an example of the:

Water Cycle

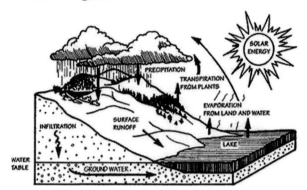

    A. geosphere.

    B. cryosphere.

    C. biosphere.

    D. hydrosphere.

8. This type of rock was originally liquid below Earth's crust and is formed by lava and magma.

    A. sedimentary

    B. igneous

    C. metamorphic

    D. fossils

9. Mr. Lopez is teaching a unit on seasons. He explains why summer days are longer and winter days are shorter. What should Mr. Lopez emphasize regarding Earth when explaining this phenomenon?

    A. revolution around the sun

    B. tilt on its axis

    C. position in the solar system

    D. distance away from the sun

10. The _____ affects the ocean tides.

    A. moon

    B. sun

    C. stars

    D. solar system

11. If a star explodes and emits light that is 13 light years away, how long will it take to be visible from Earth?

    A. 1 year

    B. 10 years

    C. 13 years

    D. 20 years

12. In the diagram below, number 6 is:

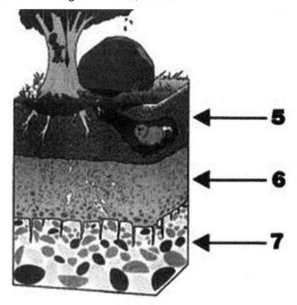

   A. topsoil
   B. subsoil
   C. bedrock
   D. mantle

13. _____ are made up of metals and rocky material, while _____ are made up of ice, dust, and rocky material.
   A. comets, asteroids
   B. asteroids, comets
   C. meteors, comets
   D. asteroids, meteors

14. This area is located around the outer edge of the Pacific Ocean and is where most volcanic activity occurs.
   A. Ring of Fire
   B. Horn of Africa
   C. San Francisco Bay
   D. Arctic Circle

15. Which of the following is the densest part of Earth?
   A. stratosphere
   B. lithosphere
   C. mantle
   D. core

16. Which of the following contains most of the world's fresh water?

   A. lakes

   B. rivers

   C. glaciers

   D. oceans

17. A giant wave caused by an earthquake is called a:

   A. tsunami

   B. tidal wave

   C. seismic wave

   D. epicenter

18. Glaciers and icecaps are all part of the:

   A. hydrosphere

   B. biosphere

   C. lithosphere

   D. cryosphere

19. Which of the following cell structures appears in plant cells but not in animal cells?

   A. plasma membrane

   B. mitochondria

   C. chloroplast

   D. nucleus

20. Mr. Rodriguez is helping students understand how the common cold is transmitted. He is most likely giving a lesson on:

   A. bacteria

   B. viruses

   C. cell structures

   D. eukaryotic cells

21. A eukaryote that does not make its own food and that does not contain cells with a cell wall is a(n):

   A. Animalia

   B. Plantae

   C. Protista

   D. Algae

22. During this stage of mitosis, chromosomes line up in the middle of the cell and spindle fibers attach to the center of the chromosomes.

    A.   prophase

    B.   metaphase

    C.   anaphase

    D.   telophase

23. Sometimes during cell division, sex cells contain three copies of chromosomes instead of two. This results in:

    A.   mutations

    B.   meiosis III

    C.   trisomy

    D.   DNA replication

24. Red plants have the dominant trait for color (R), while white plants have the recessive trait for color (r). How many red plants and white plants are produced when Rr x Rr are crossed?

    A.   3 red plants; 1 one white plant

    B.   1 red plant; 3 white plants

    C.   2 red plants; 2 white plants

    D.   All red plants

25. Which of the following is a producer?

    A.   hawk

    B.   snake

    C.   bunny

    D.   grass

26. A symbiotic relationship where both organisms benefit is called:

    A.   competition

    B.   predation

    C.   commensalism

    D.   mutualism

27. Proteins are made up of:

    A.   cells

    B.   bacteria

    C.   amino acids

    D.   mitochondria

28. Ms. Wheeler is explaining that humans have 46 chromosomes—23 from mom and 23 from dad. She is most likely giving a lesson on:

    A.   mitosis

    B.   meiosis

    C.   evolution

    D.   metamorphosis

29. This human system is responsible for the flow of blood, nutrients, oxygen, and other gases to and from cells:

    A.   circulatory

    B.   digestive

    C.   endocrine

    D.   nervous

30. Which of the following has an open circulatory system?

    A.   birds

    B.   chimpanzees

    C.   clam

    D.   humans

31. Homeostasis refers to the mechanism of the body to maintain a stable internal environment instead of changes taking place in the external environment. Which of the following contributes to homeostasis?

    A.   sweating

    B.   DNA replication

    C.   mitosis

    D.   predation

32. Who was responsible for the classification of living organisms?

    A.   Gregor Mendel

    B.   Charles Darwin

    C.   Carl Linnaeus

    D.   Louis Pasteur

33. Which organ(s) filter the blood of toxins?

    A.   bladder

    B.   kidneys

    C.   small intestine

    D.   colon

34. These make up the middle or ladder part of the DNA and code for specific genes.

   A.   phosphates

   B.   amino acids

   C.   chromosomes

   D.   nitrogen bases

35. Which of the following is a benefit to sexual reproduction?

   A.   Only one parent cell is needed.

   B.   Offspring are identical.

   C.   The DNA replicates.

   D.   It results in genetic variance.

36. Which of the following is the difference between plant cells and animal cells? Choose all that apply.

   A.   Plant cells use oxygen and water to make food, while animal cells make ATP from carbon dioxide and sugar.

   B.   Plant cells use carbon dioxide, water, and sunlight to make their own food, while animal cells make ATP from glucose and oxygen.

   C.   Animal cells go through photosynthesis, while plant cells go through cellular respiration.

   D.   Plant cells go through photosynthesis, while animal cells go through cellular respiration.

37. Which of the following is considered the least resistant to electricity and the best conductor of electricity?

   A.   wood

   B.   copper

   C.   rubber

   D.   plastic

38. Which of the following is an accurate depiction of how lightning works?

A.

B.

C.

39. Which of the following is a chemical reaction? Check all that apply.

   A.   rust forming on a bike left out in the rain

   B.   plants going through photosynthesis

   C.   water boiling on the stove

   D.   a pendulum swinging back and forth

40. At what point on the graphic below is kinetic energy the highest?

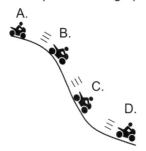

41. At what point on the graphic below is potential energy the highest?

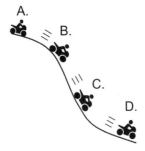

42. During which of the following is condensation occurring?

    A.   water boiling on a stove

    B.   plants sucking water up through their roots

    C.   water droplets forming on the outside of a surface

    D.   a puddle disappearing on a hot day

43. Which of the following is the least reactive element?

    A.   Lithium

    B.   Hydrogen

    C.   Carbon

    D.   Potassium

44. Which of the following phases occurs when boiling water?

    A.   sublimation

    B.   vaporization

    C.   crystallization

    D.   liquification

45. A 500 g object at 50 °C is placed into 500 *l* of 25 °C water in an insulated container. After a few minutes, what could their temperatures be?

   A. Object is 25 °C; water is 50 °C

   B. Object is 27.5 °C; water is 27.5 °C

   C. Object is 35 °C; water is 25 °C

   D. Object is 50 °C; water is 25 °C

46. Which of the following is the smallest part of an element that retains its chemical properties?

   A. atom

   B. electron

   C. proton

   D. neutron

47. In a glass of water, ice floats to the surface of the water. Why does this happen?

   A. The water weighs more than the ice.

   B. The ice weighs more than the water.

   C. The ice is less dense than the water.

   D. The water is less dense than the ice.

48. Why is it easier to compress a gas rather than a solid?

   A. The particles in a gas are further apart than they are in a solid.

   B. The particles in a gas are closer together than they are in a solid.

   C. The particles in a solid are moving faster than they are in a gas.

   D. The particles in a solid are moving the same speed as they are in a gas.

Use the following scenario to answer questions 49–52.

A student is conducting an experiment. She is testing the effectiveness of fertilizer A and fertilizer B. She has done research on both fertilizers and predicts that fertilizer A will be more effective than fertilizer B because fertilizer A contains more phosphorous.

She has 3 pots. In the first pot, she adds 5 seeds, fertilizer A, and 4 quarts of dirt. In the second pot, she adds 5 seeds, fertilizer B, and 4 quarts of dirt. In the third pot, she adds 5 seeds, no fertilizer, and 4 quarts of dirt. She uses the same amount of water every day to water the plants. All of the plants receive the same amount of sunlight. In two weeks, she measures the difference in growth among the three plants.

49. In this experiment, the student's prediction is called the:
    A. control
    B. constant
    C. independent variable
    D. hypothesis

50. In this experiment, the fertilizer is the:
    A. control
    B. constant
    C. independent variable
    D. dependent variable

51. In this experiment, the pot with no fertilizer is the:
    A. control
    B. constant
    C. independent variable
    D. hypothesis

52. In this experiment, the difference in growth is the:
    A. control
    B. constant
    C. independent variable
    D. dependent variable

53. The most important thing a teacher can do for students in a science classroom is:
    A. grade fairly
    B. encourage inquiry
    C. make observations
    D. conduct labs

54. When a scientist makes a discovery in an experiment, what should she do?
    A. Publish the results in an academic journal.
    B. Conduct the experiment over and over again to see if she gets the same results.
    C. Form a hypothesis.
    D. Change the variables in the experiment.

55. A student is looking at different types of rocks. He notices the texture, size, and hardness of the rocks. The student is making a(n):

    A. hypothesis

    B. observation

    C. prediction

    D. experiment

Practice Test 1 Answer Key

#	Answer	Category	Explanation
1.	D	I	Earth makes a full rotation around the sun in 365 days—1 full calendar year. Earth rotates one full rotation on its axis every 24 hours—1 day.
2.	A	I	Aquifers are below Earth's crust, below the water table, and above the bedrock. The mantle and the core are very deep below Earth's crust.
3.	C	I	A solar eclipse happens when the moon moves in front of the sun.
4.	D	I	During both the fall and spring equinox, there are exactly 12 hours of daylight and 12 hours of night.
5.	A	I	Venus and Earth are similar in size, density, and mass.
6.	C	I	Earth remains in an orbit around the sun because of the gravitational pull of the sun and the other planets.
7.	D	I	Hydro means water. The picture is of the water cycle; therefore, it is the hydrosphere.
8.	B	I	Igneous rocks are formed from magma or lava.
9.	B	I	The seasons are caused as Earth, tilted on its axis, travels around the sun. Summer happens in the hemisphere tilted toward the sun, and winter happens in the hemisphere tilted away from the sun.
10.	A	I	Tides rise and fall because of the gravitational forces of the moon on the oceans of Earth.
11.	C	I	A light year is a unit of astronomical distance equal to the distance light travels in one year.
12.	B	I	The top layer of soil is called topsoil. The layer under topsoil is subsoil (sub means under). The rock below the subsoil is bedrock. The mantle is not pictured here.
13.	B	I	Asteroids are made up of metals and rocky material, while comets are made up of ice, dust, and rocky material.
14.	A	I	The Ring of Fire is a ring of volcanoes around the outer edge of the Pacific Ocean. These volcanoes are a result of subduction of oceanic plates beneath lighter continental plates. Most of Earth's volcanoes are located in the Ring of Fire.

#	Answer	Category	Explanation
15.	D	I	The center of Earth is also the densest part of Earth. Therefore, Earth's core is the answer.
16.	C	I	Glaciers contain 68.7% of Earth's fresh water.
17.	A	I	A tsunami is a giant wave cause by an earthquake.
18.	D	I	The cryosphere includes all the masses of frozen water. Frozen lakes, frozen rivers, frozen oceans, and glaciers are part of the cryosphere.
19.	C	II	Chloroplasts are only present in plant cells. Chloroplasts are used in photosynthesis to absorb light.
20.	B	II	Viruses cause diseases like the common cold. Therefore, Mr. Rodriquez is most likely teaching the students about viruses. Eukaryotes, bacteria, and cell structures do not relate to the common cold.
21.	A	II	Animalia (or animals) do not make their own food. Instead, animals got through a process of cellular respiration, where they eat food. Answers B, C, and D all make their own food during photosynthesis.
22.	B	II	Metaphase is the stage where the chromosomes move the middle of the cell and prepare to be separated. An easy way to remember this is to think middle when thinking metaphase.
23.	C	II	Trisomy means that each cell in the body has three copies (tri) of a chromosome instead of the usual two copies.
24.	A	II	When Rr and Rr are crossed, it results in 1 RR, 2 Rr, and 1 rr. RR and Rr show red. The only way to show white (recessive) is if the offspring inherit rr.
			(Punnett square: R/r across top, R/r down side) RR, Rr, Rr, rr
25.	D	II	Grasses go through photosynthesis; therefore, they are producers. They produce their own food and are at the bottom of the energy pyramid. Bunnies eat the grass; snakes eat the bunnies; and hawks eat the snakes.
26.	D	II	A symbiotic relationship where both organisms benefit is called mutualism. Predation and competition benefit only one organism. Commensalism is a symbiotic relationship where one organism benefits and one does not benefit but is unharmed.

#	Answer	Category	Explanation
27.	C	II	Amino acids are organic compounds that form proteins.
28.	B	II	Meiosis ensures that humans have the same number of chromosomes in each generation. It is a two-step process that reduces the chromosome number by half—from 46 to 23—to form sperm and egg cells.
29.	A	II	The circulatory system is responsible for the flow of blood, nutrients, oxygen and other gases, and hormones to and from cells. This system contains the heart, arteries, veins, and coronary and portal vessels.
30.	C	II	Open circulatory systems are usually present in invertebrates. Clams are mollusks, which are invertebrates with open circulatory systems.
31.	A	II	Humans will sweat when they are hot. This is an example of maintaining a stable internal environment, regardless of the heat outside.
32.	C	II	Mendel – Genetics Charles Darwin – Natural Selection Carl Linnaeus – Classification of Living Things Louis Pasteur – Germ Theory
33.	B	II	All of the answer choices are part of the digestive and excretory system. However, kidneys filter the blood.
34.	D	II	The four nitrogen bases (adenine, thymine, cytosine, and guanine) make up 3 billion combinations running down the human DNA molecule.
35.	D	II	Genetic variance allows species to survive and reproduce. Genetic variance only occurs in sexual reproduction. Answer choices A, B, and C all occur in asexual reproduction.
36.	B & D	II	Animal cells go through a process of cellular respiration, where they make ATP from glucose and oxygen. Plant cells go through photosynthesis, where they make their own food using carbon dioxide, water, and sunlight.
37.	B	III	Copper is a type of metal and therefore the best conductor of electricity of all the choices. A good conductor of electricity resists the electricity the least.

#	Answer	Category	Explanation
38.	D	III	Lightning occurs between opposite charges in the cloud and on the ground (cloud-to-ground lightning). + + + + - - - - + + + - - - - + + + + - - - -
39.	A & B	III	A chemical reaction is a process that involves rearrangement of the molecular structure of a substance. Rust and photosynthesis both involve the rearrangement of molecules.
40.	D	III	Kinetic energy is at its highest when potential energy is at its lowest. When a motorcycle is traveling down a hill, the bottom of the hill is the highest kinetic energy.
41.	A	III	Potential energy is at its highest when kinetic energy is at its lowest. When a motorcycle is traveling down a hill, the very top of the hill is when the highest potential energy occurs.
42.	C	III	Condensation is when water collects as droplets on a cold surface when humid air is in contact with it (gas to liquid).
43.	B	III	In metals, reactivity increases down and to the left on the periodic table. In nonmetals, reactivity increases up and to the right on the periodic table. Hydrogen is a non-metal and is on the left of the periodic table. Therefore, it is the least reactive of the choices.
44.	B	III	Vaporization occurs when water boils. It is the steam coming off the top of the water in the pot.
45.	B	III	This is a conduction question. Conduction is the transfer of heat from particle to particle. For example, if a cold spoon is placed in hot soup, the spoon will get hotter until the soup and the spoon become the same temperature.
46.	A	III	Atoms are the smallest part of an element that retains its chemical properties. Electrons, protons, and neutrons are parts of the atom.
47.	C	III	This is a density question. In this case, because the ice is floating in the water, the ice is less dense than the water.

#	Answer	Category	Explanation
48.	A	III	Particles in a gas are more spread out and move more freely than in a solid.
49.	D	III	A hypothesis is a prediction based on evidence. She conducted research on the fertilizers before making the prediction. Therefore, she made a hypothesis.
50.	C	III	The independent variable is the variable that is changed in the experiment. In this case, it is the fertilizer. Everything else remains the same.
51.	A	III	The control is what is kept the same throughout the experiment. In this case, the pot with no fertilizer is the control. Having a control is essential. It is difficult to see the difference in growth between fertilizers without having a pot with no fertilizer.
52.	D	III	The dependent variable is the thing that changes because of the experiment. In this case, the growth was affected by fertilizer A, fertilizer B, or no fertilizer.
53.	B	III	Science is all about inquiry. A science teacher should always encourage inquiry in a science classroom.
54.	B	III	Scientific theories are based on a body of evidence and many experiments, trials, and tests. Therefore, when a scientist makes a discovery, she should replicate the experiment repeatedly to make sure the results are not a random occurrence.
55.	B	III	An observation consists of receiving knowledge of the outside world through the senses.

1. The sun appears bigger than other stars because of:

    A. the size of the sun.

    B. the size of the solar system.

    C. the distance Earth is from the sun.

    D. the distance the sun is from Mars.

2. This is when plants suck water from roots to the small pores in leaves, releasing the water vapor into the atmosphere.

    A. evaporation

    B. transpiration

    C. condensation

    D. convection

3. The Earth is getting hotter because:

    A. high levels of oxygen trap the sun's radiation in the atmosphere.

    B. high levels of sodium trap the sun's radiation in the atmosphere.

    C. high levels of carbon monoxide trap the sun's radiation in the atmosphere.

    D. high levels of carbon dioxide trap the sun's radiation in the atmosphere.

4. In a lunar eclipse, what is the order of Earth, the sun, and the moon?

    A. moon, sun, Earth

    B. Earth, moon, sun

    C. moon, Earth, sun

    D. Earth, sun, moon

5. What causes Earth's magnetism?

    A. Earth's rotation around the moon

    B. the moon's rotation around Earth

    C. the inner and outer core rotation

    D. Earth's rotation around the sun

6. Tectonic plates slide against each other in opposite directions, causing a(n):

    A. subduction

    B. earthquake

    C. mountain

    D. volcano

7. _____ happen when warmer, lighter air at the Equator moves toward the cooler air at the poles.

    A. convection currents

    B. conduction currents

    C. atmospheric currents

    D. jet streams

8. This event in history was pivotal in that it galvanized the U.S. space program and started what is known as the Space Race:

    A. building of the Russian Space Station

    B. U.S. astronauts walking on the moon

    C. Challenger explosion

    D. launch of Russia's Sputnik

9. _____ are formed when Earth's plates pull apart.

    A. Convergent plate boundaries

    B. Subjective plate boundaries

    C. Volcanic plate boundaries

    D. Divergent plate boundaries

10. Which of the following is the sphere where are all living things are contained?

    A. cryosphere

    B. biosphere

    C. lithosphere

    D. hydrosphere

11. During the Scientific Revolution, Copernicus introduced his theory that Earth revolves around the sun.

    A. heliocentric

    B. geocentric

    C. cryocentric

    D. biocentric

12. When the full moon starts to appear smaller as each night goes on, the moon is:

    A. waning.

    B. waxing.

    C. new.

    D. old.

13. What part of Earth receives the most sunlight in a year?

    A. the Western Hemisphere

    B. the desert

    C. the Equator

    D. the South Pole

14. This theory suggests Earth's continents were all once one big landmass. Over time, the continents separated because of plate tectonics.

    A. natural selection

    B. halogenic theory

    C. continental drift

    D. Earth's magnetism

15. The hotter a star is, the closer to this color it is.

    A. blue

    B. red

    C. orange

    D. yellow

16. During this eon, prokaryote life (the first form of life) emerged. The atmosphere is composed of volcanic and greenhouse gases.

    A. Hadean

    B. Archean

    C. Proterozoic

    D. Phanerozoic

17. The following gases are present in Earth's atmosphere from most present to least present.

    A. carbon dioxide, argon, oxygen, nitrogen

    B. argon, oxygen, carbon dioxide, nitrogen

    C. oxygen, nitrogen, carbon dioxide, argon

    D. nitrogen, oxygen, argon, carbon dioxide

18. This type of rock is made from heat and pressure.

    A. igneous

    B. granite

    C. sedimentary

    D. metamorphic

19. As random genetic mutations occur within an organism's genetic code, the beneficial mutations are preserved because they aid survival. This is called:

    A. common ancestry.

    B. natural selection.

    C. dominant traits.

    D. recessive traits.

20. The six different kingdoms are:

    A.   Plantae, Animalia, Fungi, Protista, Eubacteria, Archaebacteria.

    B.   Phylum, Animalia, Fungi, Protista, Eubacteria, Archaebacteria.

    C.   Plantae, Animalia, Fungi, Protista, Eubacteria, Prokaryote.

    D.   Plantae, Animalia, Fungi, Protista, Eukaryote, Archaebacteria.

21. Ms. Jackson wants students to understand the diet of an owl. The best way for students to understand this is by:

    A.   dissecting an owl pellet.

    B.   researching owls in an encyclopedia.

    C.   reading a chapter on owls in the textbook.

    D.   using a Venn diagram to compare and contrast the owl diet with the hawk diet.

22. Eukaryotic organisms are _____ , and prokaryotic organisms are _____.

    A.   single-cellular, multicellular

    B.   multicellular, single-cellular

    C.   multicellular, multicellular

    D.   single-cellular, single-cellular

23. A byproduct of cellular respiration is:

    A.   carbon.

    B.   oxygen.

    C.   carbon dioxide.

    D.   carbohydrates.

24. In a 3rd grade class, students learn that the black moth has a genetic make-up that makes it difficult for predators to see it against the dark trees. The white moth does not have the same genetic make-up and is easily seen by predators and eaten. The students are learning about:

    A.   dominance.

    B.   recessive.

    C.   natural selection.

    D.   classification.

25. In the energy pyramid below, which section contains the most energy?

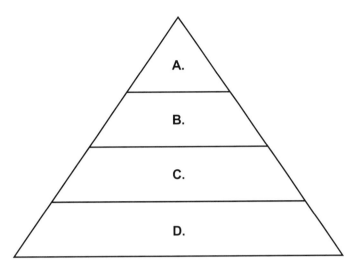

26. Select the correct order of the organization of living things:
    A. cells — tissues — organs systems — organs — organisms
    B. cells — tissues — organisms — organ systems — organs
    C. cells — tissues — organs — organ systems — organisms
    D. cells — organs — tissues — organs systems — organisms

27. Ms. Demming wants to introduce her students to the structure of cells. What would be the most appropriate tool to use to enhance student learning of this concept?
    A. an online virtual tour of a cell
    B. microscopes so students can observe cells in onion skin
    C. the science textbook
    D. a guest speaker on the uniqueness of cells

28. Mr. Parker is teaching students that cells divide to make more cells. What topic is Mr. Parker covering?
    A. cell theory
    B. photosynthesis
    C. cellular respiration
    D. organization

29. For a species to be in the same class, it must also be in the same _____.
    A. phylum
    B. species
    C. genus
    D. family

30. What do plant cells have that animal cells do not?

    A. cell wall and plasma membrane
    B. cell wall and chloroplasts
    C. nucleus and plasma membrane
    D. nucleus and DNA

31. This is the maximum population of a particular organism that a given environment can support without detrimental effects.

    A. ecosystem
    B. adaptation
    C. biosphere
    D. carrying capacity

32. This type of cell division happens during sexual reproduction and ensures the offspring have the same number of chromosomes in each generation.

    A. trisomy
    B. DNA replication
    C. mitosis
    D. meiosis

33. Prokaryotic cells reproduce by:

    A. asexual reproduction
    B. sexual reproduction
    C. genetic mutation
    D. DNA replication

34. This is when one animal feeds on another, like a lion eating a zebra.

    A. symbiosis
    B. commensalism
    C. predation
    D. parasitism

35. The brain and spinal cord make up this system.

    A. skeletal
    B. circulatory
    C. nervous
    D. digestive

36. These are herbivores that eat the producers in a food web.

    A. primary consumers
    B. secondary consumers
    C. tertiary consumers
    D. quaternary consumers

37. This is a single-celled organism found everywhere that can be beneficial (like when it aids in digestion) and dangerous (like when it causes infection).

  A. virus

  B. bacteria

  C. eukaryote

  D. mitochondria

38. A cook leaves a metal spoon in the pot of hot water. When the cook grabs the spoon a few minutes later, the spoon burns the cook's hand. What process is happening?

  A. conduction

  B. convection

  C. evaporation

  D. radiation

39. What would be the best way to demonstrate friction? Check all that apply.

  A. Roll a skateboard down the sidewalk and then on the grass to show the difference in speed.

  B. Have students rub their hands together rapidly to observe the heat produced.

  C. Have students rub a balloon on their heads and watch their hair stand up.

  D. Observe how opposite poles attract.

40. _____ are atoms that have lost or gained one or more _____ .

  A. compounds, electrons

  B. compounds, protons

  C. ions, protons

  D. ions, elections

41. The image below shows what type of circuit?

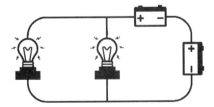

  A. The batteries are on a series circuit, and the light bulbs are on a parallel circuit.

  B. The batteries are on a parallel circuit, and the light bulbs are on a parallel circuit.

  C. The batteries are on a series circuit, and the light bulbs are on a series circuit.

  D. The batteries are on a parallel circuit, and the light bulbs are on a series circuit.

42. Which of the following is not a part of Newton's Laws of Motion?
    A.   An object either remains at rest or continues to move at a constant velocity, unless acted upon by a force.
    B.   Force is equal to the change in motion (mV) per change in time. For a constant mass, force equals mass times acceleration ($F = m \times a$).
    C.   For every action, there is an equal and opposite reaction.
    D.   Opposite poles attract.

43. These are made up of atoms that are held together by chemical bonds:
    A.   molecules
    B.   electrons
    C.   protons
    D.   particles

44. On the periodic table, these are the columns.
    A.   periods
    B.   groups
    C.   metals
    D.   nonmetals

45. This is considered a homogenous mixture.
    A.   orange juice
    B.   gel
    C.   salad dressing (oil and vinegar)
    D.   cereal

46. This is the unit of measure for force and motion.
    A.   joule
    B.   watt
    C.   newton
    D.   volt

47. This characteristic of water allows it to have cohesion and adhesion.
    A.   high heat
    B.   temperature moderation
    C.   magnetism
    D.   polarity

48. A teacher is showing students how to identify elements by looking at the number of protons each element has. What should the teacher emphasize?

    A.   atomic number

    B.   number of electrons

    C.   isotopes

    D.   ions

49. When salt is dissolved in water, it disappears. However, you can still taste the salt. This is called a:

    A.   compound

    B.   solution

    C.   colloid

    D.   suspension

50. What would be the best way to demonstrate the difference in speed of two cars on two different types of surfaces?

    A.   line graph

    B.   pie graph

    C.   bar graph

    D.   splatter plot

51. This part of an atom is a negatively charged particle that spins around the atom in a cloud.

    A.   proton

    B.   neutron

    C.   electron

    D.   nucleus

52. Which of the following is most acidic?

    A.   bleach

    B.   coffee

    C.   water

    D.   vinegar

53. A 5th grade student is skeptical about a theory presented in class. What can the teacher do to help the student understand the validity of a theory?

    A.   Remind the student that the person who established the theory is very famous in science.

    B.   Emphasize that for something to become a theory, it must be tested multiple times resulting in the same results.

    C.   Tell the student that the theory is aligned with the state standards.

    D.   Guarantee the student that if it is written in the textbook, then it is a theory.

54. Which of the following is a noble gas?

    A. Lithium

    B. Helium

    C. Iron

    D. Calcium

55. A student is testing different surfaces to see which one creates the most friction. The student is rolling model cars over the surfaces and timing each trial. What is the independent variable in this experiment?

    A. model cars

    B. friction

    C. timing

    D. different surfaces

#	Answer	Category	Explanation
1.	C	I	The sun is a star 93 million miles away. However, it appears bigger than other stars because Earth is closer to the sun. Other stars are 100,000 times farther away than the sun.
2.	B	I	There are small holes in plants' leaves that allow water vapor to enter and exit the leaves. When plants suck up water through the roots and then emit water vapor through the leaves, the process is called transpiration.
3.	D	I	Increased levels of carbon dioxide have caused a gradual increase in the average temperature of Earth's atmosphere and its oceans.
4.	C	I	A lunar eclipse occurs when the moon passes directly behind Earth into its umbra (shadow). During a lunar eclipse, the order is moon, Earth, sun.
5.	C	I	The Earth's outer core is made of iron. The outer core rotates around the inner core, causing magnetism on Earth.
6.	B	I	An earthquake happens when two tectonic plates suddenly slip past one another in opposite directions.
7.	A	I	As the cold, heavy air at the poles moves toward the Equator, a constant flow of air convection currents occurs.
8.	D	I	The Russian launch of Sputnik began the Space Age. On October 4, 1957, the Soviet Union successfully launched Sputnik, and everything about space exploration changed. It launched the U.S. into the Space Race.
9.	D	I	Diverge means to separate. When plates separate, a divergent plate boundary is formed.
10.	B	I	The biosphere is the global sum of all ecosystems, meaning all things living. Bio means life.
11.	A	I	Heliocentric is when the sun is stationary, and Earth revolves around the sun. This is what we believe today. However, long ago, people believed Earth was stationary, and the sun and other planets revolved around Earth. That is called a geocentric theory. Copernicus is credited with this discovery.
12.	A	I	As the moon appears smaller after a full moon, it is waning. As the moon appears bigger after a new moon, it is waxing.
13.	C	I	The Equator receives the most sunlight on Earth. The further away from the Equator you go, the fewer number of hours of sunlight you receive.

#	Answer	Category	Explanation
14.	C	I	First proposed by Alfred Wegener, continental drift suggests Earth's continents were once one big landmass. Over time, the continents separated because of plate tectonics.
15.	A	I	Blue stars are the hottest, followed by white, yellow, orange, and red.
16.	B	I	During the Archean eon, prokaryote life emerged. The atmosphere was composed of volcanic and greenhouse gases.
17.	D	I	Nitrogen – 78% Oxygen – 21% Argon – .09% Carbon dioxide – .01%
18.	D	I	Metamorphic rocks are made by heat and pressure and a have crystal-like appearance.
19.	B	II	Natural selection is the process whereby organisms that are better adapted to their environment tend to survive and produce more offspring.
20.	A	II	The six kingdoms are: Plantae, Animalia, Protista, Fungi, Archaebacteria, Eubacteria. Phylum is a rank above class and below kingdom. Prokaryotes and eukaryotes are types of cells not kingdoms.
21.	A	II	Dissecting owl pellets (undigested parts of a bird's diet that some bird species occasionally regurgitate) is the best way to see the diet of an owl. In the pellets, students will often find small bones of tiny rodents.
22.	B	II	Eukaryotes are multicellular and contain membrane-bound organelles, such as the nucleus. Prokaryotes are single-cellular and do not contain membrane organelles.
23.	C	II	Animals use a process called cellular respiration. Animals breathe in oxygen, a byproduct of photosynthesis, and breathe out carbon dioxide, a byproduct of cellular respiration.
24.	C	II	Natural selection is when species of a certain phenotype (genetic make-up) survive and pass those favorable traits to their offspring. The moths have favorable traits if they are black. They blend into the landscape, and predators cannot find them. They survive and pass on those traits.
25.	D	II	Most energy is stored in plants. Plants are on the bottom of the pyramid. As you move up the pyramid, energy is lost.

#	Answer	Category	Explanation
26.	C	II	The smallest unit of life is the cell. Cells come together to form tissues. Tissues form organs. Organs form organ systems. Finally, organ systems (circulatory, skeletal, etc.) make up the organism.
27.	B	II	Having students look at real cells is the best approach. Bringing science education into the real world is key.
28.	A	II	The three parts of cell theory are: the cell is the basic unit of life; all cells come from pre-existing cells; all living things contain cells. All cells come from pre-existing cells means cells divide to make more cells.
29.	A	II	Phylum is above class in the classification pyramid. Therefore, to be in the same class, organisms must be in the same phylum.
30.	B	II	Only plant cells have chloroplasts. Chloroplasts are used for photosynthesis; animals do not go through photosynthesis. The cell wall keeps the plant rigid and upright, much like a skeleton does in animals. Animals have a cell membrane, not a cell wall.
31.	D	II	Carrying capacity is the maximum population of a particular organism that a given environment can support without detrimental effects.
32.	D	II	Meiosis happens during sexual reproduction and ensures that humans have the same number of chromosomes in each generation. It is a two-step process that reduces the chromosome number by half—from 46 to 23—to form sperm and egg cells.
33.	A	II	Prokaryotic cells reproduce asexually, typically through binary fission. While prokaryotes do not go through mitosis, the cell does split into identical copies.
34.	C	II	The lion eats the zebra. The lion is the predator; the zebra is the prey.
35.	C	II	The nervous system is the master control system and contains the brain and spinal cord.
36.	A	II	Primary consumers are herbivores; they eat plants. In the energy pyramid, a bunny would be a primary consumer.
37.	B	II	Bacteria are microscopic living organisms, usually one-celled, that can be found everywhere. They can be dangerous, such as when they cause infection, or beneficial, as in the process of fermentation (such as in wine) and that of decomposition. There are bacteria in the stomach that aid in digestion.
38.	A	III	Conduction is the transfer of heat from particle to particle. For example, if a metal spoon sits in hot water, the spoon will eventually reach the same temperature as the boiling water.

#	Answer	Category	Explanation
39.	A & B	III	Both choices A and B demonstrate friction. Choice C demonstrates static electricity. Choice D demonstrates magnetism.
40.	D	III	An ion is a charged atom or molecule. It is charged because the number of electrons does not equal the number of protons in the atom or molecule. It has lost or gained an electron.
41.	A	III	A parallel circuit has two or more paths for an electric current to flow through. A series circuit has only one path.
42.	D	III	Answer D is about magnetism, not motion. Answers A, B, and C are all part of Newton's Law of Motion.
43.	A	III	Molecules are the smallest particle in a chemical element or compound that has the chemical properties of that element or compound. Molecules are made up of atoms that are held together by chemical bonds.
44.	B	III	Groups in the periodic table are the columns in the table.
45.	B	III	A gel is a homogenous solution because the particles in a gel do not settle and cannot be separated out by ordinary filtering.
46.	C	III	A newton is used to measure force and motion. It is named after Newton, who is responsible for the Laws of Motion. A joule measures energy; a watt and a volt measure electricity.
47.	D	III	Water's polarity allows is to attract other molecules, which causes water to have cohesion and adhesion.
48.	A	III	The atomic number is how an element is identified. It is also the number of protons in the nuclei of its atoms.
49.	B	III	A solution is a liquid mixture in which the solute (the salt) is uniformly distributed within the solvent (the water).
50.	C	III	A bar graph can compare multiple variables in multiple situations.
51.	C	III	Electrons are negatively charged subatomic particles that circle around the atom's nucleus.
52.	D	III	Vinegar has a pH closest to 1 out of all the choices. Therefore, vinegar is most acidic. Coffee is around a 6. Water is neutral with a number of 7. Bleach is alkaline with a number of 13.
53.	B	III	Scientific theories are based on a body of evidence developed over time and after many experiments where the results are duplicated.

#	Answer	Category	Explanation
54.	B	III	Helium is the only gas in the answer choices. In addition, Helium is part of the noble gases.
55.	D	III	The independent variable is the variable the scientist manipulates. In this case, the student is using different surfaces. Therefore, the surfaces are the independent variables. The time is the dependent variable because it depends on the surface.

This page intentionally left blank.

Bibliography

Center for Disease Control (CDC) (2019). National Health Education Standards. Retrieved from
   https://www.cdc.gov/healthyschools/sher/standards/index.htm

NASA (2017). Magnetic Pole Reversal Happens All The (Geologic) Time. Retrieved from
   https://www.nasa.gov/topics/earth/features/2012-poleReversal.html

NASA (n.d.). Earth. Solar System Exploration. Retrieved from
   https://solarsystem.nasa.gov/planets/earth/in-depth/

NASA (n.d.). Newton's Laws of Motion. Retrieved from
   https://www.grc.nasa.gov/www/k-12/airplane/newton.html

NASA (n.d.). Our Solar System. Retrieved from
   https://solarsystem.nasa.gov/solar-system/our-solar-system/overview/

National Geographic (n.d.). Continental Drift. Retrieved from
   https://www.nationalgeographic.org/encyclopedia/continental-drift/

National Geographic (n.d.). Ecological relationships. Retrieved from
   https://www.nationalgeographic.org/activity/ecological-relationships/

National Geographic (n.d.). Magnetism. Retrieved from
   https://www.nationalgeographic.org/encyclopedia/magnetism/

National Geographic (n.d.). The atmosphere. Resource Library Retrieved from
   https://www.nationalgeographic.org/encyclopedia/atmosphere/

National Oceanic and Atmospheric Administration (NOAA) (2019). What is a Tsunami? Retrieved from
   https://oceanservice.noaa.gov/facts/tsunami.html

National Oceanic and Atmospheric Administration. (n.d.). Stratospheric Ozone. Retrieved from
   https://www.ozonelayer.noaa.gov/science/basics.htm

National Research Council (2012). *A framework for k-12 science education: Practices, crosscutting
   concepts, and core ideas.* Washington, DC: The National Academies Press.
   https://doi.org/10.17226/13165.

National Severe Storms Laboratory (NSSL) (2019). Lightning Basics.
   https://www.nssl.noaa.gov/education/svrwx101/lightning/

NC State University (n.d.). Prokaryotes: Single-celled Organisms. Retrieved from
   http://projects.ncsu.edu/project/bio183de/Black/prokaryote/prokaryote1.html

Penn State University (2019) College of Earth and Mineral Science: The structure of the Earth. Retrieved
   from https://www.e-education.psu.edu/marcellus/node/870

Pidwirny, M. (2006). Organization of life: species, populations, communities, and
   ecosystems. *Fundamentals of Physical Geography, 2nd Edition.* Date Viewed.
   http://www.physicalgeography.net/fundamentals/9d.html

Schaum's outline of theory and problems of physics for engineering and science (Series: Schaum's
   Outline Series). McGraw-Hill Companies. p. 58. ISBN 978-0-07-008498-8.

Temming, M (2014). What is a star? *Sky and Telescope.* Retrieved from
   https://www.skyandtelescope.com/astronomy-resources/what-is-a-star/

U.S. National Library of Medicine (2019). How do Cells Divide? Retrieved from
   https://ghr.nlm.nih.gov/primer/howgeneswork/cellsdivide

U.S. National Library of Medicine (2019). What is DNA? Genetics Home Reference. Retrieved from
   https://ghr.nlm.nih.gov/primer/basics/dna